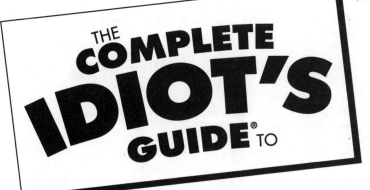

The Oceans

By *Joe Kraynak and Kim W. Tetrault*

ALPHA

A member of Penguin Group (USA) Inc.

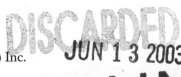

To Cecie, the mermaid who seduced me to explore the seas.
—*Joe Kraynak*

Copyright © 2003 by Joe Kraynak and Penguin Group (USA) Inc.

International Standard Book Number: 0-02-864462-X
Library of Congress Catalog Card Number: 2003102291

05   04   03   8   7   6   5   4   3   2   1

Interpretation of the printing code: The rightmost number of the first series of numbers is the year of the book's printing; the rightmost number of the second series of numbers is the number of the book's printing. For example, a printing code of 03-1 shows that the first printing occurred in 2003.

Printed in the United States of America

Most Alpha books are available at special quantity discounts for bulk purchases for sales promotions, premiums, fund-raising, or educational use. Special books, or book excerpts, can also be created to fit specific needs.

For details, write: Special Markets, Alpha Books, 375 Hudson Street, New York, NY 10014.

Publisher: *Marie Butler-Knight*
Product Manager: *Phil Kitchel*
Senior Managing Editor: *Jennifer Chisholm*
Acquisitions Editor: *Mikal Belicove*
Development Editor: *Michael Koch*
Senior Production Editor: *Katherin Bidwell*
Copy Editor: *Rhonda Tinch-Mize*
Illustrator: *Chris Eliopoulos*
Cover/Book Designer: *Trina Wurst*
Indexer: *Heather McNeill*
Layout/Proofreading: *Svetlana Dominguez, Mary Hunt, Ayanna Lacey*

Contents at a Glance

Appendixes

Contents

Foreword

We live on Earth, but perhaps our planet should be called Ocean. Life thrives on Earth because we have oceans, and sustaining life—and the quality of life—depends on our understanding of how they work.

As the heart and lungs of our planet, the oceans circulate heat around the globe to regulate Earth's climate. They provide rainfall for our rivers, forests, and farms and replenish the essential chemicals and nutrients that allow life not only to survive but to thrive. They are home to the largest and smallest life forms on earth, from the blue whale to single-cell microbes. They are a place of both still, deep waters and the greatest releases of energy on our planet, earthquakes and volcanoes.

The oceans cover 71 percent of Earth and truly are our last frontier, our inner space. Without oceans, Earth would resemble the Moon or Mars. The essence of Earth is the oceans. Yet our explorations of Earth have barely scratched the surface. More than three decades ago men landed on the moon some 240,000 miles away, an amazing technological achievement. Yet on our own planet we have seen little more than 5 percent of the sea floor and less than a fraction of 1 percent of the water column above it, which averages two and a half miles in depth—more than 10 Empire State buildings!

More than 80 percent of all the phyla of life are found only in the sea—many in the dark depths. Human occupied submersibles, remotely operated vehicles, and now autonomous underwater vehicles are enabling us to reach those depths. Permanent observatories cabled to shore are providing us with information 24 hours a day, seven days a week. New tools and technologies have enabled oceanographers to make great strides in learning what is out there. We learn something new every day, yet much remains to be discovered.

Oceanography, the study of the oceans, is not a discipline—it is the study of nature. Biology, chemistry, geology, physics, and math are all applied to our understanding of this vast underwater realm. Until recently, the oceans held many secrets and hid species and ecosystems whose discoveries have shattered long-standing notions of where and how life can exist not only on this planet but possibly on other planets. New knowledge transforms our understanding of the planet and life upon it, offering hints of discoveries yet to come.

Understanding the oceans has never been more critical to society as increasing global populations require more food, fuel, and potential cures for a growing number of diseases. Clogged harbors, coastal pollution, beach erosion, declining fisheries, and toxic red tides are but a few of the problems we face as society increasingly moves to the coasts and utilizes its resources. As individual citizens, we all need to know how the oceans work. They have more impact on us than ever before, and we have significantly more impact on the oceans. The oceans offer untapped resources and opportunities—if used and managed wisely—for many generations to come. Our survival as a species depends on it.

As a chemical oceanographer for more than 30 years, I have participated in more than a dozen research cruises and field programs around the world and now head a major independent research and higher education organization dedicated to advancing the frontiers of ocean science. I can tell you it is indeed an exciting time for ocean exploration and discovery. Come join the expedition!

Dr. Robert B. Gagosian
President and Director
Woods Hole Oceanographic Institution

Introduction

Star Trek fans might believe that space is "the final frontier," the only romantic and mysterious region of our galaxy that remains unexplored. But for those who never have studied the oceans, the secrets of the sea can be just as alluring. The colorful plant and animal life below sea level is as dazzling and spectacular as any heavenly light show. The creatures that lurk in the ocean depths are as beautiful and as ugly, as gentle and as vicious as any space aliens you might encounter beyond our solar system.

Fortunately, you don't need to board a spaceship or even leave the comfortable confines of your home to explore and understand this amazing water wilderness. Everything you need to know is right here in *The Complete Idiot's Guide to the Oceans*.

This book takes you on a guided tour of our oceans, from the dingy mud flats to the vibrant coral reefs, from the bright, wind-whipped surface to the dark, still abyss. It introduces you to some of the most incredible creatures you will ever meet, including the mantis shrimp, which can shatter inch-thick glass with a single tap of its claw, and the angler fish, which dangles a lamp in front of its face to lure unsuspecting prey into its gaping jaws.

Along the way, you learn basic oceanography as we explore the composition of seawater and how variations in salt content, temperature, and depth drive evolution in various ocean environments. You learn about the effects of the sun and moon on tides and how tides and currents control the food supplies and migration routes of various species. And, as you proceed from the surface to the abyss, you encounter amazingly complex ecosystems where scientists previously had thought no life could possibly exist!

How This Book Is Organized

This book is broken down into the following five parts that start with ocean basics and proceed to cover increasingly complex organisms and marine systems:

Part 1, "Cruising Through Vast Ocean Environments," provides a brief introduction to some key concepts in understanding the forces that drive the evolution of ecosystems. It then takes you on a brief tour of the most important and interesting marine environments.

Part 2, "A Garden of Marine Plants," goes to the bottom of the food chain to describe and explain the various single-cell and multi-cell plants that provide food and habitats for diverse marine creatures.

Part 3, "The Marine Invertebrate Collection," focuses on the simplest form of animal life in the sea—animals that do not have spines. These include single-cell animals, sponges, jellyfish, worms, starfish, clams, crabs, lobsters, squid, and other creatures without backbones.

Part 4, "The Marine Vertebrates: Backbones to Prove It!" takes one step up the evolutionary ladder to explore animals that have spines. These include the most popular sea creatures—fish (including sharks and rays), mammals (including dolphins, whales, and seals), reptiles (including sea turtles and marine iguanas), and birds of many species.

Part 5, "Man, Woman, Child, and the Sea," shows how we humans interact with the sea. Here, you find a brief overview of how people past and present have exploited and continue to exploit the vast ocean resources for fuel, food, and fun. This part also explores famous pirates and shipwrecks and helps you understand some of the laws that govern the high seas. You even learn how to become an ocean advocate!

Extras

Extras offer additional bits of wisdom and insight that go beyond the basics. These extras are flagged with special icons and are presented as boxed notes to capture your attention.

Log Entry

Log entries provide definitions of key terms and concepts that might confuse the novice marine biologist.

Ocean Alert

The ocean can be a dangerous place, so check out these ocean alerts to avoid trouble.

Captain Clam's Comments

Captain Clam has sailed the seas and speaks with the voice of experience. Look for his notes to pick up nuggets of valuable knowledge and insights.

Underwater Eye

The underwater eye reveals little-known facts about the ocean and its inhabitants. If you're a trivia buff, you'll love these notes.

Acknowledgments

Several people toiled laboriously to create and produce this book. We owe special thanks to Eric Heagy and Mikal Belicove for choosing us to author this book and for handling the assorted details to get this book in gear. Thanks to Michael Koch for guiding the content of this book and keeping it focused. Thanks to Rhonda Tinch-Mize for ferreting out all our typos and fine-tuning our sentences. Kathy Bidwell deserves a round of applause for shepherding the manuscript (and accompanying art) through production. And thanks to the Alpha Books production team for transforming a loose collection of electronic files and sketches into such an attractive, bound book.

Special Thanks to the Technical Reviewer

The Complete Idiot's Guide to Oceans was reviewed by an expert who double-checked the accuracy of what you'll learn here to help us ensure that this book gives you everything you need to know about oceans, oceanography, and marine biology. Special thanks are extended to Margot Stiles.

Trademarks

All terms mentioned in this book that are known to be or are suspected of being trademarks or service marks have been appropriately capitalized. Alpha Books and Penguin Group (USA) Inc. cannot attest to the accuracy of this information. Use of a term in this book should not be regarded as affecting the validity of any trademark or service mark.

Part

Cruising Through Vast Ocean Environments

The oceans have captured your curiosity and stimulated your imagination. You're ready to dive right in and explore the ocean mysteries for yourself, but if you wander too fast too far from shore, you're likely to get swept out to sea in a tidal wave of information.

This part eases you into the topic, introducing the oceans and explaining some key concepts in plain English. In this part, you learn about the locations of the earth's five oceans, the forces that drive the ocean's tides and currents, and the factors that contribute to ocean diversity. You then take a brief tour of three dynamic ocean areas: the coastline, coral reefs, and the open ocean.

Earth: The Ocean Planet Revisited

In This Chapter

- ◆ An eye-in-the-sky world map of our oceans
- ◆ Understanding why oceans are salty
- ◆ Following the movement of water around the globe
- ◆ Understanding waves, currents, and tides
- ◆ Exploring the various ocean zones

Picture yourself floating through space and looking down on our planet. You see a big blue marble ringed with wispy white clouds. Zoom in a little closer to bring the continents and oceans into view. Assuming that you have an accurate mental image of Earth, you soon realize that the planet is waterlogged. Sure, several continents spatter the globe, but for the most part, Earth looks like a huge swimming pool with a few rafts bobbing about on its surface. And that's not a mistake in the design or engineering of our planet. The fact that Earth's surface consists mostly of water is a primary factor in making it such a perfect place for life to flourish. This chapter provides a brief overview of our oceans, points out their locations, and explains the key concepts you need to know to understand how the oceans work. By examining the physical nature of the ocean itself, you can begin to understand the incredible array of life forms it supports.

Welcome to Oceanus

When you take a close look at Earth and its oceans, you might begin to wonder how anyone could possibly think of naming our planet "Earth." Just look at a globe's profile from the Pacific Ocean side, and you won't see much "earth" at all—just little old Tahiti and some assorted specks that you have to squint at to see. At first glance, you might think that the Pacific Ocean covers nearly half the planet. Look a little closer, and you come to realize that the Pacific Ocean actually covers *more* than half the planet! Now, add in the Atlantic, Indian, Southern, and Arctic Oceans, and other bodies of saltwater and freshwater, and you have a blanket of water that covers approximately 71 percent of the world's surface! As you can clearly see, a more appropriate name for our planet would be *Oceanus*, the ocean planet. And here are the numbers to prove it:

◆ The total surface area of the earth is about 510 million square kilometers (197 million square miles).

◆ The total surface area of land is about 150 million square kilometers (57 million square miles).

◆ The total surface area of water is about 360 million square kilometers (140 million square miles). (Earth's water supply consists of 97 percent saltwater; 2 percent ice; and 1 percent freshwater, half of which is underground and half in the form of lakes, rivers, and streams.)

Captain Clam's Comments

Oceanus is from the Greek meaning "the river that flows around the earth." Oceanus was a titan and god of the seas who, along with Prometheus and Zeus, overthrew Cronus, the original head honcho of Greek deities. "Oceanus" has been used frequently in marine-related contexts such as in titles for scientific journals (such as *Oceanus* magazine), in the names of research vessels (such as Woods Hole's R/V Oceanus), and even in the titles of entire governments (such as Oceania, another name for the Pacific Islands).

Wherefore Art Thou, Oceans?

Before you begin to explore the nature of the oceans, you should look at a map of Earth's surface and pinpoint the locations of its five oceans.

Earth's Oceans

The world's five oceans.

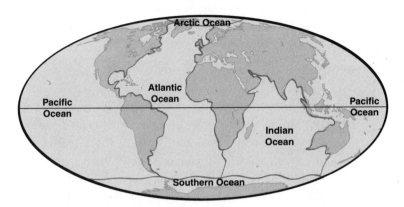

The Pacific Ocean, which lies between Asia and the Americas, is the largest ocean on the planet by far, covering approximately 155,557,000 square kilometers (64,000,000 square miles). That's more area than all the land areas combined and nearly double the surface area of the next largest ocean—the Atlantic Ocean. The Pacific Ocean also claims the award for having the deepest point on the ocean floor, the Mariana Trench, which is 10,924 meters (36,200 feet) deep—nearly 7 miles down!

The Atlantic Ocean, which lies between North America and Europe (in the north) and between South America and Africa (in the south) is the next largest ocean, covering approximately 76,762,000 square kilometers (33,420,000 square miles) of Earth's surface. Best known for its tempestuous relationship with seafarers, the Atlantic Ocean is the resting place of the *Titanic, Lusitania,* and other famous and infamous wrecks. More importantly, the North Atlantic Ocean is *by far* the most thoroughly explored, best understood, and most heavily fished of the five oceans. Compared with the Atlantic Ocean, scientists know very little about our other oceans.

The Indian Ocean, which is nestled between Africa (to the west), Asia (to the north), Australia (to the east), and the Southern Ocean (below it) is slightly smaller than the Atlantic Ocean—it covers 68,556,000 square kilometers (approximately 28,350,000 square miles) of Earth's surface. In addition to supporting the fishing industries of many of the surrounding countries, the Indian Ocean is responsible for approximately 40 percent of the world's offshore oil production and provides important sea routes for travel and trade.

The Southern Ocean is a band of water that wraps around the southernmost portion of the globe, below 60 degrees south latitude (just below the southern tip of South America) and north of Antarctica. The Southern Ocean is relatively small, covering just less than 20,327,000 square kilometers (about 8,000,000 square miles), but its average depth is greater than the average depth of any of the other four oceans—4,000 to 5,000 meters deep! The Southern Ocean is best known for its strong, sustained winds, its huge waves, and its frigid environment; during its winter, nearly the entire surface Southern Ocean is frozen.

The Arctic Ocean, the other frigid ocean, surrounds the North Pole and borders the northern edges of North America, Asia, and Europe. Most of this ocean is located within the Arctic Circle, from the North Pole down to 90 degrees northern latitude. The smallest of the five oceans, the Arctic Ocean covers 14,056,000 square kilometers (slightly more than 5,000,000 square miles), and most of its surface area consists of ice 1 to 10 meters (3 to 33 feet) thick. The Arctic Ocean is best known for its wildlife (including polar bears, whales, and seals) and for its natural resources (primarily oil). It also has a reputation, as does the Southern Ocean, for attracting some of the most fearless explorers.

Although we humans like to think of Earth as having five distinct and separate oceans, the oceans are connected, essentially making them a single, unified ocean. When a sea turtle swims from the Indian Ocean to the Pacific Ocean, for example, it hardly thinks of itself as crossing from one ocean to another. To the sea turtle, the ocean is one huge body of water. While it is helpful for us to designate certain areas as distinct oceans for study and research, always keep in mind that the oceans are connected and that the water and organisms from one ocean can mingle with the water and organisms from the others.

Don't Forget the Gulfs, Bays, and Seas

Though the previous section provided fairly clear boundaries for the various oceans, near the shores of any landmass, boundaries begin to fade and other, smaller bodies of saltwater beg for their own identities. This is particularly evident in areas where the oceans appear to extend inland to form *gulfs* and *bays*. When locating oceans on a map, note the gulfs, bays, and seas that are extensions of these oceans, and soon you will notice that distinctions between bays, gulfs, and seas can be puzzling. Look at a map of the world and try to figure out why one body of water is called a "bay," another is called a "gulf," and still another is called a "sea." The apparently arbitrary distinctions will make your head spin.

A gulf or bay is any concavity in the shoreline into which a neighboring ocean or sea extends its reach. For instance, the Bay of Bengal is a concavity of the Asian shoreline into which the neighboring Indian Ocean extends.

A *sea* can be a unique subdivision of an ocean, such as the Sargasso Sea, which is characterized by its dense mats of floating seaweed, called *sargassum*. A sea can also be a body of water that branches off from one of the oceans and might be partially enclosed by land, such as the Mediterranean Sea and the South China Sea.

> ### Underwater Eye
>
> When determining the surface area of the various oceans, neighboring gulfs, bays, and seas are assigned to a particular ocean. For example, the Atlantic Ocean includes the Mediterranean Sea, the Caribbean Sea, the Gulf of Mexico, and the North Sea.

The Water Cycle of Life

You are probably aware that plants and animals have life cycles, but did you know that water has a life cycle, too? Following the rule of "what goes up must come down," the life cycle of water, commonly referred to as the *hydrologic cycle*, describes the way water travels around the globe from ocean to air to land and back again to the ocean. During the course of its life, water transforms from its solid state (ice), to its liquid form (water), and ultimately to its gaseous state, in which it evaporates and becomes humidity. When humidity-packed air is cooled, the water forms droplets and falls back to the earth as precipitation—either in liquid form (as rain) or in solid form (as snow or hail).

The important point to keep in mind when looking at marine systems is that when salt water evaporates, only the water part goes up; the salt stays behind. This ingenious "design" enables the oceans to retain their salt content while clouds transport fresh water (salt-free) to land and to freshwater lakes and rivers. It also causes variations in the salt content of different seawater habitats, giving rise to a greater diversity of wildlife.

Captain Clam's Comments

Unlike most liquid substances, which contract as they cool and become solids, water contracts as it cools only until it nears its freezing point. As water begins to freeze, it expands, making it less dense and causing it to float on top of the water beneath it. If water contracted during freezing, it would become denser and would sink, and the process would continue (the surface water freezing solid and sinking) until eventually the Arctic and Southern Oceans would become frozen solid (no liquid water below the ice)!

The hydrologic cycle shows the movement of water from the ocean to the skies to land and back to the oceans.

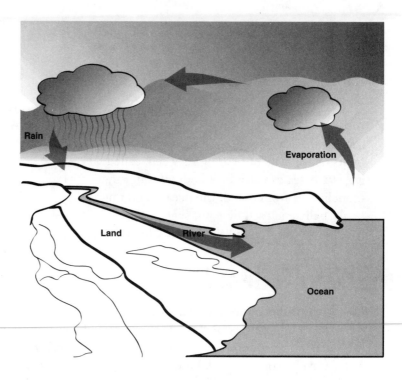

What Makes Seawater Salty?

The salty nature of the oceans inspires an obvious question: Where did all this salt come from? The answer to the question is that the salt actually comes from the fresh-water rivers and other runoff from land. As the water moves over the land and rocks and through the earth, it picks up minute traces of salt and other minerals, which it then carries to the oceans. Because the salt never leaves the oceans when the water evaporates, it continues to build up in the oceans, making them salty.

Salt Concentration Variations

As you might imagine from looking at a diagram of the hydrologic cycle, the constant movement of water around the planet can cause variations in the *salinity* (salt concentration) in different ocean areas. As water evaporates from a particular area, salinity increases because the same amount of salt is dissolved in less water. For example, in open ocean areas where no rivers flow to the sea and evaporation is significant (such as in tropical and subtropical areas), salinity can reach as high as 37 *parts per thousand* (*ppt*). Open ocean salinities in nontropical areas are the most stable because of the sheer magnitude of the water volume. The salt content is about 35 ppt in the middle of the Atlantic Ocean (not the middle depth but the middle, as in the middle of nowhere far from land).

In coastal areas where rivers empty into the oceans, salinity is low and can reach nearly freshwater levels in some cases. When the salinity dips, the water is often called *brackish*. Ocean water typically decreases in salinity toward the shoreline and up into the inlets, and as the salinity decreases, the plant and animal life changes considerably. This is especially evident in *estuaries*—unique environments created where freshwater rivers enter the salty seas.

Log Entry

Salinity refers to the amount of salt dissolved in a liquid and is typically expressed as *parts per thousand*, or *ppt*. 1 ppt equals .1 percent, so, for example, a salinity of 37 ppt is equivalent to 3.7 percent.

Underwater Eye

The saltiest water bodies in the world are salt lakes. Great Salt Lake in Utah has salinities ranging from 150 to 280 ppt depending on the lake's level. Natron Lake in Tanzania can attain a *super-saturated* salinity (cannot dissolve any more salt into the solution) of close to 340 ppt.

Three factors contribute to making these lakes so salty: First, the lake was formed by many rivers flowing into it rather than by melting glaciers (such as those responsible for creating the Great Lakes). Second, the water in a salt lake has no way to flow out of it. And finally, salt lakes exist in arid regions, where water evaporates quickly. Of course, if the land around a lake is salty, that can contribute significantly to the salt content of the lake as well.

More Than Mere Salt Water

The recipe for cooking up an ocean seems quite simple. First take a cup of tap water, add a tablespoon of salt, heat to desired temperature, and add fish. Add a few more ingredients and a dash of pepper, and you could have a nice *zuppa de peche* (fish soup). However, seawater is a little more complex than mere salt water. The composition of seawater is made up of essentially six constituents: chlorine (Cl-), sodium (Na+), sulfur (SO_4), magnesium (Mg), calcium (Ca), and potassium (K+), which make up about 99 percent of the total. The remaining 1 percent is made up of 80 or so elements that compose a list almost as long as the periodic table. Of the first 99 percent, a full 86 percent is made up of Na+ and Cl-, the stuff we fondly refer to as *table salt* (sodium chloride). The chemical composition of dilute seawater has been said to resemble vertebrate blood, the very stuff that flows through our veins.

Of course, the concentrations of all these chemicals vary in different parts of the oceans. And these variations, along with variations in water temperature, currents, nutrients, and other factors provide the driving force behind the evolution of the various plants and animals that inhabit the oceans. Throughout this book, you will see evidence of these factors at work, as we examine the diverse species of ocean life.

Hey, I Can Float!

Salinity affects more than the flavor of your food and the types of organisms that can live in a particular ocean environment. It also affects the density of the water. Saltwater is denser ("heavier") than freshwater. In other words, if you were to carefully place a layer of freshwater atop a layer of saltwater, the layer of freshwater would remain on top. If you placed a layer of saltwater on top of a layer of freshwater, the saltwater would sink to the bottom. Another way to look at it is that you can float more easily in saltwater than you can in freshwater. In water that is high in salt, such as the Great Salt Lake and the Dead Sea, you don't even need to know how to swim—the water carries you.

As explained later in this chapter, the salinity/density variations of seawater provide a driving force behind deepwater currents. Cold, salty water is denser than warmer, less salty water, causing the denser water to sink and the warmer water to rise. This moves water around the globe in huge underwater "rivers," carrying nutrients from one area of the ocean to other areas and influencing the migrations of many species of sea creatures.

Going with the Flow: Tides, Waves, and Currents

Although the hydrologic cycle explains the movement of water from the oceans to land and back, it does little to explain the way that water moves *within* the oceans.

> **Log Entry**
>
> An **eddy** is a current that rides along the side of another, usually greater current and in the opposite direction of the main current. Eddies often flow in a circular motion like a whirlpool. They can be small and short lived or can be hundreds of kilometers across, up to 2 kilometers deep, and swirl for as long as 3 years.

Water flows into bays and harbors during high tide and out to sea during low tide. It spins in *eddies* and even crashes down upon itself in violent waves. Some motion, such as the movement of tides, is predictable and cyclical in nature. Other motion, such as the raging chaos of wind-whipped seas in a sudden squall, is difficult to understand and can be unleashed at any given moment. Ocean water moves at the surface and moves below, often working in concert to create a perpetual flow of water from the surface to the ocean floor and back to the surface and from one coast to another. This constant churning erodes coastlines, stirs up nutrients, transports food, mixes salt- and freshwater, and even influences much of the weather and climate that we experience across the continents.

Throughout this book, you will see how this constant motion of the ocean affects the evolution, migration patterns, and survival of many species (both plants and animals). Because of this, understanding the various forces that control the movement of water in the oceans is critical in understanding ocean life.

The Ebb and Flow of Tides

Tides are incredible and very reliable at displacing water, sometimes causing the daily disappearance and reappearance of entire beaches and sandbars. On most coasts, the tides change the water level by 1 to 3 meters (3 to 9 feet) daily, but on some shorelines, the tide can change the water level by as much as 15 meters (50 feet) in a single day!

What on Earth could cause such a variation in sea level? Actually, the moon and the sun are primarily responsible for causing the tides. Each of these cosmic bodies has its own gravitational force that tugs on the earth. When the moon is on one side of the earth, for instance, it tugs on that side, causing the water to bulge out and creating a high tide.

You might think that the opposite side of the earth would then experience a low tide, but that's not the case. The opposite side of the earth actually experiences a high tide as well. The moon's gravitational pull is weakest on the far side of the earth (the side opposite the moon), where it is outweighed by the centrifugal force of the spinning earth. The high tide on the far side is caused by the spinning earth, which causes the ocean to lift up away from the earth just like the tassels on a figure skater's costume flare out during a spin.

When both the sun and the moon are aligned, they each contribute their tugging power to create even higher high tides and lower low tides (called *spring tides*). When the sun and the moon are at right angles to each other in relation to the earth, their forces work against each other, resulting in less tidal variation around the globe (called *neap tides*).

Captain Clam's Comments

This explanation of tides is very simplified. Actually, many factors contribute to controlling the behavior of tides in any given location, including the rotation of the earth and landmasses that restrict water movement. However, the gravitational pull of the moon and the sun on the earth are the primary forces that drive tides. The sun's pull is only half as strong as the moon's, because the sun is so much farther from the earth. (Landmasses also experience tidal variation, but the variation is typically too small to notice.)

The gravitational pull of the moon and the sun causes the tides.

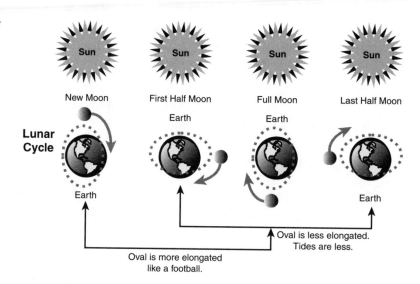

Riding the Waves

Although tides are responsible for a good share of the ocean's motion, on the surface of the ocean, waves rule. There's nothing like a large wave, rising high above the ocean's surface, to inspire awe and fear in sailors and landlubbers alike.

The size and shape of a wave depend on the force and duration of the wind that rides over the surface of the water and on the shape and composition of the ocean floor that slows down the mass of water (*pile*) as the wave gets closer to the shore. The uninterrupted distance or extent of area over which the wind blows, the *fetch*, adds still more to the wave's final form.

The wind pushes the surface of the water up into a wave. As the water falls back down under its own weight, it pushes up the water in front of it, causing the wave to *propagate* (travel), and to grow as more energy is added to it. When it nears the shore or a shallow location (a *shoal*), the friction from the bottom begins to pull back at the bottom of the wave while the top of the wave continues to move. Eventually, the wave becomes too tall for the bottom of the wave to support, and then the wave curls forward and *breaks*. The same thing happens to you when you run full force into the ocean: The water slows down your legs, but your upper body keeps moving forward until you finally fall facedown into the water.

More waves follow in an unending series. The amount of time that passes between the tops of the waves (the *crests*) or the bottoms of the waves (the *troughs*) is called the *period*, and the distance between the center points of two neighboring troughs or crests is the *wavelength*. A wave begins to break when the water depth is less than one half the wavelength.

Although waves appear to move massive amounts of water, very little water is actually displaced. When you see a wave, you actually are witnessing the energy of the wind passing through the water, causing the water to rise and fall as the wave passes through it.

Captain Clam's Comments

Huge waves, such as tidal waves or *tsunamis* (pronounced *sue-nah-mees*), are typically caused by earthquakes that occur below sea level, near a coastline, or by volcanic activity at the bottom of the ocean. Although it is true that tidal waves can cause more damage at high tide, the name "tidal wave" is inaccurate because tides do not cause tidal waves. A more accurate name is tsunami, which comes from the Japanese *tsu* (harbor) and *nami* (wave).

Current Events

Although tides and waves cause dramatic water movements that anyone lying on a beach can witness, currents are the major water movers. Currents drive water from one coast to another, spin it in circular directions (called *gyres*), and even move it from the surface of the ocean to the bottom and back again. Driven by currents, the same water eventually cycles through all five oceans (the Pacific, Atlantic, Indian, Arctic, and Southern).

Several factors contribute to the formation of currents, including tides and waves. For example, a high tide near a bay causes strong currents that carry water from the ocean into the bay. Waves also cause currents called *rip currents* (or *riptides*) that develop as wind pushes water up on shore and the water flows back toward the sea.

Log Entry

A **rip current** is created when strong winds blow directly into shore. A strong rip current can make you feel as though someone is trying to pull you underwater by your ankles and can carry even a strong swimmer out to sea.

Although tides and waves are responsible for currents that develop close to shore, currents in the open ocean are much stronger and move much more water. Open ocean currents can be classified as two types: *surface currents* and *subsurface currents*.

Surface currents account for approximately 13 to 25 percent of the water movement and are powered primarily by the wind. Near the equator, strong winds, called the Northeast Trade Winds (in the Northern Hemisphere) and the Southeast Trade Winds (in the Southern Hemisphere) push the surface water from east to west around the globe. Away from the equator, winds push the water in the opposite direction (from west to east). In addition, the rotation of the earth causes an interesting phenomenon called the Coriolis effect that deflects the wind and water currents to the right (clockwise) in the Northern Hemisphere and to the left (counterclockwise) in the Southern Hemisphere.

These forces combine to power the flow of surface currents in the ocean basins. As these currents flow, they eventually bump into landmasses that further influence the direction of the water flow and cause the ocean basins to develop currents that flow in elliptical patterns, called *gyres*. These gyres typically flow clockwise in the Northern Hemisphere and counterclockwise in the Southern Hemisphere. (You might have heard that water spirals down a drain clockwise in the Northern Hemisphere and counterclockwise in the Southern Hemisphere. This is untrue. The forces that cause the creation of gyres act on a global scale, but do not affect the water in your sink or toilet.)

One exception to the formation of gyres is in the Southern Ocean, where the current primarily flows from west to east around the entire globe. This is possible because the current has no major obstacle, such as a continent, to deflect the water. Another exception is at the equator, where the Coriolis effect is essentially zero and the water flows in the direction of the wind—east to west.

In the Northern Hemisphere, gyres flow clockwise. In the Southern Hemisphere, gyres flow counterclockwise.

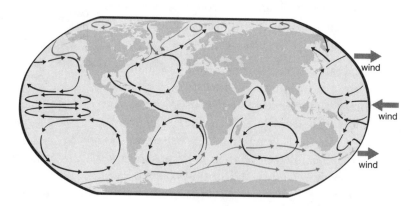

Unlike surface currents, which are driven by wind, subsurface currents are driven by variations in water density, which is determined by water temperature and salinity (or *thermohaline* conditions). The densest water masses originate near the North and South Poles—in the areas around Antarctica, Greenland, Iceland, and Norway. In these areas, cold, dense waters dive down to the ocean floor and follow a path toward the equator. In the Northern Hemisphere, the North Atlantic Deep Water sinks directly to the bottom and flows toward the equator. In the Southern Hemisphere, the dense water forms two layers—the Antarctic Bottom Water that flows north toward the equator along the ocean floor and the Antarctic Intermediate Water that flows in a layer nearer to the surface. The North Atlantic Deep Water eventually meets and flows between the Antarctic Bottom Water and the Antarctic Intermediate Water. In between the deep, cold layers and the lighter surface waters, warmer bottom water from ocean areas near the equator flows back toward the poles, carrying nutrient-rich waters to the polar regions. (Deep water also flows from seas that have high salt concentrations, such as the Mediterranean and Red Seas, as evaporation leaves behind salty, dense water.)

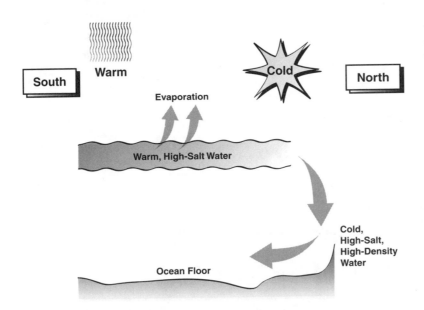

Subsurface currents develop because of variations in water density.

Captain Clam's Comments

Some of the densest water in the oceans forms near Iceland, Greenland, and Norway. As warm seawater from the Gulf Stream moves north along the surface, it becomes more and more salty because of the high level of evaporation. When it reaches the northern seas and begins to cool, it becomes very dense (because of its high salinity and low temperature), dives to the ocean floor, and heads south, generating a very powerful subsurface current.

Mixing It Up with Upwellings and Downwellings

As water moves, particularly near coastal areas, deep, nutrient-rich water often rises to the surface, causing an *upwelling*. As a surface current approaches a coast, the Coriolis force deflects the current away from the coast. Deep, nutrient-rich water rises up to replace the water carried away from the coast, causing an upwelling.

Upwellings typically occur off the coasts of California, Chile, South Africa, and elsewhere, where they transport minerals and nutrients from the ocean floor up to levels where plants and animals thrive. Hence, upwellings are often responsible for *plankton blooms*—production of massive amounts of microscopic and tiny plants and animals that feed larger, more complex organisms, including fish and whales.

Upwellings bring nutrient-rich waters to the surface, where plants and animals feed.

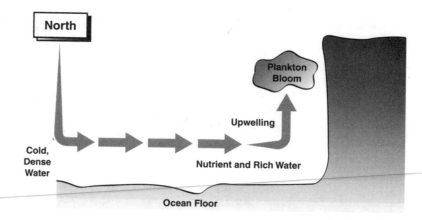

Downwellings typically occur near coastlines, when strong winds blow toward the coast. As the winds push surface water toward land, the water masses onshore, piles up, and sinks, pushing back the deepwater and causing a downwelling.

Following the Contours of the Ocean Floor

When studying ocean basins, currents, upwellings, and downwellings, you should be aware of some of the geological forces and features at work on the ocean floor. If you look at a cross section of the globe, you can see that the earth consists of layers of solid and molten rock that surround a solid *core*. The outermost layer consists of solid rock called the *lithosphere*, on which the continents and oceans ride. The lithosphere consists of several plates (about a dozen) that ride atop a layer of molten rock, called the *asthenosphere*. The theory of how these plates move is called *plate tectonics*.

According to plate tectonics, as the asthenosphere heats up, it rises and pushes up on the edges of the plates, forcing the plates apart and widening the ocean floor. As a result, the ocean basins widen and the continents drift further apart (by a few centimeters a year). This plate movement also creates a ridge along the line where the plates meet. As some edges of the plates drift apart, other edges bump against one another. When this occurs, one plate commonly pushes below another plate, causing a phenomenon known as *subduction*. As the plate dives down, carrying its rock with it, the rock heats up as it enters the asthenosphere and becomes molten rock (*magma*).

In some cases, the magma is forced up through cracks in the earth's surface, causing volcanoes.

As you can imagine, these plate movements and the resulting geological events cause dramatic changes to the contours of the ocean floor. And the shape of the ocean floor has a tremendous influence on how the water flows from one area to another.

The Ocean as a Weather Machine

The most direct and obvious effect the oceans have on our lives as land-dwellers is the effect of the oceans on our *weather* and *climate*. Without the oceans, Earth would experience dramatic fluctuations in temperature on a daily basis. Whenever the sun was beaming down on our side of the continent, we would bake to a crisp. At night, we would freeze solid. And I'm not talking normal temperature variations; I'm talking about being able to boil a pot of water in the sun during the day and freezing that same pot of water at night!

The ocean plays three important roles in keeping our planet at a steady temperature—it stores heat during the day, releases heat at night, and transports heat around the globe. In short, it keeps the planet's overall temperature fairly stable. Of course, it's not that simple, and the ocean doesn't do this all by itself; it works together with the atmosphere to establish climates and influence the ever-changing weather patterns.

Log Entry

Weather is the day-to-day variations in temperature, pressure, humidity, and wind for a given area, whereas **climate** is the long-term, statistical measurements of those weather patterns. Think of weather as that which can be measured by rain gauges, thermometers, and barometers, and climate as being defined by statistical records.

The Great Heat Absorber and Transporter

As the sun shines down on earth, most of the energy that strikes the ground is reflected back into the atmosphere. However, most of the energy that strikes the oceans and other bodies of water is stored in the form of heat. Some estimates claim that the top 3 meters of the ocean surface store as much heat as Earth's entire atmosphere! And, considering that the ocean has an average depth of nearly 4 kilometers, you can imagine just how much heat it can store.

As water moves around the globe, it carries this heat to different regions, affecting weather patterns and climates around the globe. The Gulf Stream, for example, is responsible for heating much of Eastern Europe. Without the Gulf Stream, Eastern Europe would be as frigid as northern Canada. Instead, it is more temperate than the central United States. Likewise, El Niño is a strong current that brings warm water to the coasts of Peru and Ecuador, influencing climates and weather patterns throughout the world.

The Ocean and Atmosphere Connection

The ocean and the atmosphere work hand-in-hand to control climates and weather patterns and to distribute heat around the globe. Our atmosphere actually deflects much of the sun's rays, preventing the planet from overheating. It also traps some of the energy that passes through in what is known as the *greenhouse effect*. In addition, at the interface between air and sea, the ocean and the atmosphere constantly exchange vast amounts of energy and chemicals.

One of the best ways to see how the heat exchange functions is to spend a day (and night) at the beach. During the day, when the beach is hot and the water is relatively cool, the warm air from the land rises, creating a low pressure area that pulls cool, denser air from the water over the land. This cool, incoming breeze is called a *sea breeze*. At night, the ground loses its heat quickly, while the ocean, which has been storing heat all day continues to heat the air above it. This causes a low-pressure area above the water, which pulls cooler air from the land out away from the beach. This breeze is known as a *land breeze*.

The beach breezes are a microcosmic example of what happens on a global scale. As the oceans store and release massive amounts of energy, and as air rises and falls and blows around the globe, these forces interact to influence weather patterns and establish climates around the globe.

Letting Off Some Steam: Hurricanes and Cyclones

When oceans have stored vast amounts of energy, typically near the equator during the summer months, they frequently release this energy in dramatic and sometimes very destructive ways through the creation of hurricanes (in the Atlantic Ocean), typhoons (in the Pacific Ocean), and cyclones (in the Indian Ocean).

In tropical and subtropical areas, surface water temperatures often rise to 27 degrees Celsius (80 degrees Fahrenheit), which heats the air above the surface, causing it to rise. As this warm, humid air rises, it begins to form clouds, which create a huge donut-shape storm cloud above the ocean. Heat energy continues to feed this spiraling mass of clouds, causing it to spins faster and grow larger and larger until it finally spins out over a colder body of water or over land. As soon as it moves away from its energy source (the warm ocean water), it dissipates, but before it does, it is capable of devastating any island and coastal communities that happen to be in its path.

Ocean Ecology 101

Our planet is basically an enclosed system, a big terrarium in which various natural processes work together to ensure the evolution of life and the constant recycling of nutrients. Plants transform carbon dioxide and oxygen into simple sugars. Herbivores eat the plants. Carnivores eat the herbivores. Scavengers and detrivores eat the leftovers (dead plant and animal matter). And decomposers break down any wastes to return valuable nutrients to the system. Nature wastes nothing.

To get a start and continue to flourish, every ecosystem requires an energy source and a *primary producer* (an organism that can use the energy to transform surrounding chemicals into edible matter for other organisms). In most cases, the sun provides the essential energy, but deep in the ocean and in other extreme environments, the energy source consists of chemicals that spew out of cracks or holes in the earth's crust. The primary producer typically is a photosynthetic organism, such as a plant or photosynthetic bacteria called *cyanobacteria*. In extreme environments, such as the deep sea or around hot springs, special bacteria called *archaebacteria* can play the role of primary producer, using a process called *chemosynthesis* to convert carbon dioxide and oxygen into edible, organic material.

The primary producer composes the base of the ecosystem's food pyramid, a model that represents the relative biomass that each group of organisms contributes to the ecosystem. Each step in the food pyramid is considered a *trophic level*. One step up from the plants and archaebacteria are the *primary consumers*—herbivores that eat the primary producers. The next level up consists of first-level carnivores. The next level up consists of second-level carnivores, and so on. In general, each trophic level contributes one tenth of the biomass contributed by the next lower level. For example, the primary producers might account for 100 units of biomass; the primary consumers represent 10 units, and the first-level carnivores contribute 1 unit. Another way to look at it is that it takes 100 pounds of plants to grow 10 pounds of vegetarian fish to grow 1 pound of carnivorous fish.

Because the ocean ecosystem is closed, it requires additional processes to recycle the wastes and return them to the system as useable nutrients. This is the role of the scavengers, detrivores, and decomposers. Scavengers, such as crabs and seagulls, grab what they can use, and detrivores consume the rest, essentially converting them to wastes. Worms, shellfish, and other organisms that eat dead plant and animal material are detrivores. Decomposers, typically bacteria and fungi, complete the breakdown of wastes and are responsible for releasing much of the nitrogen stored in waste products back into the ecosystem.

Underwater Eye

Every milliliter of saltwater contains approximately 1,000 to 10,000 protozoa, 1 million bacteria and archaea, and between 1 million and 100 million viruses. Think about that the next time you take a dip in the ocean!

Of course, no food pyramid or food chain is so simple and linear. Some creatures eat plants, animals, detritus, and even members of their own species. Creatures compete for the same food source, as well. Because of these complexities, scientists prefer to describe the food cycle as a *food web* that shows the interrelationships of the various creatures in a community and creates a map showing who is eating whom.

As energy cycles through the various ocean ecosystems, the physical processes that move the ocean waters continue to churn this ocean soup, mixing the nutrients, breaking down the wastes, and transporting nutrients throughout the oceans. In addition, the movements and migrations of various ocean fish and other creatures also help to transport nutrients and energy through the system. As you can begin to see, the physical features of the ocean play a critical role in the evolution and survival of the various living organisms and their ecosystems.

Zoning In on Marine Systems

Ocean ecology also focuses on the various biogeographical areas, commonly called *zones*, which help scientists classify organisms and understand the evolutionary factors at work in the various ecosystems. To designate an area as a zone, scientists look at several properties, including the zone's daily exposure to tides and currents, its topography, its depth, and the amount of sunlight it receives. The unique nature of each zone helps to determine the types of organisms that can populate the zone.

Ocean areas are designated as zones.

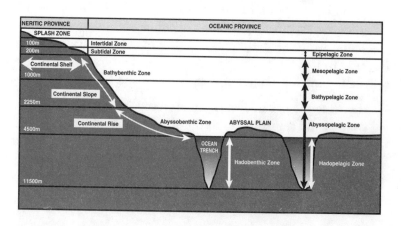

Familiarize yourself with the ocean zones in the following list, so you can quickly identify them when they crop up in later chapters. Note that zones ending in *-benthic* describe the ocean floor, whereas zones ending in *-pelagic* represent zones in the open ocean.

- **Splash zone** is the area where the high tide doesn't reach, but ocean water can actually splash up on shore or on surrounding rocks. This is the driest zone.

- **Intertidal zone** (also called the *littoral zone*) is the area between low and high tides. During high tide, this zone is covered with water. During low tide, it is exposed to the air.

- **Subtidal zone** (also called the *sublittoral zone*) is the area beyond the intertidal zone, but typically no deeper than 30 meters (98 feet) and within 1 kilometer of the shoreline.

- **Euphotic zone** (also called the *photic* or *epipelagic zone*) is the zone that sunlight penetrates well enough to support photosynthesis. This is typically no deeper than 100 meters but extends over the entire ocean surface.

- **Aphotic zone** (also called the *mesopelagic zone*) is an open ocean zone that extends from the bottom of the epipelagic zone down to about 1,000 meters (328 feet). Some light, but not much, reaches this zone.

- **Bathypelagic zone** is an open-ocean zone that extends from the bottom of the mesopelagic zone to approximately 2,250 meters (7,380 feet), but does not include the ocean floor.

- **Continental shelf** is the submerged edge of a continent, which includes some of the most biologically and geologically rich areas of the ocean. The width of the shelf varies from 1 kilometer to up to 750 kilometers (466 miles). Near the end of the shelf, the shelf has a drop-off, called the *shelf break*. Strong currents commonly cut deep canyons into the continental shelf and slope that run perpendicular to the shoreline.

- **Continental slope** is the furthermost edge of the continental shelf beyond the shelf break. In some cases, the slope dives straight down to the ocean depths. In other cases, it slopes somewhat gradually.

- **Abyssal zone** is the sea floor where the sun doesn't shine. This zone reaches from approximately 2,250 meters (7,380 feet) down to the ocean floor. This is where the movie *The Abyss* was set. This area is characterized by cold, high-pressure, pitch-dark waters.

- **Trenches** are special areas where the seafloor dips to form a valley.

Although zones provide a tool for understanding the various ocean environments, these zones are not neat little subdivisions. Creatures commonly found in one zone often spend a good portion of their lives in other zones. Many fish that swim the open oceans, for example, lay their eggs and spend their early days in salt marshes or mangrove swamps. The larvae of many benthic organisms can spend several months of their lives as plankton, floating in the surface waters before settling to the bottom. In addition, many organisms, such as various seaweeds and corals actually *build* unique biohabitats, in which other organisms live.

It's Getting Deep

Before oceanographers had a clear picture of the ocean floor, most envisioned it as a huge, flat wasteland—and for the most part, they were right. The abyssal plain is a fairly uniform area that covers nearly 84 percent of the ocean floor. Abyssal hills, made up of soft sediment, and lined up in rows lend some diversity to this region. Occasionally this corrugated landscape is broken up by a *seamount* (an underwater volcano) which can be a literal and figurative hotbed of marine diversity. Many seamounts have their own species that live only around that particular volcano.

Where the tectonic plates grind together you can find more dramatic variations in ocean floor topography. When one plate dives below another, it forms a *trench* or depression, and some of these trenches, such as Marianas Trench, represent the deepest parts of the ocean. In other areas where the plates drift apart, molten rock oozes up between the plates forming underwater mountain ranges called *mid-ocean ridges*. Many of the mountains below the ocean surface are actually taller than the mountains on land! (The tallest mountain as measured from its base to its peak is Mauna Kea, in Hawaii. It's 10,204 meters (33,480 feet) from its base to its tip, though only a small portion is above sea level. Mt. Everest, commonly known as the tallest mountain, is 8,848 meters (29,030 feet) above sea level.)

Log Entry

An **estuary** is an area where freshwater sources, such as rivers and tributaries, mix with saltwater from ocean. A **salt marsh** is a coastal area where tides have deposited sediment and grasses have begun to grow. **Mangroves** are salt-tolerant trees that grow in coastal areas of tropical and subtropical regions where rivers empty into the ocean.

Estuaries and Other Coastal Environments

Although the various oceanic zones cover all areas relating to the oceans, some unique habitats deserve some special attention, particularly *estuaries*, *salt marshes*, and *mangrove forests*. These coastal habitats form where freshwater rivers empty into saltwater seas or saltwater from the oceans forces its way inland (or both actions work together). These coastal ocean environments provide unique habitats for many interesting and diverse species of both plants and animals. You will learn more about them in Chapter 2.

The Least You Need to Know

- Seventy-one percent of the surface of Earth is covered with water, and, of that, 97 percent is saltwater.

- Earth has five oceans: the Pacific, Atlantic, Indian, Arctic, and Southern Oceans.

- The movement of water from oceans to air to land and back to the oceans is called the hydrologic cycle.

- Salinity is the measure of the concentration of salt in water and is typically measured in parts per thousand (ppt).

- The gravitational pull of the moon and the sun controls the tides.

- Surface currents are caused primarily by the winds, whereas subsurface currents are driven by variations in water density.

- The ocean and atmosphere interact to influence weather and climate around the world.

- Ocean ecology is the study of how organisms interact with their environment and with one another in a community.

- Scientists divide the ocean into zones that extend from the splash zone out to the middle of the ocean and from the surface to the ocean floor.

Chapter 2

The Most from Coast to Coast

In This Chapter

- ◆ Up close and personal with the world's coastlines
- ◆ Estuaries and other places where land meets sea
- ◆ A treasure trove of mangroves
- ◆ Good-bye bay nutrients, hello sea
- ◆ Rocky intertidal and seashore ecosystems

Before you set sail for the open sea and begin plunging its depths, spend some time on shore exploring the place where land meets sea—the place oceanographers like to call the *land-sea interface*. This is where the action is, where the most happenin' sea creatures just happen to be. In this chapter, we start to explore the coastline and check out some of the more interesting and well-populated ocean habitats: estuaries, mudflats, salt marshes, bays, beaches, tidal pools, rocky coastlines, and mangrove forests.

Estuaries: Where Freshwater and Saltwater Mix

Take a look at a large aerial photograph or map in which any substantial river reaches the end of its journey and drains into an ocean. This opening, which generally begins to widen toward the sea, is often referred to as an *estuary*. The water in an estuary is much more salty than the river and much less salty than the sea, but no two estuaries are the same. They differ primarily in how well the freshwater from the river and the saltwater from the sea are mixed. Estuaries generally fall into one of the following three categories:

- **Salt wedge estuary** Where a large river, such as the Mississippi, empties into the ocean, its flow overpowers the tidal currents and creates a wedge of freshwater that lays on top of a wedge of denser saltwater. The freshwater wedge is widest near the river and then tapers off out to sea. The narrow edge of the saltwater wedge pushes inland near the bottom of the river.

- **Partially mixed estuary** When a relatively large river empties into an ocean where the tidal activity is fairly strong, such as at the mouth of the Thames River in the UK, the freshwater becomes fairly well mixed from the surface to the ocean floor. Salinity also varies both as you move toward shore and vertically where the fresh and saltwater layers meet, but a stagnant layer of salty water remains at the bottom.

- **Well-mixed estuary** Where relatively weak flowing rivers empty into active tidal areas, such as near the mouth of the Columbia River, between Washington and Oregon states, the freshwater and saltwater become very well mixed, and salinity variations are more continuous as you move toward shore and upstream. Well-mixed estuaries are typically shallow and have a high tidal range.

A salt wedge estuary exhibits a clear division between salt-water and freshwater.

What makes estuaries so unique is that they have a tremendous amount of nutrients. River water itself is high in nutrients, but when it pours into the sea, much of the nutrients are deposited as sediment at the bottom of the estuary. When the tides come in, they churn up this sediment, mix it with the water, and carry it inland. This creates nutrient-rich, highly productive ecosystems that account for nearly half of the living matter in our oceans!

Although estuaries offer an amazing quantity of living matter, they feature a relatively narrow range of diversity. Because of the salinity variations, few species have found ways to cope in estuaries and take advantage of their resources. Instead, relatively few species have found ways to exploit and dominate these harsh environments.

One of the most dominant creatures in the estuary is the *tunicate*, a colorful blob of a being that looks like a ball of Jell-O. Though tunicates look more like *invertebrates* (creatures lacking a backbone, such as slugs) they actually are more closely related to *vertebrates*, like you and me. Tunicates can readily be seen fouling up anything that floats, such as buoys or mooring or the bottoms of floating docks. Tunicates are excellent at dealing with fluctuations in water quality, making them one of the best *osmotic conformers* in the sea world.

Captain Clam's Comments

An osmotic conformer (or *osmoconformer*, for short) is any living creature that can tolerate a wide range of salinity variations without stressing out. They do this by regulating and maintaining a stable internal environment regardless of the changes in their surroundings. Organisms that can tolerate very high as well as very low salinities are said to be *euryhaline*. When an organism cannot handle the highs and lows but can tolerate a certain limited range of fluctuation, it is called *stenohaline*.

One Kicking Raw Bar

Whenever I think of the estuary, I picture the animals I hold most dear, the *bivalves*. Bivalves are clams, oysters, and other squishy *molluscs* that live in shells consisting of two hinged halves. Anyone who loves to eat shellfish should know that estuaries can be home to one of the most happening raw bars in town, for man (or woman) and beast alike. (A *raw bar* is a counter where raw shellfish are served. They're also called "oyster bars.")

Many of the world's estuaries are famous for their estuarine seafood fare, such as the oysters from Wellfleet, Massachusetts and Blue Point, New York and the Belon oysters from the Brittany coast of France. The estuaries provide some of the best habitats for scallops, hard and soft shell clams, mussels, and an international host of other delectable notables. Estuaries provide these creatures with the proper water quality and nutrients they need to thrive and be safe for humans and other predators to consume.

The estuary's raw bar certainly was not put there solely for us. Many hungry customers were already waiting in line for their share of the slurpable shell food, long before humans developed a taste for clam chowder. Estuaries are teaming with crabs, often the main predator of the bivalve. That makes sense because most crabs have a pair of lobster crackers for hands. Other major bivalvavores include the sea stars (starfish) and various snails, such as the aptly named *oyster drill*.

More Productive Than Wheat

Estuarine environments are among the most productive ecosystems on Earth, creating more organic matter each year than equivalent areas of forest, grassland, or even wheat fields! In Part 2, which covers sea plants, you will explore just how important the estuaries are in regard to *primary production* (production of food that supports the bottom of the food chain).

One reason estuarine environments are so productive is because they represent diverse habitats, including shallow open waters, freshwater and saltwater marshes, river deltas, sandy beaches, mud and sand flats, creeks, rocky shores, oyster reefs, wooded swamps, mangrove forests, tidal pools, and seagrass and kelp beds. And every one of these areas provides an exceptional environment for producing *autotrophic* biomass (plant matter). This plant material, especially the leafy stuff that biodegrades quickly, forms a component at the base of the food pyramid, which fuels the development of other plant and animal populations. In addition, estuaries provide plenty of nutrients for their terrestrial inhabitants as well as serving as a spawning area and nursery for many pelagic fish and other sea critters.

The Buffer Zone

The estuarine environment is a relatively protected area, and is buffered from the elements by the vegetation and/or geological features that form its borders. In the case of marshlands, the production of plant materials also acts as a trap for the accumulation of the broken down matter. Over long periods of time (basically between glacial events), this buildup eventually creates a layer of peat that expands seaward. Like the peat moss sold in garden centers, this peat is very spongy and porous and acts as a buffer between the mainland and the storms and waves that come ashore. The wetlands, especially the salt marshes and mangrove forests, act as a natural barrier that dampens the energy unleashed when harsh weather comes ashore.

Welcome to the Wetlands!

Along the coastlines, especially near estuaries, and in any low-lying inland areas, water-soaked ground or *wetlands* are common. In the past, many people considered wetlands to be wastelands—smelly, useless land that needed to be filled in and planted (in the case of farms) or built upon to be any good. Relatively recently, however, people have come to realize that the wetlands perform several critical functions in our environment—purifying our water, providing habitats for many diverse species, acting as a breeding and nesting grounds for other species, keeping our air clean, and providing some of the most beautiful scenery on Earth.

Along the coasts, the wetlands take on several unique forms, the most common of which are mudflats, salt marshes, and mangrove forests. In the next few sections, you learn more about each of these important environmental areas where the distinction between land and water begins to fade.

Life on the Flats: Mudflats and Sand Flats

Coastal areas where sediment builds up can eventually form *mudflats*, some of the ugliest, muckiest, most foul-smelling places on the planet. If you've ever visited a mudflat at low tide, you won't forget the stench that wafts in from it. It smells like a combination of rotten eggs and raw sewage and plays host to dozens of the most notoriously annoying pests, including flies and mosquitoes. The green head flies in some mudflats are often mistaken for mini vampire bats wearing goggles! Even so, the mudflats are not at all bad; they're just smelly, underappreciated wetlands, which is why much of this precious resource unfortunately has been filled in or drained to make way for more human-friendly habitats such as Manhattan and Miami.

The putrid odor comes from the swamp gases, methane (CH_4) and hydrogen sulfide (H_2S), produced by the bacteria who are busy decomposing massive amounts of organic material. The decomposition of dead plant and animal matter involves many chemical and biological processes, which produce these pungent gases. *Anaerobic bacteria*, which do not require oxygen, thrive on the dead and decaying organic matter. They have a unique way of keeping out the competition by flourishing in an oxygen-free environment and by producing gases that are toxic to most marine life. These bacteria proliferate in the zones of dark black ooze that stains like charcoal and smells like matches. This is the *anoxic* layer where only the chosen few species endure and serve the rest of the community by creating a food source out of otherwise useless matter.

Where the shore has a steeper slope and wave action and tidal activity is strong enough to carry away the fine particles of mud, different type of flat forms—the *sand flat*. Because many of the nutrients on the sand flats are carried off or deposited in deeper layers, sand flats are slightly less populated than mudflats, but they do host an abundant collection of burrowing bivalves, worms, and other creatures that can dig down in the sand to find food and moisture. As in the mudflats, the deeper areas of the sand flats are populated with anaerobic bacteria that break down the dead plant and animal matter and provide a useful food source for other organisms.

The Salt Marsh

As tides and rivers continue to deposit sediment on a mudflat, the mudflat reaches a height at which saltwater grasses can take hold and spread. The network of grasses and their root systems eventually stabilize the land and create an efficient trap for additional sediments. As these grasses die and decay and sediments accumulate, they lead to the formation of salt marshes—rich habitats for hundreds of diverse species, including terrestrial animals, such as rats, snakes, insects, and birds. For more about salt marshes, skip to Chapter 9.

Mangroves: Bounty Within the Roots

In the tropics, the coastline wetlands commonly take the form of mangrove forests—dense collections of the most salt-resistant trees on the planet. Like the mudflats and salt marshes, mangrove forests have gotten a bad reputation as being smelly, mosquito-infested swamps. And if that's not bad enough, many mangrove forests are known to be infested with crocodiles. But the mangroves serve many of the same positive functions as salt marshes, buffering the coastline and providing a nutrient-rich habitat for many species.

Under water, the mangrove roots act as a protective house for the fish and invertebrates that thrive in the highly productive waters. Just about every invertebrate phylum is represented in the roots, including mangrove oysters, brittle stars, and multitudes of worms and crustaceans, all vying for a particular niche. Large populations of a wide variety of fish eat these smaller animals and use the mangroves as both hatchery and nursery. As the fish mature and grow, they eventually venture out from the mangrove's protective web of roots into open water, carrying the nutrients they consumed in the mangroves with them to other ecosystems. For more information about mangroves, see Chapter 9.

A mangrove forest is rich in nutrients and wildlife.

(Photo Credit: Ben Mieremet, Senior Advisor OSD, NOAA)

Bay Watching

Like an estuary, a bay is a semi-enclosed body of water with an outlet to a larger body of water. Bays are in the neritic province, which includes the water over the continental shelf. These bay waters can be somewhat deep but are considered quite shallow when compared to the oceanic province. Here, the bigger fish start to eat the smaller fish. With the additional volumes of water made available to them, schools of secondary consumers travel with the tides to feed upon much of the smaller individuals that have left their estuarine nursery grounds. Because of their close proximity, the bay and estuary provide an environment in which life from both ecosystems can intermingle and in which creatures that are more tolerant of varying conditions can extend their range and take advantage of increased opportunities.

The geography of the bay system is also conducive to *upwelling*, the rising up of nutrients from the bottom back up to the surface. These nutrients help sustain and feed the many tiny life forms that, in turn, become food for larger animals. Because of all this activity, the bay systems are often some of the most biologically productive areas in the ocean.

The bays are not just a hot spot for marine life; humans like them as well. In addition to providing some of the best fishing holes in the world, bays function as huge watery playgrounds, where boaters, swimmers, skiers, and other sea lovers can find a safe haven in which to frolic. One of the primary factors that make bays so safe is that they are protected from the harsh environment of the open ocean. In bays, waves are typically smaller, currents are weaker, the undertow is negligible, and lifeguards are much more relaxed. I'm not saying that bays cannot be pummeled by storms, only that bays are usually much more tranquil.

A Day at the Beach

When you first hit the beach, face the water, close your eyes, and take a deep breath. The salt air mixes with the scent of dried marine life that lies baking in the sun. The surf laps the shore as the tide continues its daily march, depositing its catch of floating debris and unfortunate victims du jour. Now open your eyes. A sea gull flies by with something in its beak; it looks like a crab. High up on the beach is a *wrack line*, alive with tiny, hopping bugs. Even the beach hoppers have found a home that few others wanted or were hearty enough to inhabit. These are amphipods that are related to a more recognizable marine arthropod—the shrimp (see Chapter 12 for details). If you dig down in the sand, you find it much cooler and moister than the surface sands scorched by the sun. Here you might discover larger arthropods; amphipods (*Orchestoidea spp.*), sand or mole crabs (*Emerita*), isopods (*Excirolana*), and possibly a worm or two. But, for the most part, few species choose to settle this unique combination of desert sand and rolling sea.

> **Log Entry**
>
> The **wrack line** is the band of marine matter consisting of seagrasses, litter, and other refuse, pushed up on shore by waves and tides. It is deposited at the daily high tide line and can build up landward at higher tide intervals.

Beach Formation

Beaches are formed by deposits of whatever geological, and sometimes biological, material is readily available. This material typically originates at some distance from the beach, and is left behind by receding glaciers, deposited by rivers and currents, or washed ashore by waves and tides. The waves and tides that hit the shoreline wash away the fine sediments that form mud or silt but leave the heavier sand and gravel behind.

Beaches vary in both color and consistency. White sand beaches are typically formed by pulverized limestone or coral. Yellow sand beaches are primarily made up of pulverized quartz. The black sand beaches, commonly found in the Pacific Ocean, are comprised of pulverized volcanic rock.

Although beaches vary widely in color and in consistency, all beaches have the same basic form—consisting of a *foreshore* and *backshore*. The foreshore is the area between the high tide and low tide levels. The backshore extends from the high tide level to the top of the beach—where you find most of the beachfront property. On some windy beaches, sand dunes (hills) form beyond the backshore where blowing sand settles and accumulates.

In cases when the tides and winds are too weak to carry the sand to the coast, barrier beaches develop just beyond the mainland. If you look at a map of Southwest Florida, you can see several barrier beaches along the coast, such as the beaches of Sanibel Island, Fort Meyers Beach, and Marcos Island. Barrier beaches are some of the most beautiful beaches in the world and have become very popular recreational areas.

Olympic Beach Combing

One of the best ways to begin your exploration of the oceans, without even setting your foot in the water, is to go *beach combing*. Beach combing consists of walking along the beach, usually along the wrack lines of a season's high tides and the day's fresh contribution of waterlogged matter, searching for interesting debris. Just pretend that you're on a deserted island in the middle of the ocean and you're searching for anything you can use to survive until you're rescued. The wrack consists primarily of various seagrasses and seaweeds, remnants of dead or dying sea creatures, and a lot of debris, including seashell shards and pop bottles. If you're lucky, you might even discover some *flotsam* and *jetsam*.

Log Entry

Flotsam is the wreckage or cargo that remains afloat after a ship has sunk. **Jetsam** is the cargo or equipment thrown overboard from a ship in distress and has washed ashore (or sunk to the bottom). Once it washes up on the beach, it all looks just about the same as it originally did, except that it is now tangled and covered with all kinds of living and deceased marine matter.

A Large Seashell Collection

A good portion of everything that washes up on a beach is in the form of seashells, homes discarded by living sea creatures or left behind by their deceased owners. Serious shell collectors comb shores and sandbars for these vacated homes and often find a bounty from which to choose.

Some devoted shell collectors even decide to turn their hobby into a profession, specializing in the field of *conchology* (a branch of zoology dealing with shells) or *malacology* (a branch of zoology focusing on molluscs). Big names go with big numbers. The number of gastropod species alone is about 90,000 if you include the 15,000 fossil representatives. Now add the other shell contributors such as the bivalves, and the species list really starts to climb.

Ocean Alert

The taking of live animals in many places of the world is illegal and punishable by jail and fines. In 1999, a Florida man and his company were sentenced in the first ever successful felony prosecution for illegal coral trafficking. The smuggler was sentenced to 18 months incarceration for his role in an operation that used false declarations, invoices, and shipping documents to circumvent U.S. and Philippine laws and international trade restrictions protecting corals and other marine species. His company was fined an additional $25,000 and given five years probation.

The Fragile Land of Sand Castles

Many coastal areas are castles in the sand—fragile areas that are subject to change and are often altered drastically by the presence of humans and our increasing impact on the marine environment. Few areas are as unstable and vulnerable as the sand beaches and dunes—the places where everything from sand castles to million-dollar cottages are at risk of sinking back into the sea as the tides fight to reclaim their land. Many prime waterfront properties, attempting to fend off the ocean's relentless attacks, fall victim to the same finality—sinking below the surface or surrendering to the unrelenting onslaught of the sea. Efforts to protect these houses by armoring beach with sea walls can cause erosion farther down the beach.

The Rocky and Barnacle Show

Now it's time to walk on solid ground—really solid ground! I'm talking about the *rocky intertidal zone*—a stony area at the shoreline between the low-tide and high-tide levels. This zone is formed not of transient material, such as sand or mud, or living matter, such as peat, but rather is made of cold, hard stone thrown up on shore by dramatic geological disturbances.

As a result of the tectonic activity that gives the earth a continuous facelift, these rocky protrusions have been pushed up out of the earth's crust and exposed to the oceans. These areas and areas formed by exposed *sedimentary* rock are now well established are teeming with life that's well adapted to the harsh conditions on the rock.

Log Entry

The term **tectonic** refers to geological activity that results in changes to the earth's crust and leads to molten rock that cools into new forms. Sedimentary rock is formed when layers of mud become compressed and turn into rock.

Chitons, Barnacles, and Other Tough Hombres

Life on the rock is no walk in the park. Only the toughest survive, and two of the toughest representatives of the rocky intertidal zone are the barnacles and the chitons (pronounced *KITE-ins*).

Barnacles are *sessile* (attached to a surface) crustaceans that you commonly see encrusting rocks, piers, bridges, and the hulls of boats. From a distance, a colony of barnacles looks like a rough layer of concrete; but on closer inspection, you can see tiny animals reaching out to grab any morsels of food that float past.

Chitons are mobile animals that look like a cross between a cockroach and an armadillo, and are the closest thing to living fossils that you'll ever see. This species of mollusc has remained unchanged for hundreds of millions of years. Lack of a typical molluscan larval stage suggests that the chitons might have diverged early from the main line of molluscan evolution.

Zones Within the Zone

The rocky intertidal region is marked by four zones based on the various levels of wetting in each zone. The zone closest to land (farthest inland) is the *spray* or *splash zone* (informally referred to as the *barnacle belt*), an area that typically gets wet only at extreme high tides and during periods of jumbo wave action. Very few creatures call this zone home because you can't grow much on dry rock. Is this land or sea? Only the well-armored creatures, such as the barnacles, limpets, and the Littorina snails, can eke out a living here.

One step down from the splash zone is the *high intertidal zone*, which extends from mean high water to slightly below the mean sea level (where the higher of the two daily low tides reaches). This area remains exposed to the air for long periods of time twice a day and is flooded only during high tide. The high intertidal zone is abundant with Balinoid barnacles and several species of snails, chitons, limpets, and algae.

Down from the high intertidal zone is the mid-intertidal zone, which is covered and uncovered twice a day by the tides. Although more turbulent than the first two zones, this zone provides the moisture needed to support a wide range of plants and animals, including mussels, algae, sea lettuce, sea palms, starfish, crabs, and even some anemones.

Down one more step is the *low intertidal zone*, which is exposed to air only during the lowest tides and can start to support larger plant species such as *Laminaria*. Here, you can find abalone, brown seaweed, limpets, sea stars, some mussels, nudibranchs, sculpin and other fish, sea cucumbers, sea urchins, shrimp, whelks and other snails, sponges, surf grass, tube worms, and other species that require a stable supply of water.

Below the rocky intertidal zone is the subtidal zone. No, this isn't where the subtitles are displayed in foreign oceans! The subtidal zone is never exposed to air, though it can get pretty shallow at low tide. Here, life is even more abundant and varied, but is still limited to species that can keep a tight hold on the ground.

Captain Clam's Comments

The names of zones vary depending on the source. In the rocky intertidal zone, the highest zone is called the *splash*, *spray*, *supra-littoral*, or *Littorina*; you might even encounter combinations of these labels, such as "supratidal splash zone." The *high intertidal* zone is also known as the *Balinoid* or *mid-littoral* zone. The mid-zone is also called the *lower mid-littoral*, *Mytilus* (mussels), *lower Balinoid*, or *mid-intertidal* zone. The low zone is referred to as the *Laminaria*, *low intertidal zone*, and *infra-littoral fringe*. There is sometimes even a sub-intertidal zone. Are you confused yet? What was wrong with just high, middle, and low? Well, the Latin-sounding zones are based on the dominant species located in these regions and act as indicators of how much exposure to the air the zone is expected to get each day, season, and decade.

Taking Hold of the Situation

The rocky intertidal shoreline is one of the slimiest, slickest places you'll find on the ocean's edge. If you have ever tried to get your footing on these algae-covered rocks, especially when the waves are crashing it, you know just how slippery the rocks can get.

The animals and plants that make their home in the rocky intertidal zone know the meaning of the verb to "attach." They must literally "hang on for dear life." They are holding on to the bare essentials: a home, a job, something to eat; it's all right there, but they have to survive the trials and tribulations of having to live in an environment that constantly pulses from wet to dry and pounds them with violent waves. Just look at the tenacious grip of the common mussel, using its beard to anchor itself to anything it can find. The beards on these things would make ZZ Top proud.

> **Captain Clam's Comments**
>
> The tough, hairy beards of mussels are made of byssal threads, which are secreted by the byssal gland in the mussel's foot. The secretion flows onto the substrate and hardens, thus anchoring the mussel firmly in place.

Any creature that intends to set up shop on the rock must find some way to get a grip. Sea stars and anemones use powerful suction cups to hang on. Still others can secrete a bio-cement that superglues them to the rocks. The barnacles, which look more like oysters than crabs but are more closely related to crabs, manage to do this with their body armor quite effectively. Even the plants have managed to develop strong holdfasts at the base of their stalks, which take a great deal of force to dislodge. But that's the point. If they couldn't hold on, they wouldn't be there; they would be washed out to sea to compete with the other, less tenacious creatures. Once again, a deserving assemblage of plants and animals effectively fills a niche and succeeds in adding to the biodiversity and character of the marine environment.

Wading in the Tide Pools

Tide pools are bodies of water near the ocean that remain filled with seawater even when the tide subsides. These pools can be as small as a cup of coffee or as big as a bathtub and can be found a few feet from shore or at the furthest reaches of high tide. Regardless of their size or location, they manage to hold a special gallery of life, as John Steinbeck described so well in *Cannery Row:*

> It is a fabulous place; when the tide is in, a wave-churned basin, creamy with foam, whipped by the combers that roll in from the whistling buoy on the reef. But when the tide goes out, the little water world becomes quiet and lovely. The sea is very clear, and the bottom becomes fantastic with hurrying, fighting, feeding, breeding animals.

Tide pools exist in areas between the high and low tide levels. When the tide goes out, these pools are left behind, along with a diverse collection of little critters. Visit a shoreline at low tide, and you'll find dozens of tide pools, some as small and shallow as puddles, teeming with life—everything from barnacles and tiny fish to crabs and starfish! Tide pools are home to many sedentary critters who sit at home and rely on the tides to deliver them the food, water, and oxygen they need to survive.

Captain Clam's Comments

When exploring tide pools, follow these rules of etiquette:

- ◆ Wet your hands before touching the wildlife.
- ◆ Handle the critters gently and put them back where you found them when you're done looking.
- ◆ If you cannot pick up an animal easily, leave it alone.
- ◆ If you move a rock to look at something underneath it, put the rock back in the same location.
- ◆ Don't take any wildlife home unless you have a license to do so.

Man Comes Calling as Usual

In real estate, location is everything, and waterfront property is the most coveted of all. Waterways support shipping and trade, fishing, tourism, and countless opportunities to earn a living and appreciate some of the most beautiful places on Earth. For this reason, people flock to the coastlines, making human populations one of the most dramatic features of the modern coastline. It is certainly the most recent feature in terms of geological and evolutionary history, as well.

In the United States, 55 percent of the population lives near a coast and by 2005, that figure likely will climb to 75 percent. Add in the population growth, and you have some areas along the coast that are expected to more than double their current densities. China, the most populated country in the world, has an average coastal population density of 600 people per square kilometer (1,560 per square mile) and densities more than three times that in cities like Shanghai. These numbers themselves are alarming, but the most disturbing aspect of coastal population explosion is that people don't just hang out on the coasts like harmless horseshoe crabs; they build stuff and they pollute their surroundings. Companies build manufacturing plants, people build homes and apartments, and the shipping industry builds docks. In addition, people need infrastructure—roads, gas lines, sewers, and so on. And when people run out of room to build more stuff, they start filling in the wetlands, clearing the mangrove forests, and building bulkheads, jetties, groins, and breakwaters to fend off the sea. Private property rights often give owners the right to completely alter environments that were established over the course of eons. We humans sure know how to leave our mark on the environment.

Filling in the Spaces

To use the edge of the sea, developers filled in and built on much of the low-lying areas and inconvenient places. Manhattan, Miami Beach, Key West, Venice, and many other coastal settlements stand as monuments to human ingenuity and achievement, but they also represent monumental losses to native vegetation and our natural habitats. In California alone, more than 90 percent of the original salt marshes have been destroyed. Most tropical countries have lost more than half of their mangroves either from urban development, logging, or conversion to rice fields, cropland, or fish-farming ponds. The search for new shoreline continues to encroach on an already taxed environment and seriously outcompetes native flora and fauna.

Glimpses of Paradise

We have filled in the wetlands and destroyed priceless habitats, but we humans are capable of understanding what it means to preserve the beauty and the bounty that the world has provided. Many coastal communities have banned further development and set aside some areas as nature preserves, assuring their protection for future generations. You can still catch a glimpse of paradise if you take the time to look. There's a certain euphoria felt when immersed in the prismatic glory of a teaming coral reef or the thrill of examining walls of anemones and bryozoans 25 meters down while schools of squid gracefully whisk by.

You can also find paradise on a clam flat during low tide, where unique and assorted species vie for a layer of the precious bottom. You can view paradise from a deck overlooking a perfect burning cirrus sunset on the bay as you dine on the catch of the day. Paradise might be that perfect day at the tide pools with your kids and watching their inquisitive smiles light up the ripples at their feet. As long as the coastal areas remain, you will always be able to catch a glimpse of paradise.

The Least You Need to Know

- ◆ Estuaries form where freshwater rivers pour into the saltwater seas.
- ◆ Mudflats, salt marshes and mangrove forests are unique coastal communities—collectively referred to as wetlands—that share the qualities of both land and water.

- ◆ Beaches are relatively unstable areas whose size and shape are at the mercy of the weather and the currents.

- ◆ The rocky intertidal zone is divided into four zones: the splash zone and the high, middle, and low tidal zones.

- ◆ Tide pools are small bodies of water between the high and low tidal ranges that typically support unique communities of organisms.

- ◆ As the human populations along the coasts increase, natural coastal environments face greater and greater risks.

An Overwhelming Garden Paradise

In This Chapter

- ◆ Diving on a pristine coral reef
- ◆ Corals, hard and soft
- ◆ Reefer madness: exploring the reef community
- ◆ Who invited the sharks?
- ◆ Tours of the oceans' riches

We used to think the oceans were a little drab, like black and white photos. We would walk along the beach and see a few light gray dolphins swimming in seemingly black water at sunset, or we'd stir up a dingy brown stingray while looking for sand dollars. Then one day, we took our first snorkeling trip to a small coral reef. Oh, brave new world! It was as though someone had suddenly painted the ocean with every color imaginable: brilliant yellows, neon blues, vibrant greens of every shade, bold reds, iridescent oranges, and colors we had never imagined! And this sea of color was all in constant, shimmering, graceful motion—a veritable ballet of pastels!

This chapter invites you to take your own virtual snorkeling adventure, so you can experience the beauty of the reef for yourself. So, pull on a mask, kick up your fins, and dive right in!

Welcome to the Coral Reef

The coral reef is a unique ecosystem that consists of materials, primarily calcium, deposited by living animals. The *corallite* (calcium carbonate) that forms the structure of the reef is secreted by animals in the cnidarian family, which also contains jellyfish (more properly called jellies, because they're not really fish) and anemones (see Chapter 10 for details). The different species of coral polyp (the animals that create the coral) construct homes for themselves on the surface of these rock-like formations and continue to grow outward over time at a rate of 1 to 20 centimeters per year. The end product is a collection of statuesque formations that make the reef look like the sculpture exhibit at your local art museum.

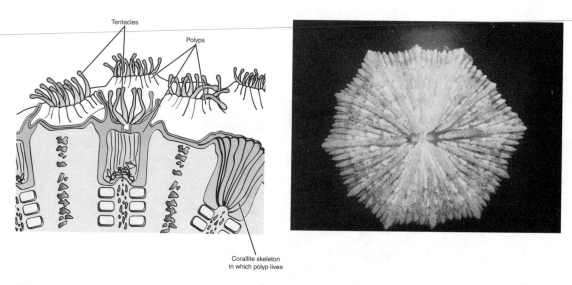

The coral polyp lives inside the limestone skeleton it creates for itself.

(Photo Credit: Photo Collection of Dr. James P. McVey, NOAA Sea Grant Program)

The Soft and the Hard Kind

When your eyes have adjusted to the exquisite beauty of the coral garden, take a closer look at the types of corals that make up the reef. The hard corals, including the brain and boulder corals, compose most of the reef's real estate and actually build outward. These corals are said to be *hermatypic* (reef building) and are found only in tropical and a few subtropical regions where water temperatures stay above the high 60s (18 degrees Celsius) and they have access to consistently intense light. Hermatypic coral polyps have a symbiotic relationship with photosynthetic *zooxanthellae* (pronounced *ZOE-a-zan-thel-ee*) that require light to survive. The zooaxanthellae actually live inside the coral polyps and, through photosynthesis, provide much of the food that the polyps need to survive. Ahermatypic coral do not require zooaxanthellae to survive. These polyps catch their own food using their stinging tentacles and although they also live in shallow waters, they can live in much colder, deeper, darker regions, as discussed in the next section.

Log Entry

The phylum *Cnidaria,* (pronounced *nye-DARE-ee-uhns*) representing the most abundant animals on the reef, includes the corals, jellies, hydroids, and anemones. Cnidarians can zap prey and predator alike using their stinging cells called *nematocysts,* which are produced by *cnidoblasts,* cells that are unique to the phylum.

Ocean Alert

Watch out for fire coral! Like all cnidarians, these corals have nematocysts (stinging cells), which they use to paralyze their prey. The sting of the fire coral is much stronger than that of other coral species—not that you should be touching any coral. They are more easily harmed by our touch than we are by theirs.

Far more species of reef-forming corals are in the Pacific and Indian Oceans than in the Atlantic—about 85 percent more. These hard corals secrete calcium carbonate similar to chalk, which forms cups in which the coral animal, or *polyp*, lives. Two types of hard corals often found in the protected lagoons of the reef are the Elkhorn and the Staghorn corals. These species form what look like underwater forests of stone and eventually take on the appearance of many racks of antlers.

The other type of coral you're likely to encounter when diving or snorkeling is the soft coral. Soft corals also secrete calcium carbonate, but they do not act as true reef builders. Their structure is based more on a spine-like skeleton called *spicule* than it is a cup. Soft corals, which include the sea fans and sea whips that form stunning displays of color, are often called *gorgonians* and are very abundant in the Caribbean. The soft corals, as the name implies, are delicate and are more often found in areas where the wave energy is dampened by geological barriers. Although they don't add significant structure to the reef, soft corals contribute their spicules as sand deposits. They also provide a habitat for other reef dwellers that can utilize the complex designs of soft corals to their advantage.

Coral Reefs of the Cold and Deep

All of the most famous coral reefs are the shallow-water varieties. The Great Coral Reef, off the coast of Australia, the reefs in the Red Sea, the Caribbean, around the Hawaiian Islands, and in other areas of the world all grow in fairly shallow water. However, many coral reefs exist in deeper, darker regions of the sea, as well. These ahermatypic coral do not require warm water or light to survive, and are quite capable of making a living wherever they have access to small fish and other creatures they can catch in their tentacles.

Fishermen have known about these deep-water coral for years, because their lines and nets commonly get caught up in the coral branches, sections of which break off and are brought to the surface. These deep-water reefs are common off the East Coast of the United States and the coasts of Canada, Tasmania (Australia), Norway (where the reefs are nationally protected). These reefs are under severe threats by bottom-trawling and dredging, which continues today and has done extensive damage to them for many years ... before oceanographers and marine biologists even knew they existed.

Technicolor Reef Fish

When snorkeling above a coral reef, you might begin to feel as though you just dunked your head in an overstocked tropical fish bowl. Healthy reefs host a conspicuous abundance of fish, both in terms of numbers and species, making it almost impossible for even experienced divers to remember all their names. If you ever decide to explore a reef, be sure to pack one of those underwater identification keys. Many of the most beautiful fish have names that match their dazzling color combinations, including the juvenile Harlequin Sweetlips, the Jewelfish, and the Fairy Basslet, but these names are still tough to remember.

Of course, fish don't wear their colors solely for our visual edification. These color combinations make the coral reef fish masters of disguise, helping them blend into their surroundings, strut their stuff for the opposite sex, or look more menacing than they really are. In the coral reef's moving collage of eye candy, various species have developed their own unique ways to disappear into the reef or use disruptive coloration to confuse and frustrate would-be attackers. As you identify the fish species of the reef, make note of their color combinations, and then try to speculate about why each fish sports a particular look.

Some species can actually change their color patterns to match their surroundings. This is often the case with bottom dwellers, such as stingrays and flat fish. Any distinct banding, shading or spotting can make the fish look less like a fish and more like a piece of the scenery.

Other species have big spots on their rear ends that look like eyes, making their posteriors look more like their faces, thus scaring away any potential predators. (I guess the rule of survival here is to never eat anything whose rump looks like its face.) But seriously, this four-eye defense makes it much more difficult for predators to figure out how to attack from behind. The Four-Eyed Butterfly fish is a perfect example of a fish that uses this disguise. Not only does this fish have an extra pair of "eyes" on its backside, but also its real eyes are camouflaged by a black stripe that runs from the top of its head, through the eyes, and down to the bottom of its "face."

Coral reefs are teeming with life.

(Photo Credit: Florida Keys National Marine Sanctuary)

Steering Clear of Predators

Hiding within the twists and turns and bumps and depressions of the coral maze are a multitude of assorted microcommunities. At every turn, the casual observer of the reef notices little skirmishes, tiny surf wars where various creatures vie for a spot on the reef. In a very quiet way, the reef is abuzz with noisy communications—some friendly and some not so friendly.

In order for smaller fish and invertebrates to survive, they must find a safe haven—a protected hole or crevice. Leaving the safety of home base can mean a chance meeting with the sleek neighborhood bully—a hungry carnivore, such as the moray eel or the barracuda.

Nightlife on the Reef

The reef is extremely busy during the day, when the sun shines bright and the water is as clear as mountain air, but the real party doesn't get rolling on the reef until the sun goes down. Only then do the nocturnal creatures awake from their daytime naps and leave their shelters in the complex coral structure to search for food. As the sun sinks behind the horizon, coral polyps extend their delicate tentacles to capture their tiny planktonic meal, a sight that no reef lover should miss. Many fish also take advantage of the low light conditions to catch up on their nutritional needs. And for every fish that's looking for a midnight snack, a predator is waiting. The hustle and bustle of the nighttime reef is like being on Times Square in New York City, complete with spotlights, because without a good dive light or camera lighting, you won't see a thing. Add artificial lighting, and you end up with an underwater extravaganza that's hard to top.

Living Together on the Reef

In some territories in which few competitors contend for a spot, a nook or cranny is easy to secure. In other territories, two species might form an alliance that helps them both survive. The clownfish and the anemone, for instance, work together to defend themselves and ensure that they both have enough to eat. The clownfish swims around inside the "mouth" of the anemone, protected by the anemone's stinging cells—it has found a way to live inside the menacing anemone without being killed. In return for protection, the clownfish acts as bait for the anemone, luring other unsuspecting fish into the anemone's poisonous grip. The clownfish then gets to chow down on the anemone's table scraps. (The clownfish also eats plankton and dead anemone tentacles.)

The clownfish and the anemone provide only one of many examples of the strange bedfellows that live together and help each other on the reef. Let's take a look at a few more relationships that are prime candidates for the *Jerry Springer Show*.

Me and My Jelly

Many of the most successful symbiotic relationships, such as the relationship between the clownfish and anemone, involve a select species working alongside a cnidarian. As you might recall, cnidarians have stinging cells (known as nematocysts) that can pack a powerful punch, making cnidarians excellent sea creatures to have on your side. For this reason, many more vulnerable sea creatures have figured out clever ways to harness the weapons stash of the cnidarians.

One such opportunistic creature is a sea slug, or *nudibranch*, called the Blue Glaucus. This clever critter has figured out a way to take advantage of a particularly potent jelly—the infamous Portuguese man-of-war. The Blue Glaucus has the ability to steal unfired nematocysts from the tentacles of the Portuguese man-of-war. By nibbling carefully on the jelly's stingers, the nudibranch is able to detach the stingers and deposit them in special pockets in its skin. This enables the slug to acquire a built-in zapper of its own.

Other creatures use the tentacles of the Portuguese man-of-war in a different way. Certain fish, including the aptly named man-of-war fish (clownfish), have learned to swim within the potentially deadly tentacles without harm. The Nomeus is generally capable of avoiding the sting of this dangerous jelly, as well, and actually eats the tentacles of the jelly, which are constantly regenerated. However, occasionally, the man-of-war will eat the Nomeus. Other fish, including the yellow-jack, have acquired a partial resistance to the toxin that is released by the jelly.

Will Clean for Food

Strange as it may seem, some species of fish (and some shrimp) have figured out a way to eke out a living by cleaning other creatures. Cleaning fish, such as the bluestreak cleaner wrasse (*Labroides dimidiatus*), form symbiotic relationships with neighboring reef fish by cleaning them of unwanted and harmful parasites. Oftentimes, a cleanerfish sets up a "cleaning station," which other fish visit to be cleaned of parasites. Frequently, you can catch a glimpse of one of these parasite pickers cleaning a much larger fish and even going inside its mouth to pick its teeth! These extremely busy and beneficial doctors of the reef help rid their patients of *parasites* such as *isopods*, which bite the hosts and feed on their blood.

The cleaner wrasse is only one of the many varieties of fish that make their living debugging other fish. Another predominant group of cleaner animals are the reef shrimp—many species of which are conspicuously marked to advertise their presence. The banded coral shrimp, with its candy-like coloration, sure looks good enough to eat, but the reef community knows that these little guys serve a vital role in their routine hygiene.

Captain Clam's Comments

Cleaning symbiosis is a form of *symbiosis* called *mutualism* because the process is mutually helpful to both the cleaner and the cleanee. In the case of the cleaner shrimp, the shrimp gets the food, and the customer is treated to a personal grooming. As a bonus, the shrimp has a visible protective marking against predators, and the shrimps' clients have a neon sign telling them where to go for a cleaning. Maybe that's why cleaner shrimp look like barber poles!

Look, But Don't Touch

One way to survive on the reef is to be antagonistic or downright ornery. Many reef dwellers make it clear, in appearance and demeanor, that they don't like anyone invading their personal space. A quick glance at a spiny sea urchin, for example, leaves you with a clear, unambiguous message: *Don't touch!* Other creatures avoid trouble and secure their prey by packing a deadly poison wherever they go. The venom released by certain marine species is some of the most powerful in the animal kingdom. The Australian box-jelly or the sea wasp, for instance, can paralyze or even kill a human being within three minutes of contact. Another potent Australian species, the Southern blue-ringed octopus, can kill within minutes of biting its victim.

Zooxanthellae: An Enlightening Little Creature

For many years, marine biologists were perplexed as to how an area like the coral reef could be bursting with life and yet have such clear water. In other ecosystems, the base of the food pyramid is usually a plant; and in many marine environments, tiny algae make up the first major level. These algae cause the water to appear murky or *turbid* and dramatically reduce the water's clarity. During peak algae blooms, visibility can reach as low as a few inches. (See Chapter 6 for the scoop on microalgae.) Reefs, however, are famous for their crystal-clear water, where visibility often reaches hundreds of feet. So where is the plant source that makes up the base of the reef food pyramid? It turns out that one form is indeed a unicellular (single-cell), alga-like organism called zooxanthella.

Not only does zooxanthellae have a name to rival Rumpelstiltskin's, but it also has a lifestyle that is nearly as bizarre. Zooxanthella is a species of microalgae called a *dinoflagellate*, which is found in the tissues of some 80 species of marine organisms where it can take on many different forms. Scientists once believed that all zooxanthellae were the same species, *Symbiodinium microadriaticum*. However, zooxanthellae of various corals recently have been found to belong to at least eight genera (groups of species). These photosynthetic *protists* make their homes *inside* coral animals and other reef species such as the Giant Clam. This relationship of plant and animal is another example of symbiosis. In this case, the plant cells are given a protective substrate and a supply of necessary nutrients such as CO_2 (carbon dioxide) and nitrogen produced through the host's breathing. In return, the zooxanthellae provide the animals with food and consume the wastes that the animals produce. In a way, this upgrades the animals on the reef to partial solar power by courtesy of a plant additive. Zooxanthellae will be reappearing in later chapters because of their unique and important role in the tropical marine regions where they are found.

Great Visibility, Great Cinematography

What could go better with taking pictures or making movies than natural light? The sunlight that shines on and through the hermatypic reefs acts as the reef's energy source—the single most important contributor to the reef's survival and growth. All true hermatypic (reef-building) coral is restricted to areas of the world that have consistently warm, well-lit water. That's why the warm, sunny tropical and subtropical waters are home to these beautiful, shallow, reefs. The location must be in a relatively warm, sunny area and shallow enough so that the sunlight can reach it.

Within this warm, well-lit zone, colors come alive in their full spectrum. With little few or no particles in the water to block, bend, or otherwise distort the light and the optics, the reef retains the brilliant reds and oranges that normally are absorbed and drop out of vision in most other marine settings. This enables photographers to capture the spectacular, shimmering rainbow that's so characteristic of the reef. In particular, the color patterns and brilliance of the *nudibranchs*, a kind of sea slug, offer visual sensations not unlike fireworks on the clear summer night. The corals also flash iridescent hues of blues and purples so regal they make the queen angelfish look like a hobo.

Coral reefs will always rate very high on the list of places to visit because of the richness of their display. The claustrophobia sometimes felt by newly certified divers can be easily washed away in the lush aquamarine splendor of a healthy coral head teaming with life. Cameras do a great job of catching the intricacies that unfold within each convolution of coralline mass, but nothing compares with a real life encounter with the reef. Take a long, slow look at the reef and photograph every piece with your mind's eye. Soon it begins to look like a huge collage. The flame fish ignites the fire coral, kept aglow by the gentle swaying of sea fans. Juvenile reef fish dart about like multiflavored Popsicles in the hands of children. Orange clownfish frolic in the flowing fingers of anemones. This is the coral reef in all its picturesque glory.

> ### Underwater Eye
>
> The first underwater camera was devised by Louis Boutan in 1898. He managed to take a self-portrait at 165 feet (55 meters) deep a year later—a depth record he maintained for 40 years. Underwater movies were being made as early as 1914 by J. E. Williamson, who went on to make the first version of Jules Verne's *Twenty Thousand Leagues Under the Sea*.

Many Reefs from Which to Choose

As coral reefs develop, die back, and rebuild themselves, they form distinctive structures that are typically grouped into three categories: fringing reefs, barrier reefs, and atolls. Let's take a look at each reef type, starting with the fringing reef.

The three types of coral reefs.

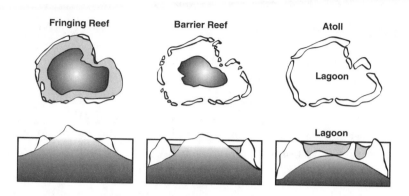

The fringing reef commonly forms a skirt around an island or other landmass and appears as an extension of the landmass. No lagoon, channel, or other body of water separates the reef from the landmass it surrounds. At the base of the fringing reef is one of the most essential components of the reef: a hard surface that enables the larvae of coral animals to settle and begin their development. The fringing reef supports a host of different coral species, but no one species dominates the scene (although boulder corals make up a large portion the reef).

The most popular of the coral reefs, barrier reefs are separated from the land by a shallow lagoon with a sandy bottom and patches of vegetation. The lagoon or channel that separates the reef from the land it surrounds is created over time by the natural growth of the reef. The corals on the seaward side of the reef obtain more food and nutrients than the corals on the inside edge. As the corals on the inside edge die back and the corals on the seaward edge grow, a low sloping area develops between the reef and the landmass, creating a lagoon or channel. Barrier reefs are more fully developed than fringing reefs and typically feature a more diverse community of creatures. Most barrier reefs are so extensive that scientists commonly divide them into relatively distinct zones, which are separated into even smaller zones in turn.

The third major type of coral reef is the atoll, or coral island. An atoll consists of a ring or partial ring of coral with a lagoon in the middle. Atolls likely began as fringing reefs around the base of a volcano or other steep geological formation. As the sea level rose and the volcano receded back into the sea, the reef grew to the surface, and the center of the reef, defined by the volcano's crater-like top, remained in the middle to form a lagoon. Atolls prefer the deeper, more balmy seas found in the South Pacific and Indian Oceans. Although rare in the Atlantic, atolls do exist off the coast of Belize. One such atoll was explored by Jacques Cousteau in 1970—a legendary blue hole with the bottom of the central lagoon being reaching 135 meters (400 feet) deep!

A more recent study of coral reefs in the Atlantic and Caribbean identifies a fourth type of reef: the bank/barrier reef, which is sort of a cross between a fringing reef and a barrier reef. Scientist currently theorize that bank/barrier reefs were formed when coral development was stopped during a recent glacial period (about 20,000 years ago). In the tropical Atlantic and Caribbean waters, temperatures dropped to a point at which coral communities died back. When water temperatures climbed back above 20 degrees Celsius or 68 degrees Fahrenheit, corals began to reestablish themselves on top of the preexisting coral base. Unlike full-fledged barrier reefs, bank/barrier reefs are much closer to shore and have much shallower lagoons or channels separating them from the mainland.

Theories of Reef Formation

When Charles Darwin was checking out the Galapagos Islands, he managed to float past some coral reefs along the way. Not one to pass up a natural habitat without expounding some hypothesis about it, he developed a number of theories regarding the origins and the ultimate configurations of the various types of coral reefs. (For more information about Charles Darwin and his journeys, refer to Chapter 18.)

According to Darwin, these reefs must have formed following volcanic activity that created islands. When the islands slowly sank back below sea level, corals settled and began to establish themselves. Darwin didn't know about global plate tectonics, but if he had, he could have used it to further support his theory. According to global plate tectonics, islands commonly form and sink back into the sea in areas associated with volcanic activity. His theory went on to explain that the various forms of reefs were really all the same but at different levels depending on how much the landmass had sunk.

Later studies have hypothesized that corals are controlled by glacial activity, which causes major sea level changes. As the earth warms and the ice caps melt, the sea level rises, covering previously exposed landmasses; when more water is trapped in the ice caps, sea level drops, making some previously deep areas shallow enough to support a coral reef. Global warming can also affect coral reef development by changing the temperature of the water—making some waters too warm for coral to survive, and making water that was too cold warm enough for coral reefs to start rebuilding. Perhaps all of these theories are correct. Whatever the case, we do know that the types of coral reefs vary depending on the unique forces that work on each reef type.

Through the Great Barrier Reef

The Great Barrier Reef of Australia is the largest reef system in the world and the single largest biological feature on the planet. (The Great Barrier Reef actually consists of more than 3,000 reefs of various sizes.) It stretches some 2,000 kilometers (1,200 miles) along the northeast coast of Australia. The lagoon or channel separating the reef from the mainland ranges in width from 10 miles (16 km) to 150 miles (240 km). Within this area, more than 1,500 species of fish, 4,000 types of mollusc, and more than 200 species of bird life join other wildlife including dugong (sea cows that are similar to manatees), green turtles, and a variety of dolphins and whales. (The second largest barrier reef is Mesoamerican Reef, which extends along the east coast of Central America.)

Log Entry

In the *Phylum Cnidaria*, the life cycle has a stage called the **polyp**. In some species, like corals and hydroids, the polyp stage is the dominant or only stage. The polyp looks like a tiny stalk of celery.

Great Barrier Reef Marine Park and World Heritage Area is one of Australia's biggest tourist attractions. Because hordes of people (in excess of two million) visit the reef every year, park managers have had to tighten control around the reef to protect its fragile nature. Just brushing up against a healthy coral can damage the surface where the *polyps* live. As long as everyone is aware of the rules for diving on the coral reefs, we can all enjoy the reef without destroying its fragile, pristine beauty.

The Marine Park headquarters, or Reef HQ, boasts the largest live coral aquarium in the world. There, visitors can see hundreds of species, including the extremely dangerous animals, such as the blue-ringed octopus and the sea snake. Reef HQ acts as the main educational center for the Great Barrier Reef and offers a wide range of programs and opportunities relating to the coral reef system. These programs make learning about the reef a lot of fun.

Look at That Bikini

One of the best-known atolls in the world is famous more for its name than for its notoriety as a nuclear testing site. The Bikini Atoll, located in the Sunset chain of the Marshall Islands in the South Pacific Ocean, is relatively small, having a total area of 2 square miles (5 square km). From 1947 to 1958, the Bikini Atoll was the site where the United States tested its thermonuclear weapons, exploding 23 nuclear devices in all, many of which were many times more powerful than the bombs detonated in Hiroshima and Nagasaki during World War II. Before blasting away at the atoll, the United States relocated the 200 or so Micronesian inhabitants to other islands. In 1968, the United States declared the atoll safe for human habitation and started to bring the native people back to their homeland. Ten years later, scientists discovered that the amount of strontium-90 in the bodies of the inhabitants was well above the danger level.

Currently, the Bikini Atoll remains uninhabited except for a few employees of tourism, as well as construction companies and a handful of employees from the United States, yet this atoll has become one of the most popular dive sites in the world. This is primarily because the United States didn't just set off bombs on the atoll, but it blew up an entire fleet of old and captured warships, including the famous USS *Saratoga*. Divers visit the site primarily to explore the wrecks. However, wildlife has returned to the atoll, and the wrecks function as an excellent surface for new coral reefs!

Although known by divers primarily for its wrecks, Bikini Atoll is home to a generous population of marlin, sailfin, and dolphin, and one of the few undisturbed collections of grey reef sharks and silvertips. Fishing boats avoid the area, giving the wildlife, primarily the local sharks, free reign.

Some Really Cool Reef Representatives

It's nearly impossible to point out a part of a coral reef that's the most spectacular. The overall appearance of the coral heads themselves, along with multitudes of phosphorescent beings darting in and out of the caves and crevices, is enough to take your breath away. At one turn, the graceful swaying of a sea anemone catches your eye. Swim a little farther, and the inky black cloud left behind by the frightened octopus draws your attention. Farther still, and the hyperventilating green head and menacing jaws of the moray eel fill you with dread.

Captain Clam's Comments

Moray eels are nocturnal animals that inhabit the waters of the Indian, Pacific, and Atlantic Oceans. The 100 identified species of moray eels range from 2 to 10 feet in length. The giant moray can reach up to 10 feet in length and weigh 75 pounds. Morays have muscular, snake-like bodies with thick skin and no scales. The moray has poor eyesight but a very good sense of smell that it makes full use of when hunting down midnight snacks. The moray keeps itself tucked away in between ledges and cracks, but divers commonly see the head sticking out, constantly pumping water through its mouth. They are an awesome sight at night when they wriggle past displaying their full body length. Don't mess with morays; their jaws are incredibly strong.

If you're lucky, an eagle ray may "fly" past. This fairly large ray is common to see during the day; its graceful body glides through the water as smoothly as a ghost. The eagle ray is one of the larger reef creatures, but you needn't fear this gentle giant—just float in place and witness its majestic beauty. Eagle rays have a wingspan of up to

2 meters (7 feet) and are said to sometimes leap out of the water like other large rays. The stingray is found in areas of the reef, as well, but prefers a sandier bottom where it can partially bury itself. (For more details on rays, refer to Chapter 13.)

Spotlight on Reef Sharks

Sharks are major players on the reef scene. After all, it's a great place for them—plenty to eat, excellent visibility by day, a lot of activity at night. What shark could ask for anything more? They don't need rhythm and music because they don't rely on hearing to navigate or track their prey, and they don't require 20/20 vision, either. To navigate the reef and hunt prey, they rely primarily on their sense of smell and on *electro reception*, a technique sharks, skates, and rays use to sense the changes in the electrical field that surrounds their bodies. The moral of the story is that when you swim with the sharks, don't be stinky, don't splash around too much, and leave the sharks alone. Most sharks are harmless creatures that have no intention of attacking humans. For more information about sharks, see Chapter 13.

Sharks in all shapes and sizes represent 400 to 500 different species, depending on the classification system. Some sharks, such as the tiger and hammerhead, are more common on the reefs than others. The following sections provide an up-close-and-personal encounter with some of the more common and intriguing reef sharks.

The Tiger of the Sea

Some divers go to the reefs just to see big game like the tiger shark. These sharks are considered one of the bad boys of the ocean, ferocious man-eaters (and women-eaters, too) with a voracious appetite. Tiger sharks are "everythingavores" (actually called *omnivores*) meaning that they chow down on food of any texture and flavor, including crabs, fish, turtles, and chunks of leftover boat parts. It's not that they can't make out what they're eating; they just really don't care what they eat. That's what makes them so dangerous.

In the ferocious shark department, tiger sharks rank second only to the great white shark, with the bull shark coming in closely at third. The worst part is that tiger sharks like to feed in shallow tropical waters where they gobble up everything they come across, including surfers, swimmers, and tourists. Talk about a tourist trap! The good part is that they usually travel alone. They command a wide berth, so to speak. During the day, the tiger shark prefers deep water around fringe reefs, where it has quick access to somewhat shallower waters for its nighttime feedings. When the reef comes alive at night, with its nocturnal creatures coming out to play, the tiger shark has a veritable smorgasbord from which to choose.

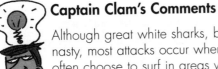

Captain Clam's Comments

Although great white sharks, bull sharks, and tiger sharks have a reputation for being nasty, most attacks occur when humans encroach on the shark's territory. Surfers often choose to surf in areas where sharks feed, divers occasionally harass sharks, and people feed sharks in such a way that the shark cannot possibly determine if the person is presenting food to the shark or trying to take it away. Sharks usually attack humans only when confused or confronted.

The Hammerhead Bizarre

If tiger sharks represent the bad boys of the beach, hammerheads are the freaks. These big-headed wonders look more like something you'd find in your garage rather than your fish tank. Nine species of sharks make up the hammerhead clan, including the bonnet heads and shovelheads. (They're weird looking no matter what kind of tool they resemble.) As a group, hammerheads are considered to be some of the most highly evolved sharks, exhibiting an array of pronounced modifications that make them masters of their domain. Twenty-five million years or so ago, somebody decided that stretching out the shark's face and dangling an eye and a nose at the end of each lobe was a good idea. Well, it sure gave these sharks an ugly, scary countenance, but it also provided them with multidirectional site and smell, which is always helpful for tracking down prey.

Unlike most sharks, hammerheads like to swim in schools, and they prefer warm, tropical waters. Cocos Island, off Costa Rica, is renowned for its hammerhead sharks. Here, residents and visitors commonly witness hundreds of scalloped hammerheads cruising around in the deep, warm currents that rise up from the volcanic topography below. During the day, hammerheads commonly gather in schools, but at night each wanders off to hunt alone. One of their favorites on the menu are stingrays, which have a tough time fending off the elongated, toothy grin of the oncoming hammerhead. That ferocious smile is just another one of the many gifts bestowed upon the shark by thousands of years of evolution.

The Reef Sharks by Name

You know you're spending too much time on the reef when people start tacking the word "reef" onto your name. A number of shark species that frequent the reef have earned this designation as "reef sharks." Two of the most common species that hang out on the reef, the Great Barrier Reef in particular, are the black-tipped and the white-tipped reef sharks. Grey reef sharks are also a common variety. These sharks generally show little aggression toward humans. They look mean, but they're more like big friendly dogs that won't bite unless you pull on their ears. As long as you don't poke these sharks with a stick, take their food, or tug on their fins, they usually leave you alone.

Who would provoke a shark attack, you might ask? You would be surprised at the number of attacks instigated by divers who were trying to get a rise out of a relatively reclusive shark. No animal likes to have its tail pulled, but some divers apparently think that harassing sharks is good, clean fun. Reading through the many documented reports about bites from small reef sharks makes you wonder who started the fights. Reef sharks are sluggish in appearance, but when they get stirred up, they rev up into high gear in a hurry. So if you're a diver looking for excitement on the reef, go chase after a black-tip reef shark and tug on its tail. But if you want a more peaceful encounter with these gentle creatures, just leave them alone and watch from a distance.

Protecting and Preserving National Treasures

Coral reefs are like huge underwater china shops that require visitors to be exceptionally careful. Any careless activity, such as brushing against the coral, collecting live coral, or dropping an anchor on a coral head can damage the reef and destroy decades of development.

Posing even greater threats to the coral reefs are the waste, silt, and pollution that flow to the reef from neighboring landmasses. With increasing populations along many coastlines, the associated development typically damages coastline habitats, leading to excessive runoff. With the land barriers removed, rain water and coastal flooding carry huge amounts of waste, sediments, and pollution to the reef. When silt and sediments cover a reef or make the water *turbid* (cloudy), the sun-loving corals die.

Over the past 20 years or so, coral bleaching has been an ever increasing threat to the reefs. Coral bleaching is the loss or reduction of photosynthetic pigment in the zooxanthellae that live inside the coral polyps. With the loss of pigmentation, the zooxanthellae produce less than the required amount of food for the polyps, causing the polyps to die off and slowing or stopping the growth of the reef. Several factors may cause coral bleaching, including

Log Entry

When the water is **turbid**, it is full of suspended particles that make the water murky. In diver lingo, it means the visibility stinks. In many waters, turbidity can be a good thing, meaning that plenty of plankton is available for all to consume. On the reef, however, water clarity means the difference between life and death for corals.

global warming and the thinning of the ozone layer, which increase the water temperature and the amount of sunlight reaching the coral. Many other factors may be at work, including overfishing (removing the fish that clean algae and sediment off the coral) and increased sedimentation and nutrients from river runoff. Perhaps a combination of all of these factors is causing a cumulative stress that the coral can no longer tolerate.

To protect existing coral reefs, President Clinton established the U.S. Coral Reef Task Force (CRTF) in June 1998. The CRTF is responsible for mapping and monitoring U.S. coral reefs; researching the causes of and solutions to coral reef degradation; reducing and mitigating coral reef degradation from pollution, overfishing, and other causes; and implementing strategies to promote conservation and sustainable use of coral reefs internationally.

However, good intentions without significant actions typically result in few benefits. In some areas, such as the Florida Keys National Marine Sanctuary, the government has set aside and enforces no-take marine reserves, where a diverse collection of species can get a foothold and begin to re-establish themselves. Another area in the Northern Hawaiian Islands was named as a marine protected area during the Clinton era, but this designation was primarily symbolic. Until a global network of significant no-take, no-catch zones is established, the coral reefs and other valuable habitats, salt marshes and mangrove forests, will likely remain at risk. (See Chapter 20 for details about the ecological importance of no-catch zones.)

The Least You Need to Know

- The coral reefs consist primarily of animals that are related to jellies but form stone-like skeletons for protection.

- Shallow coral reefs rely on warm, clear, well-lit water to develop and survive.

- Deep water reefs are populated by ahermatypic coral, which do not require intense sunlight or warm water.

- Hermatypic (reef-building) coral has a symbiotic relationship with photosynthetic protists called zooxanthellae that form the base of the reef's food pyramid.

- Reefs are commonly classified into three types: fringe reefs, barrier reefs, and atolls.

- Reef diving is and will continue to be an extremely popular activity internationally.

- Coral reefs undergo major changes over thousands of years due to changes in sea level, water temperatures, and other conditions.

- Reef systems are extremely delicate and in need of active protection from human threats.

4

Living on the Frontier

In This Chapter

- ◆ Who's living out at sea and where
- ◆ How animals make a living in the open ocean
- ◆ Searching for the big game sea creatures
- ◆ Behind the scenes with ocean mysteries
- ◆ Migration routes of the worldwide waterways

As with most ecosystems, the ocean has a significant population that chooses to live in the comfort zone—the shallow, shore-hugging regions, where they find abundant sunlight, moderate temperatures, and food aplenty. A good chunk of the population, however, chooses to live offshore in the ocean's great frontier, where life poses an entirely different set of challenges. Here, space is freely available for any species that has an urge to travel; but at the deeper depths (300 feet or more), plant life begins to dwindle, because of a lack of light, and only the most specialized animals have what it takes to survive.

This chapter examines the life forms that have adapted to living in the open ocean. It ignores the bottom dwellers for now and focuses mainly on life in the water column. (Don't worry, bottom feeders; future chapters explore life on the ocean floor in greater detail.) Ready? Let's head out to sea to find out what the open ocean has in store for us.

Call of the Open Ocean

Chapter 1 introduces you to the concept of zonation and illustrates how the ocean waters are divided into various regions called *zones*. The largest division, called the *pelagic zone*, includes all waters off the immediate shoreline and above the ocean floor—the *benthic zone*. This is the realm in which the inhabitants are more or less independent of the ocean floor. As you move down through the pelagic zone, you pass through several zones that divide it into various subzones. The following sections explain these divisions in greater depth.

Life in the open ocean, the pelagic zone.

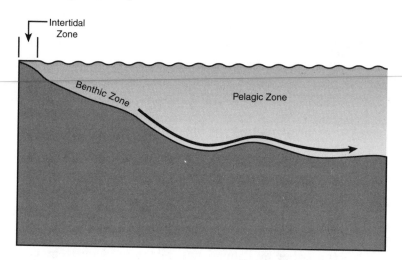

Where Is Everyone?

The ocean is like a birthday cake—the topmost layer holds the icing, the richest portion. In the case of the ocean, the topmost layer is the *photic zone*, the most productive portion of the pelagic zone, the surface layer through which light can penetrate and fuel photosynthesis. In this zone, plankton rule; the sunlight fuels the phytoplankton, which, in turn, feed the zooplankton that end up being one of the most abundant life forms on the planet. (Zooplankton include the shrimp-like *copepod* and the ever popular *krill*.)

Because plankton have no way to propel themselves through the water, they tend to sink; and if you're a plankton, sinking is bad. If they sink too far, it's "bye, bye plankton." For phytoplankton, falling out of the photic zone places them in dark where photosynthesis does not take place. When zooplankton fall out of the zone, they starve from a lack of phytoplankton. Either way, no light, no food, certain death. To keep themselves afloat and stay in that nice, productive top layer, plankton have developed several interesting modifications, including shapes that keep them afloat (flat or parachute shapes to increase resistance in the water), increased oil content to make them lighter, hairs or spikes to increase water drag, and air pockets to make them more buoyant.

Log Entry

The depth to which sunlight can penetrate is called the **photic** zone and reaches only about 100 meters (300 feet) deep in most ocean regions. Beyond this zone, little plant life can survive. Deeper regions rely on alternative food sources, including the wastes that settle to the ocean floor—dead fish and whales, copepod doo-doo, and other organic "wastes." Other deep sea ecosystems establish themselves around bacteria that use chemical synthesis rather than photosynthesis to survive, as explained in the next chapter.

The planktonic plants and animals might seem tiny and insignificant, but they play a critical role in the development of other ocean species. Blue whales, for example, are *krillavores*; their diet consists entirely of krill (small shrimp-like creatures, officially known as *euphausids*). Other whales, such as the Baleen whales, also enjoy these bite-sized morsels, as explained later in this chapter.

Although plankton dominate the photic zone in number, many diverse species represent this zone and showcase a variety of adaptations. Some swimmers, such as the flying fish and the manta ray, have the ability to leap completely out of the water to traverse extra distance.

Underwater Eye
Life is so abundant in the *epipelagic*, or upper, layer of some oceans that sound waves can actually bounce off it. The general term is called the *deep-scattering layer*, and it can be made up of many different components including fish and shrimp-like copepods. At times, the assemblage of animal life becomes so dense that it takes on the color of the dominant members.

Some, such as spinner dolphins, fly out of the water possibly to shake off parasites or herd fish, but maybe sometimes just for the fun of it. (At least it looks like they're having fun.) Other critters, such as the ocean sunfish (also called a mola mola or headfish), prefers to use the surface to relax. The ocean sunfish flattens itself out on the ocean's surface and basks in the sun. These comical-looking floating rafts can weigh more than a ton! Billfish, tuna, and other game fish also enjoy hanging out in the photic zone. But that's not all. Let's keep scanning the water column to see what else is flappin' around a little deeper.

The Vastness Continues

Rod Serling made the *Twilight Zone* a human sensation. This half-hour television show featured stories from the zone between day and night, light and darkness, life and death, and reality and fantasy. It was an eerie world where humans explored their deepest fears and experienced life-changing phenomena; a world populated with peculiar people, strange creatures, and some of the world's finest up-and-coming actors. The ocean has its own twilight zone, the mesopelagic region—the area where light and darkness merge to create a neighborhood that has an eerie glow at best. This is the area where creatures flash their own lights in order to see and be seen.

In the mesopelagic region, light isn't the only feature that dwindles; food supplies decline as well. Some phytoplankton manages to trickle down to this level along with some additional edible debris, but the pickings are slim, indeed. During the day, some zooplankters hang out here, where they provide an important food source for the denizens of the middle region. But at night, they take a pronounced elevator ride (called a *diurnal vertical migration*) up to the higher levels, where they can secure additional food for themselves.

Log Entry

A **diurnal vertical migration** occurs when a group of animals move to higher ocean levels at night and return to lower levels during the day, possibly to avoid predators. During the evening hours, for instance, copepods (tiny relatives of crabs and shrimp) rise like clouds from the middle regions up to epipelagic levels. The migration is followed by many of the primary inhabitants of the mesopelagic zone, including the lantern fish. For additional details about copepods, see Chapter 8.

While training on a research vessel during a semester as a college undergraduate, one of the authors did a study looking at the gut contents of mesopelagic fish in the middle of the Sargasso Sea. He conducted a series of mid-water net tows during a 24-hour cycle. The thought of sampling fish at depths of 1,000 to 2,000 feet brought back images of hatchet fish that he had formed as a child. Well, he did catch a hatchet fish, and just as they said in the old ocean books, the hatchet fish had eaten an entire fish whole. This alien from the depths that used to give him nightmares as a landlocked youth turned out to be a whopping 15 millimeters long (less than half an inch), and the lantern fish it had eaten was about half that.

The only stress he experienced during his encounter with this dreaded sea serpent was the strain on his eyes as he peered through the dissecting scope at three o'clock in the morning. It made perfect sense, however, that these fish needed to be that small. The modifications required to handle excessive pressure changes during daily migrations and the basic lack of available food at that level of the water column limit the size and shape of most mid-water fish.

These fish have been modified further to create different lighting arrangements for different occasions. The family of lantern fishes called myctophids has more lumines-cent species than any other, but other groups, including hatchet fish, might be more abundant in number. Many fish also depend on help from bacteria to keep the lights burning.

Underwater Eye

Organisms that can produce their own light are said to be *bioluminescent*. They pro-duce the nonheat-generating light chemically in special organs called *photophores*. (Some fish carry around light-producing bacteria.) This light is very similar to the light given off by those little plastic glow sticks that kids like to play with—both sources of light are created by chemical reactions. Photophores are generally lined up along the side of the fish, forming a straight string of holiday lights that look like tiny, illuminated portholes on miniature submarines. Mid-water fish use their light structures for various purposes including concealment, advertisement, and disguise.

Elevator Down

If you thought life was tough down deep, just wait until you reach the abyss and the trenches—the zones where the proverbial sun don't shine. How dark is it down there? It's so dark, even the fish need flashlights. Here, you can find the angler fish with an appendage extending from its nose that dangles a tiny light bulb in front of its mouth—just the thing to wear to your next New Year's Eve party. Don't underesti-mate the importance of its luminescent lure. Without its dinky glow worm-on-a-stick, this little guy would go hungry. Many deep-water fish also use these glow stick appendages for flagging down mates. If you were as homely as most of these fish, you would need a little help too. Thank goodness the lights are turned down low.

Another deep-water fish that's striving for that gargoyle look is the viperfish. These foot-long monsters look like something that just stepped off the set of a 1960s horror flick. You couldn't ask for a more terrifying combination of needle sharp fangs, huge jaws, and an overall dark, menacing demeanor. A typical viperfish sports about 350 photophores in its mouth alone to attract prey—"swim toward the light, swim toward the light ...." And to think that all this horrific hype is rolled into a body that rarely exceeds 2 feet (.7 meter) in length. Just looking at these gothic guppies, you would never think that they could be classified in the same order as salmon and trout. The viperfish looks more like a cross between a barracuda and a moray eel.

Captain Clam's Comments

In the deep, dark regions of the sea, creatures must conserve the little energy there is. One way they do this is by using very little energy for growth. Remaining relatively small, the creature needs less to survive. Many creatures also conserve energy by restricting their movement and eating large meals infrequently rather than many small meals. Conserving energy in these ways provides the deep-sea creatures with more energy for metabolism and light production.

Let's look at a couple more remarkable fish before we move on. Have you ever heard of an animal that can swallow something larger than itself? Well, the bathypelagic black swallower or chiasmodon can do exactly that. This creature is only about a foot (25 to 30 cm) long with an underbelly that looks like one of those rubber hot-water bottles. And boy, does that belly stretch when the swallower gulps down its prey. Sound impressive? Well, that's nothing compared to what the gulper eel can do. The gulper eel looks like nature's attempt to cross a pelican with a fish. Its hinged jaw can gape open and suck in prey that's larger than its own head! The gulper eel can reach a full 2 meters (7 feet) in length, which is fairly large for the bathypelagic zone.

Spinning 'Round in the Sargasso Sea

In the Atlantic Ocean, off the southeast coast of the United States, is a mysterious (and very weedy) body of water known as the Sargasso Sea, an elliptical sea that covers nearly 5 million square kilometers (2 million square miles)—approximately two thirds the size of the United States. The Sargasso Sea gets its name from the sargassum seaweed that's unique to this area of the ocean. Although it has no significant currents of its own, the Sargasso Sea is surrounded by the strong currents of the North Atlantic Gyre that lazily rotate the Sargasso Sea clockwise and keep it relatively warm.

Within this relatively tranquil sea is a unique environment altogether—an area packed with some of the thickest mats of seaweed found anywhere in the world. When Columbus was making his trek toward the new world, he came upon the Sargasso Sea, which was socked in with seaweed. He figured he must be close to land and probably came close to claiming the sargassum island in the name of Spain. Well, his crew couldn't find bottom for a few miles down, so he moved on to firmer territory, and the creatures of the Sargasso Sea were free from Spanish rule (and still are today). Fifteen species of sargassum seaweed are found throughout the world, but the dominant species of the Sargasso Sea are independent and free-floating, and they form huge mats that stay within a specific, although large, boundary (the Sargasso Sea). Within these floating islands of sargassum seaweed live communities of creatures that are completely dependent on the substrate.

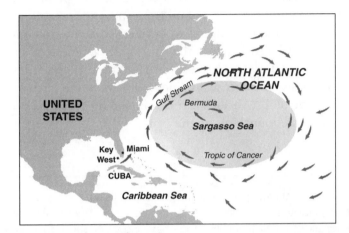

The Sargasso Sea is a tranquil sea encircled by strong currents.

Underwater Eye

The sargassum fish is a type of frogfish that inhabits floating rafts of sargassum seaweed. It grows to around 6 inches (15 cm) and takes on a form and color pattern that mimic the weed it hangs with, making it virtually invisible. The fish can stalk its prey in the weeds rather than waiting for its prey to come to it. The pectoral fins of the sargassum fish are actually prehensile and can grasp strands of sargassum weed to hold on. They aren't picky eaters and will even cannibalize their fellow sargassum fish.

Where Eels Spawn

In addition to its relationship with one of the most mysterious places on Earth (the Bermuda Triangle), the Sargasso Sea is home to another former mystery—the spawning of the American eel. When this eel was first discovered, nobody really questioned where it came from. In fact, prior to the 1950s, scientists had identified the American eel larvae as an entirely different species of fish called the *leptocephalus!* When they began to suspect that leptocephalus was actually the larvae stage of the American eel, they traced the eel back to its spawning grounds by locating smaller and smaller larvae, until they eventually reached the Sargasso Sea. Now, scientists believe that every American eel in existence was hatched from an egg laid in the Sargasso Sea. After the eggs hatch, the transparent larvae drift with the Gulf Stream toward shore where eventually they change into *elvers* or "glass eels," and begin to swim into estuaries or further into lakes and streams, depending on their sex.

Tar Ball Alley

One of the more disturbing consequences of the whirlpool that surrounds the Sargasso Sea is that the currents of the gyre suck pollution into the sea from surrounding areas. And because the Sargasso Sea itself is so calm, the pollution lingers. The most obvious form of pollution consists of oil from spills, illegal tank washes, and other sources. This oil commonly congeals to form tar balls that roll out to the Atlantic Ocean and are eventually sucked into the Sargasso Sea. These tar balls don't sink like other biodegradable material such as seaweed and dead animals. They bob around on the surface of the sea and eventually find their way to the sargassum mats, which act as filters to trap the blobs. Various animals, including green sea turtles, accidentally ingest the tar while munching on the mats.

Ocean Alert _____

Recent studies of hatchling green turtles have found that because of their indiscriminate feeding habits, about half of them have eaten tar and about a fifth have ingested plastic. The tar makes their jaws stick together, and both tar and plastic can plug their digestive systems, eventually resulting in death. Marine pollution from tar and plastic, as well as other toxins, might also hurt sea turtles indirectly by weakening their immune systems. For more information about sea turtles and the threats to their existence see, Chapter 15.

Between the tar balls and whatever plastic debris collect on the algae mats, marine life is beginning to experience an overall increase in human-based pollution that reaches even obscure areas like the middle of the Sargasso Sea. It is sad to think about turtles and tar balls colliding in an area two thirds the size of the United States, but until stricter controls are placed on offshore practices, this problem will most likely continue and even worsen. (See Chapter 21 for more information on this and other issues concerning marine pollution.)

Bermuda Triangle Meets Hollywood Square

Like Loch Ness and Easter Island, the Bermuda Triangle is shrouded in myth and mystery. This triangular area, defined by the three points of southeast Florida, Bermuda, and Puerto Rico covers more than 1 million kilometers. No sooner did Christopher Columbus lose his bearings in the Sargasso Sea than the myth first began. Christopher Columbus reported that his ship's compass went haywire and that he and his crew saw weird lights in the sky over the Bermuda Triangle. Much later, in 1945, came the disappearance of Flight 19: Five Navy Avenger bombers mysteriously vanished on a routine training mission along with a rescue plane sent to search for them. Although most reports of sunken ships, downed planes, and confused navigators have perfectly logical explanations, the Bermuda Triangle seems destined to remain a perennial pop culture icon.

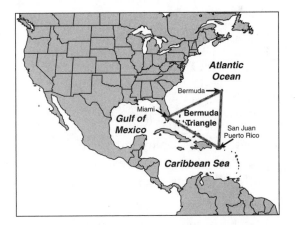

The infamous Bermuda Triangle is shrouded in mystery.

The Bermuda Triangle goes by many names, including Land of the Lost, the Twilight Zone, Hoodoo Sea, and the Devil's Triangle. In 1979, Hollywood even made a movie about this area, cleverly titled *The Bermuda Triangle*, starring Warren Vanders.

Where the Big Boys Meet

It's time to leave the mysteries of the Sargasso Sea and move on to bigger waters and even larger game. After all, the open ocean is the place that the largest animals on the planet call home—an environment that is so buoyant it can support mammals 20 times heavier than the largest land beasts! The biggest player, the blue whale, is able to attain average lengths of approximately 22 to 25 meters (72 to 80 feet) and weights of 150 tons. On land and without the support of large heavy bones, an animal this size would be crushed by its own weight. With the support of salt water, however, the blue whale needs no heavy bone structure or other adaptations that might limit its size. The lack of gravity, plus the availability of a large food supply, has made it possible for the blue whale to claim the title as the world's heavyweight champion.

To obtain enough food to support its massive body, the largest marine species eat low on the food chain, gobbling up tons of plankton and krill every day. Instead of teeth, blue whales have about 300 to 400 *baleen plates*, which they use to strain food from the ocean water. The baleen plates are like the teeth of a comb. The inside surface of the baleen plates is frayed, and the frayed edges cross to form a dense sieve through

Captain Clam's Comments

With only 1,300 to 2,000 members, the blue whale is an official *endangered species*—an animal that is facing extinction because of low numbers and loss of habitat.

which water can pass but tiny critters cannot. The whale takes a big gulp of plankton- or krill-filled water and then pushes the water out through the baleen plates, leaving the critter mush behind—in its mouth. A blue whale can eat up to 3,200 kilograms (7,000 pounds) of krill per day, so it must travel far and wide to find enough to eat!

Summering with Humpbacks

Weighing in at a mere 25 to 40 tons, the humpback whale is a minnow compared to its cousin, the blue whale, but it's still a pretty impressive beast. Reaching lengths of 12 to 15 meters (40 to 50 feet), the humpback whale can consume nearly 3,000 pounds of krill and small fish daily, using the same baleen plate technique mastered by the blue whale.

One of the best places to catch a glimpse of a humpback whale and other species is the Stellwagen Bank National Marine Sanctuary. This sanctuary protects 2,180 square kilometers (842 square miles) of ocean property and provides habitat for a variety of marine creatures including the endangered northern right whale, humpback whale, finback whale, and Atlantic white-sided dolphin. Located 40 kilometers (25 miles) east of Boston, the sanctuary stretches between Cape Ann and Cape Cod at the mouth of Massachusetts Bay. Numerous whale watching cruises depart from points around the Bank, including Boston, Cape Ann, Gloucester, and Cape Cod. These represent some of the original whale watching groups on the East coast; some even post daily sightings on the Internet. (When last checked, the tally yielded two to four humpback, three to six finback, and two Minke whales.) Considering how few whales are left in the world, it is nice to see that there are still places where sightings are almost guaranteed during certain times of the year.

Cabo, Whale Shark Central

Twelve species of whales travel the world's oceans gulping down plankton and krill, but whales are not the only animals that find this stuff tasty. The largest fish in the ocean, the whale shark, likes to chow down on krill, too. Unlike the blue whale, however, this big boy has tiny teeth instead of baleen plates. If you're looking to spot one of these bubbas of the deep, check around the coast of Baja California, particularly around the town of Cabo San Lucas.

Cabo San Lucas is a Mexican town sticking out at the southernmost tip of the Baja peninsula. In addition to being tourist friendly, this place is a top stop for whale shark diving. The coastline here is somewhat unique in that the continental shelf drops off fairly close to shore. Although whale sharks spend most of their time swimming in the open ocean, migration patterns and water temperatures often bring them near this ledge, where divers commonly catch a glance of these gentle giants—at 12 to 15 meters (40 to 50 feet) in length, they're a sight that's tough to miss. Whale sharks have distinct markings consisting of a dark background with yellowish spots or stripes that add to their mild appearance. Unfortunately, the whale shark population is fairly small (no one knows exactly how small), and in some areas (especially in South and Southeast Asia), people continue to harvest whale sharks for their fins and meat. Illegal hunting is difficult to curtail because of the extreme range of whale shark migrations.

Captain Clam's Comments

Whale shark diving sounds like a great adventure, but it certainly isn't for everyone. It is much easier to hop on a boat and look at the large members of the ocean in their natural surroundings. Baja alone has about 15 commercial shark and whale watching cruises. These cruises have become popular since the 1950s and are now an active enterprise in about 40 countries where whales are frequently sighted. We can remember swimming off of Race Point Beach in Provincetown, Massachusetts, and seeing whales spouting a few hundred yards away. Although this isn't considered open ocean, whales commonly come very close to the shore following plumes of plankton rich waters that upwell along the rising continental shelf.

Room to Roam

The ocean, like the sky, is wide open and interconnected, providing its inhabitants with unlimited travel opportunities. And, because so many of the ocean's inhabitants choose to fully exploit the waters, scientists have given them a special name—*nekton*. These world travelers include a wide variety of species—everything from whales, fish, turtles, and sharks to octopi, squid, and even shrimp. Some nekton are so well suited to travel that they can tolerate full-strength seawater, low-salt seawater, and even freshwater without experiencing much stress.

The bull shark is especially unique because it is the only wide-ranging saltwater shark known to travel far up fresh water rivers where it commonly takes up short-term residence in lagoons, bays, river mouths, freshwater tributaries, and lakes. They have been known to inhabit Lake Nicaragua, where they manage to traverse the rapids of the San Juan River while heading back out to the sea again. They have been located

Captain Clam's Comments

When a species of marine life is capable of moving from salt-water to fresh in order to breed (like salmon), it is said to be *anadromous*. Freshwater fish that migrate to saltwater in order to breed are *catadromous*. Most eels are catadromous.

2,000 miles up the Amazon River; in the Zambezi, Ganges, Tigris, and Euphrates rivers; in the coastal lagoons of Florida; and 160 miles up the Atchafalaya River in Louisiana. This shark's ability to move freely from salt- to freshwater environments, along with the fact that the bull shark is a documented people eater, makes it one nasty foe. This type of migration is slightly different from other types in that the change from one medium to another is not facilitated by the need to spawn in an alternate environment.

One of the most famous and wide-ranging nekton are the various species of tuna. Although they don't run up freshwater rivers like salmon, they commonly traverse entire oceans during migratory runs and must deal with extreme variations in water temperatures. In order to cope with the rigorous journey of thousands of ocean miles, the tuna and related species, such as albacore, have highly developed musculature that can actually help them maintain a constant body temperature—between 28 degrees and 33 degrees Celsius (in the 90s Fahrenheit), even in the chilliest waters. They achieve this feat by using their muscles and circulatory system in a heat exchanger arrangement called *whole body endothermy*. Their blood vessels retain the heat generated by the swimming muscles and circulate it around the body, keeping the entire fish warm and toasty, including important organs such as the brain and eyes.

Captain Clam's Comments

Recent research indicates that bluefin from the Eastern North Atlantic mix more frequently with bluefin from the Western North Atlantic than was previously thought. This complicates attempts to regulate tuna fishing and protect bluefin populations because the quotas are higher in the East than in the West. In other words, the West can create regulations to limit catches, but when the bluefin swim toward Europe, they're doomed—the regulations no longer protect them.

Riding the Gulf Stream

Animals are not the only things that traverse the oceans—currents can make long treks as well. One of the most powerful and influential currents on the planet is the Gulf Stream. Originating near the Straits of Florida, the Gulf Stream travels northeast, across the Atlantic Ocean, to the Grand Banks off the coast of Newfoundland. Powered by the North and South Equatorial currents, the Gulf Stream carries warm, southern waters north, moderating the temperature and weather conditions in Western Europe.

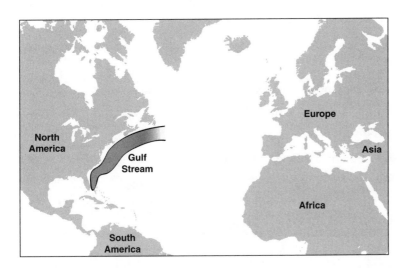

Where the Gulf Stream roams.

At its source, the Gulf Stream is approximately 80 kilometers (50 miles) wide, about .65 kilometers (.4 mile) deep, and about 25 degrees Centigrade (77 degrees Fahrenheit) at its surface. (It's a little warmer in the summer.) It travels about 5 kilometers (3 miles) per hour. As it flows northeast, the Gulf Stream gradually widens, slows down to less than 1 kilometer (.6 mile) per hour, and eventually branches off into other currents. Over most of its course, the Gulf Stream is characterized by bright blue, highly salty water (because of the high evaporation rate).

Because the Gulf Stream is so warm, it attracts warm-water seaweed, invertebrates, and fish—including billfish, tuna, mackerel, cobia, mullet, and tarpon. It also attracts any creatures that prey on these warm-water menu items, including the loggerhead sea turtle, the bottlenose dolphin, the Portuguese man-of-war, and several species of warm weather birds. In addition, the warmth of the Gulf Stream ensures the survival of the coral reef communities in southern Florida during the winter months.

Underwater Eye

The first person to map the Gulf Stream was Benjamin Franklin. When he was serving as deputy postmaster general, the English postal authorities expressed their amazement that the American ships could cross the Atlantic several days faster than the English ships could make the journey to America. They asked Benjamin Franklin if he had any theories to explain this phenomenon. Franklin did a little research, talked to a savvy sailor by the name of Captain Timothy Folger (Franklin's cousin), and together they drew up the Franklin-Folger Gulf Stream Chart.

The Least You Need to Know

♦ Most sea life is found in the open ocean—the pelagic zone—which includes all waters off the immediate shoreline.

♦ The photic zone, the zone where light penetrates, is the most productive zone in the pelagic zone.

♦ Plankton fuel the development of other species in the pelagic zone.

♦ The mesopelagic zone, just below the photic zone, supports some pretty strange fish, including the lantern fish.

♦ The Sargasso Sea, home of the Bermuda Triangle, is characterized by thick mats of seaweed and way too many tar balls.

♦ Whales and whale sharks prefer the open ocean, where they can secure the krill they need to maintain their massive bodies.

Chapter 5

Adjusting to Extreme Conditions

In This Chapter

- ◆ Coping with the icy seas
- ◆ Surviving high pressure and heat at the ocean depths
- ◆ Living in the dark ... and liking it
- ◆ The trials and tribulations of long migrations

Have you ever wondered what it would be like to live in the artic tundra, where the land is eternally frozen solid? How about pitching a tent in the middle of the Sahara Desert, where you'd have wall-to-wall sand carpeting and a permanently parched pallet? Well, many marine plants and animals live their lives in even more extreme conditions than these. And if that's not enough to deal with, they also must adapt to all of the other factors at work in the deepest depths, such as high pressure and low food supplies. In this chapter, you explore some of the most extreme ocean environments to see how amazingly well some ocean occupants can adjust and actually thrive in the most demanding places.

Arctic Inhabitants

When you're looking for extreme ocean environments, the Arctic Ocean is a pretty good place to start. Think of the coldest day you can remember, add water, multiply by five, and you can only begin to imagine the bitter arctic cold. Of course the water below the surface doesn't freeze solid. If it did, the only life there would be frozen in a solid block of ice. But the animals that live in these chilly waters, where huge ice islands bob on the waves, deal with the conditions stoically and with plenty of protective insulation—the same way humans adapt when they visit these bitter climes.

Captain Clam's Comments

The race to reach the North Pole has led many explorers to push the limits of human endurance and also human ethics. In 1909, Robert Peary and his crew made a fifth expedition to reach a spot that had yet to be attained—true magnetic north. After they reached their goal and were heading home, they heard that another explorer, Dr. Frederick Cook, had claimed to have reached the pole in 1908. Challenging the claim, Peary found out that Cook had barely left the ice pack and had paid a sea captain to fake the sextant reading. Cook disappeared and was later arrested and convicted of selling fake oil stock.

Warm-Blooded Fish

Most fish are cold-blooded animals; that is, their body temperature is at the mercy of the water that surrounds them. If the water is a balmy 30 degrees Celsius, the fish are a cozy 30 degrees Celsius. If the water is a chilly 4 degrees Celsius, the fish are 4 degrees Celsius—and at 4 degrees Celsius, most fish turn into frozen fish sticks.

So, how do tuna not only survive, but thrive in the cold polar regions? Because they're "warm-blooded" fish. A tuna can raise its body temperature as much as 20 degrees Celsius above the temperature of the surrounding water.

What makes tuna so special? This question has puzzled marine biologists for years. Most fish are cold-blooded primarily because they must circulate blood to their gills to extract oxygen from the water. As cold water passes over the gills, it quickly cools the blood, and the fish never has a chance to warm up, no matter how much energy the fish burns. Tuna have a specialized circulation system in which the warmer, used blood, on its way back to the gills, passes its heat to the colder, newly oxygenated blood instead of carrying the heat to the gills. This enables tuna to retain their heat and remain warm and cozy in the most frigid waters.

Underwater Eye

Tuna are not the only warm-blooded fish. The mackerel shark can also retain its body heat.

It's Not Heavy, It's My Blubber

Anybody who lives in cold climates knows that in order to stay warm in the winter, you need two things: heating fuel and insulation. Most creatures that visit or live in the polar regions have both, in the form of oil and/or fat (blubber). If you ever opened a can of herring, sardines, or anchovies, you know just how oily these fish can be. Whales, seals, penguins, and other polar creatures have their share of fat, as well. These fats provide the creatures with the fuel they need to make it through the day, and the more fuel they burn, the warmer they stay. In addition, these fats and oils insulate their owners from the surrounding cold waters. When the creatures generate heat by burning energy, their insulating layer of fat helps them retain more of that heat.

> **Underwater Eye**
>
> Marine mammals have adapted to the extreme cold with thick layers of fat or blubber. The walrus is a prime example. These arctic inhabitants can reach up to 2,000 pounds, much of which is in the form of oils and fat. The thermal insulation quality of this layer is more than adequate for maintaining body temperature and helps with buoyancy as well.

Built-In Antifreeze

Although insulation can help warm-blooded mammals retain their heat, it does little good for cold-blooded creatures. To keep these critters from becoming Popsicles, Mother Nature has devised another tool—an all-natural antifreeze, similar in function to the antifreeze used in cars. Automobile antifreeze is glycol (alcohol) based and is designed to provide the car with a cooling solution that has a lower freezing point than plain water. In winter, the temperature can dip well below the freezing point (0 degrees Celsius or 32 degrees Fahrenheit) before the antifreeze freezes. In fish and oysters, the antifreeze is glycoprotein, a solution that lowers the freezing point of the creature's blood, so that it doesn't freeze solid when the water temperature dips below the freezing point.

A Newly Discovered Oasis

Of course, the Arctic Ocean hosts cold-tolerant animals—it's cold there, a mass of whiteness and ice. Or at least that's how it appears to us surface dwellers. If you look deeper, however, way deeper, you find that nature has an interesting surprise in store. At the very bottom of the ocean, in an area that's supposed to have temperatures in the range of about 2 degrees Celsius and pressures of 2 tons per square inch, you would think that no being could possibly exist. In 1977, however, while studying tectonic plate shifting, geologists discovered that life not only existed here but that it flourished! Ironically, there wasn't even one biologist on board when these gardens of life were first discovered.

How could anything survive at these cold, crushing depths in near total darkness? Read on!

Captain Clam's Comments

The discovery of the first hydrothermal vents was accomplished by an incredible collection of scientists, engineers, and crews from several colleges and institutions around the world. They pooled their resources and equipment and worked together tirelessly to prove what they all believed was true—that there was warm water at the bottom of the ocean. What they found was so astonishing that it caught the research team completely by surprise. They had only enough formaldehyde on board to preserve a few specimens so they had to pickle them with Russian vodka.

Warming Up to Hydrothermal Vents

When scientists first theorized that life could not exist in the deepest, darkest, coldest regions of the oceans, they hadn't considered the fact that there could be sources of heat other than the sun. When they explored the bottom of the ocean floor, however, they found what later came to be called hydrothermal vents—holes in the ocean floor from which intensely hot water spews.

The water pouring out of these vents, called black smokers, can reach temperatures of about 400 degrees Celsius, but the high pressure keeps the water from boiling. The heat is limited to a small area around the vent opening. Less than an inch from the opening, the water temperature drops to 2 degrees Celsius, the usual temperature of deep seawater. Most creatures that huddle around these vents live at temperatures just above freezing and they feast off the chemicals that pour out of these underground fissures.

Underwater Eye

More than 300 new species of vent organisms have been identified since the first vent was discovered in 1977. Among the most abundant (around the Pacific vents) are the giant tube worms that can reach lengths of more than a meter. Mussels, shrimp, clams, and crabs are abundant at many vents but they are all very different than any species found in other parts of the ocean. To survive, these vent creatures establish symbiotic relationships with bacteria that feast off the nutrients supplied by the vents.

Where Sulfur Rules

In most ocean ecosystems, oxygen and sunlight power the development and evolution of the system. No light, no plants, no animals … no kidding. So, how can there be life around hydrothermal vents, in which both light and oxygen are scarce? The ecosystem surrounding these vents plays by a different set of rules; it is powered more by chemicals than by the energy of light.

The searing water that pours from hydrothermal vent holes is packed with chemicals, especially hydrogen sulfide, a gas that smells like rotten eggs. (This chemical is produced when seawater reacts with sulfate in the rocks below the ocean floor.) Generally toxic to most marine life that uses oxygen, hydrogen sulfide is the food of choice for vent bacteria. They suck this stuff up, grow, reproduce, and in turn, sustain larger organisms that sit higher up on the food pyramid. In short, instead of having plants at the bottom of the food chain using sunlight to convert chemicals into an edible food source, in vent communities the base of the food pyramid consists of bacteria chowing down on sulfur.

> **Log Entry**
>
> Hydrothermal vent organisms rely on a special kind of bacteria, called **chemoautotrophs** (chemo = source of energy from chemicals; auto = synthesize their own food; trophs = type of feeding). Chemoautotrophic bacteria are able to use the energy of chemicals within the vent water to synthesize the carbon compounds they require to grow and reproduce.

Xtreme Worms

A major reason why a biologist wasn't on board the submersible that discovered the hydrothermal vents was because nobody thought that abundant life could exist at such titanic pressures. Prior to the discovery, the most anyone ever found on the ocean bottom were a few species of sea spiders (see Chapter 12) and an occasional stray jellyfish, shrimp, or crab. Then came the vent animals—jumbo sea creatures bigger than most similar creatures that evolved in what scientists had considered the most optimal conditions.

One specimen that best represents the vent clan is the giant tubeworm called Riftia (in the group *Vestimentifera*). This highly specialized vent worm has lost its mouth and digestive system, and instead packs its insides with bacteria. Now that's what I call extreme living! It's bad enough that the water smells of rotten eggs and the pressure is enough to squeeze the life out of you, but then you have to fill yourself with bacteria in order to survive!

Who Turned Out the Lights?

Light can dive, but it can dive only so deep. At about 600 meters (much shallower in murky waters), you can't even see the back of your own hand. So how do other marine creatures manage to navigate the deep and find food and mates? They use a variety of tools and techniques, as explained in the following sections.

Those Betty Davis Eyes

Some organisms have a logical solution for seeing in the dark—bigger eyes. Larger eyes let in more light, enabling the creatures to see in very low-light conditions. The giant squid, for example, the largest invertebrate in the world, has the largest eye in the animal kingdom. The eye of a 50- to 60- foot squid can be 10 inches in diameter—about the size of your average dinner plate! The squid has a diving range of about 700 meters (2,300 feet), an extremely low-light region. The squid is a voracious predator that uses its vision and other tactile senses to navigate the deep and hunt its prey.

> ### CAUTION Ocean Alert
>
> When oceanographers sample deepwater fish, they usually can't take them alive unless they bring the animals up under pressure. During the ascent, the pressure change is heavy enough to distort the organism, causing organs to pop out of places they shouldn't.

> ### Underwater Eye
>
> A giant squid that was washed up on the shores of New Zealand in 1933 had an eye that measured 40 centimeters (16 inches) across!

Squid are not the only bug-eyed beasts of the deep. Most fish that hang out in the mesopelagic region (the twilight zone) have oversized and/or specially adapted eyes to see in these low-light conditions. Nearly all mesopelagic fish, for example, have pure-rod retinas, which increase their night vision while making them entirely colorblind. Another adaptation, exhibited in the Gigantura (telescope fish) and other mesopelagic fish, is the development of tubular eyes, designed to give the fish binocular vision. In many deep species, the eyes point upward, possibly to see prey and predators as their bodies are silhouetted against the brighter upper waters.

The squid uses a larger eye to let in more light.

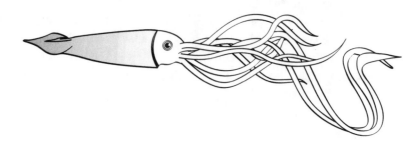

Eyes Not Included

Another way to deal with the absence of light is to forgo eyes altogether. This is the option of choice for the hagfish (slime eel), and many other fish that navigate the deepest depths. Hagfish hang out near the ocean floor where they feed on the remains of less fortunate members of the water column that sink to bottom. The blind hagfish uses its sense of smell and touch to locate its food and has abandoned the use of eyes altogether.

In most cases, fish that have nonfunctional eyes use the lateral line system to navigate and hunt for food. The lateral line system is similar to underwater radar, enabling a fish to sense variations in water pressure. The key feature of the lateral line system is a sensory organ called the neuromast, which consists of hairs encased in a gelatinous cap. Neuromasts are typically arranged in grooves that run the length of the fish's body, but can be located as individual units or in small groups called pit organs. As the fish swims, it creates pressure variations in the water and bounces waves off surrounding objects. These pressure variations and waves move the caps of the neuromasts, which bend the hairs inside the neuromasts. This movement triggers nerve impulses, which signal the fish to move in a particular direction. Of course the neuromasts can detect the movement of other creatures in the vicinity as well, helping the fish find prey and avoid predators.

> **Underwater Eye**
>
> In all blind fish, the eyes are much smaller and are usually covered with skin but are rarely totally missing. Most blind fish are associated with caves or very murky water and are usually freshwater species. Some species, when reintroduced to light, manage to regenerate their once useless eyes.

Sending the Right Signals

When you live in a place that has no light, little food, frigid temperatures, and staggering, bone-crushing pressure, the last thing you need is to be misunderstood by members of your own group. At this level, the key to survival is communication—sending out the right signals.

One of the primary ways that deep water fish communicate is through their light-emitting organs, called photophores. Every species has a set of its own glowing dots and dangling lures arranged in a unique pattern that sends very different messages, almost like Morse code. Each denizen of the dark has its own personal neon sign advertising that it's ready for business.

Captain Clam's Comments

Some African fish emit weak electrical discharges from special organs to communicate, identify objects and other fish, navigate murky waters, and survive at night with fewer predators. It's sort of like mental telepathy with a little more zing to it.

But light organs aren't the only way of communicating in places where visibility is limited. Another way is to use electricity. The majority of fish that use strong electrical current do so not for communication but to stun their prey. (The electrical discharge is so strong, nobody really wants to "listen" to the message it has to convey.) Only the weakly electric fish use current as a means of communication or identification. Each species has a unique electrical discharge that helps the members of the group communicate with one another. Members of another species use a different electrical discharge. Think of it as radio stations broadcasting at different frequencies. As long as the members of a particular group communicate using a unique pattern of electrical discharges, they can talk with one another without interference from the communications of other species.

Going the Distance

Some marine creatures can't sit still. By instinct, they're driven to follow specific, often extreme, migration patterns that require them to be some of the toughest, most adaptable creatures on the planet. In some cases, the migratory trip is so exhausting that it ends in certain death.

So, if migration is so challenging, why do animals migrate at all? Why not pick the perfect place, settle down, and raise a family? Animals migrate primarily for three purposes: to find or follow a food source, to locate a comfortable water temperature, or to spawn. After all, that's what most animals want: food, comfort, and sex. In most cases, the animals commonly follow the same pattern year in and year out for as many years as they're alive. In other cases, such as the annual migration of salmon, the migratory trip is a one-way ticket to the morgue. The salmon fatten themselves up, swim like mad upstream, find a mate to spawn with, lay and fertilize their eggs, and then die in the same headwaters where they were born. The nutrients they bring from the ocean enrich the streams and forests as their bodies decompose.

In order to survive, migratory creatures must be able to adapt to ever-changing environments and must overcome some extremely difficult challenges. As they move from place to place, these creatures cope with drastic changes in water temperatures and chemical makeup without going into shock. They don't pack winter coats or even wet suits; they carry only the scales on their backs. In addition, wherever they go, predators follow, posing an ever-present danger. Frequently, just as a migratory creature is nearing its destination, a stalker appears out of nowhere and puts a premature end to the creature's journey. But even with these drawbacks and limitations, migratory creatures keep making their regular treks across the ocean and up the rivers.

Swimming Upstream

The migrations of certain species of Sockeye Salmon are legendary. These relentless swimmers recognize the smell of their home river and have been known to swim the entire length of a long river, such as the Columbia River, upstream! That's right; before the hydroelectric dams cut off their primary route, these fish would swim from the Pacific Ocean through the state of Washington and all the way up into Canada! Known as anadromous creatures, the Sockeye Salmon begins life in freshwater, goes to the ocean, and then returns.

Hundreds of years ago, many parts of the journey posed quite a challenge to these fish. Waterfalls, rapids, and extremely shallow regions of the river stood as hurdles between the fish and their ultimate goal. But these majestic powerhouses could catapult themselves over nearly every natural barrier—rocks, rapids, and even small waterfalls were no match for the leaping power of the salmon. Now with hydropower dams and other modifications to the river system (including channel straightening and the removal of log jams), the salmon face much tougher challenges that are sometimes insurmountable. Even so, these persistent creatures are driven by their natural instinct to return to the same stream from whence they came and attempt the journey once again.

The Great Tuna Treks

As mentioned in Chapter 4, tuna are famous for their long migrations. These voracious eaters will swim anywhere for a bite to eat, intelligently using the currents and seasonal temperatures to assist them in their quest for more food. Wherever you find a stash of tuna food, you find a crowd of tuna helping themselves to the bounty. (Maybe they should be called pigs of the sea, rather than chicken.)

Tuna are remarkably talented travelers—muscular fish with missile-shaped bodies that make them some of the fastest moving animals in the sea. Many species are capable of attaining speeds of up to 80 kmph (50 mph)! Because of their energy expenditure and size, tuna are voracious eaters, typically consuming the equivalent of 10 percent of their body weight in a single day. Yet many species of tuna can go for several weeks without a meal.

> **Underwater Eye**
>
> If a tuna were to stop swimming, it would die from lack of oxygen. To survive, a tuna must swim a distance equal to its body length every second. Tuna swim with their mouths open to pass a steady stream of oxygenated water over their gills.

Tuna migrations are remarkable, often ranging from coast to coast, from the Pacific to the Atlantic. This is no small task for a fish of its size. Of course, whales commonly migrate long distances, as well, but they're much larger and have more room to pack reserves for their long journeys.

Migrating with the Eels

When most people think of eels, they think of sedentary animals that would rather stay home than take an ocean cruise. However, some eels, such as the leptocephalus (the American and European eels), make incredibly long treks during the course of their existence. These eels spend their first four to seven years, the better part of their lives, swimming around in freshwater streams off the Atlantic Ocean. While there, they are in their nocturnal, yellow eel phase. Just before migrating to the Sargasso Sea, the eels stop feeding, their eyes and pectoral fins become larger, and their body color takes on a silvery sheen. The eels swim downstream, across the ocean, and to the Sargasso Sea, where they lay and fertilize their eggs.

Once spawned, the baby eel drifts with the ocean currents for 9 to 12 months before entering coastal waters. When it reaches approximately 2.4 inches in length, the young eel metamorphoses into a transparent, "glass" eel or elver, and then reenters the fresh water. These eels are thought to have the most diverse habitat ranges of any fish species.

The Least You Need to Know

- To survive in near freezing water, Arctic marine animals have increased fat content, higher levels of fatty oils, specialized circulatory systems, and other unique modifications.

- Hydrothermal vents support communities of animals that use a sulfur-based, bacteria-assisted metabolism to survive.

- Fish living in the deepest parts of the ocean have light-emitting organs called photophores that help them trap food and communicate with one another.

- The lateral line system enables fish in the darkest depths to navigate by sensing variations in water pressure.

- Some fish use weak electrical currents to communicate and navigate in the absence of any visibility.

- Tuna can attain speeds of up to 80 kmph, can go for weeks without food, and can tolerate frigid waters, making them well-suited for long migrations.

Part 2

A Garden of Marine Plants

Any study of the ocean starts at the bottom … the bottom of the food chain, that is. In most ecosystems, the bottom of the food chain is blooming with plant life. In the ocean, this plant life exists in two basic forms: microscopic plants that float around in the ocean's surface waters and larger plants that grow from the ocean floor up toward the surface.

This part studies the plants from various perspectives—first providing an overview of microscopic and macroscopic plants, exploring the various animals that eat the plants, and finally examining how seaweed and other plants act as habitats for various ocean critters.

6

Let's Talk Really Small Plants

In This Chapter

- ◆ My life as a plant
- ◆ Phytoplankton, the first link in a long food chain
- ◆ The swirling, churning nutrient pool and the animals it feeds
- ◆ Plants that act like animals and the animals who love (to eat) them
- ◆ The bad boys of algae blooms

When discussing plants, most people think about green leafy plants—plants you can see, such as grass, flowers, weeds, bushes, and trees. Mention ocean plants, and people commonly think of seaweed and sea grass. However, ocean plant life starts out much more modestly, with microscopic algae. Although diminutive in size, these plants play a major role in various ocean environments, using the energy from the sun to convert a handful of chemicals into an edible food source. This chapter pays homage to these microscopic plants as it examines their vast diversity, explores the pivotal role they play in the ocean's ecology, and reveals the dangers that some species pose when they grow out of control.

Exploring the Base of the Food Pyramid

A good portion of marine biology centers on the discussion of trophic levels—the study of who's eating what. Land-based trophic levels typically consist of a plant at the bottom level (such as a shrub or a tree) that is eaten by an herbivore (such as a deer) that is then eaten by a carnivore or omnivore (such as a cougar). The plant, at the bottom of the food pyramid, is considered a *primary producer* and has the job of converting carbon dioxide, water, nitrogen, phosphorous, iron, and other minerals into a food source through the process of photosynthesis. Many marine ecosystems follow this same scenario; for example, kelp (a seaweed) acts as a primary producer that is eaten by sea urchins that are then eaten by lobsters or sea otters.

Plants do not compose the bottom of all food pyramids, however. In many cases, decomposing organic matter or chemical-synthesizing bacteria fuel the ecosystem. The base of all food pyramids (as we currently understand them on Earth) consists of one of the three following primary producers: photosynthetic plants, chemosynthetic bacteria, or decomposed organic matter, called *detritus*. The following sections provide details about each of these critical primary producers.

Sun-Loving Plants

At the bottom of most food pyramids are various plants and plant-like organisms that convert water and carbon dioxide into sugar (glucose) using energy from the sun in a process called photosynthesis. The pigmentation (chlorophyll, carotenoids, or phycobilins) in photosynthetic organisms catches the sunlight, which provides energy to drive the chemical reactions that are necessary to convert carbon dioxide into glucose. Plants, which typically produce more glucose than they need for growth, store the glucose in the form of starch and other carbohydrates in their cells, roots, stems, and leaves. Animals that eat these plants use the sugars and carbohydrates to fuel their own growth, movement, and reproduction.

One of the major primary producers in the open ocean is not a plant but a photosynthetic bacteria called *cyanobacteria*. Formerly known as blue-green algae, cyanobacteria (principally *Prochlorococcus* and *Synechococcus*) are responsible for 80 percent of primary productivity by phytoplankton in the open ocean (most of the ocean). Cyanobacteria are also considered to be picoplankton because they are so tiny (which is why they were not discovered until relatively recently). Diatoms and dinoflagellates, which you learn more about later in this chapter, combine to produce the remaining 20 percent, even though they are much more abundant.

Underwater Eye

Plankton that's smaller than 10 microns is classified as *picoplankton*.

Bacteria in the Sulfur Baths

In the abyss, where the sun doesn't shine, other organisms play the role of primary producer and use a different form of energy as their source—chemical energy. Unlike photosynthetic bacteria, such as cyanobacteria, that rely on light energy to fuel photosynthesis, the bacteria that live around hydrothermal vents, called *archaebacteria*, derive their energy by oxidizing the inorganic compounds that spew out of the hydrothermal vents (primarily hydrogen sulfide). This energy fuels other chemical reactions in the bacteria to convert carbon dioxide and water into simple sugars. Clams, mussels, tubeworms, and other creatures feed directly on the bacteria, and creatures higher up in the food pyramid feed on them.

Detritus Dumps and Diners

When you examine food pyramids, it's easy to overlook the fact that the system produces a fair amount of "wastes," including uneaten plants, partially eaten and decomposing animals, and plenty of doo-doo (especially from copepods). Fortunately, nature is very efficient and does not let this material go to waste. Bacteria and fungi, nature's decomposers, break down the organic material and return it to the ecosystem as nutrient-rich matter called detritus. Many invertebrates, including mussels, clams, and other organisms feed on the detritus. As a result, detritus anchors the base of the food pyramid in many deep-sea areas and areas where plants cannot grow (such as below the surface of the mudflats).

Although much of the detritus settles to the ocean floor and washes up on shore in mudflats and other coastal areas, winds, waves, and currents carry the detritus to other areas of the ocean, as well. In areas where upwellings occur, currents carry nutrient-rich water from the ocean floor to the surface, fueling plankton blooms that feed whales and other sea creatures.

Feeding the Oceans with Phytoplankton

Both on land and in the ocean, primary production can occur in microscopic plants, as well as in larger plants. On land, you might see algae growing on shady side of a tree or rock. In the ocean (or even in your swimming pool), you might witness the waters turn red, green, or brown, as a population of microscopic algae explodes. In open water, the different forms of single-cell plant life is collectively referred to as *phytoplankton*. Most phytoplankton consist of single-cell algae that float around in the ocean's epipelagic region (the surface waters). Phytoplankton are responsible for constitute the greatest amount of carbon fixing organisms in the oceans (turning water and carbon dioxide into sugar using sunlight).

Phytoplankton makes up the foundation of the food pyramid.

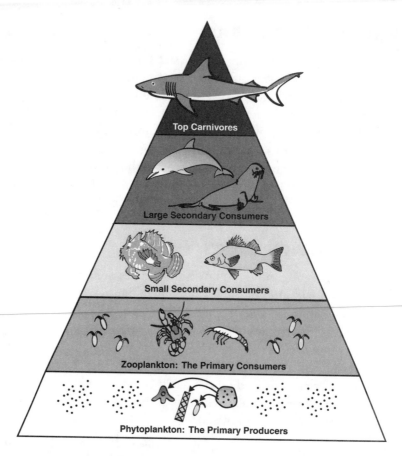

Although they are some of the tiniest organisms on the planet, as a group, phytoplankton are some of the most influential primary producers on Earth. Not only do they feed the zooplankton that feed the fish that feed the largest mammals on the planet, but they are also responsible for converting 30 to 50 percent of the carbon dioxide in the atmosphere back into oxygen. In fact, ancient phytoplankton are responsible for producing most of the oxygen that made up Earth's atmosphere in the years when life was first forming. Phytoplankton also affect climate because they remove carbon dioxide (a greenhouse gas) from the atmosphere, and they produce a chemical that affects the formation of clouds, which influence the amount of the sun's energy the earth retains.

Log Entry

Phytoplankton is generally thought of as plant plankton—tiny drifting particles that feed small animal plankton (which are called *zooplankton*).

What Are You, a "Planimal"?

Imagine a flower that can crawl out of your neighbor's flower pot and plant itself on your front lawn or a tree that can walk to the local nursery to pick up a bag of fertilizer. Weird, eh? Well, many phytoplankton have qualities that make them act like both plants, animals, or even bacteria. They have the chloroplasts and other photosynthetic machinery to make them full-fledged plants, but they also have moving parts, like animals.

This makes classifying phytoplankton very tricky: Are they plants? Are they animals? Can we just call them "planimals"? When Antoni van Leeuwenhoek, inventor of the microscope, first observed these organisms, he faced the same problem and decided to call these odd creatures animalcules. Before this discovery, anything that moved was considered an animal and anything that carried out photosynthesis was considered a plant.

Over the years, scientists developed several systems to classify plants and animals and to differentiate between single-cell and multi-cell organisms. Currently, we use a fairly simple classification system consisting of two primary divisions: *prokaryotes* and *eukaryotes*. A prokaryote is a single-cell organism that does not have a nucleus. Prokaryotes are divided into two groups: bacteria (that live just about everywhere, including inside humans) and archaebacteria (the bacteria that live around hydrothermal vents and hot springs). A eukaryote is a single-cell or multi-cell organism in which the cell structure is more complex and does contain a nucleus. Eukaryotes can be single-cell or multi-cell organisms and include plants, animals, fungi, and protists (a catch-all category for organisms that do not fit into any of the other eukaryote categories).

Captain Clam's Comments

Some algae disguise themselves as true plants. For example, macroalgae (such as kelp) look like a big plant, complete with roots, stems, and leaves. However, all the cells that compose the seaweed are essentially the same, so they are not true plants, like flowers, grass, and trees, which have different cell types for different parts of the plant.

A Diatom a Dozen

Some of the most important and prevalent single-cell plants in coastal waters are the diatoms. Think of diatoms as golden, single-cell algae with shells. A diatom's cell wall is primarily composed of silica, the same stuff used to make glass, and consists of two nearly identical halves. The rigid cell walls give the diatoms an elegant, blown-glass look. The shells vary in appearance and are often useful in helping to identify the diverse species of diatoms. This silica shell limits the conditions under which diatoms survive. They need a lot of nutrients to maintain their glass houses, and because the shell is heavy, they can only live in places where the water is well-mixed. In still water, they sink into the deep, dark waters where they cannot survive.

Diatoms have a smooth, glass-like cell well.

(Photo Credit: Dr. Neil Sullivan, USC)

Diatoms can reproduce asexually, through simple cell division, with each daughter cell getting half of the glassy shell. Each daughter cell then becomes complete by making a new half shell to match. What's funny is that the new half always fits inside the older half so that diatoms get smaller each time they divide. To keep from shrinking into oblivion, the diatom eventually sheds its shell, grows, and then secretes two new larger shell halves. Or it reproduces sexually and gives "birth" to an individual with a new cell wall.

Scientists have been studying diatoms since the eighteenth century and are still gathering new information about them. The actual number of diatom species is between 10,000 and 100,000 or more, with 1,400 to 1,800 being marine plankton. Some of these species are found in the water in such abundance that they can be counted in the millions per milliliter. During the spring, conditions are perfect for diatom blooms, especially along coastal regions. In the spring, the water is warm, the sky is sunny, and the currents and waves are strong. The churning water carries nutrient-rich water from the ocean floor to the sunny surface layer, causing diatom blooms and other algae blooms that fuel copepod blooms. Of course, wherever you find millions of copepod swimming around, you're going to find plenty of hungry animals dining on them, including fish, squid, sea birds, baleen whales, seals, and other animals.

Underwater Eye
Because diatoms have a glass-like cell wall, they don't completely break down right away when they die and decompose. Their empty shells accumulate and leave a record behind that allows paleontologists to figure out how long they have been around—about 100 million years. The shells that they leave behind are buried in sediment and are sometimes in the form of what is called diatomaceous earth, which is used for many different purposes including pool water filters and toothpaste.

On the Move with Dinoflagellates

Name a single-cell organism that carries a whip and knows how to use it. Answer: the dinoflagellate. These single-cell organisms have two flagella (whip-like tails) of different lengths that propel them through the water, using an undulating (wave-like) motion. One flagellum typically encircles the girth of the organism and enables it to spin around on its axis, sort of like a top. (That's where the dinoflagellates obtained their name: from the Greek *dinos*, rotation, and the Latin *flagellum*, for little whip.) The other flagellum dangles down from the cell's midsection along a groove in its shell and moves the organism up and down in the water column or forward and back through the water.

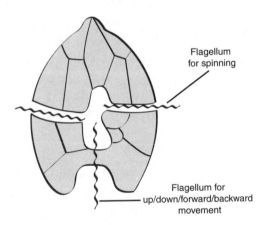

Flagellum
for spinning

Flagellum for
up/down/forward/backward
movement

Dinoflagellates can move through the water by beating their whiplike flagella.

Harmful Algae Blooms

Whenever enough light and nutrients are available, algae begin to grow and reproduce like mad, resulting in clouds of algae called *algae blooms*. In most cases, algae blooms provide a critical source of food and oxygen that fuel resulting blooms of zooplankton. In some cases, however, algae can be too successful, causing what is known as a *harmful algae bloom* (or HAB). In some cases, the bloom can last for several days, blocking the sunlight from reaching beyond the surface. If the bloom lasts long enough, it can cause plants that grow below the surface to die, resulting in reduced oxygen levels. Some species of algae release deadly neurotoxins (nerve poisons) into the ocean environment and even feed off the flesh of fish. Some algae are just plain useless on a nutritional scale but can outcompete more nutritional algae, replacing a valuable food supply with a plentiful, though useless food source. The following sections examine the more common harmful algae blooms and their less desirable effects.

Red Tide, Red Alert

One of the most infamous HABs is the so called "red tide," an occurrence that leaves the water reddish-brown and can poison animals at the top of the food chain, such as sea lions, birds, and people. In extreme cases, this toxin has also killed large numbers of fish. During a red tide, dinoflagellates that contain deadly neurotoxins (poisons that destroy nerve tissues) rapidly reproduce. Shellfish and other fish feed on the algae as it settles, ingesting and absorbing the toxins. The toxins can accumulate in fish and shellfish, and make them unsafe for human consumption. Eating fish or shellfish that have accumulated these toxic dinoflagellates can cause paralytic shellfish poisoning (PSP), a condition which can be fatal. If you live near a beach and harvest shellfish, you should contact a local or county government department of health to find out if the shellfish are safe to eat. Even if there isn't a red tide, you should ask the health department about the shellfish, because shellfish can accumulate other environmental toxins as well.

Captain Clam's Comments

No algae bloom is the direct result of tidal movements, and not all red algae blooms are harmful, so the term "red tide" is a bit of a misnomer. Even so, when harmful algae reproduce fast enough to turn the water red, many coastal residents and visitors become concerned.

In addition to tainting the shellfish and potentially killing some fish in the area, the algae can become airborne in the sea spray and cause respiratory problems in humans and other animals. The problems associated with red tides are often serious enough to require health officials to close beaches and post red tide warnings as well as to spot and track red tides to make sure that the shellfish are safe to eat.

Hello Brown Tide, Good-Bye Bay

Some harmful algae blooms pose no direct threat to human health but can seriously affect an entire ecosystem. Such a bloom, called a brown tide, occurred in 1985 off the coast of Long Island, New York. The culprit was a previously unknown species of brown algae called *Aureococcus anophagefferens*, which bloomed to such concentrations that it turned the Peconic Bay the color of coffee. These algae out-competed all other algae during certain periods of the summer months and persisted as a harmful bloom for 12 years without subsiding. During those 12 years, many parts of the Peconic estuary suffered serious damage, including the loss of critical habitats and marine species. The tide finally subsided, but the algae remain in the area, though they are found in high concentrations only in isolated regions.

Several factors contributed to making this brown tide particularly devastating. When the tide reached peak levels, the algae became so thick and dark that they actually prevented sunlight from reaching the plants at the bottom of the bay. Without sunlight, the higher plant species, including eelgrass, died out. And with the disappearance of the eelgrass, the bay scallop could not survive. The bloom not only destroyed the favored habitat of the adult bay scallop, but it also wiped out the bay scallop's offspring.

Underwater Eye

The Peconic Bay once boasted a multimillion dollar shellfish industry that included a winter fishery for the cherished bay scallop. Within two years, the bay scallop population was decimated, primarily because of the bay scallop's relatively short lifespan (18 to 24 months) and the fact that its offspring could not tolerate the unrelenting brown tide blooms. In other words, when one or two generations died off and there were no children to replace them, they were driven to virtual extinction.

The Human Contribution to HABs

Although an algae bloom is a natural occurrence triggered by several factors, human activity, especially near coastlines, contributes significantly to the frequency and seriousness of harmful algae blooms. One major cause is eutrophication—the increase in nutrients, primarily nitrogen and phosphorous, in the ocean, typically near the coastline. This increase in concentration of nitrogen and phosphorous can be composed of agricultural wastes, lawn fertilizers, human wastes from septic systems and sewers, and other sources. This nutrient-rich water flows through the ground, down storm drains, and via rivers to the ocean, where it is greeted by hungry hordes of algae. When this nutrient-packed water mixes with the sunny ocean surface waters, the algae proliferate, causing a bloom. And if the algae that are blooming are reproducing too quickly or are toxic, we call the result a harmful algae bloom.

Aquaculture and Algae Culture

Throughout this chapter, you've seen algae in the wild growing like mad, feeding the masses, and occasionally growing out of control. Their ability to grow has not gone unnoticed in the food industry. People have learned that if they can grow the right kinds of algae in controlled environments, they can use it in food supplements, as additives, and even to feed fish in hatcheries. For example, a fish farm may grow its own algae and then use it along with other food to feed shellfish and other fish, such as carp and tilapia.

Underwater Eye

Although fish farming or *aquaculture* sounds like a good way to obtain fish without over-fishing the oceans, it is not always the most efficient method. Most fisheries feed their fish ground-up fish, such as anchovies, which are pulled from the ocean. It typically requires 2 to 5 pounds of ground fish to produce 1 pound of farm-raised fish or shrimp. Fish farms are most efficient when they raise fish that eat lower on the food chain, such as catfish, carp, and tilapia.

Growing algae sounds easy, given the fact that algae loves to reproduce, but growing the right kinds of algae can be quite challenging. The algae specialist, an algologist, must know what species of algae is most nutritious and delicious and which alga is best for each stage of an organism's development. Grow the wrong algae and you can wipe out an entire generation of fish! The algae expert must also know the right conditions for raising the preferred types of algae, including the amount of light they require, the optimum water temperature and salinity, and the proper mix of nutrients (fertilizer) to feed the algae. Before you start brewing your first batch of algae, move on to the next section for a quick tour of the algae brewery.

What's Brewing in the Algae Room?

A hatchery's algae room looks like mad scientist's laboratory with vials and tanks full of different colored liquids boiling and bubbling. One tank might look like a tank of mustard, containing a supply of golden algae. Another more closely resembles a bottle of ketchup. And still another looks as though it contains a lifetime supply of green slime. Many hatcheries grow more than one kind of algae because of the different characteristics each species exhibits, including its size, shape, and nutritional value.

To start a culture of algae, you need a pure sample. You don't want a vial of seawater that might contain an alga that could outcompete with the algae you want to grow or other contaminants. To obtain a pure culture, you must contact a lab that specializes in producing and supplying pure samples. The lab can send you a sealed test tube of algae cells that, when added to larger volumes of culture media (sterile seawater complete with the proper nutrients) will divide and multiply in the presence of light.

Growing algae is relatively easy, but to develop a pure culture, you must follow the proper protocol to prevent contamination. To keep the culture pure and prevent it from growing too fast, you must transfer small amounts (inoculations) of the stock culture (pure cells of a known species) into greater volumes of culture media until the media contains the optimum amount of algae for a productive harvest. Obviously, the greater the volume, the more difficult it is to keep the culture pure. If a culture becomes contaminated, it eventually crashes—the entire culture dies and falls to the bottom of the tank.

> **Underwater Eye**
>
> Sterile culture techniques are critical for growing high-quality microalgae. The only way to grow pure cultures is to avoid introducing any foreign matter, such as bacteria, into the mix. When a culture is pure, it is referred to as axenic. Contaminated cultures are called oligoxenic, which means that the culture is full of contaminants, and that's bad.

High Lipid Strains and Pastes

As you can imagine, growing live algae is time-consuming, labor intensive, and expensive, demanding a portion of a hatchery's resources. To cut costs, some hatcheries purchase dried algae in the form of powder or pills, but this dry/dead form is less nutritious and often degrades the water quality. One product, however, is starting to gain the confidence of aquaculturists—algae paste. Algae paste is essentially the same stuff that others grow but it is then spun down into a concentrated form, which can be reconstituted when needed—sort of like frozen orange juice concentrate. Although these algae pastes still fall short when compared with live algae, paste manufacturers are beginning to develop high-lipid strains, providing a much more nutritional food source.

Captain Clam's Comments _____

Now that you can buy concentrated algae paste in a jar, why would anybody want to go through the trouble of growing their own? Two reasons: The paste isn't cheap, and the algae is dead, so it doesn't move around like the live stuff. In trials using only paste, only live feed, and a combination of paste and live feed, live feed always produces better results.

I'll Have the Phytoplankton, Please!

All this talk about phytoplankton probably has made you pretty hungry, so you will be happy to hear that phytoplankton is available for human consumption as well. In particular, a species of cyanobacteria called *Spirulina* has helped nourish people from Africa to the Americas for centuries. Recently rediscovered, Spirulina is sometimes marketed as a superfood, yielding 20 times more protein per acre than a field of soybeans. Spirulina consists of 60 percent all-vegetable protein, 5 percent fat, and no cholesterol, and it delivers an impressive array of vitamins and minerals, including B-12, beta carotene, and a fatty acid called GLA (gamma linolenic acid) that's important in maintaining proper brain development. This so-called wonder "algae" has been making health food news in a big way and is available as a dietary supplement in many different forms. Whether or not Spirulina and other forms of phytoplankton are the superfood some people seem to think they are remains to be seen, but one thing is for certain—phytoplankton will continue to play a key role in feeding the world's animals for the rest of time.

The Least You Need to Know

- Dinoflagellates combine plant-like and animal-like qualities.

- Cyanobacteria and other phytoplankton are extremely important contributors to the planet's food and oxygen supply.

- When conditions are right, algae populations can explode to produce a phenomenon called an algae bloom, which can be beneficial or harmful depending on the results (and on your perspective).

- Blooms of harmful algae can occur naturally, but are sometimes caused by coastal pollution.

- Microalgae are an important component in aquaculture operations and act as a food source for many cultures.

- People are finding new uses for algae species and are learning to use them to improve various industries.

Seaweed and Seagrass Unite

In This Chapter

- ◆ Rocking and wracking seaweed
- ◆ The towering kelp forests and the creatures they hold
- ◆ Passing around the sea lettuce
- ◆ Rock-hard red algae encrusting the coral reefs
- ◆ The seagrass saga

In Chapter 6, you encountered the tiniest "plants" on the planet—microscopic phytoplankton—organisms that float in the sunlit surface of the sea and use the sun's energy to convert water, and nutrients into a bountiful food supply. Although these microscopic wonders represent a large portion of the ocean's primary production, they're not the only photosynthesizers of the sea. Their larger cousins, the seaweed algae and seagrass, do their fair share to feed the masses. In this chapter, you begin to explore these slippery sea "plants" through the example of a few key species, and understand the critical role they play in ocean ecology.

Introducing the Macroalgae (*Seaweedus Biggus*)

Put a glass of water near a sunny window, wait a week or two, and eventually green stuff starts growing on the inside surface of the glass. These are microalgae—single-celled "plants" that can grow into long hair-like masses. Macroalgae are quite different. These algae are not true plants, but they have a plantlike structure, consisting of a *holdfast*, which anchors the algae to a substrate (surface); a *stipe*, similar to a plant's stem; and *blades*, which carry out photosynthesis like leaves.

A typical seaweed, such as the kelp shown here, consists of a holdfast, stipe, and blades.

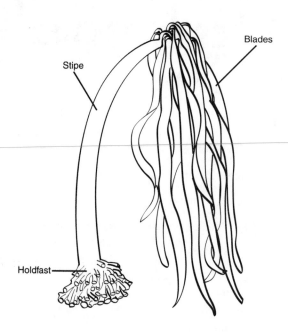

Blades

Stipe

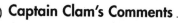

Holdfast

Captain Clam's Comments

Although kelp looks like a plant, it is really a type of algae. Its leaf-like blades are actually sheets of cells—all of which are identical in structure. In true plants, the leaves, stems, roots, and other parts are made up of several different types of cells—each of which has a distinct purpose.

Seaweed comes in a variety of colors, primarily brown, green, and red. The different species can sometimes be recognized by their colors and by the shape of their components (the holdfast, stipe, and blades). The following sections provide some guidance to help you distinguish between the general types of seaweed and seagrass. However, the mystery of how the different macroalgae are related is still unfolding, and it can be very difficult to identify particular species.

I'll Take the Brown One

When most people think of seaweed, they picture brown algae, such as kelp or rock-weed. These are the dark, tough seaweeds that remain stuck to any firm structure they can find no matter how hard the waves bash against them. Approximately 1,500 species of brown seaweed exist worldwide, including the wracks, rockweeds, kelps, and sea palms. Along nearly every shoreline that has a firm substrate on which to attach, you're likely to encounter some species of brown seaweed. Although these sea-weeds have no formal root structure, their holding power is Herculean. What gives these seaweeds their tight grip? Read on.

Floats and Anchors

Most land plants have a firm root system and stem (or trunk) to support them against the forces of gravity and winds. In the ocean, marine algae are more concerned with being pulled away by a current or sinking away from the light. Some macroalgae use strong bases called *holdfasts* to anchor themselves to any firm bottom they can find. Extending from the holdfast is a tough, cartilaginous *stipe*, which looks like the trunk of a mini palm tree and is nearly as tough. Holdfasts can stay in place for upward of 40 years and continue to produce more seaweed. This growth is often torn off at times by strong waves or when the blades become too big for the stipe. To stay afloat in the water column, many species of brown algae have little balloons, or gas blad-ders, on their blades. (In some species of kelp, the floats contain carbon monoxide gas, the same gas that comes out of the tailpipe of your car.) With the stalk-like stipe well anchored and the fronds of bladder-endowed blades well buoyed, these brown algae can stretch upward toward the brighter light and can float on the surface when the tide is high.

The rocky intertidal zone is a fantastic place to seek out one of the toughest of the brown algae, the sea palm. This sturdy seaweed, found in the Pacific Ocean, finds refuge from predators such as sea urchins by living where the waves give it a daily beating. Going 10 rounds with George Foreman couldn't compare to the pounding these seaweeds take on a daily basis. Intertidal algae not only take a beating from the waves, they also bake in the sun during low tide, which can cook 90 percent of the water out of them before they rehydrate at high tide.

Rockweeds are another tough, brown algae commonly found along the northeast and west coasts of the United States. Typically not the first algae to colonize a particular area, rockweeds wait until other algae provide a cover and grazers (such as sea snails) clear bare patches on the rocks. Rockweed then moves in to claim the cleared spots as

their own. To defend themselves from grazing predators, rockweeds secrete a chemical that inhibits the digestion of their predators, making the rockweeds a less attractive food source.

Captain Clam's Comments

Rockweed has a wide variety of uses. Because it is high in iodine, some cultures
that have low iodine levels in their foods use rockweed as a supplement. Rockweed
is also commonly used as a soil conditioner and fertilizer and is sprayed on some
crops to feed the crops directly through their leaves. Some farmers use rockweed as
a nutritious feed for their livestock. Rockweed's primarily commercial use today is to
produce sodium alginate, an extract commonly used as a stabilizer and thickening
agent in paints, cosmetics, and puddings.

Swinging in the Kelp Forest

Giant kelp and bull kelp are the largest nonvascular plants known, towering up
toward the light of the surface with the aid of gas floats. Kelp fronds can be extremely
long, sometimes stretching out as far as 100 meters (325 feet) from the base! Their
growth rates are some of the most rapid in the world, with certain species adding up
to 20 to 30 centimeters (8 to 12 inches) every few days.

About 100 different species of kelp are found throughout the oceans. The major kelp
forests sprout up in temperate subtidal waters throughout the world—where the
waves are rough in waters as deep as 30 to 70 meters (98 to 230 feet). These unique
ecosystems, especially the larger kelp forests, are restricted to temperatures below
20 degrees Celsius (68 degrees Fahrenheit), extending to both the Arctic and
Antarctic Circles. They are very well established on the west coast of the Americas, as
well as in South Africa and New Zealand. Within the
United States, forests dominated by the giant kelp
(*Macrocystis pyrifera*) are a prominent feature of the
subtidal regions in California and Alaska.

Captain Clam's Comments

Most terrestrial plants are *vascular* plants; that is, they have
a vein structure designed to
transport water, gases, and
nutrients throughout the plant.
Nonvascular plants, such as
kelp, have no vein structure running through them. In some
cases, the various cells can pass
nutrients to each other, but the
exchange is not as efficient as it
is in vascular plants.

The multilayered canopy of kelp fronds provides a
complex aquatic habitat for thousands of fish and
invertebrates. Kelp forests teem with life that uses
the vegetation as shelter as well as a food source.
Estimates show that 1 square kilometer of kelp forest
can contain as many as 67,000 animals. Among these
animals are the sea otters, which prey on many of
the fish and invertebrates that colonize the forest.
The otters actually keep one kelp predator at bay, so
to speak—the gluttonous sea urchin. If not kept in

check by otters, some species of sea urchin can defoliate even the largest kelp forests through their insatiable grazing. Other bottom dwelling invertebrates such as mussels, sea stars, and worms find a haven at the base of the forest where water currents are slow enough to allow for larvae to settle to the bottom and develop into adults.

To truly appreciate the majesty of a kelp forest, you need to slip on some diving gear and swim through the forest yourself. Second only to coral reefs, kelp beds provide a visual sensation that makes every dive a memorable event. California's kelp forests are some of the top choice diving spots for the scuba crowd. For nondivers, exhibits such as the one at the Monterey Bay Aquarium can bring people as close to the real thing as possible without getting wet. (You can check out the Monterey Bay Aquarium's website at www.mbayaq.org.)

In addition to its intrinsic beauty and the tourist dollars it brings in, kelp is commercially harvested to create industrially valuable gels, called *alginates*, which are used as stabilizers and thickening agents. Because of the size of the blade in comparison to the holdfast, kelp can be more easily uprooted than the more stubborn rockweed. After storms, large piles of dislodged kelp fronds can be found on the beaches near kelp forests.

That's Some Salty Tasting Lettuce

If you want some "salad of the sea" to accompany your "chicken of the sea," there's no better choice than sea lettuce. Sea lettuce is actually a type of green algae (known by the scientific name *Ulva*) that commonly grows in shallow ocean areas and brackish waters near the coasts. They live attached to rocks in the middle to low intertidal zone and as deep as 10 meters (33 feet) in calm, protected harbors. In some estuaries, the sea lettuce is so thick that you can practically walk across it without getting your feet wet. And, yes, some people actually add this sea lettuce to their soups and salads!

Sheets of sea lettuce are only a few cells thick—so thin that they may seem as sheer as silk, but as rubbery as a balloon. The 10 species of Ulva vary greatly in appearance, and are more delicate than the brown seaweeds we observed earlier. Some are elliptical, whereas others are long and narrow, ranging in size from microscopic to 65 centimeters (26 inches). One of the unique qualities of sea lettuce is its ability to dry up to a crispy texture when baking in the sun at low tide and then regain its normal appearance when rehydrated. Though I personally have never tasted sea lettuce, various marine creatures seem to find it quite tasty, perhaps because sea lettuce does not have the tough texture and protective chemicals contained in brown seaweeds. Chapter 8 covers the commercial use of sea lettuce and other kinds of algae in greater detail, so if you're ready to hit the salad bar now, skip ahead.

Red Algae: Friend of Coral and Abalone

As explained in Chapter 6, microscopic red algae has a pretty bad reputation as being responsible for harmful algae blooms that cause scary neurological problems in humans and marine life. But not all red algae are bad, and many of them are extremely important members of certain communities. About 4,000 species of red algae call the sea their home, making this the most diverse of all marine macroalgae. Unlike other algae, the red varieties can be found at depths of almost 2,000 feet. Red algae take on many shapes including hairy tufts of filaments, thin paint-like mats, and coralline statues.

One of the more interesting of the red algae are the *crustose* or *coralline* algae. As you might guess from their name, these algae form crusty, cement-like coatings of calcium carbonate and look more like coral than algae. Many of these species of encrusting algae completely cover the surface of whatever object they decide to settle on. Coralline algae are important in the formation of tropical reefs and have been adding structure to these areas for millions of years. They provide extensive habitats for many marine invertebrates including sea urchins, chitons, and limpets, which would be heavily preyed upon without the protection of the rocky mesh. In some Pacific atolls, red algae have contributed far more to reef structure than even the calcium carbonate of the corals themselves. Even so, their most important job on the reef is to act as the cement that binds the reef materials together. If the coral is the tile, then the coralline algae act as the grout holding it all together.

> **Underwater Eye**
>
> Ninety-eight percent of all red algae are found in seawater and comprise more species than all brown and green algae combined.

Captain Clam's Comments

Many species of red coralline algae produce chemicals that attract the larvae of abalone and other herbivorous invertebrates. One of these chemicals, GABA (short for gamma-amino-butyric acid) is very closely related to mammalian neurotransmitters (the chemicals that transport signals through the brain). Abalone graze on the coralline algae and can detect GABA and change into juveniles in its presence. Without GABA, the larvae would swim around looking for a place to settle rather than changing into adults, like a caterpillar changes into a butterfly.

Does the Grass Need Trimming?

It's time to look at some real plants—the seagrasses. Seagrasses are the only representatives of *angiosperms*, flowering plants, found in the ocean. Most closely related to lilies, seagrasses are *vascular* plants, meaning they have a network of veins to move nutrients and dissolved gases throughout the plant. Seagrasses have linguini-like or oval leaves and both male and female flowers, which produce fruit and seeds like their terrestrial counterparts. The flowers are usually borne underwater, and pollination occurs underwater as well in most cases. Seagrass also has a true root system—as opposed to a simple holdfast. The root system anchors the plant to its substrate and acquires nutrients for the plant as well. Similar to typical lawn grass, seagrass roots commonly send out rhizomes (little shoots) that sprout more grass. This root/ rhizome system creates a dense, interwoven mat that holds the grass in place.

Seagrass provides an important food source for estuarine communities.

(Photo Credit: Paige Gill)

Life in the Seagrass Meadows

Seagrass grows into extensive meadows that resemble fields of underwater wheat. Botanists estimate that these seagrass fields produce more vegetation than all the wheat fields of the grain belt combined! Seagrass fields are extremely important in providing nursery and adult habitat and feeding troughs for many species (as explained in Chapters 8 and 9). Most seagrass grazers use the broken-up and degrading leaves as their food source. Others, such as the dugong (a sea cow or relative of the manatees), eat the entire plant, and a lot of it, too. Sea cows can gulp down almost 100 pounds of seagrass a day!

In addition to supporting other marine life, seagrass meadows help stabilize the environment in which they grow. They maintain water clarity by trapping fine sediments and particles with their leaves and stems, and they help stabilize bottom sediments with their roots and rhizomes. These physical attributes work toward maintaining the health not only of the seagrass bed, but also of the surrounding areas.

Where Did Seagrass Come From?

The currently accepted hypothesis of the origins of seagrasses is that they derived from terrestrial plants, which eventually returned to the sea. Fifty or so different species of seagrass inhabit the world's oceans, 30 of which can be found in Australia. Seagrass is commonly found in shallow coastal marine locations, salt marshes, and estuaries. In tropical climates, seagrass likes to mingle with the mangroves.

Many people have a tough time believing that so few species of marine plants inhabit the oceans, but keep in mind that terrestrial environments are vastly different from marine environments. Plants with true plant structures, such as seagrasses, have a difficult time finding soil for their roots and sun for their leaves. It's much easier for plant life to survive as floating plankton or leather-tough seaweed. Few true plants can venture out into the more hostile territories of the open ocean; hence, few species of true plants can survive. Even the few existing species of seagrass have a tough time making a living in the midst of threats from disease, harsh climactic events, and human disturbances. In the 1930s, for example, an eelgrass blight called "wasting disease" decimated eelgrass beds throughout the Mid-Atlantic on both sides of the ocean, killing upward of 90 percent of all eelgrass. Most areas have never recovered from the disease, and surviving beds still can harbor the agent that caused the problem.

The Least You Need to Know

- Seaweed diversity is driven primarily by variations in available light, water, and nutrients.

- Macroalgae or seaweed are not true plants, though their structure—consisting of a holdfast, stipe, and blades—makes them look like true plants.

- Seaweed blades commonly contain gas bubbles, which buoy the plant, helping it reach closer to the surface to obtain light.

- Brown seaweed—including kelps and rockweeds—often are able to withstand brutal wave action because of their holdfasts.

- Green seaweed includes the sea lettuces, which appear thin and delicate, but are actually flexible and rubbery.

- Red coralline algae provide habitats for various animals on coral reefs and the intertidal zone, and help young abalone make the transition into adulthood.

- Seagrasses such as eelgrass are important flowering plants that have been greatly reduced in abundance worldwide.

Chapter 8

Who's Eating What Seaweed Today?

In This Chapter

- ◆ Phytoplankton feeding frenzy
- ◆ Nature's best water filters
- ◆ Cleaning up the food scraps
- ◆ Sea cows in the meadow
- ◆ Sea vegetables for human consumption

After reading Chapters 6 and 7, you might begin to think that the ocean is nothing more than an underwater greenhouse with a phytoplankton roof. Where are the crabs, clams, shrimp, urchin, manatees, and other animals? Are they hiding in the kelp forests? Lost in the seagrass meadows? Engulfed in the clouds of a harmful algae bloom?

In this chapter, botany takes a backseat and the focus turns to the secondary consumers and larger creatures that feed on the ocean's salad bar. In this chapter, you begin to explore the appetites and eating habits of zooplankton, bivalves, sea urchins, manatees, and other ocean herbivores.

The Small Eating the Smallest

In the sea, as on land, life begins on the smallest scale. In marine environments, this means that life starts at the phytoplankton level—some of which are not only smaller than the head of a pin but even as small as the pin's very tip. Although these are the smallest of the marine plankton, they are often among the most abundant.

These microscopic phytoplankton, some as tiny as 2 microns in diameter, are difficult to imagine as someone's meal. But in the eyes of the small zooplankton that feed on them, they can be a mouthful just the same. These zooplankton include some microscopic, bacteria-eating protozoans and jelly-like salps (simple, tube-shaped organisms), which are both important players in making sure that no food goes to waste.

One particular animal that takes advantage of the tiniest microalgae is the copepod, a diminutive relative of the shrimp and the crab. Copepods are the most plentiful multicellular group on the earth, outnumbering even insects, which have more species, but fewer individuals! Marine biologists estimate that copepods make up around 70 percent of the total zooplankton. The 14,000 or so species of copepods form the most important link to the oceanic food chain by swallowing the tiny microalgae and converting them into more copepod. These zooplankton then become directly or indirectly available to the consumers who eat higher up on the food chain. While microalgae constitute the greatest amount of carbon fixing organisms in the oceans (turning water and carbon dioxide into sugar using sunlight), copepods are considered to be the greatest users of that photosynthetically produced carbohydrate.

Throughout the ocean, copepods and other tiny zooplankton play an ever-impressive numbers game, making up for their diminutive size by their copious populations. The seasonal abundance of copepods closely follows the seasonal blooms of algae in ocean environments. Copepods have developed a number of physical characteristics that make catching tiny phytoplankton easy. Large antennae and paddle-like appendages sweep algae-rich water toward their "mouths" carrying in enough algae to satisfy their voracious appetites.

Stationary Feeders: Bring It On

Copepods do a pretty good job of swimming around and snaring their prey, but some creatures can do just as fine a job while acting as couch potatoes. Instead of moving around in search of food, filter feeders such as oysters, mussels, and clams prefer home delivery. They're essentially surrounded by phytoplankton, so they simply draw the phytoplankton-packed water through built-in filters to snare their food. A bivalve filter feeder, such as a clam, simply needs to open its shell to pull in a mouthful of water. A clam also can extend a pair of short tubes, called siphons, which work together to draw water into the clam. Cilia, moving hair-like structures that line the inside surface of the clam's shell, pull water in through one of the siphons and push it out through the other. In other species, such as oysters, the gills work together with hair-like cilia to draw in water and trap the tiny particles.

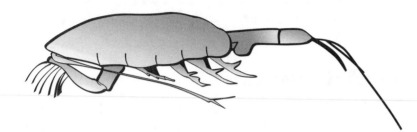

Copepods are built to find, collect, and consume mass quantities of phytoplankton.

The pumping ability of shellfish, such as oysters, is quite astounding. Microbiologists estimate that 130 years ago, the oyster populations in the Chesapeake Bay could filter the entire water column of the bay in 3 to 6 days. Today, because of a dramatic decrease in oyster population, due to overfishing, pollution, and other factors, these turnover times have increased to as long as 325 days. This has resulted in a serious degradation of water quality and clarity, reducing the amount of light that can penetrate the waters and lessening the available oxygen. The reduction in water quality has also had a negative effect on the neighboring seagrass.

Captain Clam's Comments

The siphon is a structure found in many mollusks and is most important in clams and others that live buried in the sediment; it acts as a pipeline for bringing in small food particles. In some species, the siphon has two barrels—one that brings water and algae in (*incurrent siphon*) and one that pushes the filtered water out (*excurrent siphon*). By sticking their siphon up through the sediment where they live most of their lives, clams and other filter feeders can reach the water where the microalgae drift. Oysters and scallops live above the sediment and use their gill structure to bring in the water. They have a siphon but it is greatly reduced and structurally insignificant from lack of use. Although all of them feed on the same food source, the method of retrieving this food correlates to where and how they live.

Filter feeders such as shellfish have a great affect on the water quality in the areas they inhabit. They act as nature's pumps and scrubbers, removing a great deal of debris from the water, incorporating the nutrients into their body tissues, and depositing wastes into the surrounding sediment. Their waste then becomes available to other bottom-dwelling organisms that use a different method of feeding.

As with any filter, the finer it is and the more it has to filter, the faster it can get clogged. Even good quality food particles can overload the filtering mechanism if the water contains too much of it to process. The amount of phytoplankton in the water is usually not enough to cause problems unless the area experiences a serious algae bloom. In such cases, adults typically cope by "sneezing" out a waste/mucus mixture called *pseudofeces*, but animals in their larval stage or newly metamorphosed juveniles are more vulnerable and can suffer.

Digging Through the Trash with the Scavengers

Many ocean creatures feed themselves by scraping the leftovers off the plates of other animals. These scavengers include seagulls and other birds, many species of crabs and lobsters, and most jawless fish and sharks. Amphipods, small crustaceans that live in the mud, sand, and organic matter, are less noticeable scavengers. Amphipods include sea fleas and other creatures that you can commonly find jumping around on and eating the smelly stuff that washes up on the beach.

Although they are often considered to be second-class citizens, scavengers perform a critical service for the communities in which they live; they perform the first step in a long process that breaks down wastes and returns them to the ecosystem in the form of nutrients. Ocean currents, waves, and storms also contribute to breaking down these wastes and turning them into detritus, which other animals can use as a food source.

What's So Gross About Detritus?

Whereas small animals eat live microscopic algae, other members of the ocean community settle for what some people would call the dregs. When plant and animal materials break down, they form a silty ooze that might look and smell disgusting but is packed with edible bacteria and essential nutrients. This sea gunk, called *detritus*, is an important food staple for many bottom-dwelling organisms throughout the entire ocean system. You can think of it as prepackaged food—other organisms have already processed it into a more easily digestible form. Ecosystems where detritus is plentiful include the tidal marshes, mangrove swamps, seagrass beds, and other areas where macroalgae and plant life are plentiful. Detritus is an especially important source of food in ecosystems where primary production is lacking, such as the coral reefs and the deep sea.

Detritavores do not have to be small animals that settle for the only thing available to them. Large organisms such as mullet and many other omnivorous fish use the detritus as an important source of nutrition, because it is easier to digest than the cellulose found in seagrass beds. The huge amount of detritus that is manufactured in places such as the mangrove swamps and tidal estuaries rely on detritus feeders to capture this energy source so that it can literally be exported to other ocean realms. Following this system of food flow, plants and animals that die in rich coastal waters eventually end up in the gut of the largest open ocean creatures.

Log Entry

Detritus is composed of dead and broken down plant and animal refuse that falls to the bottom of marine and freshwater ecosystems and is further degraded by bacteria (also detritivores) that feed on these leftovers as they sink to the bottom. Earthworms are the most common land detritivores. In the ocean, bacteria, fungi, and many bottom dwellers transform the valuable nutrients locked up in detritus into a food source for other creatures.

File Feeders—the Grazing Rasp

In the marine environment every available food source has a customer, no matter how difficult the food source may be to exploit. The numerous snails that slide around every corner of the ocean realm are perfect examples of how nature scrapes the plate clean. Marine gastropods, including snails, slugs, and limpets, have a mouth equipped with a rasp-like tongue called a *radula*. This organ is generally used to scrape food, typically stubborn algae, off hard surfaces, such as rock and coral. This enables snails to take advantage of a food source that most animals have no way to exploit. The radula exhibits several adaptations in different animals. In cone snails, for example, teeth on the radula act like darts that can paralyze their prey (usually a small fish); the snail then slides over to the fish and starts eating it. In oyster drills, the radula can bore through the shell of another mollusk! Now that's one powerful tongue!

A snail's radula is built to lick stubborn algae off rocks and other hard surfaces.

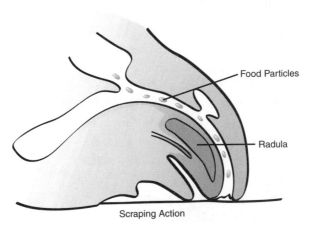

Food Particles

Radula

Scraping Action

Captain Clam's Comments _____

A number of different fish and invertebrates like to munch on coral. Parrotfish have specially modified beaks that bite off chunks of coral, crush the coral, digest the coral tissue, and pass the coral rubble out the other end. Many species of butterfly fish also eat coral, but in a more refined manner, using their long, needle-nosed beaks to pick the coral polyps out of the crevasses in coral skeletons. The zooxanthellae come along with the meal and most likely serve as a garnish. The most infamous coral predator is the crown-of-thorns sea star. It feeds by crawling over the coral and extending it stomach out of its body and over the coral polyps, leaving telltale white scars behind on living coral surfaces.

Zooxanthellae to the Rescue

On the coral reef, algae are not as abundant as in other biomes, which is one of the reasons why the water surrounding coral reefs is so clear. But coral reefs, like any marine environment, require some organism to sit at the bottom of the food pyramid and serve as a primary producer or supplier. Without visible algae or other plant life, where does the coral reef get its nutrients?

Some of the required nutrients come from nearby seagrass meadows, which supply the plant material and detritus that fuel coral reef growth. To supply the remaining nutrients, *zooxanthellae* (unicellular algae), live symbiotically inside the coral, using the coral as shelter and a sundeck, while providing the coral with important nutrients and exchanging carbon dioxide for oxygen. Without these symbiotic "plants," the coral animals would be unable to obtain enough nutrients to build their calcium carbonate skeletons.

Nature's Best Vacuum Cleaners

Though tiny animals are the primary consumers of microscopic plankton, larger animals, such as the horseshoe crab can gobble up their fair share of micromatter, as well. Horseshoe crabs are like mini marine vacuum cleaners, sucking up not only plants and algae, but also just about anything that's edible and small enough to fit in their mouths. Horseshoe crabs are so hooked on eating that their undersides simultaneously move the crabs along the ocean floor and shovel food into their mouths. A pair of appendages called *chelicerae* (pronounced *ki-lis-er-ee*), located near the front of the crab, sweep food from the ocean floor up into the crab's mouth.

Behind the chelicerae are four pairs of jointed walking legs (*pedipalps*), each ending in a claw. Following up near the back of the crab is a fifth, larger pair of legs that pushes the animal forward. The middle section of each leg is loaded with spines that macerate (grind) the food picked up by the chelicerae and pass the mashed-up food into the crab's mouth, located near the base of its legs. In horseshoe crabs, movement and feeding are closely linked, because the animal can eat only when it moves—no sit-down dinners for the poor horseshoe crab!

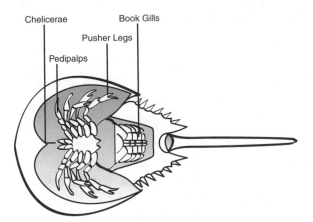

Chelicerae

Pusher Legs

Book Gills

Pedipalps

The underside of a horseshoe crab makes it an efficient vacuum cleaner.

Colossal Marine Herbivores

Second only to whales, the biggest beasts to waddle up to the ocean's salad bar are the manatee and dugong (sea cows). Manatees like to wallow in warm coastal waterways, estuaries, saltwater bays, rivers, canals, and anywhere they can find a seagrass meadow to munch on. These mild herbivores can eat the equivalent of 10 to 15 percent of their body weight daily, and they're no lightweights—some manatees tip the scales at 3,000 pounds! Being the only marine animals that feed so voraciously on the higher marine plants rather than on the more abundant algae, you can begin to understand why these species are in a precarious situation. On one hand, there isn't that much competition for the grass they eat, and on the other hand, there are few places where enough grass grows to feed the hungry manatees.

CAUTION Ocean Alert

Manatees and dugongs have a tough road ahead of them. Development projects in favorite manatee and dugong hangouts are quickly destroying the seagrass meadows that feed these beasts, making it more difficult for them to find a reliable food source. In addition, these marine mammals, which must come to the surface to breathe, are subject to frequent boating injuries and fatalities because of their slow-moving nature and the murky waters where they hang out. While protected under the Endangered Species Act, high mortalities from boat collisions still occur every year.

People Eat Here, Too

Although humans don't float around coastlines like the manatee, munching on sea-grass, we do eat a good bit of seaweed and seaweed derivatives. People consume hundreds of different seaweed species worldwide, and many are grown commercially, giving rise to a multimillion-dollar industry.

Some seaweed products are well known, such as the wrapping used to make sushi. This red algae, called *nori*, is farmed to a great extent in Japan. Dulse, another seaweed that people use as a sea vegetable, is farmed and sold internationally. However, most of the algae people consume and use in industry are not sold in their original form but are used as agents or ingredients to make other food or consumer products.

Have you eaten a bowl of ice cream lately? Gobbled down a hamburger? Drank a glass of wine? Brushed your teeth? Then you've used one of the most common seaweed products on the market—*carrageenan*. Derived from the red seaweeds, carrageenan is used primarily as a gel, food clarifier, and stabilizer. It makes ice cream creamier, beer and wine clearer, and tooth paste smoother. Most of the processed food we eat has a label that lists its ingredients, but the labels rarely list "seaweed" or "partially hydrogenated algae concentrate" as an ingredient. Instead, the label lists algae components as "carrageenan" or "alginate," names that are about as descriptive as "monosodium glutamate."

Ocean Alert

The use of carrageenan is relatively new (within the last 30 years or so). Although many tests have shown it to be safe for human consumption, a recent study (2001) has suggested that there might be a link to some forms of cancer. With this new finding, further research might restrict or modify the use of carrageenan. Researchers and consumers should stay alert as to the outcome of further tests.

The Sea Vegetable Industry

"Sea vegetable" is a glorified name for edible algae, such as dulse, nori, and sea lettuce. For thousands of years, Eastern countries have harvested and consumed these sea vegetables as part of their diets, using them in soups, salads, teas, and even as part of their main courses. Relatively recently, however, the concept of eating seaweed has reached the West, and you can now find these sea vegetables in natural food stores, specialty stores, and even in the gourmet cuisine market.

Sea vegetable farming is an old and growing industry in coastal communities that have the right conditions. The Maritime Provinces of Canada have been actively harvesting numerous varieties of sea vegetables that are now gaining popularity worldwide. During the great famine in Ireland, many families who lived along the Irish coast evaded starvation by eating Irish moss, an alga that grows in many North Atlantic regions. Nowadays, this species is harvested commercially. On Prince Edward Island, for instance, the wind blows Irish moss close to shore, and harvesters gather the masses of algae either by boat or on horse. In other parts of the world, exotic species are being harvested and used for emerging gourmet markets. Algae from all groups—red, green, and brown—are gaining popularity for their unique flavors and healthy constituents. Sea vegetables are most commonly used in soups, as salad garnishes, and as a seasoning (in flake form).

Underwater Eye

Many species of sea vegetables that people actively harvest have a holdfast that keep them firmly anchored to the rocky coasts where they grow. Harvesters sheer off the growth from the stem-like stipe without removing the base. If carefully harvested, this holdfast can continue to produce new growth for as long as 40 years. Removal of the holdfast terminates production for those individual algae. Maritime fisheries are becoming more aware and careful of their harvesting practices to avoid unnecessary loss an otherwise renewable resource.

A Note About Nuts—Coconuts

Although coconut trees spend most of their life on land, they do deserve some mention as an edible marine plant. Whenever you think of tropical island paradises, palm trees pop up on the landscape. No one really knows where coconut palms originated, although wild specimens are found growing in natural coastal forests of the Philippines and Australia. These finds support the theory that the coconut came from somewhere around the Western Pacific. From there, coconuts probably floated both east and west by sea. The coconut has the ability to germinate after some considerable time in seawater, making it a perfect traveling seed. People have no doubt sped up the dispersal process by carrying coconuts with them from place to place, either dropping or planting a few along the way. To establish themselves and survive, all they need is warm, humid temperatures, well-drained soils (such as sandy beaches), and a supply of fresh ground water. They are obviously salt-tolerant because they often grow right along the edge of the shoreline.

From the fronds and coconuts on down to the ground, almost every part of the tree is useable in some way. Coconut oil (copra) is unusual plant oil because it remains solid below 24 degrees Celsius (75 degrees Fahrenheit). Copra is widely used to make soap, suntan lotion, and cosmetics. Shredding the white meat found inside the hard shell produces dried coconut that people use for many culinary treats. Coconut milk and cream also are commonly used as cooking ingredients. Other uses of the coconut range from the production of an alcoholic drink (called *arrack*) to building materials. The fibrous husk of the coconut is excellent for making ropes, nets, mats, and brushes. It is particularly useful because of its natural resistance to water and rot. The refuse from coconut husks can serve in horticultural composts, as well. Whole or half shells are often polished and decorated for use as utensils or ornaments. The trunks and leaves can be used to build shelters.

Captain Clam's Comments

One of the best ways to enjoy a coconut is to drink its juice before the coconut ripens. An unripe coconut is known as a *jelly nut* in many of the tropical locales where it is served as a thirst-quenching drink. The name derives from the jelly-like consistency of the seed's endosperm, which hasn't yet solidified into white coconut meat. To serve a jelly nut, the server takes a green coconut, chops off its top with a machete, and then punctures the soft seed inside with a straw. Inside is the coconut milk—a slightly sweet, refreshing taste of the tropics.

The Least You Need to Know

◆ Near the bottom of the ocean food pyramid, the zooplankton eat the phytoplankton.

◆ Copepods are tiny relatives of shrimp and are the most abundant multicellular organism on the planet.

◆ Some marine creatures live by eating nutrient-rich detritus (waste and remains of other animals and plants).

◆ Horseshoe crabs are designed to scuttle across the ocean floor, sweeping up scraps of food along the way.

◆ Manatee and dugong are two of the largest herbivores in the sea, and they can gobble up hundreds of pounds of seagrass at a single "sitting."

◆ Marine algae are part of many traditional diets, and are widely used today in foods, consumer products, and industrial applications.

Plants as Habitats

In This Chapter

- ◆ Mangroves from top to bottom and everything in between
- ◆ Seagrass—wall-to-wall shag carpeting
- ◆ The kelp forest canopy comes alive
- ◆ Structurally sound coralline homes
- ◆ Blending in with the scenery

Large plants, algae, mangroves, and seagrass meadows are like oceanic gingerbread houses; these areas of lush vegetation not only feed huge populations of ocean life, but they also provide a habitat for a wide variety of ocean species. Everything from bottom-feeding bivalves, to seaweed-climbing sea urchins, to surface-swimming sea otters call these weedy wigwams home. This chapter explores various living habitats—including kelp forests, salt marshes, and seagrass meadows—and reveals the secret lives of their more fascinating inhabitants.

Wetland Subdivisions

Beachfront property is prime real estate, even in nature. Coastal wetlands—such as salt marshes, mangrove swamps, and peat lands near the shores—are nutrient-rich areas that provide food and habitat not only for fish, but also for insects, snails, crabs, sponges, snakes, frogs, turtles, crocodiles, birds, muskrat, and a host of other animals. The following sections explain the differences between the various wetland habitats and explore the types of creatures found in each *habitat*.

Log Entry

A **habitat** is the natural abode, locality, or region where a plant or animal or a community of plants and animals live. A habitat is typically the place where a plant or animal is best suited to live. A habitat also can be viewed as a structure that affords a controlled environment in otherwise inhospitable locations. When plants or other organisms create a place for other organisms to live, the place is called a *bio-habitat*.

Salt Marsh Sanctuaries

Salt marshes are located near relatively well-protected coastlines where tides carry sediment over low-lying lands and deposit it on shore. Sandbars or other barriers that stand between the sea and the marsh prevent wave and tidal action from carrying the sediment back to the sea. If left undisturbed for a long period of time, salt-tolerant grasses are able take root, stabilizing the ground, and eventually building an accumulation of live and dead grasses that serves as a foundation for other plants. In many cases, the salt marshes form around estuaries, where rivers deposit much of the sediment that gives rise to the marsh, and the salt marsh may actually merge with another, freshwater marsh further upstream.

The salt marsh is a unique area that acts as a meeting place for land and sea, a place where terrestrial plants and animals move down toward the sea while marine plants and animals move from the sea up toward the land. The types of plants and animals in a salt marsh vary depending on how dry or wet each area is. The lower marsh is a wet, salty area where only salt-tolerant organisms can live. Here, you find salt-marsh cord grass, which can grow taller than two meters; filter-feeding bivalves; several species of snails; fiddler crabs; cord-grass-loving birds, such as willets and sharp-tailed sparrows; and many species of wading of birds, including heron, egrets, and even some ducks.

In the upper marsh, plant life becomes much more diverse, and includes more land plants, featuring a shorter cord grass called salt-meadow cord grass, sea lavender, glasswort, seaside goldenrod, and black grass. Animal species also increase in diversity. Some crocodiles, which cannot tolerate the salty lower marsh, venture into the brackish (less salty) waters of the upper marsh, especially if the marsh has some freshwater input from a river or stream. Also at home in the upper marsh are diamondback terrapin (salt-tolerant turtles), raccoons, otters, muskrats, minks, snakes, insects, and various types of birds, including harriers and osprey.

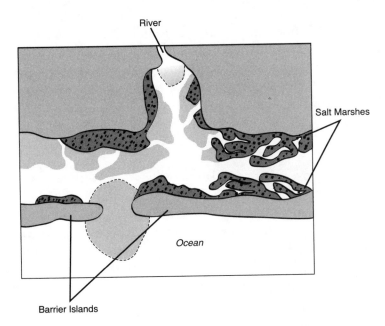

River

Salt Marshes

Ocean

Barrier Islands

Salt marshes form in protected areas along the coastline.

Mangrove Forests: The Swampy Woodlands

Unlike a marsh, which is void of trees, a swamp is characterized by its primarily woody growth—trees and shrubs. The most common type of saltwater swamp is the mangrove forest, which grows in tropical brackish waters typically near the mouth of a river. Mangroves offer something that no salt marsh can match—a leafy canopy that functions as a comfortable nesting site for many species of shore-loving birds. Birds such as great blue herons, snowy egrets, ibises, and spoonbills nest in the trees and feed in the rich muddydetritus formed by the decaying mangrove leaves. Here they find an open seafood bar stocked with delicious oysters, snails, shrimp, crabs, and the juvenile stages of

Captain Clam's Comments

Bird watching has become an important attraction in many areas of the world where mangroves are found. Bird watchers have identified hundreds of species of mangrove-loving birds and are among the strongest advocates for the protection of mangrove habitats. Their observations of reduced populations of birds in some areas have led communities to designate many of their mangrove forests as sanctuaries.

many ocean fish and other animals. The canopy also provides a home for snakes, bats, and way too many insects.

Some of the more clingy animals, including snails, crabs, and mollusks, literally hang out on the roots and trunks of the mangroves. Snails ride up and down the trunks silently stripping algae and other microscopic particles from the bark. The jingle shell, a bivalve that is not content with bottom feeding, crawls up onto the mangrove roots with its snail-like foot and attaches itself to the mangrove with its byssal threads. Hermit crabs and other climbing crustaceans are frequently seen marching along the limbs of the mangroves as well.

Breathing Out of Water

From the water level up, mangroves are typical land-dwelling trees with trunks, stems, leaves, and flowers. Their root system, however, is adapted to enable the submerged root system to breath and to help it survive in the anoxic (no oxygen) sediment in which it lives. All mangroves have root extensions that project up into the air so that the plant can breathe—think of these root extensions as mangrove snorkels. Mangroves can either have *prop roots*, structures that extend midway from the trunk and arch downward, or *pneumatophores*, structures that extend upward from the roots into the air.

Gone to Seed

The mangroves are unique in that the seed, or *propagule*, germinates (sprouts) while still attached to the tree. This cigar-shaped seedling might drop straight down, stick directly in the mud, and grow right next to its parent, or it might float miles away to find more fertile ground. The seed is encased in a protective covering, which can float for miles and survive for several weeks. When it finally washes up on a sandy beach or mudflat, it plants itself. The roots dive down, and the sprout reaches up. The plant begins to grow and actually helps to hold the land together, making more land available for baby mangroves and more area available for the various creatures that inhabit the forest.

The Mangrove Wall

Mangroves act as a living wall between the land and the sea that prevents erosion and minimizes the destructive power of waves. Because mangroves are naturally resilient and flexible, many mangrove forests have withstood the unrelenting barrage of wind, waves, and changing tides for thousands of years. In addition to protecting themselves, mangrove forests serve as a spring-loaded barricade between the sea and the coast, minimizing the loss of property and human lives in many coastal areas around the globe. The mangrove fringe itself bears the brunt of storm's energy, protecting the coast behind it. In regions where people have cleared coastal fringe mangrove forests, erosion and siltation (the buildup of sediment) often become a problem, and the loss of property and human lives rises dramatically. The mangrove fringe is a resource that needs to be protected just as it protects us. (See Part 5 to learn more about what you can do to help preserve our natural habitats and resources.)

Welcome to Mangrove Island

Although mangroves begin as modest outcroppings, they frequently develop into their very own islands, commonly referred to as *mangles*. The mangroves take hold in a shallow bay or lagoon and begin to trap sediments that support more root structures for more mangroves. Eventually, the mangroves form small patches of what is almost land. After thousands of years, the mangrove forest actually becomes a landmass, complete with its very own ecosystem. Mangrove islands can also form along inland coastal areas of land. These mangrove islands, known as *hammocks*, form elongated patterns parallel to water flow and to the coast.

Log Entry

A **mangle** is a term for an assemblage of mangroves interlocked to form patches, which can further extend seaward as a fringe around the shoreline or as a distinct island.

Living in a "Land" of Peat

In some areas of a salt marsh, the plants grow and die more quickly than they decompose. The extra plant material piles up and floats on the surface as a spongy layer of peat. Most peat floating along the coasts is from dead, decaying cord grass from nearby salt marshes. Although not known for supporting huge populations of diverse wildlife, the peat does dampen wave action and protect the coastlines from violent storms. When it eventually, washes up on shore it decays into valuable fertilizer for other plants.

Underwater Eye

Behind some mangrove forests, peat swamp forests develop as sentiment flows down river and is trapped behind the coastal swamps. The mangroves then spread farther inland as the area becomes waterlogged and as peat from the mangrove leaves builds up. The peat swamp forests are home to many interesting species, including gibbons, orangutans, and monitor lizards.

Grazing in the Grass

As explained in Chapter 7, seagrasses are flowering plants that have adapted to life in the ocean, but even this plant likes to hug the shoreline. You can find seagrass throughout the world, with different species in each location. For example, in the Northwest Atlantic, eelgrass dominates the scene. As you proceed south toward the equator, you encounter more species, including shoal, manatee, and turtlegrass. Florida is home to seven species of seagrass, four of which are widespread. Australia boasts upward of 30 different seagrass species with 25 species in Western Australia, including the largest recorded seagrass bed in the world. All seagrass beds serve as habitats for important communities of vertebrate and invertebrate species, providing food, shelter, and breeding grounds.

The House of Grass

Many fish, crustaceans, and shellfish use the seagrass beds as a permanent home, while others use the seagrass meadows as a place to lay their eggs and raise their young. Why are these seagrass meadows so popular as nurseries and adult habitats? Because they typically are nutrient-rich, calm habitats with clear water. If the water were murky, the seagrass could not obtain the necessary sunlight and would eventually die. In addition, fish, which rely heavily on their eyesight require the clear waters to see where they're going, catch prey, find a mate, and evade predators.

Only a few species of animals, including sea turtles, manatees, and dugong, feed directly on the live seagrass. Most other animals lack the digestive equipment necessary to break down the cellulose in seagrass. However, when the seagrass dies and decomposes, its nutrients become more accessible to bivalves and other animals. In addition, the live seagrass offers a surface on which *epiphytic* algae grow and other animals attach themselves or their eggs. As a result, these specially coated seagrass blades function as long, skinny, nutritious lollipops for various mollusks, fish, and other animals. (The opportunistic feeders are actually performing a valuable service for the seagrass, by cleaning bacteria and detritus off the blades that would otherwise block the sunlight they need to stay alive.)

Log Entry

The term **epiphytic** refers to an organism that grows on top of another plant, relying on it for support but not for nutrients.

Most importantly for humans, seagrass beds provide a nursery for many recreationally and commercially valuable marine fish and shellfish. Many larval and juvenile fish and shellfish species begin their life in the seagrass meadow, hiding out from predators in the lush carpet of vegetation. Juveniles then travel out to adjoining bays and eventually into the open ocean, essentially transporting nutrients from the seagrass meadows to the open ocean. This is one way that energy is transferred from more productive areas to less productive areas of the ocean.

Captain Clam's Comments

Under the Endangered Species Act (ESA), a critical habitat is one upon which a dwindling species depends and is essential to its survival and recovery. One example of a critical habitat is the greatly diminished seagrass beds that were formerly found in many parts of the world. Florida, California, and other states with seagrass communities under stress are obligated by this federal law to protect their remaining beds, which support several endangered species. These include manatee, pink shrimp, bay scallops, and saltwater crocodiles. Growing awareness of the importance of these and other marine habitats is needed, in order to increase conservation efforts and enforce these protective laws.

For Turtles and Eels Only?

A seagrass species is often named after the animal associated with it—for example, manatee grass, turtlegrass, and eelgrass. But don't let the names fool you: A turtle-grass meadow provides critical habitat and feeding grounds for many more animals than just sea turtles, and eelgrass is not exclusively for American eels. The list of species supported by a each seagrass meadow is long and impressive, as people who fish these areas often know. Many commercial and sport fishing species benefit directly or indirectly from seagrass habitats, and in areas where these habitats are diminished, a marked decline of these species follows. This is why it is so important to understand the interrelationships of various habitats.

The Kelp Canopy

Although marsh grass, seagrass, and mangroves provide most of the beachfront property, algae and seaweed, particularly kelp, dominate the real estate market in deeper coastal waters. Like mangroves and terrestrial forests, kelp forests are three-dimensional habitats, providing homes for diverse plants and animals. From the floating surface canopy, down along the vertical stipes, to the intertwined mesh of holdfasts, the kelp forest is divided into several ecological zones, each one favored by a different community of organisms.

The kelp's fronds (blades) support epiphytes (microscopic bacteria, algae, bryozoans, and other organisms), which in turn are grazed upon by larger invertebrates such as snails and urchins. In many kelp forests, the predominance of sea urchins dictates the balance of the system. Urchins actively graze on kelp and can completely defoliate a kelp forest if not kept in check. Fortunately, the kelp forest has a veritable army of sea urchin predators—most notably the lobsters, fish, and sometimes sea otters. On any given afternoon near a kelp forest, you can view an otter lazily floating on its back preparing a sea urchin for an afternoon snack. The otter typically dives down empty-handed and resurfaces with an urchin and a rock, which it uses to bash open the urchin. Despite their tough, spiny covering, sea urchins are vulnerable to other predators as well—including lobsters, crabs, molluscs, sea stars, and even some fish and jellyfish—particularly when the urchin is in its larval stage. With many predators at work, urchins are kept at bay, allowing dense patches of kelp to grow. In areas where overfishing has reduced the number and size of lobsters and fish, urchins can create large bare patches within the kelp forest.

> **Underwater Eye**
>
> After gorging themselves on urchins, mussels, crabs, and other seafood, otters often wrap themselves up in the kelp blades and cover their eyes with their paws to take a nap.

Living within the root-like branches of the kelp holdfast, invertebrates such as anemones, brittle stars, isopods, amphipods (shrimp-like creatures), and other organisms are plentiful. The structural complexity of streaming kelp blades offers security as well as food. Visiting pelagic fish often use the kelp forest and floating kelp mats as a sanctuary to hide from predatory fish. Certain fish species, such as the kelp fish, blend into the surroundings with such proficiency they become indistinguishable from the kelp itself. Other species, including the garibaldi, wear stunning, vibrant colors that make them look like swimming neon signs.

Coralline Algae—Masonry to Die For

As we all know from the story of the three little pigs, grass and wood homes are easy to build but are not the most stable of structures. For a solid home, only stone or brick will do. The same is true in the sea—seagrass, woody mangroves, and weed homes are plentiful, but they hardly provide the solid protection you can find in a home formed from rock or stone.

Some of the most solid homes are found on the coral reefs, where both the coral and some algae species provide rock solid huts for many of the reef's inhabitants. A large part of the actual structure of many coral reefs is composed of coralline algae, a seaweed that produces a calcareous exoskeleton. Think of it as algae dipped in cement. Coralline algae typically appear as a flat, reddish layer that covers the substrate or as fan-shaped growths that look like coral. The coralline algae habitat forms a concrete barrier and tightly woven mesh that functions as an ideal hiding place for scores of small invertebrates. Some of the more popular inhabitants include tube worms, sea stars, urchins, anemones, and various crabs and sponges. Some of these creatures, such as the urchin, use the coralline algae both for food and shelter, but most rely on the alga's nooks and crannies for safe haven.

Blending in with the Scenery

In any living habitat, from marsh grass to kelp to coralline algae, a few creatures take on the appearance of their surroundings, camouflaging themselves to avoid their predators or to sneak up on their prey. One creature that is particularly adept at playing hide and seek is the sargassum fish. This fish looks so much like the sargassum seaweed in which it lives that it becomes virtually invisible. It's even equipped with its own dangling, weed-like appendages!

Sargassum fish looks like seaweed with eyes.

Closer to shore, pipefish, cousins to sea horses, are masters of mimicking the eelgrass in which they live. In a police lineup, you would have a tough time distinguishing a pipefish from a blade of eelgrass. Not only does the pipefish have the same shape as a blade of eelgrass, but it also shares its characteristic bright green color. Another fish that's related to the seahorse is the sea dragon, a fish that is as extreme in its leafy appearance as the sargassum fish. The plant-like protuberances that emanate from various parts of the sea dragon's body are strictly for show—helping the sea dragon blend in with its leafy surroundings.

The trumpetfish goes vertical to blend in with the surrounding coral. This long, skinny, pale fish has a head that's almost as long as its body. Swimming head down, the trumpetfish disappears inside the coral bed, but it can still drop down on unsuspecting prey.

Most creatures are not born to look like their surroundings, but create their own disguise. Undressed, the decorator crab looks like most other crabs, but when it puts on its costume, you can't tell the difference between it and, say, a sea anemone. In fact, it might be wearing a sea anemone! Making deft use of its claws, the decorator crab snips off pieces of plants and collects other objects and creatures to adorn its shell. It's not uncommon to find decorator crabs covered with algae, anemones, sponges, and other invertebrates just like the ocean floor. You can't eat what you can't see!

Some fish that are best at blending in with their surroundings are the flatfish, particularly sole, flounder, and halibut. These fish have gone so far as to wear both eyes on one side of their heads! They begin life as a normal fish, but before they are born, one eye migrates around their head to meet the other. They can then lie down on the ocean floor and see what's going on above them. Talk about laying low! Many flatfish also are capable of changing colors and patterns to blend in with the color and texture of the ocean floor.

The Least You Need to Know

- Salt marshes typically contain cord grass and other marsh grasses that provide a habitat for fish, insects, snails, crabs, snakes, frogs, turtles, crocodiles, birds, and muskrats.

- Mangrove forests provide a three-dimensional habitat, consisting of the canopy, tree trunks, and submerged roots.

- Marine grasses such as eelgrass and turtlegrass provide important habitats and nursery grounds for many estuarine species.

- Kelp forests have some of the greatest living assemblages, because of their rapid growth and extensive surface area.

- Coralline algae and seaweed attached to rock surfaces act as barriers and protective netting for many small ocean inhabitants.

- Marine creatures often mimic their surroundings in an attempt to remain inconspicuous to predators and prey.

Part  The Marine Invertebrate Collection

What do sponges, jellies, tubeworms, starfish, crabs, squid, and clams have in common? This part answers that question as it explores a bizarre collection of sea creatures classified as invertebrates.

This part begins with some of the simplest, always fascinating, sometimes dangerous, sea creatures—jellies, sponges, anemones, and related beings. It then moves on to explore the slime daddies of the deep, mollusks; tours the wonderful world of krill, shrimp, crabs, lobsters, and other crustaceans; and finishes up with an exploration of wiggling worms and creepy-crawly starfish.

Chapter 10

Simply Invertebrates

In This Chapter

- ◆ Introducing the invertebrates
- ◆ Squeezing information out of sponges—poriferans
- ◆ Stingers one and all—cnidarians
- ◆ Steel belted radials—echinoderms
- ◆ Worms under the water—annelids

They crawl, they float, they slide, they swim, they squirm, and some just sit there looking pretty. They're the ancestral animals of the sea, the most basic of the invertebrates: the poriferans, sponges; the cnidarians, including anemones, jellies, and corals; the echinoderms, featuring starfish and sand dollars; and the annelids, the squirmy wormy critters.

Although this chapter kicks off the study of marine animals with the most primitive of creatures, don't be fooled into thinking that these invertebrates are simpletons. As you will see throughout this chapter, these curious creatures exhibit some of the most ingenious adaptations you can imagine to ensure their survival—everything from suction cups and tiny water pumps to regenerating limbs and poison darts. Some of these creatures even have mastered the fine art of cloning themselves! So wade in slowly as you begin your exploration of these "lower" life forms by looking at the history of their development.

Climbing the Underwater Phylogenetic Tree

The controversy over who came first in the animal kingdom will always be subject to debate, but students of phylogeny (the study of the origins of phyla) continue in their quest to trace the evolutionary history of the various phyla and understand the family tree of animal life. The farther back you look in history, the more difficult this study becomes. Not all life forms leave a fossil record behind, making it nearly impossible to complete the genealogical tree.

However, scientists generally agree that the earliest forms of life were the blue-green algae that appeared somewhere around three billion years ago and began to give off elemental oxygen. These algae are considered the precursors to the higher plants, which would appear much later. Single-cell organisms, bacteria, and other "simple" life forms have no doubt been around for eons. However, without tangible, physical evidence, proving who came first is a matter of conjecture.

A few billion years after the evolution of simpler, single-cell organisms multicellular animals came into being. The fossil record shows an explosion of complex animal life at the onset of the Cambrian period, roughly 600 million years ago. At this time, multicellular animals burst onto the scene and began climbing the phylogenetic tree to where they are today. This all took place in the ocean, where the primitive soup began to brew complex life forms. The theory follows that through symbiotic relationships, single-cell organisms gave rise to multi-cell organisms, which then evolved into more complex beings.

However, how particular organisms developed and where they belong in the classification scheme is under ongoing debate. Sometimes, determining how organisms are related to each other is easy based on their structure and appearance. The position of the organism in its community, the organism's metabolism, what it eats, its system of reproduction, and other factors can further clarify or complicate any attempt at classification.

Captain Clam's Comments

Primitive metazoans (multicellular animals) can be placed into three basic categories: sponge-like animals, cnidarians, and annelid worms. The cnidarians (corals, jellies, and sea anemones) and the sponges have the simplest design, with about 11 different kinds of cells. Worms and higher metazoans are more complex, with approximately 55 specialized cells. The degree of specialization and tissue structure often reflect how species are related to one another. Depending on which structure or cell type you look at, it's possible to draw branches in different directions. Scientists are constantly redrawing the picture as they make new discoveries.

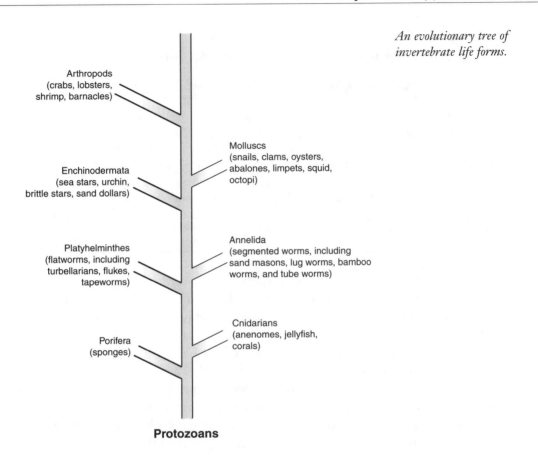

An evolutionary tree of invertebrate life forms.

Arthropods
(crabs, lobsters,
shrimp, barnacles)

Molluscs
(snails, clams, oysters,
abalones, limpets, squid,
octopi)

Enchinodermata
(sea stars, urchin,
brittle stars, sand dollars)

Platyhelminthes
(flatworms, including
turbellarians, flukes,
tapeworms)

Annelida
(segmented worms, including
sand masons, lug worms, bamboo
worms, and tube worms)

Cnidarians
(anenomes, jellyfish,
corals)

Porifera
(sponges)

Protozoans

Holiest Creatures in the Sea

What has holes but still holds water? Sponges, of course! Sponges are in the phylum Porifera, meaning porous or full of holes. Although kitchen sponges vaguely resemble real sponges, if you've ever seen or used a real sponge, you can quickly tell the difference. Kitchen sponges have smaller holes, are more springy, and don't hold nearly as much water. If you dunk a good-sized real sponge in a half-bucket of water, it can soak up nearly all the water! Try that with the synthetic variety. Although real sponges are actively harvested in some parts of the world, the synthetic version is cheaper and better for kitchen use.

True sponges have three principal components: many small chambers, a system of canals, and a fibrous skeleton that makes up most of the body. The fibers are joined together in a complex framework that supports the soft, loosely connected tissues that are pierced by many small pores. The simple structure of sponges suggests that these are some of the most ancient invertebrates of the oceans, and they're pretty resilient, as well. You can squeeze a sponge through a silk handkerchief into a bowl of seawater, and the resulting sponge cells will form new sponges through asexual reproduction.

Underwater Eye

Sponges have been harvested in the Mediterranean Sea for thousands of years. Around 1852, divers discovered that sponges growing in Florida waters were equal in quality to those being harvested in the Mediterranean, and by 1890, Key West was considered the commercial sponge capital of the world. Although the industry has had its share of problems, the sponge fishery in Key West remains active, bringing in almost 700,000 sponges each year. New regulations on sponge fishing are geared to reduce pressure on this resource. About 9,000 species of sponges grace the world's oceans, of which only a few species are harvested for commercial use.

Sponges are characterized by having a feeding system that is unique among animals. They don't have mouths; instead, seawater is drawn through the pores in the outer walls of their "bodies" by the currents that move along the seafloor. Cells in the sponge walls filter food particles from the water, which is pumped through the body and out other, larger openings. Water flows in only one direction, driven by the beating of flagella, which line the surface of chambers that are connected by a series of canals. Sponges lack any form of nervous system and essentially pump water in and out. Sponge cells perform a variety of bodily functions and appear to be more independent of each other than are the cells of other animals. Although the differentiation of cells is present, they follow a unique design unlike any other animal phylum. The complexity of this primitive animal has allowed it to succeed for hundreds of millions of years.

Please Don't Bore Me

One family of sponges goes through life in a slightly different fashion than do most sponges. These are the boring sponges—boring in terms of drilling, not in terms of their inability to entertain. Boring sponges dissolve calcareous structures such as coral and mollusk shells by secreting an acid-like substance that eats into the surface. If you have ever found a clam or oyster shell on the beach that has thousands of tiny holes in it, a boring sponge was the likely culprit. Unfortunately, these sponges can frustrate shellfish culturists whose shells lose value from the unsightly holes and brittleness that result from boring sponge attacks. Although destructive, these sponges are some of the more attractive sponges you might encounter, displaying colors of deep reds and sulfur yellows.

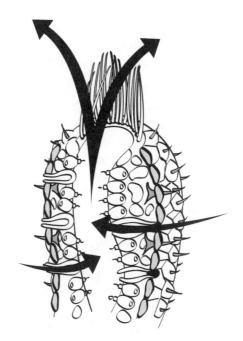

Sponges suck in nutrient-rich water to obtain food and oxygen.

Fiery to the Touch

Another species worth mentioning is the fire sponge. This sponge has a well-deserved reputation for being a nasty stinger. Fire sponges inhabit the tropical coral reef waters of the West Indies, a popular place for skin diving and scuba diving. Plenty of animals in this location can deliver painful stings, but who would expect that kind of behavior from a lowly sponge? Instead of having stinging cells like jellies and coral, the fire sponge has tiny needle-like spicules (their skeletal component) that can cause painful wounds … at first. The initial jab is like being stuck by a sea urchin, but the sponge isn't finished with its victim yet. It also produces a toxin that can cause a painful, burning skin irritation, rash, and blisters. Truthfully, you deserve this sting for touching any part of the coral reef, so grin, bear it, and sprinkle some meat tenderizer on the rash to neutralize the toxic protein. (Hey, it works!)

Logging Truck Tires?

One sponge that is hard to miss in tropical climes, to the misfortune of the wary boater, is the loggerhead sponge, the largest species in the sea. This sponge can reach a diameter of 6 feet and rises a few feet from the bottom, easily tagging passing boat props and keels. The loggerhead looks like a truck tire, complete with a big hole in the middle. Loggerhead sponges provide great places for animals to seek refuge, including the ever-popular spiny lobster. If you're looking for a loggerhead, check out hard-bottom communities near shore where the currents are fast and strong. Loggerheads count on the strong currents to bring them the food they need to maintain their massive size.

Another common sponge in this high-velocity, hard-bottom community is the vase sponge, which also reaches a respectable size. As the name implies, these sponges form large, thin vases that are extremely attractive and fairly delicate. Numerous species of vase sponges vary in both size and color. At a distance, these sponges resemble coral but upon closer inspection, it is clear that they are infinitely holier.

Cnidarians One and All

Here's a trivia question for you: What do hydra, jellies, ctenophores, sea anemones, and corals have in common? Actually, a great deal, but the primary characteristic they all share is that they all are equipped with their very own stingers. In a sense, they represent the bee and wasp family of the sea. Earlier classification schemes put all these animals in a division called the Radiata because of their basic body shape, which is radially symmetrical. The older name of this phylum, Coelenterate, is still found in literature but has more aptly been changed to Cnidarian. This refers to a cell type that is unique within the phylum—the stinging cells. These cells are described in detail in Chapter 3.

They Call Me "The Wanderer"

Jellies, more properly called *jellies* because they are not technically fish, are the great wanderers of the ocean, bandied about by the currents and waves, unable to control their own movement—jelly blobs at the mercy of the seas. However, jellies are much more complex than they appear at first glance. Though jellies can't chase down their prey or roam the ocean like tuna, they can thrust themselves through the water with their very own system of jet propulsion. Using special muscles called coronal muscles, the jelly fills up with water and then shoots it out to push itself through the water.

Most jellies basically consists of a "head," called the bell, that's equipped with dozens of dangling tentacles, complete with stingers. Inside the bell, around its rim, are special sensory organs called statocysts

Captain Clam's Comments

When an organism has a body that displays radial symmetry, it can be divided into slices like a pizza—with all of the slices coming out looking identical. Radial symmetry is a relatively rare body form compared to the more common bilateral symmetry, which humans exhibit. The phylum Echinodermata and cnidaria both exhibit radial symmetry (pronounced *STAT-a-sists*) that help keep the jellies balanced. When the jelly starts to tilt too far in one direction or the other, the statocysts stimulate nerve endings, which signal particular muscles to contract, bringing the jelly back in balance. Although they cannot see objects in the water, they can sense light and darkness. They also have chemo (chemical) receptors, which enable them to smell and taste, and they use touch receptors to "feel around" for food.

While floating around in the water column, the jelly's long, deadly tentacles dangle down, swaying gently with the currents. These tentacles are equipped with spring-loaded nematocysts, which make up the stinging organs. Unfortunate fish or other organisms that happen to touch these deadly strands are quickly stunned and swept up into the jelly's mouth, which is located at the base of the bell. Some jellies can be quite large—both in the diameter of the bell and the length of the tentacles. The Arctic lion's mane jelly can reach diameters of more than 2 feet and have tentacles as long as 100 feet!

Log Entry

Cnidocytes are a unique cell type found in all jellies, anemones, hydroids, and corals. They are especially abundant in the tentacles of many species. These cells have a bulb, or nematocyst capsule that houses a cnidocil, the dart-like stinger. The type of stinger ranges from species to species and even within a species depending on the level of defense required. Some have extremely potent toxins used to debilitate very large prey.

Little Stingers, Big Stingers

Members of the phylum Cnidaria assume two distinct body forms: the hydroid (polyp) form (early in their lives) and the medusa form (when they become adults). In the hydroid form, the animal resembles a chubby hand sticking up with its fingers waving. Some species, including all the corals and hydra, live their entire life in this form, and never morph into a medusa. These cnidarians (class Anthozoa) are very small and have a more developed polyp than in species that only temporarily pass through the polyp stage. Anthozoans like to be together and form vast colonies in which the power of numbers benefits each polyp. Coral reefs are actually the largest living structures on the planet, but they are made up of thousands of tiny polyps, waving away like mad. Each little stinger does its job to keep the community alive and growing, with the help of zooxanthellae and other symbiotic partnerships along the way. The largest solitary anthozoan is the anemone, which has managed to evolve into a bigger and more potent organism than most of its cousins. For more detail on zooxanthellae, see Chapter 3.

Cnidarians that spend most of their lives in the medusa body form tend to have more potent stingers than those that remain polyps. The medusa gets its name from Greek mythology. Medusa was a creature with snakes streaming from her hair and whose glance could turn people to stone. That description is pretty accurate for the appearance of a full-blown medusa jelly. The top section of the medusa forms a bell, under which dangles a mass of snake-like tentacles. The bigger and darker the mass underneath, the greater assemblage of polyps, which are specialized to perform various tasks. Covering the tentacles are the nematocysts that stun their prey.

Ocean Alert

Some jellies are harmless, but others can be painful or even deadly to humans. Portuguese man-of-war are blue jellies periodically seen washed up on beaches. They can give a painful sting even if the jelly is dead. Box jellies (sea wasps) are some of the most toxic of the cnidarians—their venom is 700 times more powerful than that of the Portuguese man-of-war. They might just be the most toxic of any animal! The sting from a sea wasp is excruciatingly painful, leading to shock, muscular cramps, numbness, nausea, vomiting, breathing problems, paralysis, delirium, convulsion, and ultimately, death. Fortunately, a thin layer of material—even something as thin as women's hosiery—can prevent the stingers from firing. So, the next time you take a swim in the waters off Australia, consider wearing some pantyhose … on your arms, too!

Neon Electric Watermelons

Another gelatinous sea creature that poses little threat to anything but the smallest zooplankton is the *ctenophore* (pronounced *TEEN-oh-four*). Commonly known as comb jellies, ctenophores contain eight canals called comb rows that run the length of their watermelon-shaped bodies. The comb rows are ciliated (tiny hairs moving rapidly) and help this little watermelon blob swim and eat. They also give off light in the form of chemical bioluminescence. Imagine a glass watermelon with tiny points arranged in rows spinning slowly as it swims. In the daytime, when caught in the right light, comb jellies display the electrical currents of rainbow iridescence rippling through their canals. At night, when large assemblages of ctenophores congregate at the surface, a greenish glow pulses through the drifting blobs, creating a dazzling light show.

Underwater Eye

Ctenophores are similar to jellies in appearance but they make up their own small phylum separate from medusae and other cnidarians. One reason is that of the 50 or so species of ctenophores, only one has stinging cells. They have tentacles, but these are used for movement, almost like oars rather than for defense or offense. One of the most beautiful and peaceful views during a night dive is the light show offered by this planktonic marvel.

The Ever Modest Bryozoans

Another invertebrate that's similar to the coral polyp is the bryozoan. Bryozoans are sessile creatures that can be found glued to just about any substrate, including boats, docks, kelp blades, and rocky shores. From a distance, they look like mossy mats. In some cases, bryozoans can form thick, jelly-like masses in and around water intakes that are thick enough to clog the pipes.

Like coral polyps, bryozoans are colonial animals that live inside calcium carbonate shells, typically cylindrical or box-shaped. They have tentacles, similar to those of coral polyps, but they don't use them the same way to catch food and defend themselves. They filter feed more like a sponge than a coral polyp. To feed, they extend their tentacles to form a funnel at the opening creating a current that pulls water into the center of the creature. Water passes out through tiny openings in the bryozoan's body, and any plankton are filtered out to nourish the bryozoan. The tentacles provide no defense; in fact, when they feel threatened, bryozoans retract their tentacles to protect them.

Radials All Around

The invertebrates we examined so far represent only the opening acts. Now we're ready to introduce the star of the show—the sea star and other echinoderms. Found exclusively in marine (salt water) environments, members of the phylum Echinodermata (pronounced *ee-KAI-no-der-MA-ta*) are not quite as primitive as sponges and cnidarians, and are not quite as complex as some of the other invertebrates I discuss later in this chapter.

This phylum gets its name from the spiny skin worn by some of the phylum's most exemplary members, such as the sea urchins. All echinoderms share other characteristics such as radial symmetry and the presence of an internal skeleton, or test. The test is sometimes the only remains of a defunct individual, but in the case of the sand dollar, it can appear pretty much like the living animal. Let's take a quick look at what makes echinoderms so special.

A Well-Rounded Outlook

Unlike other phyla that demonstrate examples of radial symmetry (the sponges, cnidarians, and ctenophores), the echinoderms are more highly structured. In general, their bodies are arranged in five equal parts; a characteristic called pentamerous radial symmetry. Sea stars can have more than five arms, but the central axis around which they radiate is similar throughout the group. No matter how you slice them, as long as you slice them pizza style, you get even-looking sections that in some cases can regenerate into whole beings.

Captain Clam's Comments

The sea cucumber is a slightly different member of the echinoderms, but it exhibits the same basic body structure. Sea cucumbers, representing some 900 species, are stretched out into an elongated cylinder. Sea cucumbers lie on their sides with their suction-cup "feet" radiating out from their cylindrical bodies. They are primarily deposit- and filter-feeders but some species can move around and graze. When attacked (or picked up), the sea cucumber can disembowel itself, coating the would-be attacker with sticky, rotten-smelling goo. If it survives the attack, it eventually grows a new digestive tract.

Do the Tube Foot Boogie

Echinoderms have a water-vascular system—an innovation that enables them to use hydraulic pressure to move, grab onto things, and eat. The basic plan requires a central cavity or coelom around which lies the central ring canal. Lateral canals radiate outward in five directions and connect to the outside of the animal by way of a small button called the madreporite. In sea stars, this button appears as a little red dot on the top of the body. The animal controls the internal water pressure to the tiny tube feet that run along the lateral canals. These tube feet are like mini suction cups lined up in rows that grasp and pull the animal along at a steady pace. Echinoderms' speed and power come from this water-vascular system, making them very dangerous predators.

Underwater Eye

Sea stars are voracious predators and eat many animals that are otherwise unpenetrable, including clams that can seal themselves tight in their armored shells. The sea star uses its arms and suction-cupped feet to grip the clam and slowly exert pressure to pry it open. The sea star then slips its stomach out of its mouth and into the space between the two clamshells to digest the clam meat … right inside the clam's own home. Now that's cold!

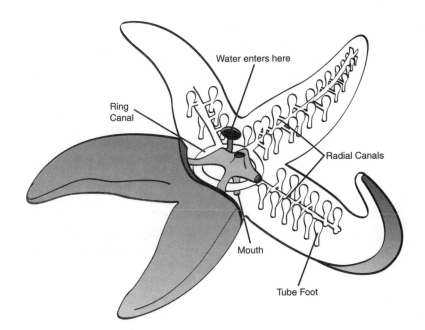

Water enters here

Ring
Canal

Radial Canals

Mouth

Tube Foot

An echinoderm's hydraulic system helps the creature hold on and move.

How *Not* to Exterminate Starfish

Back in the glory days of shell fishing in the bays, fishermen quickly realized that starfish ate clams and oysters. They figured that they could increase their harvest by eliminating the starfish, so they collected starfish at low tide, chopped them into little pieces, and scattered the pieces into the sea. Little did they realize that by chopping up the starfish, they were actually helping them reproduce. Soon after the fishermen scattered the starfish pieces into the water, they saw their starfish population explode and realized that chopping up starfish is no way to exterminate them. Starfish and many other species of echinoderms can regenerate to full form if at least one fifth of the central disc is undamaged. In many fisheries, it is unlawful to return known predators like sea stars and snails to the water. They must be held and discarded.

Brittle Brother and Spiked Sister

Two somewhat unlikely relatives in the echinoderm group are the brittle star and the sea urchin. They share the symmetry, water-vascular system, and test, but they otherwise don't look like members of the same family. The brittle star is reminiscent of a sea star, but looks and acts like a cross between a starfish and an octopus. It can use its arms like a starfish to grab onto substrates, but it can also feed without leaving its

Captain Clam's Comments

Sea stars and urchins often have pedicellariae on their body surface. Pedicellariae look like a pair of loping shears or massive crab claws and are handy additions to echinoderm arsenal. Some pedicellariae also have toxins that can paralyze small prey and keep larger predators away. Spines usually point away from the pedicellariae to leave them more exposed.

secure hideout, much like an octopus. Movement is calculated and swift, setting it apart from all other echinoderms who typically are slow and lumbering. The brittle star can also sacrifice an arm if it is seized, growing it back later. These adaptations have given the brittle star an evolutionary edge, making it one tough survivor.

Lacking the waving arms of the brittle star, the sea urchin is covered with spines as stiff as porcupine quills that run symmetrically out from the rounded body. The urchin moves along face down with a mouth on its underside. Sea urchins don't use their spines for offensive strikes, although a few species do have poisonous tips.

The Most Valuable Beach Currency

At first glance, you might not place a sand dollar in the same phylum as a starfish or sea urchin. The sand dollar looks more like a tiny UFO or a hingeless clam than a starfish. However, if you think of it as a flattened, spineless sea urchin, you can see that the sand dollar also has radial symmetry, a water-vascular system and a test. Its most unique quality is the thinness of its body—a body so fragile that you can barely pick one up without having it crumble in your hand. Sand dollars, sea biscuits, and heart urchins each have a velvety covering of short spines and pedicellariae, which help them burrow into and creep along the sandy bottom. Because they offer little edible meat, sand dollars and related species don't need to worry as much about predators as they do about wind-driven currents washing them ashore. Many a sand dollar test has washed up on the sandy beaches of the world, and is the best currency in the world for inquisitive beachcombers of any age.

Seriously Squirming Segments

Let's take a break from the stiff, inflexible invertebrates and look at a phylum that has a bit more fluidity of movement—the annelids or segmented worms. If you've ever seen a night crawler, you've seen an annelid (a terrestrial annelid, anyway). This group's most pronounced characteristic is *metamerism*—the segmentation of body into similar parts along the main trunk of the worm. The head and back are not true segments but the midsection is made entirely of like compartments. All components of each segment connect to the components of the next, including nervous, circulatory, and excretory organs. This allows the worm to contract and expand in a *peristaltic* movement that gives it tremendous burrowing power as well as the ability to retreat with lightning speed by yanking its body down a hole or tube.

Many marine worms have well-developed heads with menacing jaws, and they have long legs called parapodia, which can make the worm look feathery. Some worms can even create their very own homes, in the form of stiff, tubular structures, some of which form extensive networks below the sediments. The tube can also extend above the surface as a stalk, giving the worm a higher position in the water column. Some worms are filter feeders, others are deposit-feeders, and still others are raptorial feeders that seize unwary victims in their jaws. However they feed, annelids are critical members of most soft-bottom communities, aerating the sediments in similar ways as their Earth-bound counterparts.

> **Log Entry**
> The wavelike contractions of the annelid's tubular structure are described as **peristaltic**. In humans and other creatures with complex digestive systems, the intestines contract in a peristaltic movement to push food along. Worms use peristaltic contractions to move and burrow.

Valley of Nuclear Tube Worms

To find some of the largest of the marine worms, you need to dive down pretty deep—at least a mile or so to a hydrothermal vent, where deep sea tube worms hang out. Riftia, the icon of all deep sea worms, live inside white tubes made of chitin. These tube worms put on a magnificent ocean display when they poke their bright-red (hemoglobin-rich) bodies out from the virgin-white chitin tubes. Chitin is an extremely hardy material that provides stiff support for the massive weight of the worm's 8- to 9-foot body, and is the same material that makes up a beetle's shell.

When the worms are very tiny, they have a primitive mouth and gut through which symbiotic vent bacteria enter. As the worm grows older, the mouth and gut disappear, locking billions of the symbiotic bacteria inside the body, where they continue to process chemicals for the worm.

The red plumes of the tube worm gather ingredients such as oxygen and carbon that are needed by the bacteria to manufacture food. Energy for this food-making process comes

> **Underwater Eye**
> Riftia blood is composed of hemoglobin molecules that are 30 times larger than those found in humans and give the worms their bright red color. The blood carries all the necessary chemicals to the symbiotic bacteria, which convert them into food for the tubeworm.

from hydrogen sulfide produced by the hydrothermal vents where the worms live. As explained in Chapter 5, the process by which bacteria converts oxygen and carbon into food by using hydrogen sulfide is known as chemosynthesis, which takes the place of photosynthesis in dark regions. Because of the huge amounts of raw materials that are available around the vents, a massive food supply is prime for the taking, and Riftia is perfectly designed to exploit it.

Worm Wonders

Although starfish are the stars of our invertebrate show, certain worms can put on a magnificent show of their own. In the Turks and Caicos Islands, for instance, about four days after a full moon, the Bermudan glow worms swim to the surface of sheltered bays to perform a 15-minute light show. This luminescent mating ritual begins with the green-glowing females swimming seductively in circles and releasing their pulsating egg masses. Soon after, the males join in, also glowing green, as they swim around the eggs and release their sperm. Swarms of these glow worms gather near the surface approximately one hour after sunset for 12 days straight. If you're visiting this area near full-moon time, be sure to sign up for one of the many glow-worm cruises.

The Least You Need to Know

- The earliest forms of single-cell marine animals gave rise to multi-cell forms in a burst of evolution some 600 million years ago.

- True sponges (in the phylum Porifera) have three principal components: small chambers or pores, a system of canals, and a fibrous glass skeleton that makes up most of the body.

- Hydra, jellies, sea anemones, and corals are cnidarians, all having radial symmetry and stinging cells.

- Cnidarians have two kinds of life form, a polyp and a medusae.

- Another kind of nonstinging jelly is the ctenophore, which looks like a small glass watermelon.

- Echinoderms, including starfish, sea urchins, and sand dollars, all exhibit radial symmetry, a water-vascular system, and an internal skeleton called a test.

- The most pronounced characteristic of annelids is metamerism, the segmentation of body into similar parts along the main trunk of the worm.

A Most Diverse Phylum: Mollusca

In This Chapter

- ◆ Turning back the clock with a little mollusc history
- ◆ Exploring the softies of the sea
- ◆ Protecting soft flesh with hard shells
- ◆ Oysters, clams, mussels, and other bivalve molluscs
- ◆ Look Ma, no shell: squid and octopus

The next time you dine at your favorite seafood restaurant, order the mollusc and see what happens. Your server will probably look at you funny or tell you that the restaurant doesn't serve mollusc. If your server is ocean savvy, he or she will ask you what type of mollusc you would prefer: mussels, clams, oysters, squid, escargot (snails), or octopus. If your server simply writes something down and walks away, start worrying—you have no idea what you're going to get! This chapter serves up a little of everything, revealing the world of molluscs by examining several representative species.

Meet Father Mollusc: The Ancestral Template

Back in the days when the invertebrate world was exploding into full evolutionary glory, a whole bunch of innovative adaptations began with one simple creature. This creature was to become branded the *hypothetical ancestral mollusc* (HAM). You can almost picture a snail with a long white beard, telling stories of grazing on algae to all the young snails gathered around the mudflats. The descendants of this fictional granddaddy of the mollusc family eventually branched out to take on modern forms that most people recognize—snails, clams, sea slugs, squid, and octopuses.

HAM has all the qualities of every member of the mollusc family—even though many members of the mollusc family do not have some of the qualities of HAM (most notably the squid and octopus, which lack the characteristic exterior mollusc shell). HAM's most obvious feature is its shell, which takes on a spiral configuration in snails, a split, hinged configuration in clams, and is totally absent in the sea slugs, squid and octopus. At HAM's base is a single large "foot," which it uses to skate across surfaces. This foot is an obvious feature of most snails and their relatives (such as limpets), but has been modified into sucker arms in the squid and octopus, and remains hidden in most bivalves, except when used for burrowing. To eat, HAM uses a rasp-like tongue called the radula (described in detail in Chapter 8) to scrape algae and other microscopic food particles from surfaces. Most molluscs, including snails and octopuses, continue to use some form of radula. The main portion of HAM's body consists of the soft, fleshy mantle that is characteristic of all molluscs, although the location of the mantle cavity differs among species. The mantle cavity, a hollow area under the shell, is typically where the mollusc discharges wastes and where the gills are stored.

HAM exhibits the characteristics of all molluscs.

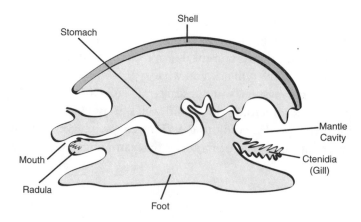

The only universal feature that all molluscs share is that at some point in their development, they have a shell-like structure called a *shell gland*. In some molluscs, such as the octopus, the shell gland appears only in the embryonic stage, and then completely disappears.

Soft in the Middle

Molluscs are commonly known as soft-bodied animals, a trait that makes them some of the most vulnerable animals in the sea. To protect themselves, most molluscs wear a hard shell that shields them from predators. Some molluscs, such as the limpet and abalone, live under a domed half shell. Others, including clams and oysters wear a dual-shelled jacket joined at a hinge. The most complex and interesting shell configuration, however, is exhibited by the gastropods, a class that comprises about 80 percent of all mollusc species. Gastropods represent more than 40,000 marine, freshwater, and terrestrial species, including many of the marine snails in everyone's seashell collections.

Gastropods have undergone three alterations from the original mollusc design; the development of a more pronounced head (cephalization), the shift from a shield-like shell to a spiral shell that the animal can retreat into, and an internal twist called *torsion*.

Captain Clam's Comments

Torsion is an evolutionary modification in gastropods that causes the soft parts, including the guts (the visceral mass), to rotate 180 degrees. Rotating the midsection 180 degrees provides the gastropods with greater balance, making them less top-heavy and providing additional protection for the creature's soft underbelly. Torsion also places the excretory organ above the head, which might seem a little disgusting but this allows the snail to withdraw its head into the shell before withdrawing its foot. Torsion was not the result of a singular evolutionary event but a series of smaller changes. Torsion can also be seen in the growth and development of the modern gastropod larvae.

A Motor Home with a Security Door

Snails take full advantage of their ancestral motor homes. Besides being able to retract head first into a hard, compact shell, most snails even have a security door they can slam shut when predators approach. This door, called an *operculum*, is a thin, hard disc attached to the foot of most snails. Snails fashion these doors out of the same materials they use to form their shells, but with a little calcium mixed in. This door not only keeps predators out, but also keeps moisture in, giving the snails a much wider travel range and allowing them to survive dry conditions at low tide.

House Without a Door

Limpets are the Rodney Dangerfields of the ocean—they get no respect. They don't have the spiral-shell-trap-door motor home of the snail, and they can't slam two shells shut like a clam or oyster. These gastropods have a single, domed shell with a wide opening at the bottom that offers them little protection. Their only option is to suction themselves tight against any hard surface they can find and lay low.

Some limpets, such as the slipper limpet, find strength in numbers, stacking themselves together like piles of upside-down saucers. Each limpet grasps the next with the strong suction grip of its foot. Although this is a great way to protect the exposed underside of the limpet, it also greatly reduces their mobility. Because of this, slipper limpets, unlike other limpets, are filter feeders, not grazers. To feed, a slipper limpet relaxes its grip to create a little space between itself and its partner, and then draws in algae-rich water from which it obtains its nutrients.

Nudist Colonies for Snails

Other gastropods that break ancestral rules are the sea hares and slugs. These creatures have either no shell at all or a very small, often internal shell beneath their fleshy body, and rely on alternate forms of defense. Sea hares get their name from their bunny-esque floppiness, all the way down to their adorable little ear-like folds. Although they have few predators, sea hares are well camouflaged to look like algae and also have the ability to squirt ink into the water to baffle the bad guys. Among the enemies of the juvenile sea hares are anemones and sea spiders.

Closely related sea slugs called nudibranchs (for naked gill) make a much more flamboyant fashion statement. Rather than using camouflage to blend in, many nudibranchs broadcast their presence by displaying brilliant Day-Glo colors that scream out for attention. Why? Because nudibranchs and their predators all know that the wild colors mean trouble.

> **CAUTION**
>
> ### Ocean Alert
>
> The brightly advertised colors of many nudibranchs remind likely predators to steer clear. Once a fish or other predator has made the mistake of ingesting a gaudily clad nudibranch, it is more likely to avoid "foods" that have the same color scheme. Some harmless marine creatures take advantage of this defense tactic by mimicking the color patterns and hues of the truly toxic.

These beautiful creatures pack toxins that make them a nasty, unpalatable treat for any predator who doesn't know better. This colorful warning is similar to the defense technique used by the brightly colored, poison tree frogs of the Amazon.

Two Valves Are Better Than One

Because their names commonly appear on most seafood menus, the bivalves are the most popular of all molluscs. Clams, scallops, oysters, and mussels representing hundreds of species have been consumed by humans for ages and still are cherished today. Bivalves are so named because they have two shells connected at a hinge by a flexible ligament. A muscle or pair of muscles hold the shells tightly closed in some species, fending off predators while sealing in moisture and the elements.

Captain Clam's Comments

Some bivalves have a remarkable ability to stay alive out of the water for very long periods of time. Cultured oysters left in growing cages to overwinter in cool garages have been known to survive for months. Their capacity to seal in moisture and retain their salt balance, coupled with their ability to hibernate during cold northern winters, make the oyster a tenacious survivor. Oysters likely developed this adaptation for life in the intertidal, where they can become exposed to air for considerable periods during low tide.

Are You In or Out?

Often, you can tell the difference between one bivalve and another by where it lives—whether *infaunal* (buried in the mud) or *epifaunal* (on or above the bottom). Infaunal species, including clams, require special adaptations to survive underground. First, in order to reach an underground location, the clam requires a powerful, well-developed foot that can dive down in the muck and yank its body and shell under. Once the clam reaches its subterranean home, it requires a long snout or feeding siphon that travels up through the sediment to reach the oxygen-rich, nutrient-packed water. The siphon works like an inverted straw, enabling the clam to suck the water down to where it lives.

Oysters and mussels prefer an *epifaunal* lifestyle, choosing to remain on or above the bottom. Finding and keeping a parking space on the ocean floor or somewhere above it requires a completely different set of tools. These bivalves don't need well-developed feet because they're not going anywhere. Instead, they need an anchor to hold themselves in place. Oysters, for example, are mobile only during their larval, free-swimming stage. When they metamorphose into juvenile "spats," they anchor themselves to a rock or other object and are permanently stuck where they chose to settle. Mussels use tenacious threads (called byssal threads) to anchor themselves to rocks and other substrates in some of the most violent seas. (See the next section, "Spider-Like Webbing," for details about byssal threads.)

Scallops practice an epifaunal lifestyle as well, but they like to move around. Because they do not have a well-developed foot, they must rely on their shells and adductor muscles for jet propulsion. When a scallop wants to move, it opens its shell and then snaps the halves together to send itself flying off to a new location. Scallops also have several "eyes" that surround the mantle and provide some rudimentary sense of sight that helps them detect the presence of predators.

All bivalves have well-developed gills that serve a dual function—they help the organism breathe and feed. As water passes over the gills, the gills extract oxygen from the water. They also catch minute food particles, primarily microscopic algae, which is then passed to the animal's mouth through special tubes. In the stomach of every bivalve and most gastropods is a saucer-shaped *gastric shield* and a rotating *crystalline style* that work together like a mortar and pestle to grind up food particles and mix them with gastric enzymes for digestion. Cilia spin the tip of the style against the gastric shield, causing the tip to erode and shed digestive enzymes into the stomach. The style also grinds up larger food particles, including the glasslike silica shells of diatoms. The style's tip is constantly regenerated as it is worn down.

Spider-Like Webbing

Unlike gastropods and other mobile molluscs, mussels and a few other bivalves prefer a more sedentary (*sessile*) lifestyle, as explained in the previous section. After their free-floating youth, mussels are determined to settle down, tying themselves to a solid surface (a rock, a dock, a cliff, a mangrove root, an oil tanker, or any other firm surface) using mats of tenacious *byssal threads*.

Many epifaunal bivalves attach themselves to rocks using tough, elastic byssal threads.

Byssal Threads

Tough as steel at the anchor end and stretchy as a tie-down at the bivalve end, byssal threads function as flexible tethers—the perfect adhesive for areas with a great deal of wave action. To attach itself to a rock or other solid surface, a bivalve first grasps the surface with its foot and produces a sticky plaque that glues it in place. The bivalve then secretes a collagen-based protein fluid from its byssal gland, which is located in the foot. This fluid travels down to the base of the foot to form a byssal thread. The bivalve might create several hundred such threads to anchor itself to its substrate. It can then relax its foot and even retract it, so it does not need to expend energy to stay in place.

Scallops use a single byssal thread in a very delicate manner. The small scallop prefers to be off the bottom away from predators and silt. In order to stick to a substrate such as eelgrass, the scallop snaps its two shells together to swim up to and push against the surface of an eelgrass blade. Once against the blade, the scallop shoots a single thread out from its hinge and glues itself in place. Frequently, scallops hang out together, spacing themselves equally in a confined area to minimize competition for food and oxygen.

> **Underwater Eye**
>
> Byssal thread material is 5 times tougher and 16 times more stretchable than a human tendon! This material is described as the first known protein having both collagenous and elastin-like properties. These tough, leathery, yet amazingly stretchy collagen threads might someday suggest strategies for developing better artificial skin and other useful biomedical materials—not to mention a superior superglue.

Bizarre Bivalve Sexual Practices

Whether they roll in the mud or hang out on rocks, bivalves lead fascinating sex lives. The clams and related burrowers are typically *dioecious*, meaning they are either male or female for their entire lives, like most animals you know. Oysters and other molluscs, however, exhibit more interesting sexual orientations. Some start out as males and end up as females, others begin as females and become males, and still others change from male to female and back again throughout the course of their lives. And they do this without a single sex-change operation!

Many species of scallop can go either way— they're considered *serial hermaphrodites*, meaning that each individual scallop can produce both male and female gametes (the equivalent of sperm and eggs) throughout their lives. As you might guess, this adaptation makes it easier to find a mate. Various oyster species are *protandric hermaphrodites*, meaning that they all start out as males but then develop into females and stay that way for the rest of their lives.

> **Log Entry**
>
> A **serial hermaphrodite** possesses both male and female sexual organs. A **consecutive hermaphrodite** changes from male to female or female to male as it matures. A consecutive hermaphrodite that changes from male to female is called **protandric**, whereas one that changes from female to male is called **protogynous**.

European oysters (genus *Ostrea*) are *rhythmical consecutive hermaphrodites;* they can change sex several times during the course of their lives. All European oysters begin life as males, but after they shed their sperm, they become females. As females, they develop eggs, which are then fertilized by males of the same species. The female carries the fertilized eggs until they become larvae, and then she sheds her newborns, and soon thereafter reverts to being a male. (European oysters are said to be larviparous, because they carry their fertilized eggs until the larvae hatch and are mature enough to release.)

Another fascinating protandric hermaphrodite is the slipper limpet, which you met earlier in this chapter. Recall that slipper limpets live in stacks like upside-down saucers to protect the limpets from predators. This protective stack influences the sexual orientation of each limpet as well. A large female typically holds the bottom spot with a small, young male at the top. The limpets in between may be male or female. As the male sheds its sperm, the sperm cells settle to the lower levels to fertilize the eggs of the females. As long as a male is attached to a female, the male can remain a male, but when detached, the male soon transforms into a female and can be fertilized by other male slipper limpets.

Captain Clam's Comments

The bay scallop (*Argopecten irradians*) typically lives less than two years, providing little time to mature, find a mate, and replicate. To compensate, the bay scallop has a large gonad capable of producing millions of eggs and billions of sperm. Every individual bay scallop has the potential to cast eggs or sperm into the water column. They appear to have hormonal mechanisms for detecting nearby spawning activity, so they can all discharge their eggs and sperm at nearly the same time (a phenomenon called *synchrony*). They even have eyes that are thought to fine-tune seasonal spawning events based on a *photoperiod*. These elaborate modifications give bay scallops a fighting chance at surviving extinction.

High-Tech Cephalo: Action Shellfish

When you see an octopus and a mussel side by side, you find it nearly impossible to believe that they're in the same family, let alone the same phylum. The octopus is an eight-legged, suction-cup–footed, master swimmer that can see and produce its own ink clouds. The mussel is a blind hunk of flesh that can glue itself to rocks, seal itself up in a shell, and sip on a straw. You would never think that the two could possibly be related.

In fact, the mussel and the cephalopod (pronounced *SEF-a-la-pod*) are distant relatives. Cephalopods, including the octopus, squid, cuttlefish, and nautilus, are, by far, the most specialized and advanced creatures of the phylum. All cephalopods have a distinct and prominent head surrounded by "feet," which earns them the name of cephalopod (Greek for "head footed"). In addition, every cephalopod has a well-developed and sophisticated brain, three hearts that pump blue blood, fairly good eyesight, a system of jet propulsion, prehensile tentacles, a sharp beak, and (in most species) an ink sac for defense.

Most cephalopods lack the distinct shell that is so characteristic of other molluscs. One exception is the chambered nautilus, which has a well-developed shell complete with air-filled chambers to help keep it afloat. The cuttlefish, which looks like a nautilus without a shell, has an internal elongated saucer-shaped shell called a *cuttlebone*, which you might have seen sold at pet stores as a calcium source for birds. The squid has an internal long, thin shell, called a *pen*.

Underwater Eye

The chambered nautilus is one of those magical creatures from out of antiquity. Everything about it looks primordial. It is a perfect blend of squid and snail, wearing a gorgeous shell of spiraling chambers. Unlike the shell of a snail, the animal occupies only the last chamber. As the nautilus grows, it shuts off its last chamber with a thin wall of shell, creating another air pocket. Besides fossil remains, these are the only cephalopods with completely developed shells.

The Sucker Punch

One of the most prominent and unique features of cephalopods are its tentacles, its prehensile "arms." On some species, including the squid and octopus, these arms come complete with rows of suction cups that can grab hold of rocks, shells, flesh, and anything else they want to put the squeeze on. In one documented case of the rare giant squid, tentacles stretching as long as 35 feet were measured on a squid with a body length of 20 feet. That's one big calamari!

Squid have ten arms including a pair of larger, extensible tentacles for swimming and for seizing prey. These twin tentacles are equipped with powerful suction cups that prevent captured prey from being swept away as the squid propels itself through the water. The tentacles act like the talons of an eagle but with suction cups rather than claws. The octopus lacks this pair of specialized tentacles. It has eight arms that work equally well to move the creature over the ocean floor and around obstacles to avoid predators and seize prey. The octopus uses its arms more deftly than the squid, preferring a slower, more methodical approach than the squid's pounce-and-swim technique.

Here's Ink in Your Eye and Other Defenses

Like their fellow molluscs, cephalopods are soft in the middle … in fact, they're soft all over. This makes them prime candidates for becoming fish food. Everything from fish to sharks to seals to humans likes to snack on the soft flesh of the octopus, and, contrary to what you see in cartoons, the suction-cup–covered arms provide little defense.

Fortunately, most cephalopods have a complete arsenal of defense mechanisms at their disposal. One of the best defense systems of the octopus is its ability to blend in with the color and texture of any surface it traverses. As the octopus crawls along the ocean floor (rock, sand, coral, or seaweed), its skin changes both in color and contrast to camouflage the creature from potential predators and prey. Cephalopods can also change color more dramatically during aggressive exchanges or to woo a coy mate. These color displays are more prominent in the cuttlefish and octopus.

The second defense that most cephalopods rely on is their ability to squeeze their skeleton-free bodies through tiny holes and crevices. An octopus with an arm span of 30 centimeters, for example, can squeeze itself through a 2 to 3 centimeter gap. Using this technique, the octopus can hide out in holes and tunnels where large predators cannot reach.

When hiding and camouflage fail, many cephalopods escape by squirting ink in the predator's eye. This ink (black, brown, or red) creates a decoy in some cases and completely obscures the exit route in other cases. In any event, it confuses the predator for at least a few seconds, giving the cephalopod time to escape. Some scientists theorize that the ink actually impairs the senses of the predator. Of course, as a last resort, the cephalopod can always grasp the predator and bite it, which is usually enough to dissuade most humans.

Maternal Momma Octopus

Cephalopod sexuality might seem prudish after studying the sexual escapades of the bivalves. Cephalopods are born (hatched) male or female; the male stays male, and the female remains female for the rest of their lives. The male uses various techniques to mate with the female, but in all species, the mating ritual consists of passing sperm to the female to fertilize her eggs.

After her eggs are fertilized, the female cephalopod begins to prove herself as the consummate devoted mother. The female common octopus, *Octopus vulgaris*, strings her eggs from rocks and crevices and remains with the eggs, cleaning and aerating them without stopping to eat, until she eventually dies from exhaustion. The female brown paper nautilus (also called the Argonaut), *Argonauta nodosa*, creates a paper-like sac to hold her fertilized eggs, which she carries to a sea grass meadow or another shallow area where they can safely hatch. Momma Argonaut then dies, as her babies head out to sea. Many other cephalopod species follow a similar pattern, in which one or both parents die shortly after the eggs are fertilized and hatch.

A Gallery of Giants

In general, the phylum Mollusca consists of a collection of featherweights. Even a large mussel, snail, or slug is miniscule when compared to a whale, shark, or even a tuna fish. However, a few monster molluscs can hold their own as heavyweights of the deep.

The largest mollusc to tip the scales is the giant squid—the largest invertebrate on either land or sea. Weighing in at 900 kilograms (1,980 pounds), this squid can stretch to 18 meters (60 feet) in length. That's about as long as a male sperm whale, its major predator. However, given the fact that an adult male sperm whale can weigh upward of 54,000 kilograms, the largest invertebrate is little more than a main course for one of the largest vertebrates on the planet.

The second largest known mollusc on the planet is the sessile giant clam, which weighs less than a third as much as the giant squid. The official weigh-in has the giant clam at nearly 230 kilograms (500 pounds), and all but about 10 kilograms of that is shell! That's not even a close second to the giant squid. However, the giant clam's shell is pretty impressive and has generated some interesting myths of these clams chowing down on divers.

The remaining "giant molluscs" are anything but giant. A horse conch, *Pleuroploca gigantea*, popular with shell collectors, can have a shell 60 centimeters (24 inches) long, which is quite impressive, but hardly qualifies the creature as a gargantuan. The California sea hare, a shell-less gastropod, can weigh in at more than 14 kilograms (30 pounds) and measure 76 centimeters (30 inches) in length. When you think "slug," that's enormous, but it's still small potatoes compared to a 900-kilogram giant squid.

The Least You Need to Know

- HAM stands for hypothetical ancestral mollusc, a template for all species of molluscs.
- HAM is characterized by a fleshy body (called the mantle), a shell (for protection), a foot (for locomotion), a rasp-like tongue (for eating), and gills (for breathing).

◆ Most molluscs have a shell for protection, although many molluscs have an internal shell or possess a shell only during the embryonic stage.

◆ Bivalves have two shells that are joined at a hinge by a tough ligament.

◆ Bivalves commonly change sexes through the course of their lives or several times during their lives.

◆ Cephalopods include the octopus, squid, nautilus, and cuttlefish.

◆ Female cephalopods are some of the most devoted mothers—often working themselves to death to ensure the success of their offspring.

Chapter 12

A Multitude of Jointed Variations

In This Chapter

◆ Dishing up more krill

◆ Half-crab, half-scorpion, and totally freaky

◆ Luscious lobster lineup

◆ An assortment of crab cakes

◆ Rounding out the menu with sea spiders

Unless you grew up in a hermetically sealed chamber, you have encountered some form of arthropod sometime in your life. An arthropod is an invertebrate that has a hard, chitinous (pronounced *KITE-in-us*) exoskeleton. The arthropod's body typically is segmented and each segment has a pair of jointed appendages attached to it. Insects are arthropods, as are spiders, crabs, lobsters, shrimp, and other crispy creatures.

Together, arthropods represent the largest animal phylum, accounting for more than 850,000 species. Of this number, approximately 30,000 are crustaceans (crabs, lobster, shrimp, krill, copepods, barnacles, sea spiders, and related creatures). This chapter introduces the major crustacean classes and examines a few of the more interesting representatives in each class.

Characteristically Crustacean

When you start to study crustaceans, you encounter some species that just don't seem to fit in with the group. At first glance, for instance, an acorn barnacle looks more like an inverted bivalve than it does a lobster. On closer examination, however, it becomes obvious that the barnacle is more crustacean than mollusc. So, what makes a crustacean a crustacean?

The first quality that all crustaceans share is bilateral symmetry; if you draw a line down the center of a crustacean's back, the left side is a mirror image of the right side. One small exception is the fact that some crustaceans have a left and right front claw that differs significantly in size and shape. Humans exhibit bilateral symmetry, as well.

Like all arthropods, crustaceans have the requisite exoskeleton and the segmented body with each segment having a pair of jointed appendages. These appendages vary from species to species; for example, lobsters have eight walking legs and two larger claws for eating and defense. Because the exoskeleton does not grow with the animal, a crustacean must molt as it grows and discard the exoskeleton it just outgrew. In most species, the body is divided into distinct areas, including a head, thorax, and abdomen. Although in some larger species, such as lobsters, the head and thorax are combined into a single unit called the cephalothorax, which is protected by a large, shield-like carapace. The cephalothorax contains most of the business parts of the crustacean, including its antennae, eyes, mouth, gills, and internal organs. The remaining portion, the abdomen, is used primarily for locomotion (swimming).

Unlike shrimp, lobster, crabs, copepods, and other crustaceans designed to crawl and swim around the ocean, barnacles are sessile creatures; they glue themselves to a surface and stay put. Hence, their anatomy is completely different. Instead of using their legs to crawl, they lie on their backs and flail their legs in the current in an attempt to gather any food that might be floating past.

Barnacles use their legs to collect food that floats past.

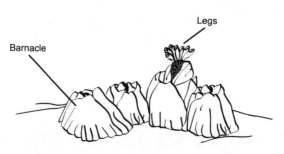

Legs

Barnacle

A Most Abundant Life Form

Take a drop of water from the epipelagic zone and examine it under a microscope. Chances are good that you see some tiny shrimp-like animals darting around and gobbling up specs of phytoplankton. Most of these shrimp-like zooplankton are crustaceans—copepods, amphipods, isopods, and other "pods" that are tough to spot, let alone identify and name. These microscopic marvels compose a huge portion of the bottom of the food pyramid. In sheer numbers, the crustacean zooplankton represent the largest group of animals on the planet—not just in the ocean, but on land, as well!

> **Underwater Eye**
>
> Zooplanktonic crustaceans have certain characteristic traits that scientists use to identify them. Size, body form, and appendages (such as antennae) are often the most conspicuous features that vary among species. Although all crustaceans have five pairs of legs, their specific configuration can be used to identify particular species.

Combing for Krill with Blue Whales

Commonly known as whale food, krill, also known as *euphausiids*, is a group of about 85 species of crustaceans found in open oceans. Krill look like smaller versions of familiar crustaceans such as prawns or lobsters. Antarctic krill is one of the most abundant and successful animal species on the planet, frequently found in such abundance that they turn the sea a reddish brown color. Although many whales can opportunistically add small fish to their diet, blue whales are as finicky as house cats, eating only krill and feeding mainly in the cold Antarctic waters, which seasonally boom with at least five major species of krill.

> **Captain Clam's Comments**
>
> One of the greatest predatory pressures placed on krill comes not from the whales but from a species of Antarctic seal called the crabeater. Crabeater seals are the most numerous pinniped species (seals, otters, walrus) in the world, found throughout the pack ice that surrounds the Antarctic continent. (Despite their name, crabeaters prefer krill over crab.) These seals, whose population is estimated at more than 10 million, track the cyclical swarms of krill. During breeding season, the seals stay close to krill blooms so that pups weaned from mother's milk can gorge on the krill and quickly bulk up.

The dominant Antarctic krill, *Euphausia superba* (sounds delicious, doesn't it?), not only feeds the massive blue whale, but it also serves as the middleman in a simple three-link food chain that links tiny phytoplankton to most of the Antarctic whales, seals and penguins, as well as other birds. They serve as a food source in all seasons but bloom in response to increased microalgae blooms, which typically occur during warmer, sunnier months.

Eat or Be Eaten

When you think of edible crustaceans, you never picture a guy wearing a bib with a krill on it, do you? A mouthful of krill just isn't all that appetizing to the average seafood lover. People prefer meatier crustaceans—lobsters, rock crabs, blue claws, and king crabs. These armored beasts crack the appetite of seafood lovers wide open.

Log Entry

Most crab and lobster species are opportunistic feeders. They are scavengers that eat just about anything that crosses their paths, including members of their own species! So don't feel too sorry the next time you see some sad-looking crustaceans in a restaurant's lobster tank—it's a crab-eat-crab world out there!

As a group, these crustaceans share many characteristics, but upon careful examination, they are also quite diverse. Some crustaceans are swimmers, whereas others prefer to walk. Some are elongated like lobsters, whereas others are short and squat like flying saucers. Many of the better-known crustaceans have a pair of massive claws that they use as their main feeding tools, whereas some lobsters and crabs have only dainty pincers. The following sections explore these differences in greater detail as they examine some of the more crab-like and lobster-like crustaceans.

Line-Up of Lobsters

Two types of lobsters crawl around the ocean floor—lobsters with claws and lobsters without claws. The famous Maine or American lobster is one of about 25 species of crustaceans that has claws it can brag about. This lobster lugs around two strong claws: a big shell-crusher claw for cracking open clams and other shellfish and a smaller, serrated claw for cutting and tearing its food into bite-sized chunks. The position of the two claws can vary. A lobster that carries its crusher claw on the right side of its body is a "right-handed" lobster. Those that carry the crusher claw on the left are "lefties." (The next time you order a lobster, order a left-handed or right-handed lobster, and watch the look on your server's face.)

Some lobsters, such as the spiny or rock lobster, forego the big front mitts, preferring mobility over heavy-duty weaponry. The spiny lobster, which prefers to live closer to the equator than its cousin from Maine, has no large claws up front. For defense, the lobster relies on its spiny exoskeleton and two huge, armor-plated antennae. When provoked, the spiny lobster can whip the antennae furiously against its opponent, inflicting some serious lacerations. Spiny lobsters don't display the voracious cannibalistic tendencies of their clawed counterparts and are periodically found marching single file along the ocean floor in seasonal migrations.

Of course, all lobsters can use their powerful tails to evade potential predators. When confronted face-to-face with a potential predator, a quick flick of its tail can shoot the lobster several feet back, usually into a crack or crevice in a rock. Young lobsters make even greater use of their tails, spending much of their early lives swimming above the ocean floor. Only when they become adults do they settle down and start using their legs for locomotion.

Captain Clam's Comments

Lobsters haven't always been considered a delicacy. Native Americans commonly used lobsters as fertilizer for their fields and as fish bait. In colonial times and well into the 1900s, lobsters were commonly served to servants, prisoners, and children as a second-rate food. Poor kids were given lobster sandwiches to take to school for lunch. Not until the middle 1900s did people begin to consider lobster a delicacy.

Swimmers and Shredders

You might think that one primary difference between lobsters and crabs is that lobsters can swim. In reality, however, some crabs can swim as well. Swimming crabs hold a special place in the complex world of crustaceans. They are modified to travel quickly and efficiently in the pelagic zone (the open ocean) rather than being limited like most crabs to life as a bottom feeder near the shore. When a swimming crab is about to take off, it positions its body and claws to look like a fish, converting to a fusiform or torpedo-like shape. It then uses its rear, paddle-shaped legs, to ascend and "fly" through the water. They actually look like little flying saucers.

One of the best-known swimming crabs in North America is the blue crab. The blue crab, whose Latin name, *Callinectes sapidus* (pronounced *kal-i-NEK-tes-SAP-i-dus*) literally translates as the "beautiful" (*calli*) "swimmer" (*nectes*) that is "savory" (*sapidus*) is one species that lives up to all of its names. But the blue crab could just as well have been called the Jack the Ripper crab or Freddy Kruger crab. Of course, they are strikingly beautiful in their brilliant blue armor and succulently sweet to eat, but they are also some of the nastiest bullies to brutalize the estuaries.

As with any species of swimming crabs, the blue crab has a pair of feeding claws that do a thorough job of crushing and tearing apart its prey. One claw handles the crushing and one handles the shredding—similar to lobsters but with a narrower profile.

Handling these crabs can be a nightmare even for seasoned crab hunters. Fortunately, the crab can't reach every part of its own body with its claws, so if you know these spots and can grab the crab where it can't reach, you're generally safe.

Underwater Eye

Soon after a female blue crab molts, it mates. A male crab typically cradles the soft-shelled female as they mate and continues to hold her until her shell hardens. This may sound sweet, but scientists believe that the male continues to hold the female to ensure that she doesn't mate with another male when he lets her go.

As swimming crabs grow, they eventually outgrow their shells and must molt, giving up their old armor for a newer, larger suit. Right after the crab sheds, it is most vulnerable—open to attack by any of its many predators, including humans. Soft-shell crabs are one of America's favorite seafood delicacies. Although all crabs shed their shells to grow, only a few species of crab, including the blue crab, are actually edible in this form. Another edible soft shell is the mangrove soft-shell crab. Raised on Asian crab farms, these delicious crabs are caught by local fisherman, brought to the crab farm, and then maintained until they molt. Within one hour of shedding their hard shells, the crabs are harvested, making for a very tender crab that can be consumed whole.

The Cancer Crabs

Cancer crabs are the crabs most people picture when they hear the word "crab." These crabs have bodies like flying saucers and typically shuffle from side-to-side. Cancer crabs include the many varieties of rock crabs, stone crabs, Dungeness, Jonah, and other crabs of similar appearance and behavior. These crabs typically inhabit bottom-dwelling communities and favor areas rich in geological features—such as big rocks and crevices in which they can hide.

Underwater Eye

If you're interested in astrology or astronomy, you've certainly heard of the zodiac sign of Cancer or Cancer the constellation. In Greek mythology, Cancer was the crab that Hercules crushed when it pinched his toes while he was fighting the Hydra, a nine-headed sea monster.

Unfortunately for humans, most species of cancer crabs are major predators of valuable seafood items and have no commercial value themselves. The mud crabs and shore crabs eat many wild and cultured shellfish. Being opportunistic, these hearty scavengers always find plenty to eat, and when their natural predators, such as fish and other crabs, are thinned from the system, few factors keep the cancer crab population in check.

To compound the problem, new nuisance species are constantly being introduced to fragile ecosystems.

The Asian shore crab is the latest non-native crab to invade the North American coast. Its appearance was first recorded in New Jersey in 1988. This species is now well established and exceptionally abundant along the Atlantic intertidal coastline of the United States from Maine to North Carolina. Because the species is tolerant of a wide range of environmental conditions, the invasion likely will continue along the North American coastline. On the West Coast of North America, the green crab has become a particularly nasty menace, threatening the shellfish populations in the United States and Canada.

 **Ocean Alert**

Some areas have established new voluntary requirements for ships to discharge ballast water before entering port, but this can't be done in rough weather and enforcement can be difficult. Recreational boaters can help prevent the spread of invasive species like the zebra mussel by carefully washing and scrubbing their boats anytime they go to a new body of water.

How non-native invader species are introduced to different regions often remains an unsolved mystery, but many incoming ships frequently import foreign species in their ballast water and dump them into a new body of water at their next port of call. An infamous freshwater mussel (the Zebra mussel) pulled such a stunt in the Great Lakes at the same time that Asian shore crabs were invading the Atlantic. In any case, one more aggressive crab on the ocean's bottom is more than enough to tilt the already unbalanced predator-to-prey ratio.

Crab Legs Express

If you had to live on a diet of crab legs from any of the crabs covered so far, you would starve. The legs are relatively tiny and contain very little meat. Spider crabs, however, have legs that are packed with juicy strips of meat. This group of crabs includes the world-renowned Alaskan King crab, the snow crab, and the Tanner crab—the latter of which has become quite rare. These crabs are actively fished in Alaska, Canada, Russia, Japan, Korea, New Zealand, Australia, South Georgia and Falkland Islands, Argentina, and Chile. Historically, the red king crab fishery has been Alaska's top shellfish fishery, but with the sharp decline of red and blue king crab populations, some commercial fishers have targeted golden king crabs. Red and blue king crab populations have been slow to recover from a combination of overfishing and a period of poor survival of young crabs. The demand for this type of crab, which is prepared using only the long, meaty claws, has put significant pressure on the fishery.

Spider crabs, including the king crab, shown here, have long, meaty legs.

(Photo Credit: OAR/National Undersea Research Program, Texas A&M University)

Too Many Crustaceans to Cover

With tens of thousands of arthropods swimming, floating, and crawling around in the ocean, this chapter cannot possibly provide even a brief description of every creature. All this chapter can hope to do is explore some of the most interesting creatures—the few that exhibit modifications that are uniquely fascinating and have managed to survive for eons. The following sections examine some of the more intriguing crustaceans. Think of these sections as the sample platter—the appetizer plate that will fuel your hunger for further exploration.

Mantis Shrimp Madness

Mantis shrimp (fondly known as *stomatopods*) are the shell bashers and fish spearers of the sea. In some species, tucked just beneath the shrimp's head is a large, heavy claw that it uses like a sledge hammer to crack open clams, mussels, and other well-protected seafood items. A mantis shrimp can "swing" this hammer-claw so quickly and land it with such force that it can smash the thick safety glass used in many large aquariums. Other species of mantis shrimp more closely resemble their land cousin, the praying mantis, in the way that their front claws are specially modified for stabbing and grabbing their victims. Like a praying mantis, the mantis shrimp waits patiently for its victim to approach and then snaps its arms forward to snatch its victim.

Most of the 400 species of mantis shrimp live in burrows one to two meters beneath the bottom sediment or in rock crevices—where they can defend themselves and execute surprise attacks. In tropical regions, the mantis shrimp likes to hang out in coral alcoves. Mantis shrimp tails are considered as fine a treat as jumbo shrimp, their close relative.

You're Outgrowing Your Old Digs

Hermit crabs always provide a curious diversion for beachcombers and marine biologists alike. The hermit crab has a chitinous body like most crabs, but its body provides little protection for its internal organs. Instead, hermits rely on the discarded shells of other animals, preferably snails, for their protection. When a crab grows too big for its shell, it scrambles around until it finds a nice new one, tries it on, and then leaves the old one behind for some other runt.

Matching the spiraling structure of the snail shell, the hermit crab's abdomen is permanently bent to fit deep inside the shell. To enable the hermit to retreat completely back into its shell, hermits have only a single pincher claw, which is the last appendage the hermit retracts. The large claw acts as the hermit's security door. Hermits grow as large as their next shell allows, which in the case of a large conch shell, can equate to a pretty large hermit. The transfer from one shell to the next is what makes a hermit crab what it is—a wary but proud homeowner.

Captain Clam's Comments

Hermit crabs are very opportunistic. Not only do they take full advantage of discarded homes, but they also enlist the help of anemones for protection. Many hermits can coax an anemone to relax its pedal disc, which anchors the anemone to its substrate. The hermit can then lift the anemone onto its back. When the hermit crab changes shells, it coaxes the anemone off the old shell and moves it to the new one!

Filter Feeding Foulers

Look near the water line around any saltwater dock, boat, or rocky area, and you're sure to see some barnacles cemented to the surface. In most cases, you see some species of acorn barnacle—the short, squat, cone-shaped barnacles. The other type of barnacle, called the goose barnacle, grows on a stalk, making it look more like a sprouting lima bean than a crustacean.

Most barnacles are free living, attaching and cementing themselves to anything and everything that is firm enough to settle on, and once they settle, they remain in place. These crustaceans deal with lack of mobility the way that

Captain Clam's Comments

Barnacles commonly settle on a boat's hull or propeller, causing serious drag and slowing down the boat. They can also damage the metal surfaces. To prevent barnacles from settling, special no-foul coatings are applied to the boat's hull and sometimes its propeller, and the boat is cleaned regularly. In some cases, high-frequency vibrations are used to repel the barnacles and prevent them from taking hold.

most sessile sea creatures do, by filtering food from the water. Barnacles have a fan-like feeding attachment that grabs plankton from the water and rams it down the pipe (into their mouths) for digestion.

A hermit crab without a shell has little protection.

(Photo Credit: National Oceanic and Atmospheric Administration/Department of Commerce)

A Living Marine Fossil

Some things never change, and the one sea creature that has changed very little in over 500 million years of evolution is the lowly (and very common) horseshoe crab. More closely related to spiders than to crabs, the horseshoe crab actually evolved from the trilobite, an ancient arthropod that looks like an armor-plated roach.

From above, the horseshoe crab resembles a cross between a tank and a submarine. It has a huge, shield-like cephalothorax, called the prosoma, complete with seven eyes (three in front, two well-developed lateral eyes, and two rudimentary lateral eyes). Beneath the prosoma are the horseshoe crab's mouth and legs, which it uses to creep across the ocean floor and suck up food particles. Behind the prosoma is the crab's abdomen or opisthosoma. The opisthoma's horned plate provides protection for the crab's gills (called book gills), which assist in the crab's movement as well as acting as its breathing apparatus. At the tail end is the horseshoe crab's telson (or tail), which also contains photoreceptors to help the horseshoe crab navigate. (For more information about horseshoe crab anatomy and a description of how they eat, refer to the section "Nature's Best Vacuum Cleaners" in Chapter 8.)

Horseshoe crabs take approximately 9 to 11 years to reach sexual maturity, at which time they stop molting and begin undergoing annual spring migrations to inshore spawning areas. (All the horseshoe crabs you see on a beach in the spring are mature.)

Few hatchlings make it through the natural predator cycle but if they survive this and other rigors, they can live for almost 20 years.

A horseshoe crab has a simple design when viewed from above.

(Photo Credit: Mary Hollinger, NODC biologist, NOAA)

Underwater Eye

One of the most valuable parts of the horseshoe crab for humans is its blood, which is used to test the purity of some medications. This blood is particularly sensitive to bacteria, and when a horseshoe crab is wounded, the blood cells swarm to the wound, form a clot, and destroy the invading bacteria. Scientists have isolated these cells and created an extract called *Limulus Amebocyte Lysate* (LAL), which they can use to test medicines for the presence of toxins that can be fatal to humans. Horseshoe crab blood is also useful in cancer research and in other medical research and applications. Blood is collected from more than 200,000 crabs each year and can command a price of more than $15,000 for a single quart!

Slim Pickin's for Pycnogonids

The Wiriest Arthropod Award would certainly have to go to the pycnogonids, including the daddy long legs of the deep, the sea spider. Sea spiders are some of the most bizarre-looking arthropods on the planet—they almost look like they're formed out of twisted pipe cleaners. Sea spiders are common throughout the ocean, even in its deepest locations, but you might have trouble spotting them, because most sea spiders are only about 10 millimeters across. However, some species that live in the deep waters off Antarctica can have a leg span of near one full meter! Although some sea spiders have been known to munch on algae, most are carnivores, feeding on anemones, soft coral, polychaete worms, and other animals with suitably soft flesh.

One species is known to prey on juvenile sea hares, which most predators find thoroughly disgusting.

The Least You Need to Know

- ◆ Arthropods are invertebrates with exoskeletons and jointed appendages.

- ◆ Krill represent a key food source in the Antarctic food chain and directly support many of the world's largest creatures.

- ◆ Most commercially harvested shellfish are crustaceans, including lobsters, crabs, and shrimp.

- ◆ Horseshoe crabs are a small and ancient form of arthropod that has adapted well to ocean life and has remained virtually unchanged for 350 million years.

- ◆ Sea spiders live in a wide variety of ocean environments and are capable of eating even the unpalatable sea hare.

Part 4

The Marine Vertebrates: Backbones to Prove It!

When you're born with a spine, you automatically win a lifetime membership to the vertebrate club, where you get to rub elbows with the most highly developed creatures on the planet. In the ocean, this includes the most popular fish, including tuna, mackerel, sharks, and rays; reptiles, including sea turtles and marine iguanas; birds, such as sea gulls, pelicans, and penguins; and mammals, including dolphins, whales, seals, and otters.

This part introduces you to your fellow sea-loving vertebrates and explores the fascinating lifestyles that many of them have developed to survive and thrive in various ocean environments.

Chapter 13

Celebrating Fish Evolution and Diversity

In This Chapter

◆ The earliest known vertebrates evolve

◆ Lines of fish that survived the fishing lines

◆ Trawling the seas for a variety of species

◆ The many sides of sharks

◆ Skates and rays fly by

Jellies, crabs, clams, and the other invertebrates you met in the previous chapters are beautiful creatures, and they display some fascinating traits, but, quite frankly, they have no backbone. Not until about 500 million years ago did creatures evolve that had anything resembling a backbone. These first vertebrate prototypes were fish, which eventually developed into all sorts of other vertebrates, including amphibians, birds, lizards, whales, and even humans. This chapter takes you on a journey through time to explore the evolution of the first fish and examine some theories of how these evolutionary pioneers evolved into current species (or failed to evolve and became extinct).

Chordates and Vertebrates

Any discussion of vertebrates must begin with a description of the larger group that includes vertebrates—the *chordates*. Chordates are any animals that have, at some stage in their existence, a *notochord*—a rigid muscular rod that lies between the animal's gut and the *dorsal nerve cord*—which runs down the back of the animal. The phylum Chordata is further broken down into the following three subphyla:

- **Cephalochordata** consists of about 25 species of eel-like lancelets, which are frequently referred to as *amphioxus* (meaning "pointed at both ends"). They look like toothpicks. These creatures spend most of their time with their heads (and the rest of their bodies) buried in the sand. Their importance lies in the fact that they represent the most basic of chordates—possibly the link between the invertebrates and vertebrates.

- **Urochordata (formerly called Tunicata)** consists of approximately 2,000 species of tunicates, which you met briefly in Chapter 2. Commonly called sea squirts, adult tunicates look like plastic bags or tubes with two holes in them: one for sucking water in and another for pumping it out. You would never guess from looking at an adult sea squirt that the animal could be a chordate, but the tunicate has a free-swimming larva that looks very similar to a tadpole, complete with a notochord and dorsal nerve chord characteristic of the chordates.

- **Vertebrata** is the largest subphylum of chordates and includes more than 41,000 species. To belong to this club, each member must have, at some stage in its life, the following four characteristics: pharyngeal slits (for gills), a notochord made of bone or cartilage, a hollow dorsal nerve chord, and a tail. In vertebrates, the notochord is surrounded by a spinal column, and the dorsal nerve chord has evolved into a very complex central nervous system, complete with a skull-protected brain. Vertebrates include fish, amphibians, reptiles, birds, and mammals. Although most of these animals lose their pharyngeal slits early in development, they do have them at some stage of their lives.

Look Ma, No Jaws

To understand the revolutionary impact that fish had on evolution, put yourself way back in time. Imagine an ocean that was just beginning to teem with life, not only primitive life, such as algae and bacteria, but also some relatively sophisticated invertebrates. Then, all of a sudden (in a period of just a few million years), an animal with a backbone appears—an animal with a tail that can swim from one place to another, giving itself a virtually limitless range to feed and populate. So, what did this evolutionary wonder boy look like? Fossil remains reveal that this 500 to 540 million-year-old creature was an armored, jawless fish.

Armor-Plated Ostracoderms

Scientists labeled these ancient, armor-plated fish *ostracoderms* (which means "shell skins"). What is most interesting about ostracoderms is that they provide a logical transition from the invertebrates (many of which have shells or exoskeletons) to vertebrates (which wear their skeletons on the inside). Ostracoderms had both—a bony external skeleton that provided most of the supporting structure for the fish, and a rudimentary "backbone" of cartilage.

Like today's lampreys and hagfish, ostracoderms had poorly formed fins and no jaws. For this reason, many scientists group lampreys, hagfish, and ostracoderms together as Agnatha (meaning "without jaws") and no longer acknowledge "ostracoderm" as a separate group. However, "ostracoderm" is still used to describe this archetypical, primitive fish. Because ostracoderms were not only the first fish, but also the first animals to have a backbone, most scientists believe that the history of all other vertebrates can be traced back to these armor-plated fish.

Ostracoderms are armor-plated vertebrates.

Between about 450 and 350 million years ago, during the Silurian and (even more significantly) the Devonian periods, fish evolution peaked. In the middle Silurian period, which lasted from 438 to 408 million years ago, the jawless fishes had spread far and wide, had developed more advanced fins and tails, and had given rise to the first fish with jaws near the end of the period. The Devonian period (408 to 360 million years ago) marked the "Age of Fishes," when the true diversity of fishes exploded. This period saw the rise of several species of primitive sharks (*Placodermi*), lobe-finned fish and lungfish (*Sarcopterygii*), and the bony fish or ray-finned fish (*Actinopterygii*). At this point, the jawless fishes still outnumbered their jawed relatives, but about 380 million years ago the balance tipped in favor of the jawed vertebrates or *gnathostomes*. Currently, gnathostomes represent the majority of all living vertebrates, including sharks, rays, chimaeras, ray-finned fishes, lobe-finned fishes and land vertebrates.

Scientists generally agree that toward the end of the Devonian period, the first tetrapods (four-footed vertebrates that evolved true legs for walking on land) had evolved from one specific group of fish. Fish continued to specialize and establish their respective niches during both the Silurian and the Devonian periods, and part of this evolution resulted in the introduction of the first amphibians—vertebrates that have legs and live both on land and in water. The theoretical progression flows like this: The ostracoderms gave rise to jawed fish with backbones, which gave rise to the first tetrapods, which led to the evolution of *amphibians*, which eventually led to the evolution of all land vertebrates.

Captain Clam's Comments

Ostracoderms were small, heavily armored fish that probably reached the peak of their development about 400 million years ago. About the same time, two other groups of fish were developing—one that became the first known jawed fish and the other called the *placoderm* group, which included the primitive sharks. Some members of this now extinct line of fish were the largest fish of that period. One such species, the *Dunkleosteus*, grew to 23 feet (7 meters) long and had powerful jaws and sharp bony plates that served as teeth.

Agnathsty Hags and Lampreys

Today's jawless fish can be some of the nastiest creatures in the sea. For example, the aptly named hagfish is an eel-like, beady eyed, toothless, finless, slime-oozing parasite that makes a living by sucking the blood out of its victims. The 20 or so species of hagfish all live on or in muddy sea floors in very dense groups. Although hagfish have a partial skull, they have no true back bone, so technically they are invertebrates. What skeleton they do have is made of cartilage. In Korea, almost 5 million pounds of hagfish meat are consumed each year. The hagfish skin is processed into "eelskin" boots, bags, wallets, purses, and other products. Overfishing in Asia has decimated its local hagfish stocks, so the Asian hagfish fishery has focused on the shores of North America, where these "slime eels" are considered a worthless bycatch—a fish that is never a "keeper."

Another despicable Agnath is the lamprey "eel." Lampreys are primitive eel-like fish that have no jaws or paired fins and have gill pockets in place of the standard fish gills. These fish, together with the hagfishes, are frequently called *cyclostomes*, meaning animals with round mouths. Most of the lampreys are parasitic, attaching themselves to other fish and aquatic animals. They also feed, to a certain extent, on dead organic material. Some species of lamprey have caused significant problems in recent times—particularly the sea lamprey. Sea lampreys are predaceous fish that don't know when to stop. They latch onto a host using their dagger-like teeth and then suck out the host's bodily fluids, usually leaving the host dead or dying. Sea lampreys fall into two groups: anadromous (which can live in both salt and freshwater) and the freshwater lamprey, which is limited to rivers and freshwater lakes.

Ocean Alert

The sea lamprey is an invading non-native species that has had a serious negative impact on fish communities, fisheries, and fishery management in the St. Lawrence River and the Great Lakes of North America. Sea lampreys are native to the Atlantic Ocean and probably entered the Great Lakes by way of the Hudson River and the man-made Erie Canal, which was opened to Lake Ontario in 1819. The fishery declines related to the invasion of sea lamprey were best documented in Lake Superior, where lake trout production held at 1.8 million kilograms from 1930 to 1952. In the following decade, with the lamprey present, production dropped 90 percent, whereas the number of sea lampreys caught in a fixed number of assessment weirs rose from 1,000 to 70,000!

The Original Jaws

When real fish started showing up in the oceans, it became obvious that ostracoderms were destined for extinction. They couldn't possibly compete with the placoderms (pronounced *PLAK-oh-durms*)—primitive, armored sharks with real jaws and paired pectoral and pelvic fins (for improved balance and mobility). The placoderms' real jaws allowed them to eat more than the filter-feeding ostracoderms, enabling them to grow faster and larger. Their paired fins improved their swimming and mobility, making them very capable hunters. In many placoderms, a strong armor of rigid and fused bony plates covered the head and front part of the body. One species of placoderms, antiarchi, even had external bone-covered "arms." Placoderms were typically small but some, such as the dunkleosteus and dinichthyids, were massive and most likely vicious.

Although the placoderms first appeared during the early Silurian period, they did not become common or widespread until the Devonian period when they experienced massive evolutionary modification and *radiation*. They soon came to dominate most brackish and near-shore ecosystems and spread to marine and freshwater environments, as well. Fossil records identify more than 250 genera of placoderms, making them the most diverse and important of early marine vertebrates.

Placoderms were armor-plated sharks with advanced fins.

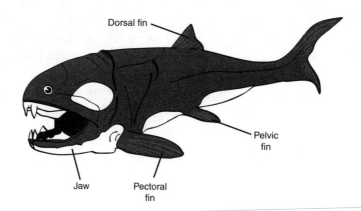

Dorsal fin

Pelvic fin

Jaw

Pectoral fin

Placoderms were not the only fish in the sea that had jaws and fins. At about the same time, another group of fish were competing for pool time and for their place in evolutionary history—the acanthodians (pronounced *AK-anth-oh-dee-uns*). These fish were actually more fish-like than the placoderms, possessing both a jaw and fins, but trading in their large bony plates for smaller, lighter scales. The acanthodians also took on a more fish-like, tapered form and had large eyes positioned toward the front of their faces.

Log Entry

The term **radiation** refers to the spreading of organisms into different locations and habitats. When an organism populates a habitat that later becomes isolated, that population begins to follow its own course of evolution and *diverges* to create a separate species.

Late in the Devonian period, an apocalyptic event occurred that wiped out nearly 75 percent of all marine life. Some scientists theorize that a large meteor struck the earth, but not all scientists agree. Whatever the cause, the earth apparently cooled down considerably and sea levels dropped, killing off most ocean life. Placoderms were some of the few to survive the crisis, but between the Devonian and Carboniferous periods, even the placoderms died out, leaving no direct descendents. The acanthodians outlived the placoderms through to the Permian period and are the likely early ancestors of today's bony fish.

Fish Out of Water

Near the end of the Devonian period, the earth became a fairly dry place. Sea levels were sinking and rivers and lakes were drying up, making it tough for fish to make a living. Gills, fins, and a tail, will get you only so far on land. To make a living as a land-dwelling vertebrate, you need lungs and a good pair of legs. Well, current theory has it that some ancient fish had the bare essentials to survive at least a brief time on land; they had lungs and stiff, rounded fins that acted like flippers. Scientists have identified three possible candidates as having the necessary equipment to crawl up on shore—and all of them are lobe-finned fish (*Sarcopterygii*): the lungfish, the now extinct rhipidistian (pronounced *RIP-i-dis-tee-un*), and the coelacanth (pronounced *SEE-la-kanth*).

Coelacanth: The Walking Fish?

The coelacanth stole the show when a specimen was discovered in 1938 in the net of an African fisherman. (Coelacanths were thought to be extinct for 70 million years.) When scientists saw an actual coelacanth, they tripped over each other trying to be the first to name the link connecting the fish to the first amphibians—a coelacanth looks like a fish that could walk. One small detail was lacking, however—nobody has witnessed a coelacanth walking, even underwater.

Even if the coelacanth cannot (or does not) walk, it has additional characteristics that qualify it as a possible link to the first land vertebrates. The coelacanth is quite different from all other living fishes in that it has an extra lobe on its tail, paired lobed fins, and a fully functional *intercranial joint*—a division that separates the ear and brain from the nasal organs and eye. This enables the coelacanth to lift the front part of its head to feed. Another interesting characteristic of the coelacanth is that it has paired fins, which move in a similar fashion to arms and legs.

> **Underwater Eye**
>
> According to a report in the June 1988 edition of *National Geographic*, Hans Fricke and a team of researchers filmed coelacanths in their native habitat hoping to catch them dancing (or at least walking) around on the ocean floor. They did catch the fish doing headstands, but had to confess that they had not witnessed any walking.

Lungfish Landing

Another candidate considered to be a possible link between marine and terrestrial vertebrates is the lungfish. It's not the lungfish's fins that make it a candidate but rather its lungs, which enable it to breathe out of water. Where did it get these lungs? Most fish have air sacs that help buoy the fish in the water. Over millions of years, these sacs developed into full-functioning lungs in some fishes. The lungfish is a living relic of some of the first vertebrates to develop lungs. However, the evolution of lungs does not prove beyond a doubt that the lungfish is the link between sea and land vertebrates.

The Rhipidistian Revolution

Once the coelacanth was proven to be less than the ideal candidate as the missing link, paleontologists turned their attention to another group of fishes, the extinct rhipidistian. Some lineages of rhipidistian fishes are anatomically more closely related to tetrapods than either the lungfish or the coelacanth. Paleontologists who pick rhipidistian as the likely link from water to land vertebrates site the following similarities between this fish and its more advanced amphibian descendents: The pattern of bones in rhipidistian's skull is similar to the pattern in the amphibian skull; rhipidistian's have labyrinthodont teeth (enamel and dentine appear folded in) like amphibians; and the complex bone structure in rhipidistian's fleshy fins give the fins a foot-like structure similar to amphibian feet.

Rubber-Boned Chondrichthyes

As various species of fish were specializing and diversifying, one group diverged to test a different kind of skeleton, using the softer, more flexible cartilage rather than brittle bone. This was an unfortunate choice of building material for paleontologists because soft stuff such as cartilage doesn't leave behind a very clear fossil record; but for the fish themselves, cartilage proved to be a winning alternative. It's sort of like that new space-age metal that enables you to twist your glasses into the shape of a pretzel and have them bounce back to their original form. The fish who tested this innovative new material included sharks, skates, and rays, and as a group they earned the clever label Chondrichthyes (pronounced *khan-DRIK-thees*), or "cartilaginous fish."

Making their debut on Earth almost 450 million years ago, cartilaginous fish today include the largest ocean fish (the whale shark), some stretching to over 15 meters long, as well as many tiny species that grow barely as long as a pencil. Worldwide, more than 450 species of sharks and 400 to 500 species of rays cruise the ocean waters. The numbers keep changing as marine biologists and oceanographers continue to identify new specimens with subtle differences. Various oddities make up the balance of this group, including guitarfish, ratfish, and elephant fish. The 950 to 1,100 or so species of cartilaginous fish primarily inhabit the marine realm, but a few have ventured into freshwater rivers and lakes.

Characteristically Chondrichthyan

In addition to a cartilaginous skeleton, chondricthyes share a number of uniquely chondrichthyan characteristics. Most chondrichthyes are gray and have five gill slits, typically located right behind the head. Most species lack a swim bladder like those that other fish use to control their buoyancy, so they must swim continuously to keep from sinking. Males have reproductive appendages called *claspers* near the inner margins of their pelvic fins. To mate with a female (and hold on to her while mating), the male shark inserts one of the claspers into the female and inseminates the female. Fertilization of eggs is always internal.

Chondrichthyan skin is covered with tooth-like scales, called *placoid scales*, which take the form of spines in some species, such as the rays. Placoid scales (also called *dermal denticles*) are pointed like tiny teeth, with the points all facing the same direction, toward the tail. So if you pet a chondrichthyan from head to tail, the skin feels smooth, but rub your hand from tail to head and the skin feels like sandpaper. Unlike the scales on most fish, placoid scales do not become larger as the animal grows. Unlike the teeth of most vertebrates, which are locked into sockets in the jaw bones, most chondrichthyan teeth are attached to the jaw with fleshy tissue. Many species have rows of teeth that continue to be replaced—some as many as tens of thousands of teeth in a lifetime.

One class of chondrichthyes, the holocephali, has an upper jaw that is completely fused to the braincase and enamel-free grinding plates instead of teeth. They generally lack a true stomach and bottom feed on small items. This class includes the *chimaera*—ghost sharks, ratfish, and elephant fish. About 30 to 35 species lurk in the deep, cold waters. As their common names imply, these species hardly pass as conventional fish.

Underwater Eye
In Greek mythology, the Chimaera (or Chimera) was a fearsome fire-breathing monster having a lion's head, a she-goat's body, and a serpent's tail. It was killed by the hero Bellerephon riding on the winged horse, Pegasus.

The cartilaginous fish you are most likely to see are elasmobranchs (pronounced *i-LAZ-mu-brangk*), including all the sharks, skates, and rays. Each fish in this class has five or more gill slits on each side of its head, often a pair of openings called *spiracles* on the top of the head, and an asymmetrical tail fin (known in the industry as a *heterocercal* or caudal fin). You will meet several members of this class as you proceed through this chapter.

Sensory Overload

Like most vertebrates, chondricthyes have the standard five senses—sight, smell, touch, hearing, and taste. Although their sense of sight is not the greatest, chondricthyes have two additional sensory systems to help them compensate. The first is the lateral line system of navigation, which is explained in the section "Eyes Not Included" in Chapter 5. Along the left and right side of the fish, buried under the skin, is a lateral line or canal that contains a series of sensory organs. Tiny tubes lead from this canal to pores on the surface of the skin. This system enables the fish to pick up on vibrations in the water and changes in water pressure caused by the fish's movement in relation to objects and other fish.

Chondricthyes can also sense weak electrical signals using a system called the *ampullae of Lorenzini*. Sharks and rays have electrical receptors located near their snouts that open to facial pores. Whenever a fish or other animal moves in close proximity to the face of a shark or ray, the shark or ray can detect the very weak electrical signals emitted by the animal's muscle movements. This is useful especially when a shark attacks, because sharks typically roll their eyes back or close them tight when they initiate an attack to protect their eyes. Using the ampullae of Lorenzini, the shark can still "see" its prey during the attack.

The ampullae of Lorenzini are specialized jelly-filled organs that enable sharks and rays to detect electric impulses given off by the muscle contractions of prey.

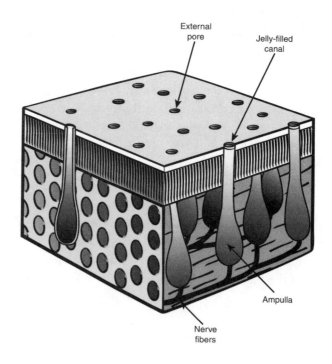

External pore

Jelly-filled canal

Ampulla

Nerve fibers

The Mating Game

Unlike bony fish, such as tuna and salmon that spawn and lay eggs, most sharks rely on internal fertilization and give birth to a litter of offspring, typically numbering far fewer than 100. To mate, the male inserts one of its claspers into the female to fertilize the eggs. Although rarely observed, mating typically occurs on the ocean floor, with the female lying on her back, but occasionally (as with the great white), the sharks mate side-by-side near the surface. Which clasper the male uses depends on his relative position to the female.

Mother shark typically carries the fertilized eggs for six or more months until they develop into fully-formed sharks, at which time she swims to calm, shallow waters to get away from the male sharks, and gives birth. Some sharks, such as the dogfish, carry their young for up to two years and can give birth to "babies" that are as long as 1 meter (3 feet)!

Although most sharks are ovoviviparous (bearing live young), about one third are oviparous, such as the bony fish, laying eggs that later hatch into baby sharks.

Underwater Eye

In January 2002, at the Henry Doorly Zoo in Omaha, Nebraska, a bonnethead shark gave birth to a baby shark even though the mother hadn't been in a tank with another male of the species for more than three years. Scientists are still investigating this case, but they have two guesses as to how this could have happened. The first is that the female was inseminated before entering the tank and carried the sperm for more than three years. The second, more fascinating, guess is that the female shark was able to reproduce asexually (without mating)!

Who's the Baddest Shark in Town?

Sharks are notorious for being the bad boys of the seas, chomping on surfers, attacking divers, and terrorizing the beaches. Although sharks deserve some of this bad press, the horror stories are greatly exaggerated. In addition, people deserve some of the blame for shark attacks. Nearly all shark attacks are precipitated by people who encroach on shark territory or make dumb decisions, such as feeding sharks, knowingly surfing in shark-infested waters, and even tugging on a shark's tail. In many cases, sharks attack because they're confused—when a diver puts on a wetsuit that makes him look like a delicious seal, you can hardly blame a shark for attacking. Of course, some sharks are menacing predators. They're designed to hunt down food, grab it, shred it, and swallow it. They've been doing it for millions of years.

Any discussion of shark attacks inevitably leads to the question of which shark is the most dangerous: Which shark is the biggest, baddest shark, the one shark you don't want to cross? Of the 40 or so documented species implicated in shark attacks, about 10 species account for most attacks, and only the top three are particularly notorious for unprovoked attacks. Here is the list of the top 10 sharks to avoid:

- **Great white**   By far the shark with the worst official record, the great white is responsible for more reported shark attacks and deaths than any other shark on the list (according to records at the International Shark File at the Florida Museum of Natural History). Although the great white is responsible for the major percentage of shark attacks, its kill rate (percentage of fatalities per attack) is comparatively low at 26 percent.

- **Tiger**   Running a distant second in number of shark attacks and deaths, the tiger shark has a higher kill rate than the great white; that is, a higher percentage of attacks result in fatalities. The tiger sharks kill rate is 35 percent.

- **Bull**   Considered by many to be the meanest, most ornery shark, the bull shark is responsible for nearly the same number of attacks as the tiger shark, but its kill rate is only about 17 percent. Two factors make the bull shark a contender for top billing as the baddest shark—it tolerates brackish water, often finding its way into estuaries and rivers, and it's just plain mean. The bull shark has a higher concentration of testosterone in its blood than any other shark, giving it a short, raging temper. This shark has been known to attack boats—and that's no Hollywood hype.

- **Sand tiger or grey nurse**   Relatively disinterested in humans, the sand tiger is not particularly aggressive, but it is big, and it has sharp teeth, which are reasons enough to avoid it.

- **Requiem (unspecified)**   Requiem sharks include the great white, bull, and sand tiger. Some requiem sharks other than the sharks already covered in this list are responsible for a fair number of attacks.

- **Shortfin mako**   Primarily dangerous to humans due to the fact that humans like to fish for these sharks; shortfin mako put up a good fight and are known to jump out of the water like marlin. However, shortfin mako are pelagic, so you needn't worry too much about them when you're at the beach.

- **Great hammerhead**   Not considered particularly aggressive, the great hammerhead is considered dangerous primarily because of its size and its voracious appetite.

- **Blue**   This long, slender shark is considered a potential threat to humans, but does not actively pursue human flesh.

◆ **Nurse**   Considered a fairly gentle shark, the nurse shark poses a danger to humans only because of its size and the fact that when it latches onto a person, it doesn't let go. Attacks from nurse sharks have increased over the years, mostly because their populations are on the rise.

◆ **Wobbegong**   Also known as carpet sharks, these pudgy, toad-faced, moss-skinned bad boys like to lie on the bottom, where they stay fairly well camouflaged, and that's what causes problems. Divers and swimmers commonly don't notice the wobbegong and end up kicking it or stepping on it. When that happens, these sharks do what any respectable sharks would do—they bite. And like the nurse shark, when the wobbegong bites, it doesn't let go.

Captain Clam's Comments

Statistics show that more people are killed each year by dogs than have been killed in more than 100 years by great white sharks. In fact, bees are responsible for far more attacks and human fatalities per year than all sharks combined. In contrast, if the sharks posted a list of the top 10 most dangerous shark predators, we humans would have no trouble securing the top spot.

Breaking Free of the Stereotypes

Great white, tiger, and bull sharks steal the spotlight and often leave people with a stereotypical image of sharks. When someone says the word "shark," most people picture the long, missile-shaped fish with the menacing, toothy grin. However, the shark family is very diverse and contains some very gentle species, including the largest fish in the world, the plankton-eating whale shark. The whale shark, which could easily swallow a person whole, prefers to pick on the little guys. It swims around with its mouth open to scoop up and filter out plankton.

Other fascinating species include the ornamentally striking wobbegong, mentioned in the previous section; the eel-like frilled shark of the abyss; the goblin shark, whose long snout makes it look like a cross between a shark and a swordfish; the sawshark, which has a long, toothy snout like that of the sawfish; and the harmless, slender bamboo shark, which is primarily a bottom-feeder. These sharks, along with many others, are mild and beautiful creatures that pose no threat to humans.

Winging It with the Rays

Rays are those weird-looking, flat fish that look like floppy stealth bombers. Like sharks, rays are elasmobranchs, but from looking at them, you would never guess that they were members of the same family. The most obvious difference is that the ray's pectoral fins have been stretched out to form wings, one on each side of its "head." Because of this arrangement, their gills end up being in front of and below the wings. In many bottom-dwelling species, the ray takes in water through the spiracles at the top of its head rather than through its mouth, because the mouth is on the bottom or ventral side along with the gills. The 400 to 500 species of rays differ from each other in various configurations and alterations of tail and dorsal fins, body shape, jaw structure, and other features. The following sections explore the more intriguing adaptations by examining a few fascinating species of rays.

The Stingers

The aptly named stingray has an infamous defense mechanism—a tail that it can whip up at the slightest sign of danger to inflict a painful sting to its victim. As long as a stingray is swimming around, it's not dangerous. You can even pet the slimy swimmers as they swim past. However, when a stingray is lying on the bottom, any pressure from above triggers the tail to whip up against whatever, or whoever, is applying that pressure. Unlike a bee sting, which leaves a stinger in the victim, the sting from a stingray is more like a puncture wound. A barb at the base of the tail inflicts the wound and leaves behind no stinger. This serrated spine has venom-secreting tissue in its underside and can inflict a serious wound. The stingray's venom consists of proteins that can cause respiratory complications, which can be fatal, even to humans.

Ocean Alert _____

Most stingrays are generally considered to pose no threat to humans, but if you step on one and it manages to swat you just right, you're going to be in a world of hurt. To prevent stings, shuffle your feet when you walk in the water. If you kick a ray, you'll be okay; you just don't want to step on one. If you do get stung, seek medical attention immediately.

The Zingers

Electric rays and a number of other fish, including the electric eel, can produce electric charges from specialized organs. almost 70 species of electric rays can regulate their electrical discharges depending on the situation. Low voltage pulses can ward off many predators, whereas high-voltage bursts can stun prey and even jolt a human into unconsciousness, which could result in drowning.

Electric rays are found in various oceans. The torpedo ray, *Torpedo californica*, of the Pacific Ocean, can stun its prey by administering a shock from a pair of electric organs. These modified muscle tissues are designed to deliver a concentration of electrical voltage ranging from low to fairly substantial (over 200 volts in some species). The electric organs can direct the discharge in either of two directions: to below the fish to stun prey or through the back of the fish to make predators back off. Torpedo rays typically hang out in deeper water, so you're not likely to step on one at the beach; even divers rarely catch a glimpse of a torpedo ray.

The Real Humdingers

The devil rays, commonly known as mantas, are the largest of the rays and are anything but "devils"—devil rays are actually gentle vegetarians. An adult manta can weigh up to 1,350 kilograms (3,000 pounds) and have a wingspan of more than 7 meters (23 feet). Mantas are known to leap from the water, sometimes even performing somersaults, and then falling back to the surface, making a big splash. Some marine biologists theorize that the mantas splash around to remove irritating parasites, but others think the mantas are just having a little fun. Whatever the reason, when a 1,350-kilogram flying saucer slaps down on the surface next to you, the show is well worth the ticket price.

The Least You Need to Know

- To be a vertebrate, an animal must have, at some stage in its life, pharyngeal slits (for gills), a notochord made of bone or cartilage, a hollow dorsal nerve chord, and a tail.

- The first vertebrates were fish, and the first fish were ostracoderms—armor-plated, jawless fish.

- Ostracoderms were eventually replaced by placoderms—primitive, armored sharks with real jaws and paired pectoral and pelvic fins.

- In an attempt to establish a link between water and land vertebrates, scientists examine three possible links: the coelacanth, the lungfish, and the now extinct rhipidistian.

- The Chondricthyes include the elasmobranchs (sharks, skates, and rays), as well as an odd assortment of other fish with cartilaginous skeletons.

- Although sharks have a bad reputation as being ill-tempered and vicious, most are relatively harmless creatures who attack only when provoked … or really hungry.

Chapter 14

Boning Up on the Bony Fish

In This Chapter

- ◆ Bones rule in land and sea
- ◆ Fascinating fish physiology
- ◆ Meeting some special specimens
- ◆ On the coral reef and in pet shops and aquariums

When you think about all the animals in the world—in the oceans, on land, and in the air—most larger creatures have one trait in common: Bones. And most of these creatures have real bones, hard bones, not just that rubbery cartilaginous stuff. This hard material provides superior protection for the brain and spinal column, giving bony animals a competitive edge … except, maybe, when it comes to sharks.

Fish with bones dominate the oceans, composing a group of more than 24,000 species that populate virtually every part of the world's oceans (and lakes and rivers and streams). These fish are not dominant in the sense that they're the biggest and strongest. Place a bluefin tuna and a great white shark in the same tank, and you know who's going to come out on top. However, in terms of population size and range, the bluefin wins. This chapter provides an overview of some of the members of the oceans' ruling class, and examines how their modifications have led to such tremendous species diversity.

Bony Fish Taxonomy

Historically, zoologists have grouped the bony fish in the class Osteichthyes (pronounced *aw-stee-ICK-theez*, *oste* "bony," *ichthy* "fish"). However, this class structure has proven to be inaccurate, so throughout this chapter, I refer to these fish simply as "bony fish." The bony fish consist of two groups: *Actinopterygii* (pronounced *act-i-NOP-ter-i-jee-ee*), ray-finned fishes that include most of the fish we know and love; and *Sarcopterygii* (pronounced *sahr-KO-pter-i-jee-ee*), a smaller group of lobe-finned fishes and tetrapods that includes coelacanths and lungfish.

It's worth keeping in mind that the official taxonomy guidelines are constantly in flux. Taxonomists are always trying to ensure that each name is monophyletic, meaning that the taxonomic group contains all the descendants of a common ancestor, that no unrelated species are included, and no descendants are left out. This means that the discovery of just one new species may be enough to cause the groups to be redefined. For example, the *Actinopterygii* and the *Sarcopterygii* were formerly referred to collectively as Osteichthyes, but this name was eliminated when it became clear that it was not a monophyletic group.

Not Just Skin and Bones

The previous chapter introduced the jawed placoderms. The ancestral fish that gave rise to placoderms also gave rise to cartilaginous fish and bony fish. The cartilaginous fish (primarily sharks and rays) consist of a small family of about 1,000 species. The bony fish, on the other hand, are comprised of nearly 24,000 species! The ray-finned fish, *Actinopterygii*, can be divided into *Neopterygii* and *Chondrostei* (sturgeons and paddlefish). Finally, *Neopterygii* includes *Teleostei* and two other groups. Most of the fish covered in this chapter are part of *Teleostei*, commonly referred to as *teleosts*.

These fish exhibit a number of special modifications and adaptations that have given them the competitive edge they needed to achieve their dominant status. The following sections explore these adaptations in greater detail.

Made to Move

Unlike the lumbering sharks and whales, bony fish are made to move quickly and efficiently through the water. Most fish exhibit a fusiform (missile-like) shape that's tapered in the front to shoot through the water. They also possess a large, streamlined tailfin, called the *homocercal caudal* (pronounced *HO-mow-SER-KAW-dull*) fin, that has a symmetrically crescent shape. To further increase their speed, these later fish developed a lighter, coating of scales that creates less drag than the teeth-like dermal denticles characteristic of the *Chondrichthyes*. These new and improved fish also secrete a glandular slime that covers their bodies to reduce drag even further. Inside, the fish's flexible, bony skeleton gives them the agility they need to change direction quickly.

One of the major improvements in the design of the bony fish is the air-filled swim bladder that makes the fish more buoyant. Think of the swim bladder as a pair of water wings for fish. The swim bladder helps the fish conserve energy, because the fish doesn't need to swim constantly to stay afloat, as does its cousin, the shark. The fish can regulate the amount of air in the swim bladder to remain at the desired depth.

In addition to these design innovations, the ray-finned fish also have fin adaptations that make them much more agile. The fins actually consist of a thin membrane stretched over fanlike spines. A ray-finned fish can move each fin independently, using them as paddles or as tiny rudders to move quickly up, down, forward, or back, or even to tilt their bodies as they swim. In addition, the fish can use the spines in its fins as weapons against predators. Freshwater catfish are especially infamous for jabbing careless fishermen with their spike-like fins.

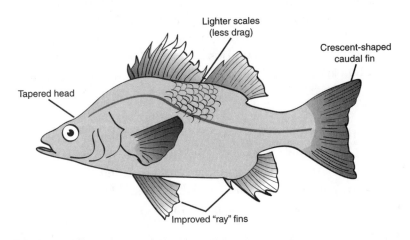

Lighter scales
(less drag)

Crescent-shaped
caudal fin

Tapered head

Improved "ray" fins

Bony fish, especially the ray-finned fish, are built to swim.

Captain Clam's Comments

Tuna are perhaps the most thoroughly evolved open-ocean cruising fish. Their bodies are sleek, compact, muscular rockets. Their tails are designed for rapid movement—consisting of a lunate (crescent-shaped) caudal fin and a thin caudal peduncle (which attaches the tail to the body). The body surface of the tuna includes recessed areas where the fish can tuck in its fins to reduce drag. Even the tuna's eyes are recessed into the sides of its head. Extra finlets, on the top and bottom directly in front of the peduncle, function to reduce turbulence created by water flowing over the fish's body.

Pumped-Up Gills

You can be the fastest creature on the planet, but if you lose your breath, you're not going anywhere. To complement their improved equipment for moving through the water, these fish also have improved gills. Most ray-finned fish have a gill cavity typically containing four gill arches covered by thin membranes. Covering the gills on each side of the head is a layer of skin called the operculum. This gill design is far superior to the gill design of Chondricthyes, and results in a much less bulky gill. To draw water over the gills, some fish, such as the tuna, use a ram ventilation system, which consists of swimming through the water with their mouths open. If they stop swimming, they quickly lose oxygen and die. Other fish can open and close their gill covers to draw water in through their mouths and over the gills to pump out the water, creating a more uniform flow of water and enabling them to breathe when at rest.

Improved Jaws

When studying the evolution of fish, always keep in mind that fish are primarily carnivorous predators. You won't find most fish bellying up to the salad bar to chow down on a bowlful of seaweed. They prefer seafood, usually in the form of other fish. So, to make it as a fish and to endure the travails of survival of the fittest, every successful predator needs a good pair of jaws. The rapid rise of the bony fish can be attributed, at least partially, to the development and diversification of its jaw muscles and structure.

Today's fish exhibit a wide variety of adaptations in their jaws for exploiting diverse food sources. The parrotfish, for example, seems to have evolved its strong beak-like jaw and teeth mainly for the purpose of grinding up pieces of coral. Parrotfish use their specialized mouths to peck algae off the surface of the reef and frequently bite off chunks of coral to chow down on the coral polyps themselves.

Underwater Eye

Marine ecologists originally thought that parrotfish were destroying the reef by chipping away at it with their beaver-like teeth, but studies have shown that when parrotfish are prevented from feeding on the reef, the coral is suffocated by the unchecked growth of algal mats. Parrotfish have molar-like teeth in their throats that chew up coral so that stomach acid can digest the algae found in and around the coral. The ground-up coral is then released as sand, helping to create the sandy bottom and white beaches associated with coral reef ecosystems.

Unlike the parrotfish with its coral-crushing beak, most fish have normal jaws complete with teeth. Variations in the size of the jaws and the size of the teeth are the distinguishing factors. Many fish, for example, have big jaws with a lot of tiny teeth that make them look relatively harmless, but don't let the reduced dentition fool you. Bluefish in a feeding frenzy can chop other smaller bluefish in half. They have large, well-developed jaws equipped with extremely strong muscles that give the bluefish an incredibly vicious bite. Other fish, such as the wolf eel, have normal sized jaws with conspicuously large teeth—the better to eat hard-shelled treats such as clams and crabs, which the wolf eel crushes with ease.

Some fish have teeth and jaws that are completely out of proportion with the rest of their bodies. Remember from Chapter 4 that some of the deepwater fish have mouths large enough to swallow larger fish whole! The gulper eel, for example, engulfs its prey in its huge, pelican-like mouth. Usually the gulper eel eats small, slow fishes and shrimp, but it can unhinge its enormous jaws and stretch its stomach to consume a fish as large as itself.

New and Improved Sensory Tools

The sharks and rays you encountered in the previous chapter rely primarily on a keen sense of smell and hearing as well as a decent sense of sight to navigate the waters and hunt for prey. They also use the lateral line system of navigation, which functions as underwater radar, enabling the shark to sense variations in water pressure. In addition, sharks have electro-receptive sensors called ampullae of Lorenzini that they can use to sense the weak electrical pulses generated by nearby fish.

Like the cartilaginous fish, the bony fish have an exceptional sense of smell and hearing and use the lateral line system of navigation to pick up vibrations or sounds in the water. However, bony fish also have a well-developed sense of sight. In most fish, the eyes are set apart, one on each side of the head, and the eyes are well developed to enable the fish to find and hunt down prospective prey.

Assorted Shapes and Sizes

As explained earlier, the standard and typically dominant fish shape is the fusiform—the torpedo or missile shape that enables quick fish, such as the tuna and mackerel, to fly through the water with ease. However, not all shapes are the best for all lifestyles. Fusiform is perfect shape for tuna, which frequently make transoceanic treks, but for a fish that plans to spend its life on the bottom, such as a flounder, the fusiform shape would be a death warrant. In addition, many fish, such as the sargassum fish, rely on a strange, irregular shaped body to blend in with their surroundings. The following sections explore some of the more interesting and successful fish shapes.

Not Quite Fish Shaped

For fish that hang out in the weeds eating plankton, being able to maintain a fixed position and blend in with the background are essential skills. One fish that specializes in hovering in position and blending in is the seahorse and related species, such as the pipefish. These fish are perfectly adapted for clinging onto aquatic vegetation with their prehensile tails as they eat tiny plankton with their tube-like snouts. They perform movements not unlike a helicopter and hover in place with the aid of dorsal fins for propulsion, ear-like pectoral fins for stabilization and steering, and a small anal fin. Because they need to go nowhere fast, they have relinquished the large caudal (tail) fin and the pelvic fins (for balance).

Another oddity is the ocean sunfish, or mola mola, which is the world's largest known bony fish. These fish have been estimated to weigh up to a ton and a half and span 11 feet from fin tip to fin tip. They hardly resemble any other fish and look more like a fish head with wings, which is why they are commonly called headfish. Ocean sunfish lack any tail fin and have a modified structure called a clavus, which connects and extends the dorsal and anal fins. They seem to work more on the principle of a manta ray, with their flattened body and strangely paired fins stuck towards the rear of the fish. Ocean sunfish are usually open ocean species that are often seen at the surface where they might be mistaken for sharks, because of the large dorsal fin. These fish have earned the name sunfish, because they commonly lie on their sides on the surface of wide open waters to work on their tans.

Flatfish Floozy with a Floy-Floy

Speaking of fish that resemble door mats, the flatfishes certainly fit the bill and are often called that name by anglers who land a big one. (You should have seen the door mat that got away!) Flatfish include flounder, halibut, fluke, sole, and tonquefish. A flat fish starts off looking normal enough but early in its life, it begins to swim on its side. Then one eye migrates from one side of the head to the other side, which then becomes the top of the head. In some species, the eyes always end up on the left side of the head; in other species, the left eye migrates to the right side of the head; in other species, the eyes have no preference for which side of the head they land. The largest of the flatfish are the Atlantic halibut. They can weigh more than 600 pounds, making them a valuable catch in what is a major fishery. Flatfish are configured for bottom feeding and are often camouflaged to blend in with the sea floor. Certain flatfish can alter their skin color and even match patterns to perfect their camouflage.

Almost all fish contain some mercury in the form of methyl mercury, which can cause neurological problems in humans, especially in developing fetuses. Large predatory fish (including shark, swordfish, king mackerel, and tilefish) can build up high levels of methyl mercury in their bodies, but tuna have been shown to have significant mercury concentrations as well. To avoid risks, the FDA recommends that pregnant women avoid eating shark, swordfish, king mackerel, and tilefish and eat limited amounts of fresh tuna fish. Canned tuna is safer because it is made from smaller tuna fish.

Marlin, Swordfish, and Other Beaky Freaks

Some of the strangest and most strikingly beautiful ocean fish are the billfish, which include the marlin, swordfish, spearfish, and sailfish. All have long modified rostrums (snout-like projections) in the shape of formidable lances. A typical swordfish snout, which is actually an extension of its upper jaw, can account for a third of its body length. This stiff snout serves as a deadly weapon for the billfish. The billfish stalks its prey in a wide range of ocean depths, including the deep, cold, poorly lit regions of the open ocean, where it hangs motionless in chilly water waiting for unsuspecting prey. It then darts out and impales its prey to create its own sushi shish kebab.

To maintain mental and visual acuity, the billfishes (and some mackerel sharks) have an organ that warms their brains and eyes, enabling them to hunt in very cold waters. The process is called *regional endothermy*, which means that only a specific area is capable of maintaining temperatures above that of the surrounding water. In swordfish, and other billfish, their huge eyes possess a specialized ocular heater mechanism—a modified muscle that generates heat. The cells that make up this tissue contain the greatest amount of *mitochondrial mass* of any cell in the animal kingdom. At higher ocular temperatures, vision typically becomes keener; and for these fish, keen vision is essential for catching prey. Unlike other fish that can regulate temperature, the billfish can increase the temperature of only its brain and eyes.

Log Entry

The term **mitochondrial mass** refers to the material in a cell that controls the genetic code and enzymes required for cell division and for maintaining a cell's metabolism. Mitochondria helps a cell convert food into energy.

The Amazing Technicolor Reef Fish

The fish we examined so far in the previous chapter and in this chapter wear some fairly drab colors. Sharks and rays are typically gray or brown on top and white on the bottom. Tuna dress up a little with shimmering silver and pale blues, yellows, and greens. The flatfish try to blend in with the mud and sand by wearing splotchy browns, blacks, and grays. Even the billfish appear formal, wearing their dark blue suits.

When you visit a coral reef, however, it looks as though the ocean inhabitants decided to celebrate Mardi Gras; the reef's crystal clear waters are bursting with explosions of colors. Only in the reef will you find a fish as boldly red as a squirrelfish, as brightly yellow as a longnose butterflyfish, or as pretty in pink as the fairy basslet. Reef fish come in all shapes and sizes as well—from the slender angelfish to the chubby spiked porcupinefish that can blow itself up into the shape of a pincushion, complete with pins! On the reef, there's no excuse for not being able to eke out a living, and there is no limit to the innovative adaptations creatures use to exploit the reef's resources.

> **Underwater Eye**
>
> Eighteen percent of all identified fish species (an estimated 4,000 species) make the reef their home.

Choosing What to Wear

Most reef fish wear vibrant colors that help them blend in with their surroundings, confuse their predators, sneak up on their prey, warn potential enemies of their deadly weapons, or make themselves look much more menacing than they really are. The surgeonfish, for example, has two bright orange spots near the base of its tail that advertise the presence of razor sharp spines. The bright coloration of some fish functions as a more positive advertising tool. The dazzling colors of the cleanerfish, for example, announce to its customers that it is open for business—ready to pick the parasites and other nasty stuff off its client's skin. Some fish exhibit a technique called aggressive mimicry to match the coloration and even the movement of beneficial fish, such as the cleanerfish, in order to attract and then attack their prey. The saber toothed blenny, for example, is as brightly colored as the cleanerfish and has even learned how to dance around like a cleanerfish. When a larger fish drops by for its free cleaning, the saber-toothed blenny chomps a chunk of flesh out of the fish and takes off.

Of course, bright colors do not always stand out. When a red squirrelfish is swimming near a rock covered with red algae, the fish blends in with the backdrop. Many reef fish also exhibit a camouflage design known as *disruptive coloration* that uses patterns and lines to break up the outline of the fish and help it blend in with the background. Many of the more brightly colored reef fish, such as the butterflyfish have their colors arranged in vertical bands, such as black and white zebra stripes. Against a backdrop of bright, branching coral, the stripe pattern helps the fish blend in. Many fish also use countershading to help them "disappear." Countershaded fish are typically dark on top and light on the bottom. When seen from above, they seem to disappear by blending in with the darker, deeper water. From below, the light belly blends in with the brighter, sunlit surface waters. Countershading is more common in the open ocean than it is on the reef, but some reef fish do make use of it.

Captain Clam's Comments

Some color selections seem illogical, but when you examine the possible function of the color, it makes perfect sense. Red, for instance, seems a poor option for a fish that's trying to keep a low profile and hide from predators, but many red fish hang out in deep water where red light does not penetrate, making the fish look a dull gray. Some brightly colored fish are also active only at night, when brilliant colors don't call attention to the fish.

Clowning Around with Darts

Some of the most dazzling, comical looking fish on the reef are the anemonefish, best represented by the clownfish. Most anemonefish have a distinct pattern of bright orange and white (or red and white) stripes that help them blend in with the coral and with the anemones in which they live. That's right: The anemonefish chooses to live right inside a waving mass of poison-dart–packed anemone tentacles.

Anemonefish can safely brush up against the anemone's poisonous tentacles.

(Photo Credit: Mr. Mohammed Al Momany, Aqaba, Jordan)

The anemone's tentacles are capable of killing most fish that swim too close, but the anemonefish can brush up against the tentacles without harm, apparently immune to the anemone's poison darts. Some scientists theorize that the anemonefish might be coated with a special mucous that protects it from the nematocysts that lay within the anemone's tentacles. The anemone protects the anemonefish from most predators, who know not to go near the anemone's tentacles. The anemonefish helps the anemone by cleaning it of any detritus that settles on it and perhaps by scaring away predators of the anemone.

You can find anemonefish in most tropical waters, except in the Caribbean. Even with anemones as their body guards, anemonefish are still preyed upon by other reef fish and are becoming scarce in some areas.

A Prize for Wildest Design

If you sponsored a contest for the reef fish with the most dazzling colors and bizarre design, the competition would be pretty stiff. Swimming down the runway would be the buck-toothed parrotfish and heart shape angelfish wearing flamboyant colors that would make die-hard hippies blush. Perhaps you would vote for the queen angelfish with the blue lipstick or the bright orange yellowtail wrasse. My vote for wildest design and coloration would definitely go to the lionfish—a creature that wears a lion's mane of spiked pectoral fins, a branched dorsal fin and brightly striped body. They can grow up to 17 inches long, and they have maroon bodies with vertical white stripes. So many attachments are hanging off this fish that it is impossible to tell where the spikes end and the body begins or even how big its body really is. The eye-catching coloration is there for a reason as well. It warns potential enemies that the lionfish's grooved spines are laced with potent venom, which can inflict serious, perhaps fatal wounds, even to humans.

Lionfish are usually found in depths of at least 80 feet and in waters warmer than 25.55 degrees Celsius (78 degrees Fahrenheit) and are native to the Indo-Pacific. Lately, however, lionfish have been turning up in the Caribbean and Florida. The lionfish thus joins the ranks of invasive species whose better-known and widely despised members include the Asian eels and the snakehead. Ecologists believe that someone introduced the fish to these areas by releasing their aquarium fish; they don't think that the lionfish migrated to the Caribbean naturally. Warnings have gone out to swimmers and divers to be alert to the presence of this toxic fish, but as far as the lionfish is concerned, its body language does a sufficient job of issuing warnings.

The lionfish's body tells predators to back off.

(Photo Credit: Mr. Mohammed Al Momany, Aqaba, Jordan)

The Grimacing Barracuda

In terms of color and design, the barracuda is a fairly dull member of the reef community. However, its long, tapered body, massive jaws, and menacing grimace make it a dazzling fish, all the same. Barracudas are the quintessential torpedoes, with a streamlined body that can grow to 6 feet in length. The barracuda uses its sleek physique to race through the water after schools of helpless fish with its blade like teeth. After it injures and immobilizes some of the fish, the barracuda returns to gobble them up.

Despite its threatening appearance, which clearly represents its place as a top predatory fish, barracuda rarely attack humans. They typically attack only in turbid water in which visibility is low and whenever a swimmer or diver is wearing or carrying something shiny. Most divers and swimmers are usually cautious enough to stay out of harm's way, which, in the case of barracudas, can actually be quite close.

CAUTION

Ocean Alert

The main threat to humans posed by barracuda comes in the form of barracuda meat, some of which can contain toxic ciguatera, a toxin produced by some dinoflagellates (algae species) similar to the ones that cause paralytic shellfish poisoning. Marine finfish most commonly implicated in ciguatera fish poisoning include groupers, barracudas, snappers, jacks, mackerel, and triggerfish. Many other species of warm-water fishes harbor ciguatera toxins as well. The occurrence of toxic fish is sporadic, and not all fish of a given species or from a given locality will be toxic.

Eighteen species of barracuda, including the great barracuda, are found throughout the tropical and subtropical waters of the Atlantic, Indian, and Pacific Oceans. Most species prefer the clear, warm waters of coral reefs, whereas other smaller species favor muddier, shallower waters. These smaller species also favor swimming in large schools for protection from predators and to find food more effectively. Larger species, such as the great barracuda, live a solitary existence.

Aquarium Checklist: Fish to Know

The most popular saltwater aquarium fish is the clownfish—most likely because of its beautiful coloration and its affinity to anemones. Other popular saltwater fish are the angelfish, royal gamma, hamlets, spotfin butterfly, yellowtail damsels, and blue tangs. The neon goby from Florida and the Caribbean is one of the most easily recognized and popular saltwater aquarium fish. This fish is a cleaner species that picks parasites and other debris from the mouth, gills, and skin of larger fish. Think of it as part fish groomer and part veterinarian. The neon goby is small, reaching about 2 inches in length, and is black with a white belly and two neon blue stripes running along its back.

People unfamiliar with saltwater aquariums should take care to find out what species are compatible. Unlike life on the reef, territorial space within a tank is limited and competition for what is available can lead to the needless loss of valuable specimens. We can tell you from experience that putting a scallop and a hermit crab in the same tank is a mistake; the poor scallop didn't have a chance.

Numerous volumes are written about the care and compatibility of saltwater fish, including *The Complete Idiot's Guide to Saltwater Aquariums* by Mike Wickham (Alpha Books, 1999).

The Least You Need to Know

- Most familiar fish are part of the *actinopterygii*, or ray-finned fishes, which derived from the same ancestral group as the *sarcopterygii*.

- Bony fish make up the largest group of living vertebrate animals, claiming territory in every part of the ocean and in rivers, streams, and lakes.

- Bony fish exhibit several improvements over cartilaginous fish, including an air-filled swim bladder, tapered body, scales, and advanced gills.

- Because of their structural complexity, coral reefs contain nearly one fifth of all the known species of fish.

- The most popular aquarium fish are generally tropical species that are found on the coral reef.

15

Marine Reptiles—the Good, the Bad, and the Ugly

In This Chapter

- ◆ Ancient reptile roots
- ◆ Rare marine turtles struggle onward
- ◆ Real live sea serpents
- ◆ The lone living sea lizard
- ◆ Estuarine crocodiles out at sea

Most modern reptiles avoid saltwater at all costs, choosing to make their livings in lakes, streams, forests, swamps, fields, under rocks, and even in the most arid desert environments. The only vertebrates who hate saltwater more than modern reptiles are the amphibians, but given the amphibian's permeable skin, you can understand why they might want to avoid salt. Even though most reptiles avoid the salty seas, a handful of reptile species (approximately 80 species in all) prefer a marine existence. Some, such as the sea turtles, live their entire lives in the oceans, crawling up on land only to lay their eggs. Others, including the marine iguana, hang out on rocks most of the time, diving down in the water primarily to feed. This chapter is devoted to these reptiles that have made a successful transition to the marine environment.

The Ancient Age of Marine Reptiles

About 250 million years ago, after the vertebrates successfully made the transition from sea to land, a line of land reptiles began to move back to the sea. Going by the name of ichthyosaurs (pronounced *ICK-thee-uh-soarz*), these "fish-lizards" were the first major group of reptiles to return to the sea. The ichthyosaurs consisted of a collection of related species with fish-shaped bodies, ranging in size from 1 meter (3 feet) to more than 15 meters (50 feet). The early, air-breathing ichthyosaur probably lived its entire life in the water like a seal and had not yet developed the shark or dolphin shape that was to come later. It had a lizard-like tail as opposed to a lunate (crescent-shaped) tail fin, and its pelvic bone was still attached to its backbone, limiting its range of motion. As these marine reptiles adapted to open ocean swimming, they developed more dolphin-like features (including the long snout) and spread through the oceans. Paleontologists estimate that ichthyosaurs could travel up to 30 miles per hour—about as fast as a modern dolphin.

Arriving on the scene a little later than the ichthyosaurs and sticking around a little longer were the plesiosaurs (pronounced *PLEE-see-uh-soarz*), which came in two models—one with an egg-shaped body, long neck, and small head (sort of how you might imagine that the Loch Ness Monster would look) and the other with an elongated body, short neck, and large head. Both models had razor-sharp teeth. Some were more than 25 meters (82 feet) in length and weighed as much as 100 tons!

Captain Clam's Comments

Paleontologists constantly dream of finding living relics that prove a link between prehistoric and modern animals, and these dreams exist for reptiles as well. These dreams are what fuel the mystery of Loch Ness—that a discovery as significant as coelacanths and megamouth sharks will take place for other marine species, including the reptiles.

Plesiosaurs swam rapidly through the water using four triangular flippers—unlike anything living today. The closest living reptiles resembling these ancestral sea lizards are the alligators and crocodiles, which have diverged very far from the pelagic lifestyle of their ancient cousins.

About 135 million years ago, for unknown reasons, the populations of ichthyosaurs and plesiosaurs started to dwindle and then became extinct about 35 million years later. Populations of other sea reptiles also declined during this era, and with the exception of a few species of turtles and snakes and a few lizards marine reptiles went extinct about the same time as the dinosaurs, nearly 65 million years ago.

Icthyosaur

Ichthyosaurs and plesiosaurs were the water lizards of the Triassic and Cretaceous periods.

Plesiosaur

Old Timers in Armored Tanks

With their armor-plated mobile homes, thick, scaly skin, and lumbering gait, turtles look like miniature prehistoric beasts. In fact, the first land turtles evolved more than 200 million years ago, shortly after the first dinosaurs appeared on Earth. Sea turtles followed some 50 million years later, possibly at a time when the landmasses drifted further apart. One of the largest of the prehistoric sea turtles was the Archelon, fossils of which were discovered in North America (in South Dakota of all places). Archelon grew up to 4.5 meters (15 feet) long with massive flippers and a voracious, carnivorous appetite. Like today's leatherback turtle, Archelon's shell was made of a leathery material rather than bony plates.

Sea turtles exhibit a few important modifications that help them survive in the ocean environment. The first and most obvious is the turtle's "legs" which are more like fins. When sea turtles crawl up on land, they can barely walk, but these fins are perfect for swimming. Another important modification is the shell design. Unlike most turtles and tortoises, which can retract their arms and head completely into their shells for protection, the sea turtle cannot. The shell has a more streamlined design that enhances the sea turtle's ability to move through the water. Most sea turtles have the standard turtle shell complete with bony plates, except for the leatherback, which has a leathery shell similar to the shell of the prehistoric Archelon.

Sea turtles have streamlined shells and long flippers.

(Photo Credit: OAR/National Undersea Research Program; University of North Carolina at Wilmington)

All marine reptiles, including sea turtles, require one additional adaptation to enable them to tolerate the ocean's salinity—salt-secreting glands, typically located somewhere in or around the animal's head. In the case of the sea turtle, the glands are tear ducts that ooze highly saline tears to carry excess salts out of the turtle's body and protect its eyes.

Most species of sea turtles prefer warm tropical waters. After all, like all reptiles, sea turtles are cold-blooded animals. If they find themselves in waters colder than 18 degrees Celsius, they start looking for a place to take a winter nap. The one exception is the leatherback turtle, which has the ability to raise its own body temperature 18 degrees Celsius above that of the surrounding water! This gives the leatherback a wider range to roam—some have been spotted as far north as the Mediterranean Sea.

Underwater Eye

When most people think of marine turtles, they picture the big, pelagic sea turtles, such as the leatherback. However, several other species of turtles take advantage of ocean and coastal habitats, such as the diamondback terrapin, which lives exclusively in brackish salt marshes. Some freshwater turtles also use the coastal areas as nesting sites or even migrate over bodies of saltwater to nesting sites on distant beaches.

Eggs Aplenty

Sea turtles spend most of their lives at sea, but must return to land to lay their eggs. Because they have evolved to become strong swimmers, sea turtles can undergo long migrations from seasonal feeding sites to natal nesting grounds. Some species travel more than 1,600 kilometers (995 miles) to deposit their eggs. Females can be seen in the summer far up on the beaches late at night digging deep holes in the sand. Each sea turtle then deposits 50 to 100 soft-shelled eggs about the size of Ping-Pong balls in the hole it dug. After laying its eggs, the female then gently pushes sand over the eggs and returns to the sea, ready to recharge her spent energy. Over a single breading season, a female sea turtle might repeat this egg-laying ritual two or more times. The turtles might not return for several years afterward. Two to three months after the eggs have been deposited, the hatching turtles use their tiny egg tooth to crack the shell, and then they spend about three to five days digging themselves out of the hole their mom buried them in.

First Mad Dash for Life

When newly hatched sea turtles finally claw their way to the surface and scramble toward the sea, it is an event that is, unfortunately for the turtles, hard to miss. The hatchlings wait until after sunset to increase their survival odds, and then they burst out and make a mad dash toward the beach. The outcome is almost as devastating as the Charge of the Light Brigade. Every hungry predator from miles around heads to the beach to scoop up these poor, defenseless babies; crabs, birds, raccoons, foxes, and even cats and dogs join the attack. The turtles fortunate enough to pass this first gauntlet of land predators then enter the sea only to face a host of hungry fish, ready to gobble them up. It's unknown exactly where the few survivors go next, but they may spend up to three years drifting somewhere in the open sea, feeding on jellies and other small floating organisms. Following the ocean currents, they later return to coastal waters where they feed on shellfish and other marine animals. Although marine turtles appear to have the potential to reproduce abundantly, laying as many as 1,000 eggs each breeding season, estimates show that only 1 or 2 turtles out of every 1,000 eggs make it to maturity to possibly lay eggs on that same beach.

Humans often contribute to the sea turtle's high infant mortality rate simply by leaving their lights on. Baby turtles have a natural instinct to head toward the brighter horizon over the ocean after sunset. However, lights from beach cottages, condos, and restaurants can confuse the tiny turtles and make them head inland. Some areas where sea turtles commonly lay their eggs have strict ordinances that prohibit residents and businesses from shining any lights in the direction of the beaches during times when turtles are nesting and hatchlings are likely to emerge.

Captain Clam's Comments

The only place in the world where it is legal to harvest turtle eggs is on the beach of Ostional, one of the 60 nesting beaches in Costa Rica. On this beach, a massive nesting phenomenon called arribada occurs, in which the endangered Olive ridley marine turtles hit the shores to lay their eggs. So many turtles visit the beach in such a short time span that later turtles destroy many of the first nests. Because of this, the government initiated a project to allow local people to collect and sell a percentage of the eggs from the first three days of each arribada. This practice was designed to prevent poaching and to help the local community.

Stranded on the Beach

To make matters worse, sea turtles commonly become stranded on the beach because of natural causes or human activity. Occasionally, a person will run over a sea turtle with a boat or the turtle will get tangled up in a net or other fishing gear. Shrimp nets alone claim the lives of thousands of sea turtles every year. Because turtles are air breathers, they can easily drown if kept from surfacing over a long period of time. Natural strandings of adult turtles occur most frequently during the nesting seasons when adult males and females have migrated to an area for egg laying. Some turtles travel to climates that become too cold for these reptiles to tolerate. As winter approaches, turtles that have lingered too long at northern latitudes become too sluggish to continue the journey south to safe, warmer waters. These turtles are often found stranded on the beach and can freeze to death.

Captain Clam's Comments

In many parts of the world where sea turtles commonly become stranded, ecologists have set up active networks to rescue and return these stranded turtles to the sea. Heightened awareness of the precarious situation facing sea turtle populations has had a positive effect on victims of strandings. Facilities and trained personnel are recovering and releasing individuals with a greater rate of success in communities that post stranding information. With populations at critical levels, every turtle's life is important.

Reckless Endangerment

Sharks, especially the tiger shark, occasionally prey on adult sea turtles, but humans are the sea turtle's main predator. Humans hunt the turtles for meat, for their shells (to make combs, eyeglass frames, and aphrodisiacs), for their fats and oils (for food and cosmetics), and for their eggs. Litter poses additional risks. Discarded plastic bags and other litter often wash into the ocean from beaches and city streets. Plastic bags may resemble jellyfish, causing problems for turtles that mistake this trash for food. In addition, as humans claim more and more beachfront property, the sea turtles' natural nesting sites are quickly disappearing, further depleting the sea turtle population.

Only seven species of sea turtles are alive today, and their dwindling populations give sea turtles the dubious ranking as some of the world's most endangered species. The following list names the seven species and provides one or two important facts about each species:

◆ **Green**   Endangered around the world, but some populations in Florida are significant. Green sea turtles are especially susceptible to a disease called fibropapilloma, which causes tumors to develop around sensitive areas of the turtles' bodies.

◆ **Leatherback**   Largest living turtle, reaching weights of more than 1,300 pounds. This species is on the Endangered Species list.

◆ **Olive ridley**   Commonly breeds near beaches in Costa Rica and Mexico. This species is on the Endangered Species list.

◆ **Kemp's ridley**   Smallest and most endangered species.

◆ **Loggerhead**   Two major nesting grounds with 25,000 each.

◆ **Hawksbill**   Hunted almost to extinction for its shell.

◆ **Flatback**   Found in Northern Australia and New Guinea.

Ocean Alert _____

Fibropapilloma is a tumor-forming, debilitating, and often fatal disease of sea turtles. It has rapidly emerged in the past decade as a serious threat to sea turtle populations worldwide. The disease is manifested by formation of multiple fibrous masses of tumors growing from the eyes, flippers, neck, tail, in the mouth, and in the intestines. Although most fibropapilloma tumors are considered noncancerous, they can seriously affect a turtle's breathing, digestion, sight, and ability to swim. In advanced stages of the disease, turtles often become lethargic and are prone to becoming stranded on shore.

Six of the seven species of marine turtles are listed as endangered or critically endangered, and the latest numbers are not very promising. All seven species of marine turtles are listed in Appendix I of the Convention on International Trade in Endangered Species of Wild Fauna and Flora (CITES), thus prohibiting international trade by more than 140 CITES member nations. In many nonmember nations, where people harvest sea turtles for meat, eggs, and shells, reductions in numbers continue. Some villages have strong cultural and economic ties to hunting these animals, and have trouble relinquishing their reliance on sea turtles.

The Real Sea Serpents

From the myths of the ancient Greeks to the current folklore of Loch Ness, people have imagined huge sea serpents ruling the sea, terrorizing sailors, and smashing boats. No one really knows how these legends started. Perhaps a sailor mistook an odd wave or current for a serpent. Maybe some seaweed near the surface took on the form of a huge snake. Or maybe a sailor saw an eel swimming alongside the boat and spun a yarn about it. Or maybe there was just a little too much rum on board.

Although these stories continue, the real sea serpents, sea snakes, are much less spectacular and far less treacherous. The 70 or so known species of sea snakes account for nearly 86 percent of all marine reptiles. Most of these snakes are tiny compared with their land-based cousins, such as the anaconda—the largest sea snake reaches only about 2 meters (6.5 feet) in length and most are much shorter. The only real threat posed by a sea snake is its venom—sea snake venom is 2 to 10 times more potent than that of a cobra.

Sea snakes are found primarily in tropical waters. The greatest variety is found between Singapore and Borneo, where 27 identified species live. Australia's coastal waters also provide habitat for a diversity of sea snakes—between 17 and 21 species.

Adapting to Ocean Life

To make the move from land and trees to a life in the ocean, sea snakes have had to tweak their overall design and manifest a few innovative adaptations. The most obvious adaptation is their flattened tails—perfect for propelling the snakes through the water. Sea snakes do not have enlarged ventral scales on their bellies as do land snakes for gripping the ground. To stay under water for long periods of time, the sea snake has an elongated right lung that extends nearly the entire length of its body and valves that enable it to seal its nostrils. Some species can remain underwater for approximately two hours depending on how active they are. The sea snake rids itself of the excess salt from seawater by using a salt excreting gland located under the tongue.

As reptiles (cold-blooded creatures), sea snakes are incapable of regulating their body temperature to deal with environmental temperature changes, so if they get cold, they become sluggish. If they overheat, if their body temperature rises above 35 degrees Celsius (95 degrees Fahrenheit), they're likely to die. To keep their bodies at a steady temperature, sea snakes, like terrestrial snakes, change their location. In warm, tropical waters, sea snakes commonly swim lower in the water column to cool themselves off. When the skies are overcast and they obtain little heat from the sun, they stay nearer to the surface. Most sea snakes remain relatively close to land; if they wander too far out to the cooler waters of the open ocean, they don't last long and eventually their dead or dying carcasses are washed ashore. If you come across a sea snake on the beach, avoid it; it might look dead, but if it has any life in it at all, it is still capable of inflicting a lethal bite.

Potent Poisons

As mentioned earlier, sea snake venom is a particularly potent neurotoxin capable of shutting down the central nervous system. Most sea snakes pack about 10 to 15 milligrams of venom, and a dose of about 1.5 milligrams can be lethal to humans. Fortunately, the sea snake is not particularly aggressive, unless, of course, you step on one, tug on its tail, poke it with a stick, or do anything else to annoy it. Sea snakes rarely attack divers. Most attacks occur when a fisherman accidentally catches a sea snake or a swimmer inadvertently steps on a snake.

Even if a sea snake manages to bite you, the risks of being poisoned are slim—about a one in four chance. Although sea snake venom is potent, only a few species have an effective delivery system for injecting the venom into their victims. In most sea snakes, the fangs lie at the back of the mouth rather than in front, so the sea snake would need to get a pretty good chunk of your flesh in order to puncture your skin with its fangs. In general, sea snakes have small front teeth they use to subdue and immobilize prey while the toxin acts to paralyze the victim. Eating the snake would cause a predator worse problems than if the snake were to bite it. Sea snakes commonly have brightly colored stripes or bands that warn would-be predators to steer clear or prepare themselves for a nasty treat.

Although sea snakes are dangerous predators and formidable foes, they have their share of enemies including birds, sharks, moray eels, fish, crocodiles, crabs, and humans. Sea snakes are often caught as bycatch during the shrimp harvest and are used for food, leather, and medicine. Some Asian cultures consider the meat from a sea snake to be an aphrodisiac. Some countries including Australia have regulated sea snake harvesting in their waters.

Sea's One and Only Lizard

Although turtles and snakes have made a fairly successful transition from land to sea, lizards haven't done so well. In fact, only one species of lizard calls the ocean home—

the marine iguana. This sole specimen inhabits the Galapagos Islands, which form an archipelago off the coast of Ecuador, South America. These mini-Godzillas, which look like menacing carnivores, are actually vegetarians, feeding primarily on algae that they gnaw off the rocks. Although iguanas prefer the rocky coasts, some like to hang out in mangrove swamps and on beaches, as well.

Marine iguanas seem to be living a life of eternal retirement. They hang out on the rocky shore all day, sunning themselves and keeping their lumbering bodies warm. As soon as they're warm enough (and hungry enough), they ease themselves into the water and swim out to the nearest mass of seaweed to grab some lunch. When they're done eating or get too cold to continue, it's back to the rocks for more warm sun and relaxation. Occasionally, some of the more ambitious iguanas, typically the males, swim out beyond the surf and dive down to feed, some diving as deep as 15 meters (50 feet). A typical dive lasts only a few minutes, but iguanas have been known to stay down for up to a half-hour!

Seaside Iguana Adaptations

To live this docile, seaside life, marine iguanas required a few changes to the overall iguana design. Specifically, they needed long, flat tails for swimming, long claws for hanging on to rocks and grabbing hold of seaweed, and some way to get rid of all that salt in their diets. The marine iguana exhibits all three of these special adaptations. If you were to compare a marine iguana with a land-based species, the first two adaptations would be readily evident. The marine iguana's tail is much flatter and more powerful, and its claws are longer and stronger.

The third adaptation (the ability to secrete salt) is just as obvious, assuming you know what you're looking for. When you examine most marine iguanas, you notice that the very tops of their heads are white. This white cap is not part of the marine iguana's natural coloration—it's actually a crust of salt. Like other marine reptiles, the iguana has a special gland that removes excess salt from its system. This gland is located between the iguana's eyes and nostrils. When enough salt accumulates, the iguana blows the build-up out its nostrils, and the discharge typically settles on the lizard's head. Eventually this forms the white cap that adorns the heads of many marine iguanas. Marine iguanas often blow out a spray of salt to ward off any annoying intruders.

In addition to its flattened tail, long nails, and ability to blow excess salt out of its nose, the marine iguana has a characteristically blunt snout, hence its name *Amblyrhynchus* (*amblys* "short," *rhynchos* "snout"). This makes it easier for the marine iguana to scrape algae off of rocks.

Not Too Hot, Not Too Cold

Have you ever had the feeling that you just can't get the right temperature? You put on a sweater and become too warm. Take it off and you become too cold. Well, that's the way most reptiles feel all the time. They rely on the temperature of their surroundings to regulate their own temperature. That's why so many turtles and snakes are killed on the roadways. They're just looking for a little warmth, and a tar-black highway often seems to offer just the source of heat they need to keep their bones warm. Possibly, this inability to regulate their own temperature is the major reason why so few reptiles have moved to the sea.

As you might guess, an inability to regulate body temperature could seriously limit an animal's ability to dive, especially in the relatively cool waters surrounding the Galapagos Islands. Marine iguanas possess some physiological adaptations that help them cope. They can direct their blood flow away from the surface of their skin to conserve heat, and they can drastically reduce their heart rate. Upon returning from the sea, marine iguanas perch themselves on the black rocks to warm up. At night they can be found huddled together in large piles to stay warm. Although chilling out is a problem, overheating can also be an issue, and the iguanas use several techniques to avoid this. They cool themselves off either by swimming or by perching high up on the rocks in an elevated pose to increase the amount of body surface exposed to the cooling breeze.

Checking Out the Local Colors

A cruise around the Galapagos Islands reveals that not all marine iguanas are the same. Although only one species inhabits the islands, several races have developed on the various islands. Most marine iguanas are coal black, matching the volcanic rock on which they can be found clinging. However, green iguanas dominate Santiago Island and red iguanas are most common in the Española race. In all races, females are generally gray to black. Scientists have come to believe that diet might influence the color of the iguanas, because of the prevalence of red seaweed around Española Island.

The volcanic Galapagos has never been attached to another landmass, so paleontologists believe that iguanas rafted over from South America. Some researchers believe that the land iguanas and the marine iguana diverged from a common ancestor at least 10 million years ago on the former islands of the archipelago, which are now below sea level.

Threatening the Majestic Marine Iguana

The marine iguanas of the Galapagos, like most animals here, have evolved in the midst of few natural predators. Because of this, they have few defenses against any non-native predators who have arrived on the islands, including rats that eat their eggs, cats that eat their young, and dogs that eat just about anything. Even some areas where the iguana populations seem to be thriving are in danger. For example, Academy Bay and Volcan Ecuador have significant populations of adult iguanas, but the wild housecats have slaughtered the young, virtually ensuring the future disappearance of iguanas in these areas. On islands that the cats have not yet invaded, iguanas continue to thrive.

Rats, cats, and dogs aren't the only creatures threatening the existence of this sole marine lizard. Humans and their pollution are encroaching on these animals as well. One of the major threats to the Galapagos iguanas is a relatively minor oil spill that occurred in 2001 when the tanker Jessica ran aground off the Isla Santa Fe. At first, ecologists thought that the effects of the spill would be minimal, but they are learning that the long-term effects might be devastating. Although few iguanas were directly and immediately harmed by the spill, scientists have witnessed a significant increase in mortality rates on this population, possibly due to the effect of the oil on the iguana's food source—the algae.

Do Alligators and Crocodiles Count?

When the ichthyosaurs were still roaming Earth and the plesiosaurs were just starting to arrive on the scene, crocodiles were beginning their own lines of descent. These early crocodiles were relatively small, land-based creatures. However, by the middle to late Jurassic period, crocodiles started to migrate to water and develop into several larger species. A couple of types of the crocodiles that appeared were specifically marine oriented. One was so adapted to life in the seas that its limbs had turned into flippers, and it even had a fluke on its tail to help push itself more efficiently through the water.

Eventually, at about the same time the dinosaurs became extinct, the early crocodiles disappeared. Fortunately for the crocodiles, evolution revived the species, and now approximately 10 species of alligators and 14 species of crocodiles inhabit various areas around the globe. Although most of these amphibious reptiles prefer freshwater, many, especially the crocodile, can tolerate various degrees of salinity and can venture into estuaries and brackish systems for extended periods of time. In fact, one of the primary differences between crocodiles and their close cousins the alligator and caiman is that the crocodile possesses salt-secreting glands on its tongue that help it discharge excessive salt from its system.

One crocodile in particular—the largest crocodile on the planet (the largest reptile on the planet), the Indo-Pacific or saltwater crocodile—is a saltwater-tolerant reptile of frightening proportions. Male saltwater crocodiles can reach lengths of 7 meters (23 feet) and can weigh more than 1,000 kilograms (2,200 pounds)! Females are about half the size of males. Saltwater crocodiles have very large heads and very strong jaws capable of crushing large turtles with a single chomp. Also known locally as salties, these crocodiles are long-lived, having a maximum age of at least 70 years. Saltwater crocodiles have been known to make long treks across the seas of more than 1,000 kilometers (620 miles). Some have even been found with barnacles attached to their skin!

> **Underwater Eye**
>
> Crocodiles are the most evolved of all reptiles: They have a four-chambered heart, well-developed senses, and a natural instinct to care for their young. In many ways, they are more closely associated with birds than they are with other reptiles.

The Least You Need to Know

- Approximately 250 million years ago, the ichthyosaurs (or fish lizards) were the first reptiles to return to the sea.

- Plesiosaurs came in two models—one with an egg-shaped body, long neck, and small head, and the other with an elongated body, short neck, and large head.

- The first sea turtles evolved about 150 million years ago.

- The sea turtle population is threatened from both ends: the adults from entanglement in fishing nets, hunting, and pollution; and the young from predation and development of nesting beaches.

- Sea snakes have some of the most toxic venom in the animal kingdom but rarely cause mortality in humans because of their nonaggressive nature and small fangs in the back of their mouths.

- Marine iguanas are the only living true marine lizard and are only found in the Galapagos Archipelago.

- The saltwater crocodile is the largest living reptile on the planet.

Chapter 16

Marine Mammals

In This Chapter

- ◆ Ancient land mammals take the plunge
- ◆ Sorting out whales, dolphins, and porpoises
- ◆ Cetacean sonar
- ◆ Pinnipeds, Sirenia, and other assorted marine mammals
- ◆ World outlook on marine mammals

Some marine mammals are obviously mammalian. When you see a walrus, a seal, or an otter, you know that you're looking at a mammal. They're hairy, they have whiskers, and they spend a lot of time out of the water. Other marine mammals look like fish. They swim like fish. They eat like fish. If you weren't taught in grade school that dolphins and whales are mammals, you might still think that they're fish. And unless they get washed up on a beach, they spend their entire lives in the water, just like fish. However, all of these animals—the whale, dolphin, walrus, sea lion, seal, and otter—are mammals, just like you and me. This chapter explores the evolution and diversity of marine mammals and examines some of the factors that threaten the existence of many of our closest mammalian relatives.

Cetacean Evolution: The Dolphins and Whales Arrive

Like reptiles, *mammals* first appeared on land, where all other air-breathing creatures hung out at the time. In fact, mammals evolived from reptiles called therapsids about 200 million years ago. According to fossil records, the first mammal was approximately no more than a few inches in length. During the Jurassic period, land mammals continued to evolve alongside the kings of this era, the dinosaurs, and eventually developed into some fairly complex (and hefty) creatures. When the dinosaurs died off at the end of the Cretaceous, around 65 million years ago, mammals were well positioned to replace them as the dominant animals.

Log Entry

To be a **mammal**, you must have the following characteristics: Be warm blooded, breathe air, have hair (at least at some point in your life), give birth to live young, and nurse your babies.

Not content to dominate only the land, mammals returned to the sea some 50 million years ago, give or take a year. The first marine mammals probably looked like today's seals—their back legs starting to disappear, and the arms becoming more finlike. As these mammals became more dependent on an aquatic existence, they began to develop more fishlike features and attain massive sizes with the help of water's buoyancy and plentiful food supply.

The earliest whale-like mammals were the *archaeocetes* (pronounced *are-KEE-uh-seets*), which actually possessed several unwhale-like attributes. Their teeth, for example, like those of most land mammals, still show differentiation into several types, such as molars and incisors. Modern whales, on the other hand, have baleen plates for straining food, teeth that are essentially identical in shape and size, or no teeth at all. Instead of a blowhole on the top of its head (as is present in modern whales), archaeocetes had nostrils near the tip of their snouts. Some early forms of archaeocetes exhibited visible, external hind limbs, as well.

Log Entry

To be a **cetacean**, you must be an aquatic, primarily saltwater mammal with few hairs, front limbs modified into flippers, undeveloped rear limbs, and a flat notched tail (flukes). Members include approximately 80 species of whales, dolphins, and porpoises.

Nearly 37 million years ago, archaeocetes became extinct, and during the following Oligocene period, two new groups of ancient whales appeared—the odontocete (toothed) and cetotheriids (baleen) whales. Think of the odontocete as the hunters and the cetotheriids as the gatherers (gathering zooplankton). By the end of the Tertiary period, these two groups became extinct, as well, setting the stage for the arrival of the modern *cetaceans* (pronounced *si-TAY-shins*)—whales, dolphins, and porpoises.

Modern cetaceans exhibit several modifications to adapt to their exclusively aquatic lifestyle. The overall shape shows a streamlined design, in which the jaw and facial features are elongated and the hind limbs are virtually nonexistent. Reproductive organs have been internalized and are concealed behind small slits. External ear flaps have disappeared, leaving the cetacean with two pinhole openings for hearing. This streamlined design enables swifter movement through the water with less drag. To further reduce drag, the cetacean traded its mammalian fur coat for a layer of smooth, skin-covered blubber. The blubber keeps the animal warm, increases the animal's buoyancy, and provides some reserve fuel for long journeys. Instead of nostrils at the front of the snout, the cetacean has blow holes at the top of its head, so that it can more easily take in air at the surface. Modern cetaceans possess a pair of flukes that make up the flattened tail that propels the cetacean through the water. To balance and guide itself through the water, the front limbs of the cetacean exhibit a modified bone structure that's covered with blubber and tough tissue to form flippers.

Flukes

Flippers

Modern cetaceans are designed to move through the water.

One of the most significant adaptations that cetaceans had to make for life at sea is also one of the least obvious—the highly specialized kidneys. Cetacean kidneys allow these marine mammals to drink saltwater; something you and I cannot do. If you or I were to drink a liter of saltwater, we would need to expel one and one-third liter of fluid to dispose of the excess salt. This would eventually lead to our dehydration and deaths. When a cetacean drinks a liter of saltwater, its kidneys can dissolve the excess salt into only two-thirds of a liter of fluid, leaving the cetacean with one-third liter of pure water. River dolphins have smaller kidneys because they live in fresher water.

Thar She Blows

When you go whale watching, the first thing you look for is the whale's spout—the plume of warm, moist air that shoots up from the whale's blowhole when it surfaces and exhales. The spout results when the warm, moist air from the whale's lungs hits the cool dry air and condenses—this is the same effect that you produce when you exhale on a cold day. The spout does not consist of seawater in the blowhole, as some people think. Some spouts can shoot as high as 10 meters!

As mammals, cetaceans need to breathe air, but unlike most mammals that breathe through their nostrils, a cetacean breathes through the blowhole on the top of its head. Muscles around the blowhole open and close the hole. When a cetacean surfaces, it flexes the blowhole muscles to open the hole. It then blows the water and air from its lungs and takes a deep breath. When the cetacean is ready to dive down, it relaxes the muscles around the blowhole, enabling the blowhole to seal itself tight. A large whale, such as the sperm whale, typically can hold its breath for about one hour (50 to 80 minutes) before it must resurface. Dolphins typically stay under less than 10 minutes.

You Are How You Eat

Modern cetaceans can be divided into two subgroups determined by the structure of their teeth: the Odontoceti (which have teeth) and the Mysticeti (which have baleen plates instead of teeth). Odontocetes teeth are typically conical in shape and of roughly equal size. Most odontocetes have numerous teeth, though there are a few exceptions. The narwhal, for example, has a single tusk that protrudes from the middle of its forehead, similar to a unicorn's horn. In the beaked whales, some teeth are fanglike, giving the beaked whales an edge as hunters. The toothed cetaceans are typically hunters, using their teeth for catching fish, squid, or other marine life, which they then swallow whole. Dolphins and porpoises are examples of odontocetes, as are belugas, narwhals, killer whales, sperm whales, and beaked whales.

The Mysticeti (or baleen whales) do not have teeth as adults, although teeth are present in fetal baleen whales. In place of teeth, baleen whales have stiff, "hairy" plates called baleen plates that act as strainers. Baleen plates are made of a substance called keratin, which is very similar to the composition of our fingernails. These plates hang down from the upper jaw, and the overlapping "hairs" form a dense, permeable mat through which the whale can strain plankton-rich water. The whale takes a huge mouthful of water, closes its mouth, and then spits the water back, through the baleen plates, trapping the plankton and any other poor, unfortunate creature that got sucked into the whale's mouth.

Sensory and Extrasensory Perception

Cetacean senses are similar to ours, though different senses are more or less developed than ours. They can see pretty well, hear very well, and feel vibrations and objects that touch their bodies, but their sense of smell is likely very weak or absent, and they probably do not have a strong sense of taste. Of course, if you were eating raw fish and krill your entire life, you would probably wish you had no sense of smell or taste.

The cetacean's eyes are fairly small in relation to its body, especially in deep-feeding whales, probably because in the deeper ocean waters, little light filters down, making sight less important. However, cetacean eyes are well developed and are designed to work best in low-light conditions. In addition, in cetaceans that have their eyes positioned toward the front of their face, such as dolphins, the eyes provide the cetacean with excellent binocular vision to improve its ability to hunt and catch prey. In most whales, the eyes are positioned on either side of the head and typically are recessed, so they have peripheral but not binocular vision—this arrangement is more suited to keeping watch for predators.

Whales are known for their keen hearing, which enables them to communicate over hundreds of kilometers. They can even determine which direction the sound is coming from, which is fairly difficult to do underwater. The baleen whale has a pinhole in the skin behind each of its eyes that leads to an auditory canal. This canal is completely sealed off with a waxy plug, so scientists aren't quite sure how well baleen whales hear. The middle and inner ear structures in all cetaceans are well-developed. In the toothed whales, the waxy ear plug is absent. In addition, the bones that form the structure of the ear are covered with a foamy liquid to protect them against the high pressure conditions of the deep.

Toothed cetaceans all use a sophisticated technique called *echolocation* to navigate underwater. This technique works sort of like the ultrasound scans used to determine the location, position, and health of a human fetus. To use echolocation, a cetacean emits sounds (typically about 300 clicks or whistles per second in the case of dolphins), which then bounce off objects and return to the cetacean. As the signals echo back, the cetacean can use the reflected signals to render a mental image of its surroundings. Through echolocation, the cetacean can discern the size, shape, surface characteristics, and movement of the object, as well as how far away it is. This technique gives cetaceans an extreme advantage when searching for and catching evasive prey in total darkness. They even use it to find prey that buries itself in the soft ocean floor to escape.

Log Entry _____

Echolocation involves the emission of sound and interpretation of its echo. The animal produces the sound somewhere in its head, possibly from its mouth, blowhole, or other organs in its head. The sound reaches the melon—a fat deposit at the top, frontal area of the head—which focuses the sound into a directional beam and sends it forward. The beam bounces off an object back to a receiver on the bottom of the creature's jaw, called the acoustic window, which leads to the inner ear. Vibrations in the ear create signals that then travel to the cetacean's brain to help it form an image of the surrounding objects. Bats use a similar system to navigate through the air.

Are You a Whale, a Dolphin, or a Porpoise?

When you study cetaceans, you begin to notice that the lines between one group of cetaceans and another seem blurry. Many people, for example, think that dolphins and porpoises are one and the same and that killer whales are really whales. So, what distinguishes the whale from the dolphin from the porpoise?

Actually, the question is not that simple. Some textbooks lump all cetaceans together as whales and divide them into two groups—toothed whales or baleen whales. Under this system of classification, all dolphins and porpoises are toothed whales and all whales with baleen plates are baleen whales (or simply whales). The other system of classification, the system that this chapter follows, distinguishes between the following three types of cetaceans:

♦ **Whales** are the large cetaceans to that don't have snouts like dolphins and porpoises. This group includes all the baleen whales plus some toothed whales, including the sperm whale.

Underwater Eye

The killer whale (or Orca) is actually a dolphin. You can tell by examining its pronounced dorsal fin, and by looking inside its mouth, which is packed with sharp, conical teeth.

♦ **Dolphins** are all toothed cetaceans. Dolphins are characterized by long snouts, prominent dorsal fins, cone-shaped teeth, and long, slender bodies.

♦ **Porpoises** are toothed cetaceans that are neither dolphins nor whales. Porpoises are characterized by short snouts, spade-shaped teeth, and short, squat bodies. They're typically smaller than dolphins, breed more frequently than dolphins, and live shorter lives.

Of course, this system is not foolproof, and some whales, dolphins, and porpoises defy classification. Some beaked whales, for example, have snouts that make them look suspiciously like dolphins, whereas some dolphins, such as the killer whale have no pronounced snout, making them look more like whales.

Dolphins: The Brainy Cetaceans

By far, the most popular and lovable cetacean is the dolphin. It has the looks, the personality, and the intelligence to win over audiences, awe divers, and entertain sailors and divers throughout the world. But how do dolphins stack up against chimpanzees on an IQ test? Most people would give the chimp an edge, simply because the chimp can hold a pencil and learn sign language, but just because a dolphin doesn't have opposable thumbs doesn't mean it's dumb. A dolphin probably could learn sign language, but without hands, the knowledge would do the dolphin little good. The point here is that we tend to judge other species' level of intelligence by human standards, so any comparison between the relative intelligence of a dolphin and a chimpanzee or a human can be deceiving.

Even so, the size and complexity of the dolphin brain has led scientists to conjecture that the dolphins are very smart individuals. In addition, observations of dolphins in captivity and in the wild have supported this theory. In captivity, dolphins can be trained to perform tricks and carry out complex tasks. In the wild, marine biologists have observed that dolphins establish sophisticated societies and demonstrate advanced communication skills. The following sections introduce the dolphin and showcase some concrete examples of dolphin brains at work.

Dolphins in the Wild

One of the most attractive of the cetaceans, the dolphin is a familiar sight. It has a characteristically long, sleek body, an extended snout, and a mouth packed with more than 200 tiny, cone-shaped teeth. Like other cetaceans, dolphins have powerful tails to propel them through the water. They can maintain a cruising speed of 30 kilometers (19 miles) per hour with bursts in excess of 40 kilometers (25 miles) per hour. They typically swim near the surface, coming up for air every two or three minutes, but are capable of diving to depths of 300 meters (985 feet) and staying underwater for more than 10 minutes. Their lungs are specially adapted to cope with the dramatic pressure changes they experience by descending and ascending so quickly.

Thirty-two species of dolphins cruise the world's oceans, and several freshwater species are commonly found in estuaries and far up into rivers. Dolphins typically eat the equivalent of about one third of their body weight daily and dine on a diet consisting primarily of fish, shrimp, and squid. Dolphins typically hunt in small groups, working like a pack of wolves to herd smaller fish before attacking the school.

At the ripe old age of 5 to 12 years for females and slightly later for males, dolphins reach sexual maturity. They typically mate in the spring and give birth approximately one year later. Most females bear only one baby at a time. The baby dolphin begins swimming immediately and stays with the mother for about 18 months to nurse.

Naval Recruits

During the height of the cold war, the U.S. Navy decided to draft some dolphins into service. At first, the Navy merely wanted to study the dolphins' exceptional ability at locating objects and navigating under water and examine the dolphins' overall design to improve the speed of their naval vessels, including their submarines.

As they were studying dolphins, researchers realized that these creatures were highly intelligent and that they possibly could use dolphins and other marine animals to complete various underwater tasks and even carry out secret missions. They enlisted the help of dolphins to retrieve objects, deliver equipment to divers, carry messages, detect mines, and guard boats. They even strapped underwater cameras to some dolphins and sent them out on reconnaissance missions! Dolphins and other marine mammals performed many of these tasks in both Vietnam and the Gulf War.

Dr. Lilly and the Dolphin Classroom

While the Navy was trying to enlist the services of dolphins to attain a competitive edge, Dr. John C. Lilly was performing experiments on dolphins to prove just how intelligent they are and to attempt cross-species communication between humans and dolphins. To prove the intelligence of dolphins, Lilly adapted a system he used before to test the intelligence of chimpanzees. Lilly equipped the dolphin with a probe that could apply a pleasurable electrical current to the dolphin's brain whenever the dolphin pushed a lever. Before the system was hooked up, the dolphin already had figured out what the lever was for and started pressing it. Typically, an animal must accidentally press the lever or bump into it a few times before it "learns" the purpose of the lever. According to Lilly's previous research with chimpanzees, a chimpanzee usually experienced 100 or

> **CAUTION**
> ### Ocean Alert
> Dolphins typically are friendly creatures that have little fear of humans, so you can get fairly close to wild dolphins. However, keep in mind that dolphins are wild animals ... with teeth, and they have been known to bite the hand that feeds them. Admire these beautiful creatures as you admire most wild animals—from a safe distance.

more random tries before it figured out what the lever was for, and then it took the chimp a few more tries to learn how to push the lever.

In another experiment, Lilly attempted to make a dolphin emit a whistle at a specific pitch, duration, and intensity to obtain a reward. The dolphin quickly figured out what Lilly had wanted and then continued to raise the pitch of its squeals until they were outside the range of human hearing, and hence received no reward. The dolphin quickly adjusted the pitch to bring it back in range and never again whistled outside the range that Lilly was capable of perceiving. The dolphin was actually performing an experiment on Lilly!

One of Lilly's most advanced experiments was designed to establish "verbal" communications between Lilly and a dolphin. Lilly raised a dolphin in captivity allowing no contact with other dolphins. Only human contact was allowed. Lilly trained the dolphin to rise to the surface and emit a sound when any word was shouted over the surface of the water. Lilly taped the "conversation" and later studied the tapes and estimated that 18 percent of the sounds that the dolphin emitted were humanoid sounds or imitations of human words. I would guess that the remaining 82 percent of the sounds were dolphin for "More tuna, please," "I want my mommy!" and "Boy, do I hate humans."

Dr. Dolphin, Child Therapist

If you're looking for talk therapy for your child, a dolphin might be low on your list of options. However, for many children suffering from autism, Asperger's syndrome, Down's syndrome, and other physical and psychological maladies, dolphins have been proven to help. With Dolphin Human Therapy (DHT), children and adolescents are encouraged to swim with dolphins as part of their treatment plans. Parents, teachers, and doctors have noticed considerable improvement in many children, especially in improving their moods and social interactions with other people.

Most scientists theorize that the healing power of the dolphins is no greater than the healing power of other animals, such as horses, which are used in similar treatment programs. Simply being near a gentle animal and being able to hold it and touch it without being judged by it, enables the child to feel acceptance and open up. Some people prefer to think that dolphins have inexplicable healing powers, perhaps because of their body chemistry, energy fields, or the sound waves they emit. Whatever the case, DHT has proven effective in positively changing the lives of many long-suffering children.

The Consummate Showmen

Trained dolphins have been entertaining crowds since the first formal dolphin show was presented in Saint Augustine, Florida, in 1938. Watching dolphins perform, you might begin to believe that dolphins really enjoy performing for humans. They seem so delighted to skim across the water on their tails, jump out of the water for fish, do acrobatic flips, and wave to the crowd, but are they happy? The directors of some zoos and aquariums think not, and many have discontinued their dolphin shows because of health problems and deaths of the performers. Some directors, on the other hand, have continued the shows to increase awareness of dolphins in the hope that people will care more about preserving them and their habitats. In any event, most dolphin trainers are sensitive to the needs of their performers and are genuinely concerned about their health and well-being.

> **Underwater Eye**
>
> The Spinner dolphin, typically spotted in the Pacific Ocean, can leap into the air and make as many as seven complete flips with its body before reentry. Because of their acrobatic abilities, they were one of the first dolphins to be captured for aquariums, but they have a poor survival rate in captivity.

Whopper Whales

Dolphins might be the smartest cetaceans, but whales hold bragging rights for having the largest animal on the planet—the blue whale, which can reach lengths of 30 meters (98 feet) and weigh as much as 136,000 kilograms (150 tons). Some paleontologists believe that the blue whale is the largest animal of all time! The largest toothed whale is the male sperm whale, which can reach lengths of about 18 meters (59 feet) and weigh as much as 54,000 kilograms (60 tons). On the other end of the scale is the lightest whale, the dwarf sperm whale, which grows to only 2.6 meters (8.5 feet) and weighs only 40 to 50 kilograms (88 to 110 pounds).

Depending on the classification system in use, approximately 40 to 45 different whale species swim the world's oceans. All whale species exhibit the standard cetacean characteristics, including their large, complex brains, blowholes, broad tail flukes, and well-developed flippers. Most whales have no prominent dorsal fin. If the whale has a dorsal fin, it is typically small and located closer to the rear of the whale. In addition, whales are the only group of cetaceans to have members with baleen plates.

Of the two types of whales, the toothed whales are the more social, typically traveling in small groups or schools, called pods. Pods might consist of mothers and their calves, a dominant male and its harem, bachelor pods of multiple young adult males, or bull pods of sexually active adult males. Along with providing social connections for whales, pods help their members hunt and capture prey, and the pods protect their members. When any member of a pod is sick or injured, the remaining members encircle the individual with their heads pointing in toward the center of the circle and their tails flailing around the perimeter.

The age at which whales become sexually mature varies from species to species and ranges anywhere from 2 to 20 years. The whale's sex also influences the age at which it becomes sexually mature. The female sperm whale, for example, is ready to mate at the age of 9, whereas males must wait until they're 20 years old! When whales are ready to mate, they typically head toward warmer waters near the equator. The female carries its baby for 8 to 19 months, and then returns to the tropics to give birth. Most females bear only one baby at a time, tail first. The baby whale begins swimming immediately and stays with the mother for several months to nurse, and nurse they do—mother sperm whales produce up to 600 liters of milk per day and can nurse their babies for more than a year. And this isn't low-fat milk; sperm whale milk has a 25 to 50 percent fat content.

Natural-Born Divers

One of the major traits that differentiate whales from other cetaceans is the whale's ability to dive down deep and stay submerged for long periods of time. Sperm whales, for example, are able to stay under water for longer than an hour and dive to depths of more than 1,000 meters (3,280 feet). (Some reports place the record sperm whale dive at nearly 3,000 meters (9,840 feet). Whales have become diving champions due to several adaptations: They can slow down their respiration rate, cardiac output, and heart rate; increase their oxygen storage capacity; and direct the flow of oxygen to the areas that need it most.

The major factor limiting the amount of time an organism can remain submerged is the amount of oxygen the creature can supply to its vital organs—its brain, heart, and sensory organs. Whales exhibit several adaptations to overcome this limitation. First, their blood and muscles are capable of storing high concentrations of oxygen. Their red blood cells are larger than those of humans, and they're more highly concentrated. The whale's muscles contain a higher concentration of myoglobin, an oxygen-binding protein. Second, when a whale dives, the whale's heart rate slows and the blood flow to the muscles is restricted in order to make more blood available for the vital organs. In addition, the whale seems impervious to the pain and fatigue that typically result when a lack of oxygen causes lactic acid and carbon dioxide to build up in the muscle tissues.

Underwater Eye
When a whale takes a single breath (exhales and inhales), it exchanges 85 to 90 percent of its stored air volume. In other words, it almost completely empties its lungs of stale air and fills them with fresh air. When you take a breath, you're exchanging only about 15 percent of your air.

Cretacean Census

Nobody can say how many whales of each species populate our oceans, but many marine biologists like to estimate whale populations, especially those of endangered species. Each species is divided into populations or stocks, typically based on geographic location. The International Whaling Commission (IWC) has posted its estimates of only a few whale populations, but is careful to note that estimates can be less than reliable. The population estimates that the IWC is fairly confident to provide are listed in the following table.

Whale Population Estimates (from the International Whaling Commission)

Species	Location	Years	Population
Minke	Southern Hemisphere	1982/83–87/88	510,000–1,140,000
	North Atlantic	1987–1995	120,000–182,000
	Northwest Pacific	1989–1990	12,800–48,600
Blue	Southern Hemisphere	1980–2000	400–1,400
Fin	North Atlantic	1969–1989	27,700–82,000
Gray	Eastern North Pacific	1997–1998	21,900–32,400
Bowhead	Bering Sea Area	1993	6,900–9,200
Humpback	Southern Hemisphere	1998	5,900–16,800
Pilot	North Atlantic	1989	440,000–1,370,000

Captain Clam's Comments

Subsistence whaling has been allowed for a number of indigenous tribes in the United States and Russia. The whales are used to feed tribe members and are not sold in any way. Current quotas are 120 grey whales allowed to the Chukotka tribe, 4 grey whales to the Makah, and 56 bowhead whales allowed to the Inuit.

In 1946, the IWC was founded to help preserve whale populations, so the whaling industry would still have some whales to hunt in the future. In 1986, the IWC placed a moratorium on commercial whale hunting, which remains in place today. However, some nations that rely heavily on the whaling and fishing industries, including Norway and Japan, are seeking to have the ban lifted. As yet, they have been unsuccessful. With this ban in place and genuine, international attempts to preserve whales, populations of some species are on the rebound.

Narwhals, Unicorns of the Sea

One of the rarest (and oddest looking) whales in the oceans is the Narwhal, a creature that looks half-whale and half-unicorn. Narwhals lack a dorsal fin, and the male has a tooth on the left side of its upper jaw that grows into a long spiral tusk. The tusk can grow to a length of more than 3 meters (10 feet) and weigh up to 10 kilograms (22 pounds). The Narwhal often uses its tusk in duels with another male, typically over a female Narwhal they both desire.

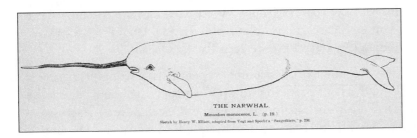

THE NARWHAL.
Monodon monoceros, L.   (p. 19.)
Sketch by Henry W. Elliott, adapted from Vogt and Specht's "Saugethiere," p. 236.

The Narwhal looks like a cross between a unicorn and a whale.

The Narwhal makes its home in the frigid waters of the Arctic and it is seldom seen further south than 70 degrees North latitude. They swim the Arctic seas from Canada to Russia through the Norwegian waters. Many Narwhals have been spotted in the Davis Strait, around Baffin Bay and in the Greenland Sea. It is one of three whale species that spend their entire lives in the Arctic—the Bowhead and Beluga being the others.

Some estimates place the Narwhal population in a range of 10,000 to 45,000. The Narwhal is not considered an endangered species and continues to be hunted by the Inuit people of Greenland and Canada for its tusk, flesh, and other edible parts. Its thick skin is boiled or eaten raw. Some of the meat is fed to sled dogs, and the blubber is used to produce heat and light. The Norwhal can also fall prey to polar bears, walruses, killer whales, and sharks.

Marine Mermaids—Manatee, Dugong, and Sea Cows

The sirenians (commonly called sea cows) are a small group of marine mammals made up of dugongs and manatees, as well as the extinct stellar sea cow. The name sirenia is derived from Greek mythology, which presented the sirens as voluptuous mermaids who would seduce sailors with their songs and cause their ships to crash into the rocky shores. One look at a manatee, however, will make you wonder how anyone could possibly call these endearing beasts sirens. They look more like a cross between an overweight walrus and the Goodyear blimp. Dugongs and manatees have relatively small heads, bulbous bodies, and large flippers located high up on their bodies. In place of the usual mammalian rear limbs is a horizontally flatted tail, similar to the tail of a walrus. Manatees vary in size from 2.5 to 4.5 meters (8 to 15 feet) in length and weigh in at 200 to 600 kilograms (440 to 1,320 pounds). Dugong are a little smaller, reaching lengths of less than 3 meters (10 feet) and topping out at 400 kilograms (880 pounds).

Despite their less than alluring appearance, the manatees and dugong are a common sight around warm coastal areas, especially in and around estuaries, where they graze on sea grass. Some even make their way up rivers. You can find manatees throughout the Amazon River basin, near the coast of tropical West Africa, in the coastal waters near the Southeastern United States, and in the Caribbean Sea. Dugongs prefer the tropical waters of the Indian Ocean and the western Pacific Ocean.

Manatees and dugong are the only marine mammal vegetarians, grazing primarily on various types of seagrass and other vegetation for approximately six hours per day. They're one of the few sea creatures capable of digesting the cellulose in seagrass. Other marine vegetarians eat microscopic algae or seaweed. Manatee and Dugong specialize in two things: floating and eating. The manatee and dugong lungs extend nearly the entire length of their bodies, giving them the lung capacity to stay submerged and making the bottom halves of their bodies as buoyant as the top halves. This enables the creature to lazily float above a field of sea grass and munch away. Manatees and dugongs typically hang out alone or in small family units of only a few members. However, they sometimes form larger groups (or herds) of 20 or so.

The manatee is anything but a voluptuous mermaid.

(Photo Credit: National Oceanic and Atmospheric Administration/Department of Commerce)

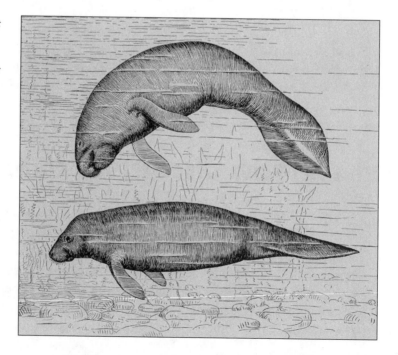

People have traditionally hunted manatees and dugongs for their meat, hides, blubber, and oil, and this has placed some strain on their populations. A more significant threat to the manatee and dugong populations, however, is the destruction of wetlands, many of which grow the seagrass that feeds these creatures. In addition, increased traffic in the waterways in and around estuaries has resulted in increased numbers of manatees and dugong being accidentally injured or killed.

Seals, Walruses, and Other Pinnipeds

Seals, walruses, and sea lions make up an exclusive group of nearly 37 species collectively known as pinnipeds or "wing footed" creatures. The sleek, fur-covered members of this club all have a wing-shaped tail, a fur coat with a blubber lining, and a set of front and rear flippers that work a lot better in water than they do on land. All are dependent on both land and water; they primarily feed and travel in water and rest, breed, molt (shed fur), and bear their young on land (or ice). According to most paleontologists, pinnipeds evolved long after the arrival of cetaceans and sirenians but before the sea otters.

Unlike cetaceans, pinnipeds haven't completely relinquished their fur coats, because fur insulates much better than blubber when you're standing out in the cold. However, in water, blubber is a much better insulating material. This combination of fur and blubber enables the pinnipeds to stay warm both on land and in the cold arctic waters. The blubber also functions as a fuel reserve for long trips or when food is scarce.

Another similarity between cetaceans and pinnipeds, especially between whales and seals, is their ability to dive to great depths. Earlier in this chapter, you learned that sperm whales can dive to depths of nearly 3,000 meters (9,840 feet). Though the southern elephant seal cannot match this record, it has gotten close with an official dive of 1,700 meters (5,580 feet)! Several seals are known to dive down hundreds of meters as well, although eared seals max out at about 200 meters (655 feet). Seals possess many of the same characteristics as whales to enable them to reach these depths: Their blood and muscles can store highly oxygenated blood; they can slow down their metabolism; and during a dive, blood is redirected away from muscle toward the vital organs.

Walrus, Seal, or Sea Lion—What's the Difference?

This family of marine mammals, Pinnipedia, includes the seals, walruses, and sea lions. So, what's the difference between a seal, a walrus, and a sea lion? Following is a list of the characteristics to use when assigning a pinniped to a particular group:

◆ **Seal** has tiny ear holes (no ear flaps); short, blunt front flippers covered with hair; claw-like nails on its "fingers"; short, paddle-shaped rear flippers covered with hair; webbed digits on rear flippers, each "toe" equipped with a nail. Seals are unable to turn their hind flippers forward to help them "walk," so they undulate their bodies and use only their front flippers to move on land. (Seals are also called true seals or earless seals to distinguish them from sea lions and fur seals, which have ear flaps.)

- **Eared seal** (sea lion and fur seal) has small, thin external ear flaps; long, wing-like, hairless flippers with no nails on flipper "fingers"; large, paddle-shaped, hairless rear flippers with webbing between the "toes"; nails on middle three "toes." The eared seals are able to turn their hind flippers forward for improved movement on land.

- **Walrus** is big with tusks. Walrus flippers are hairless, and each "finger" and "toe" contains a small nail. Like sea lions, the walrus can turn its hind flippers forward for improved movement on land.

The seal, sea lion, and walrus are obviously related, though very different.

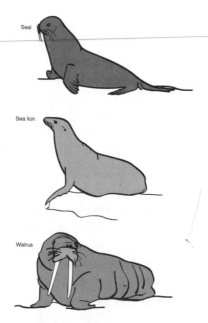

Seal

Sea lion

Walrus

Ocean Alert

Currently, four species of pinnipeds in the United States are on the Endangered Species list. These include the Caribbean monk seal (commonly believed to be extinct), the Guadalupe fur seal, the Hawaiian monk seal, and the Steller sea lion. The Caribbean monk seal and the Hawaiian monk seal are listed as endangered, whereas the Guadalupe fur seal is listed as threatened. The Steller sea lion is listed as endangered in the western part of its range but is listed as threatened in the east.

Making Babies

All pinnipeds must come ashore to breed, give birth, and nurse their young. Interestingly enough, much of this breeding activity occurs all around the same time. Typically during the spring (or early summer in more temperate regions), pinnipeds gather on shore to mate. After mating, the female carries the developing fetus for approximately one year. It doesn't take the fetus that long to fully develop, but it apparently has an internal clock that shuts down development for weeks at a time to ensure that it is born the following spring. When baby pinniped is ready to emerge, the mother swims ashore, gives birth, and starts nursing junior. At this same time, the males arrive to claim their mates, fight with other males, mate with the females, and occasionally roll on top of the babies. Yes, it can be quite a scene.

During these mad birthing-nursing-mating periods, male pinnipeds typically fight a great deal. Of course, each male pinniped wants to breed with all the female pinnipeds it can seduce, so it attempts to coerce various females into joining its harem. Male (bull) sea lions will puff up the mane around their necks to ward off competitors and attract females. Bull elephant seals can inflate their snouts like a balloon for the same purpose, and the hooded seal can inflate the top of its head. A successful bull can establish a harem of up to 50 females.

Who's Endangered Now?

Seals are as cute as babies and have generated a great deal of press for the ecology movement, but now that some populations are on the rebound, nature lovers are beginning to wonder how much protection we should afford these voracious predators. Some species of seals are actually contributing to the endangerment of other species and are destroying valuable human resources.

One case provides the perfect example of how a recovering species can negatively affect the "natural" balance. The California sea lion and Pacific harbor seal populations have reached historically high levels—with a 6 to 8 percent annual growth rate since the mid-1970s. During this period, salmon populations have declined dramatically along the West Coast, leading to this obvious question: Should we protect the seals or the salmon? Of course, the answer is "both," but people are beginning to become more selective, leaving the threatened species alone in areas where their populations are at risk and hunting the more populous pinnipeds in areas where they are overly successful.

One of the biggest success stories in rescuing endangered seal species concerns the rebound of the Guadalupe fur seal. The major cause of the Guadalupe fur seal's decline was commercial hunting in the late 1700s and early 1800s. By 1825, this species was exterminated in the waters off Southern California. Commercial sealing continued in Mexican waters through 1894. Currently the Guadalupe fur seal seems to be expanding its range, with regular sightings of animals on San Miguel and San Nicolas Islands off the Southern California coast. The Caribbean monk seal was not so fortunate and is believed to have been extinct since the early 1950s.

Captain Clam's Comments

Have you ever heard the true story of André the seal? Every spring for more than 20 years, the New England Aquarium in Boston, Massachusetts, would release André, and he would swim about 150 miles north to Rockport Harbor, Maine, to spend the summer there. André's return was always a high point for local residents. André became the honorary harbormaster, has had books written about him, and has even had his story made into a movie.

The Least You Need to Know

- Marine mammals can be divided into three groups: the cetaceans (whales, dolphins, and porpoises), sirenians (manatees and dugongs), and pinnipeds (seals, sea lions, and walruses).

- The first marine mammals, the archaeocetes, appeared on Earth nearly 50 million years ago.

- Cetaceans have a streamlined shape, elongated face, virtually hairless body, a blowhole for breathing, horizontally flattened flukes for swimming, and front arms that are formed into fins.

- Dolphins are toothed cetaceans with long snouts.

- Whales have several adaptations that make them great divers, including the ability to store highly oxygenated blood, slow down their metabolism, and redirect blood away from muscle toward the vital organs.

- The sirenians (commonly called sea cows) are a small group of marine mammals consisting of dugongs and manatees, the only vegetarian marine mammals.

- The pinnipeds include true (earless) seals, eared seals (sea lions and fur seals), and walruses.

Chapter 17

Waterfowl Wonders

In This Chapter

- ◆ Penguins and other flightless birds
- ◆ Marathon gliding with the albatross
- ◆ Dive-bombing pelicans and other aerial fish predators
- ◆ Plunging the depths with loons, grebes, and other divers
- ◆ Winging it with the gulls

The ocean scene consists not only of estuaries, tidal zones, and the open ocean, but extends above the ocean's surface to the wide-open skies, beyond the shores to the surrounding treetops and high-rise cliffs, and beyond the cold arctic waters and up onto the ice. This is the realm not of bottom dwellers and open ocean swimmers, but of some of the most beautiful and successful of all sea creatures—the seabirds. In this realm, you find penguins waddling on pack ice, heron wading in the shallows of the estuaries, gulls scavenging the shores for rejected fish, pelicans plummeting from the skies to fill their gullets, majestic albatross soaring over open seas, colorful puffins eking out a living on the rocky cliffs, and hundreds of other species exploiting the rich resources of the sea. This chapter explores the wonderful world of marine waterfowl and reveals the secret lives of some of our more interesting feathered friends.

What Makes a Seabird a Seabird?

As a group, birds constitute the second most populous class of vertebrates. Only fish have more members. Worldwide, the bird population consists of 9,000 species, but only 4 percent of those are considered seabirds. Fortunately, what seabirds lack in diversity, they make up in population. These few species that have managed to adapt to life in the oceans are highly successful and never need to share their bounty with the other 96 percent of the world's bird population that live inland.

So, what does a bird need to do to join the exclusive seabird club? For a bird to be considered a seabird, it generally meets the following requirements:

♦ **Be a bird.** Obvious, huh? To be a bird, a creature needs to be a warm-blooded vertebrate with wings; feathers; strong wing muscles; a toothless beak; a skeleton made up of strong, usually hollow bones; two legs; excellent binocular vision; and a specialized breathing system in which air flows in a continuous path through the lungs.

♦ **Depend on the sea.** Seabirds live, breed, and feed in or near the sea and depend on the sea for most of their food.

♦ **Secrete salt.** Seabirds ingest a great deal of salt when they eat and drink and must have salt-secreting glands. These are typically located in the bird's beak or near its eyes.

♦ **Breed in colonies.** All seabirds must return to land to breed, lay eggs, and nest. Most seabirds (95 percent) form colonies during the breeding season. Colonies can vary in size from 10 pairs to thousands of pairs of seabirds.

Of the 9,000 species of birds, 372 are considered seabirds; and of the 29 orders of birds, 7 contain all the seabird species. These seven orders are the *Sphenisciformes* (penguins), Gaviiformes (divers and loons), *Podicipediformes* (grebes), *Procellariiformes* (albatrosses, petrels, shearwaters), *Pelecaniformes* (pelicans, gannets, boobies, cormorants, frigatebirds, tropicbirds), *Anseriformes* (ducks and geese), and *Charadriiformes* (gulls, shorebirds, terns, skimmers, auks). Of course, this chapter cannot possibly cover all these birds, but it does examine each group and mention one or two of the more common and representative species of each order. Some *Falconformes* (eagles and osprey) catch fish near the coasts, but they are not considered to be true seabirds.

> **Underwater Eye**
>
> A bird's lungs do not expand to fill with air and contract to exhale as ours do. In birds, the air follows a circular path through the lungs—in one end and out the other. Birds typically have nine air sacs that they use to establish a continuous flow of air through their lungs.

Skating and Diving with Penguins

No seabird is more devoted to ocean life than the penguin. This chubby little bird even traded in its wings for a pair of flippers and can barely waddle let alone walk, choosing instead to hop or to sled across the ice on its belly. Although penguins are a laughing stock on land and can't even dream of flying, when they hit the water, they are among the most graceful of birds, using their strong "wings" to propel themselves through the water while steering with their feet and tails. Fairly quick in the water (up to 24 kilometers [15 miles] per hour), penguins are quite capable of catching their keep (primarily fish, cuttlefish, crustaceans, and other small sea creatures) and have actually become the most dominant water fowl in the frigid Antarctic region.

Penguins are represented by 17 species, all of which live south of the equator; most choosing to nest around the periphery of Antarctica and its surrounding islands. Several species favor nesting sites in Australia and New Zealand, and some species prefer the western or southern coast of Africa, or the western coast of South America. The Galapagos penguin marks the northernmost penguin colony, choosing to breed very near the equator on the Galapagos Islands.

Penguins are specially adapted to living in frigid water. Like cetaceans (whales, dolphins, and porpoises), the penguin's body is tapered, helping it move through the water more smoothly. Unlike most birds that have hollow bones, the penguin's bones are solid, reducing its buoyancy, so it can dive more easily. Its wing bones are fused and covered with tough skin, making them more like flippers than wings. The penguin has a double-insulated hide, consisting of a thick layer of fat on the inside covered by skin and a densely packed layer of feathers that are shaped more like needles than true, branching feathers. Their feet are positioned toward the rear of their bodies, near the tail, so the penguin can use the feet and tail together to guide itself through the water.

One of the most social of the seabirds, penguins commonly flock in the water and gather in the thousands (sometimes hundreds of thousands) on shore to breed and raise their young. These breeding grounds, called rookeries, are very influential in the life of a penguin, and penguins always return to the rookeries where they were born. During the mating ritual, the males bray, trumpet, and strut their stuff in showy performances for the females, who are in charge of selecting a mate. Shortly after mating, the female penguin lays one or two eggs (sometimes in a nest and sometimes not), which take about one to two months to hatch. Both penguins typically care for the newborn until it loses its baby fluff and grows its first real coat of feathers.

Penguins are built to survive and navigate the cold arctic waters.

(Photo credit: Michael Von Woert, NOAA)

Underwater Eye

Unlike other birds that typically breed in the spring, the emperor penguin breeds during the cold Antarctic winter, when temperatures can dip below −60 degrees Celsius (−76 degrees Fahrenheit) and winds blow at speeds of more than 124 kilometers (77 miles) per hour. (Emperor penguins breed in the winter, so that the newborns will be ready to swim when the ice begins to break up in the spring.) The mother lays a single egg and then takes off for about two months, leaving the father to hatch it. The father perches the egg atop his feet and covers it with his toasty brood pouch, standing pretty much in the same place until mom returns. Near the time when the newborn is ready to hatch, mom returns with food and cares for junior for another two months while dad grabs some lunch.

Going Down Under with Loons

Loons (called divers in the United Kingdom) are the Northern Hemisphere's answer to penguins. Although they look nothing like penguins, they exhibit some of the same adaptations that penguins have, making them remarkably gifted divers and swimmers. Like penguins and unlike other birds, loons have solid bones, which make them nearly as dense as the water on which they float. Simply by exhaling air from its lungs and air sacs and by releasing the air trapped in its wings, a loon can lower itself down below the surface like a submarine.

The loon's legs, positioned near the rear as they are on penguins, provide the loon with powerful thrust. Unlike a duck, which has webbed feet (webbing that extends between the toes), the loon has lobed feet (webbing around each toe, but not connected between the toes). Using its legs for propulsion and its wings to steer and turn, the loon can zigzag through the water, making sharp turns to nab quick prey and elude predators. The loon can dive its torpedo-shaped body down through the water hundreds of feet and stay submerged for several minutes.

The loon is a natural-born diver.

Unlike penguins, which have lost the ability to fly, loons are excellent aviators, able to achieve speeds of up to 60 miles (97 kilometers) per hour. However, with their dense bodies, solid bones, and small wings, take-offs are a little awkward. Loons must drag their bodies through the water for several yards before they get up enough speed to lift off.

Loons spend nearly all their time in water, coming to shore only to avoid violent storms or to nest. When nesting, the loon, which is awkward on land, builds its nest close to the water and creates a slide down to the water. When a predator approaches, instead of running to the water, the loon slides down its ramp and dives below the surface. In its nest, the loon typically lays only one or two eggs, which hatch in about a month. The baby loons stay close to their mother—often riding on the mother's back until they learn to swim on their own.

Underwater Eye

Although loons spend a great deal of time in the ocean, especially around northern coastal areas, loons are equally at home in freshwater lakes. The common loons commonly summers throughout Canada and the Northern United States (including Minnesota and New Hampshire), and are a common sight until they make their annual winter migration to the coastal areas as far south as the Gulf of Mexico. Some also winter inland, in and around Lake Michigan.

Grebes

Another family of seabirds that is particularly adept at diving is the grebe family. Although a little smaller than loons and having longer necks and more colorful plumage, grebes are remarkably similar to loons in both structure and behavior. Their tapered bodies are nearly tailless, and they have lobed feet set far back on their bodies to provide the necessary thrust for diving. Also like loons and penguins, grebes have solid bones that make them float low in the water and enable them to descend below the surface simply by exhaling and releasing the air from their feathers.

One of the more bizarre traits unique to grebes is their appetite for their own feathers. Grebes commonly pluck their own feathers and swallow them. Although no one is certain why grebes eat their own feathers, some scientists have guessed that the feathers assist the grebes' digestion in some way, perhaps by filtering out sharp fish bones before they reach the intestines, which the bones could potentially puncture.

Grebes also differ from loons in their nesting habits. Unlike loons, which build primitive nests on shore, grebes nest in shallow, densely weeded areas and build more intricate nests, consisting of mud and vegetation. Grebes practice a couple interesting courting rituals—one in which the male and female dive down, grab a mouthful of weeds, and then dance together, breast-to-breast, heads high in the air, wildly shaking their weeds. In another ritual, the two face off. Each holds its neck in a swan-esque S-shape. They then start running across the water for 20 to 30 meters (66 to 98 feet) and dive down below the surface.

Once the wild courtship is complete, and soon after the two lovebirds mate, the female lays two to six eggs in the nest, and the male and female take turns warming and turning the eggs. When the newborns hatch, they crawl up on the back of one of the parents and ride along until they're ready to swim on their own. Of course, one of the first meals that the newborn eats is a feather from the breast of one of its parents!

Is That an Albatross Around Your Neck?

For centuries, sailors have believed that the albatross is a sign of good luck and that killing an albatross is a sure way to ruin a good cruise. Perhaps this belief has arisen because so few birds soar above the middle of the ocean or because the albatross is such a majestic glider. If the albatross is truly a good-luck charm, though, you would think that it would be a revered bird; however, most sailors treat the albatross with disdain, assigning it nicknames such as "gooney" and "mollemok" (Dutch for "stupid gull").

Unlike the birds covered up to this point—the penguin, loon, and grebe—the albatross is more at home in the air than in the water. It has a huge wingspan, reaching 3 to 4 meters in some species; a hooked bill with tube-like nostrils; and fully webbed feet. Most species make their home in the Southern Hemisphere, where the wind blows almost constantly. Without a constant wind, the albatross is nearly grounded, because it is designed more for gliding than for flapping its wings. With wind under its wings, the albatross can lift off and glide effortlessly for hours at a time, barely twitching its wings.

The albatross has the largest wingspan of any bird.

Like most seabirds, the albatross must return to land to breed and nest. Most species choose to nest in isolated island rookeries, where the process starts with an elaborate mating ritual. The male and female first greet each other with deep bows, and then they clap their beaks together as if in a swordfight. Face to face and beak to beak, they then squawk at each other in a rising pitch of "Ahhh-ahhhh-ahhhh," after which they settle down and gently touch. The two eventually mate, and soon after, the female lays a single egg. The albatross fashions its nest out of mud, plants, or and/or soil into the shape of a small, cylindrical tower. A divot in the top of the nest holds the egg safely and securely. (In general, the albatross is monogamous, sticking with the same mate its entire life.)

Captain Clam's Comments

In Samuel Taylor Coleridge's poem, "The Rime of the Ancient Mariner," the mariner uses his crossbow to shoot an albatross that his shipmates had interpreted as a good omen. Soon thereafter, the winds die, and other ill luck follows the ship. To punish the mariner and appease the evil spirits, the crew forces the mariner to wear the dead albatross around his neck. Ever since this poem became famous, wearing an albatross around one's neck has been a symbol for the disdain one suffers when he or she lets down family members, fellow workers, or any community of individuals.

Skimming the Surface with Petrels and Shearwaters

Close cousins of the albatross, the petrels and shearwaters have a slightly shorter wingspan, a more slender body, and powerful wings. Their nostrils are fused into a single tube that runs along the top of the bill and is used for secreting salt as well as for breathing. They prefer to fly just above the surface of the ocean, which is the reason they're called shearwaters. The shearwaters are typically open ocean (pelagic) birds that spend most of their lives far out to sea. Many are known for their long migrations, some migrating from below the equator all the way up into Alaska! Like the albatross, the shearwaters prefer to glide, but when they need some power, they don't hesitate to beat their wings. Some of the smaller shearwaters exhibit more "normal" flying techniques, choosing to flap their wings more regularly.

Like the albatrosses, the shearwaters meet their mates in a large group setting to breed and lay eggs, though most shearwaters assume a nocturnal lifestyle in the rookery. I guess that's the attraction—the night life.

Storm Petrels and Diving Petrels

Some of the smallest of the seabirds, the storm petrels, look as though they don't belong in the same group as the albatrosses and shearwaters. These mini-petrels have the characteristic hooked beak and fused, tubular nostrils, but the resemblance ends there. These small birds typically prefer flapping their wings to merely gliding, and they typically perform long, annual migrations, spending their summers in the north or south and hanging out around the equator during the winters. Like the shearwaters, storm petrels become primarily nocturnal when they reach their breeding grounds.

The diving petrels are small, compact birds that are equally adept at flying and swimming. They fly fast and low, flapping their wings rapidly rather than merely gliding. These species also like to dive into the water—often entering the water directly from flight to pursue its prey. Many will fly right into the crest of a wave. The diving petrels prefer a solitary lifestyle, and are typically found at sea alone or with one or two other companions. However, like other members of this family, they congregate in the thousands to breed and nest. The diving petrels typically nest in shallow burrows and take on a nocturnal lifestyle to avoid larger birds and other predators.

Pelicans and Other Pouched Pelecaniformes

Accounting for nearly 67 of the 372 species of seabirds are the *Pelecaniformes*, which include pelicans, gannets, boobies, cormorants, shags, frigatebirds, and tropicbirds.

All these birds exhibit fully webbed feet (*totipalmate*), with webbing extending between all four toes. Most have an elastic pouch of bare skin that hangs down from the lower bill, called the gular pouch, which is most prominent in the pelicans. Most of these species live on a diet of fish, although some species in more tropical areas feed on squid, as well. The Pelecaniformes gather in colonies to breed and nest, typically laying one to six eggs. The hatchlings emerge completely helpless, born featherless with their eyes closed, and are completely reliant on the parents for several weeks.

The species that make up this group of seabirds vary widely both in physical characteristics and behavior. The following sections provide a brief overview of each species, highlighting their most characteristic features.

The Pterodactyl-Like Pelicans

Most people are accustomed to seeing pelicans perched on poles, loitering on fishing piers, or sitting in cages at the zoo, where they are best known for their huge beaks and baggy chins that stretch out like mailbags when they're filled with fish. However, in flight, pelicans look less like cartoon characters and more like modern day pterodactyls. Weighing up to 15 kilograms (10 feet) and having a wingspan of nearly 3 meters (33 pounds), these primitive-looking birds practically blot out the sun when they fly in formation overhead.

Pelicans are known for their huge beaks and baggy chins.

Although the brown pelican of the Americas often acts like a panhandler, begging tourists to throw it some fish, it is actually a gifted angler. The pelican soars in slow circles over the water, surveying the surface for schools of small fish. When it spots its prey, it tucks in its wings and plunges headfirst, diving into the ocean with mouth wide open. It then surfaces with a mouthful of fish and seawater, tilts its head to one side to drain the water (sometimes a gallon or more), and then tosses back its head to gobble up its catch.

Most other pelican species prefer fishing in groups, on the surface. These pelicans commonly gather in shallow areas, where they work together to corral a school of fish. The pelicans then move in with mouths open to scoop up their dinner.

Pelicans are communal creatures and typically build simple nests out of twigs and branches. The male supplies the building material, while the female builds the nests. Some species prefer nesting on the ground, whereas others favor treetops (including mangrove treetops). Pelicans become sexually mature at about the age of three years, and both parents contribute to hatching the egg and caring for the young.

Underwater Eye

In 1970, the brown pelican was declared endangered in the United States because it was failing to reproduce. Chemicals including DDT, chlorinated hydrocarbons, and polychlorinated biphenyls (PCBs) contaminated the food chain, accumulated in fish, and became highly concentrated in brown pelicans and other seabirds (including bald eagles). This caused the thinning of the birds' eggshells, which decreased the number of successful hatches. In 1972, the government banned DDT and other chemicals that caused the problem, and since then populations have been on the rebound.

Dive-Bombing Boobies and Gannets

Outstripping even the brown pelican, gannets and boobies are aerial dive-bombers, plummeting from heights of more than 30 meters (98 feet) to snare unsuspecting fish. Gannets and boobies frequently hunt in flocks, dropping from the sky like a flurry of arrows when they spot a school of fish, each surfacing with a fish wedged between its scissor-like jaws.

Gannets and boobies are beautiful, torpedo-shaped birds with long, thick beaks, strong necks, and a streamlined appearance. Gannets prefer a cool, northern climate and nest in rocky areas and cliffs. Boobies prefer more tropical regions. Their eyes make them look kind of dumb, but the name "booby" was probably derived from the bird's habit of landing on the decks of ships and allowing sailors to capture them easily. Both are highly social birds, especially when it comes time to breed and lay eggs. Boobies and gannets are known to gather in colonies numbering in the tens of thousands.

Spear-Fishing Cormorants

If boobies and gannets are diving torpedoes, the cormorant is a diving spear—a powerful, streamlined bird with heavy bones and a long neck tipped with a sharp spike of a beak. Like the loons and other diving birds, the cormorant sits low in the water, but unlike loons, the cormorant's feathers are not waterproof. This makes it difficult for cormorants to spend much time in the water. Typically, they fish, eat, and then find somewhere to rest on land, spreading out their wings to dry. They are commonly seen on shore, drying their wings in groups. Cormorants are some of the most efficient hunters and best underwater swimmers, commonly diving more than 10 meters down to pursue a fish. The cormorant then flips the fish in the air, catches it by the head, and swallows it headfirst, ensuring that the fish's scales don't catch in its throat. Some cormorants are flightless birds, using their powerful, fully webbed feet to dive underwater and hunt for prey.

Close cousins of the cormorants, the anhingas (or snake birds) prefer spear fishing to diving, and commonly prefer feeding in freshwater lakes and rivers and shallow coastal swamps. Anhingas float low in the water and swim around in search of prey. Instead of diving in and biting its prey, the anhinga cocks its neck in an S-shape and then snaps its head forward, spearing its prey with its sharp, slender beak. Like the cormorant, the anhinga then flips the fish in the air, catches it by its head, and swallows it headfirst.

Underwater Eye
Cormorants are commonly enlisted by humans, especially in Asian countries, to help them fish. The cormorant is forced to wear a ring around its neck, which allows the cormorant to breathe but prevents it from swallowing its catch. The cormorant is released to fish, and upon its return, its catch is removed.

Frigatebirds and Tropicbirds

The most opportunistic of the Pelecaniformes, the frigatebirds will grab a meal wherever, and from whomever, they can. Frigatebirds, with their broad wingspan and relatively light bodies, are aerial acrobats compared to the other species covered in this section. They have a wide range of tastes and are known to dine on everything from molluscs and fish to baby sea turtles and even jellies. They can snap up a flying fish in mid-flight or skim the surface for unwary prey, but some prefer to let other birds do the work for them. These forked-tail bandits commonly harass other fishing birds for their catch, pecking on pelicans, boobies, gulls, and other birds until they drop their food and then scooping it up for themselves. Frigatebirds will even snatch food out of a pelican's gular sac as the pelican is draining out the water after a catch! Because their plumage is only lightly greased, the frigatebird cannot spend a great deal of time in the water; hence, it hangs out close to shore, where it can return to rest and dry off.

> ### Underwater Eye
>
> Unlike the pelican, which uses its gular sac to trap and hold food, the frigatebird has a bright red gular sac that it puffs up to ward off enemies and attract mates.

Closely related to the frigatebirds are the tropicbirds. These graceful fliers have a broad wingspan, a relatively light body, and a forked tail, just like the frigatebirds, and spend more time airborne. Unlike frigatebirds, whose plumage is only lightly oiled, the tropicbird is designed more for an open ocean lifestyle. Like the albatrosses, tropicbirds prefer to live out at sea and return to land only to nest and breed.

Sea Ducks and Geese

The majority of ducks and geese are freshwater species, but some of these species spend at least a portion of their lives in coastal areas, which enables them to be listed as seabirds (or sea ducks to be more specific). Four species of ducks, collectively called the eider (pronounced *EYE-duhr*) ducks, are considered to be solely marine oriented. You probably have heard of "eider down" jackets or pillows, which are made from the soft, fluffy feathers of these ducks. The eider ducks use this down to line their nests, and then people come and steal it to make coats, jackets, pillows, and comforters.

Other primarily marine ducks, which live south of the equator, are the steamerducks. Four species of these large, stocky steamerducks inhabit the coastal waters around Argentina, Chile, and the Falkland Islands. Only one species of steamerduck, the flying steamerduck, can fly; the others are flightless birds. The Falkland Islands are also home to one of the few geese species that favors the ocean over freshwater habitats—the kelp goose. This goose lives in coastal areas and feeds primarily on seaweed.

Gulls and Their Close Cousins

Accounting for 131 of the 372 species of seabirds, the Charadriiformes are the most diverse collection of seabirds covered in this chapter. This order includes 50 species of gulls; 44 species of their closest relatives, the terns; 22 species of auks, some of which look more like parrots than gulls; 8 species of skuas, which look like frigate-birds; and a handful of other species, including skimmers, sheathbills, and shorebirds.

By looking at the members of this order, you would never think that they could possibly be related; however, they share many internal anatomical traits that qualify them to use the same family name. Shared characteristics include the structure of the skull and spinal column, leg tendons, and syrinx (voice box). Most of the external features vary from species to species. Some members have webbed feet, some do not. Some have narrow, pointed beaks whereas others are equipped with flattened, curved bills that look like pruning shears. Some have a wide wingspan for gliding, whereas others have short wings that they must beat rapidly in order to stay aloft. The following sections reveal the diversity of this group by examining some of its more common and interesting members.

Gulls—Survivors of the Sea

Gulls are survivors, opportunistic birds that are designed and motivated to take advantage of nearly every environment and food source available. Most live along the shorelines where they pick through whatever washes up on shore and any scraps other animals discard. They fish. They drop bivalves from the air to crack them open. They live near garbage dumps, where they sort through trash to feed on human leftovers. They follow plows through fields to feed on worms turned up by the plows. Gulls even eat the eggs and prey upon the young of other gulls.

Gulls are built to take advantage of a wide range of opportunities. They have strong, football-shaped bodies; long, powerful wings; webbed feet; and hooked bills. They cannot glide as far out to sea as an albatross; they cannot dive as deep as a loon; they cannot swim as well as a gannet. However, gulls are a complete package—a well-rounded bird that specializes in nothing but is capable of carving out a niche in nearly any ocean (and even nonocean) environment.

Ocean Alert

Gull populations explode in any areas where they find a particularly rich food source, and they can pose a threat to human health and safety. Huge populations of gulls near air strips commonly cause safety problems for airplanes taking off and landing. Gulls also have been connected to several salmonella outbreaks when populations become heavy near water treatment plants, fish-processing plants, and other places where human consumables are processed and handled.

The Slimmer, Trimmer Terns

Although closely related to gulls in both structure and appearance, terns are a bit more elegant—both in flight and in behavior. Because of their graceful flight and forked tails, they are commonly referred to as sea swallows. Terns are smaller than gulls and have a more streamlined body, making them much more adept at navigating the ocean airspace. Unlike the scavenging gulls, terns prefer to hunt for their meals, soaring over the ocean with beaks pointed down, in search of small fish. When a tern spots a fish, it dives down, scoops up its catch, and quickly returns to the air. Because terns have small, webbed feet, they are not particularly gifted swimmers and prefer to negotiate the air or land; hence, they are primarily coastal birds.

Terns typically nest in colonies on beaches, in sand pits, or other soft ground near the coast or near an inland body of water. They form small depressions in the ground, which they might line with grass or twigs or shards of shells. Some species nest in rocky cliffs or in treetops. Terns lay anywhere from one to four eggs, which hatch in about a month. The young seek cover under surrounding vegetation, where the parents feed and care for them for another 30 days or so. Approximately two to three months after hatching, the young terns set out for life on their own.

Auk Talk

The most gifted swimmers of this group are the auks—chubby, dumpy-looking birds that are relatively clumsy in the air, but talented divers in the water. The auks favor the cold northern waters in the Northern Hemisphere, commonly nesting in rocky areas and cliffs. Many have narrow, pointy bills, but a few species, including the puffins, have a heavy, colorful bill that makes them look more like parrots. Like penguins, auks use their powerful wings to propel themselves underwater, but because they are more buoyant than penguins, they have a tougher time working their way below the surface. Puffins spend most of their lives at sea, returning to land only to nest and raise their young.

The Scary Skuas (Jaegers)

Representing eight species, the skuas (in Great Britain) or jaegers (in the Americas) look like a cross between a gull and a hawk. Fully grown, they reach a length of more than a half meter. They have powerful wings, sharp, hooked bills, and bad attitudes, which make them some of the fiercest aerial predators of the sea. The South polar skuas even have the nerve to pick on baby penguins—much to the consternation of Antarctic tourists. Most species hang out south of the equator, although the great skua makes its home in the North Atlantic, and the south polar skua vacations in the north.

The puffin is a beautiful bird and an excellent swimmer.

Wading in with Shorebirds and Sheathbills

Walk along any beach, and you will encounter a host of leggy birds that enjoy playing in the waves and pecking at the sand and rocks to extract morsels of food. These birds are collectively known as shorebirds (or waders in Great Britain). This group of beachcombers includes sandpipers, plovers, oyster catchers, avocets, and stilts. With no webbing between their toes, shorebirds are not designed to spend much time at sea. On land, however, these are the most mobile birds on the beach.

The shorebird diversity typically reveals itself in the size of the birds, the length of their legs and necks, and the length and shape of their bills. Most of the shorebirds have long, narrow bills, some of which are flexible, for reaching down the holes created by worms and diving down into sand or muck to extract submerged bivalves. However, some shorebirds that feed closer to the surface have shorter bills. After feeding, shorebirds typically retreat to the trees or weeds near shore, and although they favor land to air or sea, some shorebirds experience extremely long migrations of thousands of miles. Many shorebirds are commonly found inland, where they prefer brackish or freshwater environments.

Another type of shorebird is the sheathbill, which prefers colder climates. Sheathbills look like harmless white chickens, but are some of the lowliest scavengers of the sea, living on the excrement of seals and penguins and stealing what they can from penguins—primarily their eggs and any uneaten food the baby penguins drop or refuse to eat. These relentless predatory scavengers will even pick the scabs of wounded animals.

Surface-Fishing Skimmers

Whereas shorebirds dig down to retrieve their meals, skimmers prefer surface feeding. The skimmers have beaks with a lower half that juts out from the upper half. These agile aviators fly low along the surface of the water with their mouths open—the lower half of the beak skimming the surface. As soon as the beak bumps into an object—typically a small fish, insect, or crustacean—the beak slams shut, catching and killing the prey.

Three species of skimmers glide along the ocean's surface in areas as distant as North America, Africa, and Southern Asia. During the day, skimmers typically roost on shore, heading out at night to skim for prey.

Ospreys, Herons, Flamingos, and Other Seaside Attractions

Along the coasts of many islands and continents are hundreds of species of birds that frequent ocean areas, through their migratory patterns, feeding patterns, or merely by coincidence. Although these birds are not formally considered seabirds, many people associate them with the shallow waters of estuaries, salt marshes, and rocky cliffs that neighbor the oceans. Following is a list of the most commonly spotted seaside birds that do not officially qualify as seabirds:

- **Ospreys**   Commonly called a fish hawk, this bird is a hawk that frequents the sea for fresh fish. Unlike most divers that catch prey with their beaks, the osprey prefers to use its talons.

- **Herons**   These long-necked, long-billed wading birds prefer freshwater but are commonly seen in the brackish waters of salt marshes where they commonly feed. Herons are graceful and interesting to watch, both when they spearfish and when they fly overhead, with their distinctive S-shaped necks curled up even in flight.

- **Egrets**   The uptown herons, egrets are actually herons but , usually have white plumage. The egret typically has a tuft of feathers on its heads and on the lower portion of its back. Their beautiful plumage nearly drove them to extinction because it was such a valuable commodity for making women's hats.

- **Ibises**   In the same order as the herons and egrets, the ibises are unique in that they have curved bills and when they fly they keep their necks extended rather than holding them in the tucked, S-shaped configuration. Like herons, ibises are waders; they prod the shallow waters with their long, curved bills and snap up whatever they touch.

◆ **Spoonbills**   Another relative to the heron, the spoonbill, common to Europe and India, has a distinctive, flattened bill that's rounded like a spoon at the tip. The spoonbill wades in the shallows, swinging its open bill from side-to-side, and snapping up whatever it happens to bump into.

◆ **Flamingos**   In many classification systems, the flamingo qualifies as a seabird. It likes to hang out in estuaries and salt marshes but seems to prefer living in and near saltwater lakes. To feed, a flamingo dunks its head below the water and scrapes the bottom with its huge, hooked beak. It then presses its thick tongue against the roof of its mouth, straining the water out of its beak and leaving behind a meal of small creatures and vegetation.

◆ **Kingfishers**   Short, stout birds with big heads, short legs, and long, narrow bills, the kingfishers like to pick on smaller, weaker fish. Kingfishers typically make their homes in subterranean holes and "caves" left behind by other creatures, such as bees and termites.

◆ **Crows**   A couple species of crows, including the fish crow, prefer to hang out along the coasts and eat fish. The fish crow, common in the Southeastern United States, is equally at home near fresh and saltwater, where it feeds on fish, invertebrates, road kill and other carrion, fruit, seeds, and the eggs and young of other birds, especially seabirds and other waterfowl.

Although these birds don't qualify as bona fide seabirds, they spend enough time on shore to earn them at least an honorable mention.

The Least You Need to Know

◆ To qualify as a seabird, you must be a bird, depend on the sea, secrete excess salt, and breed in colonies.

◆ Although penguins are flightless, they are well adapted to live in the sea, where they can use their "wings" to propel themselves through the water.

◆ Loons and grebes are excellent divers with dense bodies and powerful legs.

◆ If the birds in this chapter were to have a long-distance flying contest, the albatrosses would win, because they can glide for hundreds of miles barely flapping a wing.

◆ Pelicans use their baggy chins as huge nets, scooping up water and fish and then tipping their heads to one side to drain the water.

- Gulls are equally adept in air, water, and on the ground and are some of the most successful scavengers on the planet.

- Auks, in the same order as the gulls, swim better underwater than they fly in the air.

- Although many other birds rely on the ocean for much of their food, they are not true seabirds.

Part  5

Man, Woman, Child, and the Sea

Long before the Greeks sailed around the Mediterranean Sea in search of adventure and conquests, people have had a vital relationship with the sea, relying on it for food, travel, commerce, and recreation. Over many thousands of years, people have developed an even closer relationship with the seas and have learned how to exploit even more of its resources.

This part reveals the history of human interaction with the world's oceans. Here, you learn about ocean exploration and recreation, the laws that govern the seas and the pirates who have broken those laws, and the various ways humans have exploited and continue to exploit the ocean's many resources. You even learn how to become an ocean advocate and help conserve the ocean's vulnerable resources.

Exploring and Exploiting the Ocean Depths

In This Chapter

- ◆ Navigating the seas without a global positioning system
- ◆ Science goes to sea: the birth of oceanography
- ◆ The development of modern submersibles
- ◆ Discovering sunken treasures
- ◆ The ocean's mineral treasures

Early explorers viewed the sea more as an obstacle between landmasses than as a separate world to be cherished and explored. Sure, they exploited the oceans for seafood and appreciated their immensity and mystery, but for the most part, oceans were little more than big moats standing in the way of human progress and global commerce. Once humans mastered the seas and were able to traverse the oceans at will, they quickly became curious about tides, currents, and the various creatures living beneath the surface. This curiosity inspired scientists to begin formal studies of the oceans that have become more and more sophisticated with each passing year.

This chapter examines the history of our growing understanding of the sea and reveals some of the technological innovations that have improved our ability to explore its depths and exploit its resources.

The Early Days

As long as people have lived near the oceans, they have studied the oceans to more fully exploit its resources, to avoid dangerous sea plants and animals, and to better navigate the seas for travel and trade. As early as 1200 B.C.E., the Phoenicians had become seasoned sailors and had dominated trade in the Mediterranean Sea. At some point, the Phoenicians explored beyond the Straits of Gibralter and into the Atlantic Ocean sailing north along the European coast and south along the western coast of Africa. Sometime around the seventh century B.C.E., the Phoenicians may have even circumnavigated the African continent!

Although not as dexterous on the high seas as the Phoenicians, the Greeks were experienced sailors, as well, sailing primarily in the Aegean and Mediterranean Seas. Near the middle of the fifth century B.C.E., the Greeks began a more formal study of the oceans and record their observations in writing. Around 400 B.C.E. the Greek historian Herodotus recorded his observations of the regular tides in the Persian Gulf. He also wrote about the silt deposits in the Nile Delta and about the western seas, using the term Atlantic to describe this body of water.

In the fourth century B.C.E., the Greek philosopher Aristotle applied a more disciplined approach to study the oceans and their life forms to earn the title of "Father of Natural History." Aristotle is one of the first philosophers on record to conclude that the earth is spherical. Aristotle was famous for his keen observations and he used his talent to identify and describe more than 100 species of fish, 40 species of molluscs and echinoderms, and more than 20 species of crustaceans and annelid worms. Aristotle also properly classified cetaceans as mammals. Perhaps his greatest gift to modern oceanography, marine biology, and other sciences is the disciplined, thorough approach he followed in all his studies.

After Aristotle, a few scientists and philosophers throughout Britain, Italy, Arabia, and other countries preserved Aristotle's works and furthered the study of the oceans and marine life. However, during these dark ages, little progress was made in any of the arts and sciences—at least little was recorded. Not until the Renaissance period, in the fourteenth century and the arrival of the famous explorers, did the formal study of oceanography start to move forward again in any significant way.

Captain Clam's Comments

Although the European sailors steal the limelight for crossing the Atlantic, the Polynesians were sailing back and forth across the Pacific a few hundred years before the Europeans realized that the earth was round. Instead of focusing on charts and on latitude and longitude, the Polynesians turned their gaze to the skies, using their observations of the positions of the stars, planets, and moon to orient themselves. The Polynesians' cross-oceanic journeys throughout the Pacific to Hawaii, New Zealand (Aotearoa), Easter Island (Rapa Nui), Tahiti, and other remote islands would never have been successful without a keen understanding of celestial navigation.

Sailing the Seas with Some Famous Explorers

A few hundred years after Christopher Columbus crossed the Atlantic (1492) and Magellan and company circumnavigated the globe (1519–1522), people started becoming interested in ocean currents, tides, and winds and curious about the plants and animals that hang out below the surface. The exploration began with the mapping of the continents and oceans and then led to a study of the ocean winds, tides and currents. When scientists finally had a general understanding of the geography and nature of the ocean waters, the naturalists (including Charles Darwin) began to study and catalog the various plants and animals that lived in and near the sea. As technology improved, oceanographers and marine biologists dove deeper and deeper to explore more fully the ocean environments and their inhabitants. The following sections introduce some of the key explorers and events of these early years of oceanography.

Mapping the Oceans with Captain Cook

Having no satellite photographs of the earth, nobody really knew the locations of the oceans or continents, so the first priority in ocean exploration was to develop a map of the globe. However, even as late as the mid-1700s, sailors could determine only their latitudinal position at sea (by observing the elevation of the sun at its highest point in the sky). They could not determine their longitudinal position. Fortunately, around 1760, a clockmaker by the name of John Harrison developed an accurate, reliable, and portable timepiece called the *chronometer*. A sailor would set the chronometer to the time at Greenwich, England, which sits at 0 degrees longitude, and then read the chronometer at noon (when the sun is at its highest point in the sky). Given the fact that the earth spins 360 degrees in 24 hours (or 15 degrees per hour), the sailor could multiply the time difference (in hours) by 15 to determine the longitudinal position of the ship.

Captain Clam's Comments

Latitude is fairly easy to determine by measuring the elevation of the sun above the horizon when the sun is at its highest point in the sky. For example, if the sun is directly overhead at its highest point, you're at the equator (0 degrees latitude). North or south of the equator, the sun is slightly lower in the sky at its highest point. By measuring the angle between the horizon and the sun, one can determine his or her latitudinal position. At night, navigators can use the positions of other celestial bodies, such as the North Star, to determine their latitudinal positions.

Using these relatively new navigational tools and techniques, a British captain by the name of James Cook set out on the first of three voyages to map the oceans and their landmasses. His first journey, begun in 1768, was devoted to discovering and mapping the southernmost continent, which French sailors had only mentioned seeing. Captain Cook and his crew set out on the HMS *Endeavor,* and although they failed to find Antarctica, they did manage to reach the South Pacific, bump into Tahiti, chart the coastline of New Zealand, and claim for Britain the Eastern coast of Australia, which he also mapped.

Log Entry

The letters "**HMS**" that precede a ship's name stand for His Majesty's Ship or Her Majesty's Ship. It essentially means that the ship is British.

In 1772, Cook set out on a second mission to search for the southern continent. He took command of the HMS *Resolution* and was accompanied by another ship, the HMS *Adventure*. Like his first exploration, Cook failed to find the southern continent for which he was looking, but the trip was a great success, nonetheless. Cook headed south around the Cape of Good Hope and sailed east hugging the outer edge of the Southern Ocean (at about 60 degrees southern latitude). Remember, in this region the breeze blows pretty constantly from west to east. Cook did manage to dip down into the Antarctic Circle (90 degrees southern latitude) for the first time, but ice prevented him from discovering the fabled southern continent of Terra Australis (Antarctica). He did, however, discover and chart the South Georgia and South Sandwich Islands, New Hebrides, the Marquesas, Easter Island, and a few Pacific Islands, including New Caledonia.

Captain Clam's Comments

Unfortunately, the determined Captain Cook didn't live long enough to see the discovery of Antarctica. On his return to the Sandwich Islands, Cook was killed by the native Hawaiians over a dispute about one of his boats. The fabled southern continent would not be discovered until the early 1820s.

In the summer of 1776, Cook set out on his third and final voyage aboard the good ship HMS *Resolution* and accompanied by the HMS *Discovery*.

The purpose of this journey was to determine whether a northwest passage existed around the north of North America. Instead of approaching from the Atlantic, as other explorers had tried, Cook sailed in from the Pacific Ocean side and charted additional Sandwich Islands (later called the Hawaiian Islands) along the way. Cook then headed east to the western coast of North America and sailed north, mapping the western coastline of North America. Cook and his crew ultimately reached the Bering Sea, where he became the first explorer to sail in both polar seas. Unable to discover a northwest passage, and blocked by ice, Cook headed back to the Sandwich Islands.

Matthew Fontaine Maury, the Father of Oceanography

From the very beginnings of transoceanic voyages, sailors have been aware that winds and currents could help or hinder their journeys. For example, captains could cut several days off their journey by riding the Gulf Stream from North America to Europe. In the mid-1800s, a U.S. naval officer by the name of Matthew Fontaine Maury, decided that it might be a good idea to study the ocean breezes, tides, and currents to determine the safest and most efficient routes for traversing the oceans. In 1842, Maury was named superintendent of the U.S. Depot of Charts and Instruments in Washington, D.C.

Using old ship logs and other sources of data, Maury compiled information and published several articles on sea navigation and meteorology. He also created and published wind and current charts that served to improve ocean navigation internationally, and he worked tirelessly to foster international cooperation for gathering and reporting information about the oceans. In 1955, Maury published a book called *The Physical Geography of the Seas*, which is considered to be the first major study of oceanography and earned him the title of "Father of Oceanography." This book included the very first chart of the ocean basin, which Maury based on soundings (depth readings) taken with line and lead.

The Nineteenth-Century Naturalists

Shortly after Maury joined the U.S. Navy in 1825, a young British naturalist by the name of Charles Darwin was preparing to study a different aspect of the oceans—their wildlife. From 1831 to 1836, Darwin sailed aboard the HMS *Beagle*, commanded by Captain Robert Fitzroy. The purpose of this five-year mission was to collect hydrographic, geologic, and meteorological data from various locations around the globe, primarily around South America, the Galapagos Islands, and Australia. Darwin was particularly fascinated by the coral reefs, and several years after his return, he published *The Structure and Distribution of the Coral Reefs* in 1843. In this book, Darwin proposed his theory of the formation of coral reefs, which has stood the test of time.

The copious notes that Darwin took on the journey also inspired his most famous (and infamous) work, *On the Origin of Species*, published in 1859. The same ideas were independently conceived by a younger naturalist, Alfred Russel Wallace, but it was Darwin's book that became famous. This theory of how species evolve describes how variations in newborn individuals of the same species and natural selection could give rise to new, better-adapted species over long periods of time. Referred to as "the book that shook the world," Darwin's publication still stirs up controversy between die-hard creationists and evolutionists.

Another British naturalist, Edward Forbes (1815–1854), undertook several missions to dredge up life from the ocean floor, collect species from various depths, and designate distinct zones based on the fauna he collected. Forbes was also one of the first to notice that most plant life was concentrated in the first 500 meters or so of the ocean's surface, where light could penetrate. However, Forbes theorized that no life could possibly exist beyond 500 meters deep, which was later disproved by other naturalists who dredged up organisms from more than 1,500 meters, and later from 7,000 meters! The moral of the story is: Never say that something is impossible in nature.

Plunging the Depths with the HMS *Challenger*

By 1860, most scientists and oceanographers believed that ocean life existed beyond 500 meters deep. In 1864, Norwegian researches dredged up a crinoid (a disk-shaped echinoderm) from 3,109 meters below sea level; and in 1869 Charles Wyville Thompson dredged up creatures from 4,600 meters down. By the early 1870s, the British government had decided to finance a thorough exploration of the oceans, including the ocean floor. Captain Charles Wyville Thompson was placed in charge of a well-equipped ship called the HMS *Challenger*, which was staffed with six scientists. The Challenger Expedition would embark on a four-year mission (1872–1876) to explore the chemical makeup of the ocean, catalog the distribution of marine animals, map the ocean basin, and study coastal and open-ocean currents. This expedition was to be the most comprehensive and systematic study of the oceans ever attempted.

During this mission, the *Challenger* crew and scientists performed 362 soundings in the Atlantic, Pacific, and Indian oceans; collected and cataloged more than 7,000 species; discovered 4,417 new species representing 715 new genera; collected water samples from various areas; measured temperatures in various locations and at different depths; recorded meteorological observations; and mapped the major currents. The data collected during this expedition took more than 20 years to analyze and eventually resulted in the publication of 50 volumes. The Challenger Expedition was important not only for the data it collected but it also set the standards for future ocean expeditions.

Going High-Tech with Modern Oceanography

After the British completed the Challenger Expedition, several other countries, including Norway, sponsored fact-finding, data-collecting missions of their own and contributed to the vast amount of information already available. With this new information, scientists began to understand more about seasonal variations, migrations, and the truly global nature of the oceans.

In the late 1800s and early 1900s, ocean studies continued, but no country had undertaken anything comparable with the Challenger Expedition. From 1887 to 1925, the USS *Albatross* of the United States Fish Commission set out on several voyages to study fish populations, migration patterns, currents, and other aspects of the oceans primarily affecting the fishing industry. In the 1920s the British, concerned about declining whale populations, sponsored similar missions with its ships the *Discovery* and *Discovery II*. The results of these missions were later published as the *Discovery Reports*.

This lull in ocean research can be attributed primarily to the stagnation of deep-sea technology. There's only so much you can do with a net, dredging equipment, a thermometer, and a lead weight on a rope. Starting just before World War II, however, improvements in diving equipment, manned submersibles, and audio sounding equipment kicked off the development of deep-sea technology. The following sections explore some of the key developments and technologies that have driven the progress of modern oceanography.

Captain Clam's Comments _____

Much of the progress of modern oceanography actually can be attributed to several institutes that moved their labs ashore. The Scripps Institution of Oceanography, founded in 1903, and Woods Hole Oceanographic Institute, which began in 1930, enabled ships to collect specimens at sea and drop them off in more sophisticated, better-equipped labs on shore for more in-depth study. These institutes also are dedicated to teaching and training future oceanographers.

Mapping the Ocean Floor with Acoustic Soundings

During World War I, submarines became important weapons and were even used by the Germans to form a blockade around England. At one point in the war, the Germans sunk the British passenger ship, the *Lusitania*, effectively drawing the United States into the conflict. In 1915, Paul Langévin developed the first sonar device for detecting submarines, and near the end of the war, both the British and Americans had developed *sonar* devices to be used on the open seas.

Log Entry

Sonar is an acronym for "sound navigation and ranging" and it functions like cetacean echolocation. The sonar device sends out a signal and then "listens" for the echo to return. The amount of time it takes the signal to reach an object and return provides a pretty fair estimate of the distance or depth of the object.

After the war, sonar depth finders replaced the line-and-lead method for determining ocean depths. These depth finders bounced signals off the ocean floor and read the echoes to provide continuous depth readings. Sonic depth finders could be mounted on any slow moving ship to collect data from around the world. From the early 1940s to 1977, oceanographic cartographer Marie Tharp and marine geologist Bruce Heezen teamed up to map the ocean floor. Their discoveries of the mid-ocean ridges and trenches were revolutionary, proving that the ocean floor was not a flat, featureless landscape, as many had thought. Their discoveries gave rise to the theory of global plate tectonics, which explained the spreading of the ocean floor and provided conclusive evidence to support the theory of continental drift.

Improvements in Diving Equipment

One of the main limitations early oceanographers faced was the inability to observe the ocean directly deep down. Diving bells were used for centuries (and were even mentioned in Aristotle's writings in 360 B.C.E.) to increase the diving depth and the amount of time divers could stay submerged. A diving bell is sort of like a heavy, inverted trash can that's filled with air and lowered down on a rope or cable. Small bells surround the upper body of a diver, whereas some larger bells can accommodate the entire diver and even provide the diver with a place to sit. Early diving bells held only a fixed amount of air, but in 1690, Edmund Halley developed a diving bell in which air could be replenished; barrels full of air were lowered down from the surface to fill the bell. This enabled divers to remain submerged for an unlimited amount of time … or at least until they got hungry.

Near the end of the 1700s, diving suits were being developed that provided divers with a continuous flow of air from the surface and improved their mobility. In 1819, a German inventor by the name of August Siebe invented the first open diving suit, which consisted of a copper and glass helmet attached to a canvas and leather suit. A hose attached to the helmet led to a pump at the surface, which supplied pressurized air to the diver. The suit was weighted to prevent the diver from floating to the surface, so he could freely walk around on the ocean floor. Over many years, the suit was improved with the addition of a communication line, valves to help the diver control his buoyancy, and the use of rubber instead of canvas and leather for the suit part. Various adaptations of Siebe's suit was in use for nearly 100 years.

In the 1870s, inventors started developing hoseless diving suits to further improve a diver's mobility under water. Several designs were tested with varying levels of success. In 1943, Jacques Cousteau and Emile Gagnan developed and tested the first prototype of the aqualung, also referred to as a self-contained underwater breathing apparatus (or scuba). The aqualung enabled divers to carry a pressurized air supply on their backs and swim freely without being tethered to a cumbersome air hose. Because the aqualung was portable and affordable, it enabled people to dive for recreation as well as for work and exploration. It also enabled Jacques Cousteau to create those cool TV specials—*The Undersea World of Jacques Cousteau.*

Underwater Photography Becomes a Hit

As early as 1856, photographers were taking pictures underwater using standard cameras sealed in watertight, metal and glass housings. As you might imagine, these pictures were not candidates for *LIFE* magazine, but they were the precursors to the dazzling underwater photographs that are possible today. For nearly a century, from the 1850s to the 1950s, underwater photography progressed slowly but significantly. In 1915, an American photographer by the name of John Ernest Williamson made the first underwater movie of himself killing a shark. (And we thought *Real TV* went too far.)

Not until the Austrian Hans Hass started playing with underwater cameras in the 1940s was there significant improvement in underwater photography. Hass designed a superior housing for underwater cameras, which remained the standard until the early 1970s. This housing, along with improvements in optics, enabled Hass and others to take crystal clear shots underwater in a variety of conditions. Jacques Cousteau also assisted in the progress of underwater photography by helping to design the first 35-mm underwater camera. Hass and Cousteau would become famous for their individual achievements and award-winning documentaries of ocean life.

The Advent of the Submersibles

Even with the most advanced scuba diving equipment, humans cannot dive far past the 300 meter mark. In fact, only highly skilled divers attempt dives deeper than 30 meters (100 feet). To explore the ocean beyond these depths, humans must be encased in pressurized, steel-reinforced vehicles called submersibles. A submersible is an underwater vessel that's typically smaller than a submarine and is commonly used for exploration, salvage operations, and underwater rescues, as well as inspecting and monitoring underwater structures, such as bridges and dams. Two basic types of submersibles are commonly used: manned and unmanned.

The first recorded use of a submersible was during the time of 356 to 323 B.C.E., when a crude submersible (more like a diving bell) was used to lower Alexander the Great into the Mediterranean Sea. Real submersibles were not in use until the American Revolution, when an inventor by the name of David Bushnell developed a one-man, hand-powered submersible called the Turtle to try to sink British warships. Nearly 100 years later, Simon Lake developed the first true submersible, called the Argonaut First, which was designed to roll along the ocean floor on wheels.

David Bushnell's Turtle.

(Photo Credit: OAR/National Undersea Research Program)

The era of modern submersibles did not kick into gear until 1930, when American zoologist Charles William Beebe and engineer Otis Barton developed a submersible they called the bathysphere. This hollow steel ball with windows was lowered down into the ocean from a ship and enabled Beebe and Barton to descend to a depth of 923 meters in 1934. Improving on this design, Swiss scientist Auguste Piccard created the bathyscaphe (deep boat), which he named the *Trieste*, that enabled him to descend to depths of 4,000 meters. The *Trieste* could descend and surface on its own, making it unnecessary to tether it to a ship at the surface. In 1958, the U.S. Navy purchased the Trieste and hired Jacques Piccard, Auguste's son, to help operate it. In 1960, Jacques and Navy lieutenant Don Walsh descended to a depth of 10,915 meters to measure the deepest ocean point, the Marianas Trench.

Although *Trieste* was an exceptionally sturdy vessel, it was a little clunky for deep-sea exploration, so the folks at Woods Hole commissioned the design and building of a lighter, more maneuverable submersible that came to be called *Alvin* (after Allyn Vine and Alvin the chipmunk). *Alvin* typically carries three passengers (a driver and two observers), has a working depth of about 4,000 meters, and has been used in thousands of underwater expeditions, including the exciting discovery of hydrothermal vents in the 1977. Since the development of *Alvin*, several other manned submersibles (all with a working depth of about 6,000 meters) have been developed and used by various countries. These submersibles include the American *Sea Cliff II*, the French *Nautile*, the Russian *Mir I* and *Mir II*, and the Japanese *Shinkai* 6500.

Alvin *is the Woods Hole workhorse.*

(Photo Credit: OAR/National Undersea Research Program)

In addition to the manned submersibles, smaller, remote-controlled submersibles have contributed significantly in ocean research. These remote-operated vehicles (ROVs) are typically tethered to a ship at the surface or to a manned submersible, and they carry a high-resolution camera that transmits video back to the mother ship. Many ROVs also have robotic arms that enable them to pick up samples and retrieve objects. The most famous use of these ROVs was during the exploration of the

Titanic from 1987 to the present. ROVs were used not only to explore and film the inside of the Titanic but also to retrieve objects left behind by the passengers of this ill-fated trip. ROV's are more widely used for many different kinds of research, as an affordable and versatile alternative to the manned submersible.

Remote-Sensing Satellite Images

One of the most exciting and cutting edge technologies to be applied to ocean studies is remote sensing—the study of oceans from satellite and aerial images. Using remote-sensing devices, oceanographers can scan the entire globe on a daily basis to track everything from hurricanes and ocean currents to plankton blooms and fish migrations without ever heading out to sea. Using radar imaging, which consists of bouncing electromagnetic signals off the earth's surface, remote sensors can take "pictures" even through the clouds. Using infrared sensors, scientists can also create images that show temperature differences in bodies of water to track phenomena such as El Niño or identify patterns in water circulation. Marine biologists can even tag sea turtles and other animals with special satellite transmitters to track their movements across the oceans.

Diving for Dollars—Sunken Treasures

On the open ocean, one thing is certain—ships sink. And wherever a ship has sunk, something of value has probably gone down with it. At the bottom of the ocean, in the area sailors refer to as Davy Jones's locker, rest the remains of thousands of ocean-going vessels: ships full of gold, ancient artifacts, valuable antiques, unused ammunition, and, unfortunately, unspilled oil locked in the hulls of sunken oil tankers.

In the past, nobody ever dreamed of being able to reach these vessels, but with the breakthroughs in deep sea technology, treasure hunters are tripping over themselves to find these vessels and exploit their buried treasures. According to the maritime law of salvage, the treasure hunter has the right to keep whatever he or she discovers and is able to retrieve. Although some countries have laws that limit salvaging in their territorial waters (within 12 miles of their coasts), in international waters, treasure hunters have the right to pillage any ship they can reach. More than 40,000 ships have officially sunk throughout the seas, and only about 200 of these have been discovered. The following sections describe some of the more famous discoveries.

Discovering the *Titanic*

On April 14, 1912, the British luxury liner, *Titanic*, struck an iceberg and sank in the icy waters off Newfoundland; 1,513 of its 2,200 passengers died and nearly all their belongings went down with the ship. Not until 1985 was this sunken giant discovered resting on the ocean floor some 3,810 meters deep. In 1995, the French and Americans teamed up to locate and explore the *Titanic*. The French team, led by oceanographer Jean-Louis Michel and operations leader Jean Jarry, was responsible for pinpointing the *Titanic*'s location by using its side-scan sonar device, called SAR.

The American team, led by underwater archaeologist Robert Ballard, was responsible for filming the *Titanic*. As it worked out, the team from the United States actually discovered the *Titanic*, using its tow-behind submersible called the *Argo* that was equipped with underwater cameras. The team then lowered the *Argo* down to the *Titanic* to film it.

In 1996, the American team returned with *Alvin* and a smaller ROV called *Jason* to survey and photograph the *Titanic* inside and out. Both French and American crews returned to the site for several years to photograph the ship and its contents and to retrieve and preserve its artifacts. Currently, a company called RMS Titanic, Inc. is sole owner of the salvage rights for the Titanic. It has recovered more than 6,000 artifacts, which it leases to museums around the world for exhibitions.

> ### Underwater Eye
>
> The low-oxygen, high-pressure environment of the deepest ocean depths provides a great medium for preserving most ancient artifacts. Explorers are commonly surprised to find artifacts that are thousands of years old in nearly perfect condition. Of course, they usually need to scrape off the salt and mineral deposits, but other than that, the artifacts remain well-preserved. In some cases, however, worms, iron-eating microbes, and other organisms can eat away at the remains of even the sturdiest ship, making it crumble beneath the ocean's pressure.

Locating the *Lusitania*

Perhaps the second most famous shipwreck of all time is the sinking of the *Lusitania* by a German U-boat during World War I. On May 7, 1915, only 17 kilometers off the coast of Ireland the *Lusitania* was struck by a single torpedo and sank to the bottom within 18 minutes, taking the lives of 1,195 passengers and crew (123 of which were Americans). The loss of American lives provided the impetus America needed to get involved in the war. Germany insisted the ship was carrying munitions to Britain, which America and Britain vehemently denied. However, the *Lusitania* was struck by only one torpedo, and many survivors reported hearing two explosions. Perhaps the ship was carrying munitions.

For nearly a century, the *Lusitania* remained undisturbed, but the controversy over its sinking generated a host of conflicting theories. Driven by the controversy and mystery, in 1993 Robert Ballard, along with Ken Marschall and Eric Sauder decided to drop in on the *Lusitania* and check it out for themselves. They took a tiny submersible, called the Delta, down to the *Lusitania* and inspected its hull. The hull was in bad shape, damaged not only by the initial explosions but also by British warships (that had used the *Lusitania* for target practice) and by iron-eating microbes. The hull was also half-buried in the muddy ocean floor. Upon close inspection, Ballard and his crew found no evidence of munitions, and he theorized that the explosion of the torpedo might have stirred up and ignited coal dust in the ship's hull, causing a huge explosion that blew out the side of the ship. Not everyone buys this theory, so the controversy continues.

Finding the Phoenicians

Ballard was involved not only in discovering the most famous shipwrecks of all time, but also the oldest. In 1997, the Israeli government commissioned a U.S. Navy research submarine to help it search for a sunken submarine, the *Dakar*. Although the mission did not locate the sunken sub, it did take some fuzzy footage of a couple of ancient ships. The U.S. Navy contacted Ballard, who then hooked up with a Harvard archaeologist by the name of Lawrence Stager to explore the wrecks. Before they began their exploration, they knew the ships were hundreds of years old, but as they neared the vessels, they soon realized that the ships were *thousands* of years old— Phoenician ships from a period between 750 and 700 B.C.E.!

The ships themselves were not well preserved, because worms and other pests had eaten much of the wood hulls; however, both ships were packed full of cargo, much of which did withstand the test of time. Working together and with a team of students and other scientists, Ballard and Stager were able to catalog and retrieve 750 amphoras (clay jars used for shipping wine), as well as other artifacts, including incense stands, stone anchors, and pottery.

Remarkable Sunken Battleships

Although the *Titanic* and *Lusitania* are the most famous shipwrecks, several battleships decorate the bottom of the ocean floor, some of which hold the remains of more victims than either the *Titanic* or the *Lusitania*. The two most famous sunken battleships went down within days of one another: the HMS *Hood* and the German battleship the *Bismarck*.

On May 24, 1941, these two ships faced off in the Battle of Denmark Strait. The HMS *Hood* opened fire on the *Bismarck*, which then responded with its own blasts. Shortly after the battle began, a huge explosion tore the *Hood* in two, and within minutes the ship sank, taking the lives of 1,400 officers and crew with it and leaving only three survivors. Four days later, the British tracked down the *Bismarck*, battered it with torpedoes from air and sea, and then finished it off with blasts from its battleships. All but 115 of the *Bismarck*'s 2,212 man crew went down with the ship.

The Raising of the *Kursk*

One of the most recent maritime tragedies was the sinking of the Russian nuclear submarine, the *Kursk*, killing all 118 of its crew. On August 12, 2000, the *Kursk* was on a training mission in the Berents Sea, just off the coast of Norway. Less than 20 meters from the surface, one of the submarine's own torpedoes exploded near the front of the submarine and approximately two minutes later another explosion occurred, mangling the bow. The submarine quickly filled with water and sunk to the bottom, more than 100 meters down. Twenty-three members of the crew survived for days in the rear sections, but no one could reach the submarine in time, and they, too, were doomed.

In addition to the remains of the victims, the *Kursk* went down with several live torpedoes, 22 Granit supersonic cruise missiles, and 2 nuclear reactors, so salvaging the ship was imperative. Given the fact that the water in the Berents Sea is so cold, dark, and turbulent, salvage operations were delayed for the entire winter. Finally, Russia enlisted the aid of two Dutch companies, Mammoet and Smit International, to raise the *Kursk* and retrieve its contents.

From May 18 to October 23, 2001, these companies worked tirelessly to raise the *Kursk*. First, they cut off the damaged bow (front portion) of the *Kursk*, which they were afraid would come loose during the lifting operation. Working at a depth of more than 100 meters in water as cold as 0 to 6 degrees Celsius, divers used high-pressured water jets to cut several holes through the submarine's hull. In each hole, they installed a special plug for attaching a strand cable—a thick cable consisting of 54 smaller cables. A huge pontoon 140 meters long and 36 meters wide (bigger than a football field) was fitted with 26 strand jacks. This pontoon, called the *Giant*, floated above the *Kursk* and lowered down its cables. Divers attached the cables to the plugs, and the lifting began. Equalizers were used to maintain even pressure on the cables in the event of sea swells. Eventually the *Kursk* was lifted just below the *Giant*, and towed to Murmansk, where it was transferred to another boat for hauling to a dry dock.

The Ocean's Mineral Treasures

Although most ocean exploration is undertaken in the name of science—to satisfy natural human curiosity, discover more about ancient cultures, and to protect and preserve wildlife, much is done for commercial purposes, as well. In addition to exploiting fish and other wildlife for food and other useful products, more and more businesses are exploring the possibility of tapping the ocean (and below the ocean floor) for valuable mineral deposits, oil, and natural gas.

One of the earliest indications that the ocean floor stored valuable mineral treasures came from the work aboard the HMS *Challenger*. From the ocean's deepest depths, the HMS *Challenger* dredged up not only life forms but also metal balls described as "more or less circular nodules and botryoidal masses of manganese oxides of large dimensions." Commonly referred to as "manganese nodules," these metal balls are actually made up of iron, manganese, titanium, chromium, copper, nickel, cobalt, and zinc. For a time, entrepreneurs considered mining these balls for commercial purposes, but the cost of collecting, transporting, and separating out the minerals is prohibitive.

More valuable and accessible commodities that lie beneath the ocean floor are oil and natural gas, and many oil companies are actively tapping these resources through offshore drilling. The continental shelves provide promising areas for discovering oil; nearly two thirds of the total area covered by the continental shelves has sedimentary basins where oil and gas normally accumulate. Existing offshore drilling facilities already pump 25 percent of the world's oil supply. As land-based oil wells dry up and offshore drilling technology is perfected, this number is likely to rise. However, marine biologists are concerned about the effects of increased offshore oil drilling. Initial studies of soft sediment communities surrounding offshore oil rigs have found that different animals are present at different distances from the rig, with fewer species closest to the structure. In other words, sea creatures are not too happy about the oil rigs.

The Least You Need to Know

♦ Early ocean exploration was carried out using celestial navigation, ocean mapping, and descriptions of natural history.

♦ Using sonar, cartographer Marie Tharp and marine geologist Bruce Heezen were able to develop an accurate map of the ocean floor.

♦ Diving equipment enables humans to explore the ocean to a depth of only about 300 meters, whereas submersibles enable humans to explore the deepest depths to nearly 10,000 meters.

♦ Improvements in technology have enabled scientists to locate and explore shipwrecks that were previously irretrievable.

♦ The oceans contain valuable minerals, oil, and natural gas.

Maritime Laws and the Villains Who Break Them

In This Chapter

◆ Understanding the need for maritime law

◆ The players who make the rules

◆ A brief history of the development of maritime law

◆ Crime on the high seas past and present

◆ Can't we all just get along?

Except for a few landlocked countries, most countries have some beach-front property, and all countries have an interest in how the oceans and their resources are managed. To ensure the safety and security of vessels, including their crews, passengers, and cargo; to provide equitable distribution of the ocean's resources; and to keep the oceans and their wildlife healthy for future generations, various governments have enacted laws and signed international agreements between nations. Because worldwide consensus is rarely reached, individual nations and people frequently choose to ignore the laws. The ocean has been and remains a place that falls between the cracks of different nations' territories, and there is no clear governing framework to either create or enforce laws of the open sea. This chapter provides a brief overview of the laws that govern the seas and how they originated. It also highlights ongoing crimes and the villains who commit them.

The Major Players: Maritime Powers

As with most aspects of international relations, the players with the biggest ships and most powerful navies rule the seas and make the laws that everyone else must follow. In ancient times, the Phoenicians—and then the Greeks and Romans—dominated the shipping industry, and they were the ones to call the shots. In the late 1400s and well into the 1500s, Spain and Portugal ruled the seas, exploring various trading routes to the East and eventually discovering and exploiting the New World to the West. In the 1600s, England and the Netherlands took turns reigning the high seas, until England finally achieved total dominance around 1690 and continued to dominate the seas until the mid-1900s.

Captain Clam's Comments

It's no surprise that Britain and the United States value a strong navy. Britain is an island state that must be able to defend its entire coastline. Likewise, except for its northern border, much of the United States borders the oceans and the Gulf of Mexico.

With the fall of the British Empire and the military buildup of the United States after World War II, the United States achieved naval superiority and continues to hold it today. However, several other nations have well-equipped navies and strongly influence international maritime law, including Britain and Russia. In addition, through the United Nations, nearly 150 governments have come together to agree on some basic rules for sea travel, exploration, and resource use.

The U.S. Navy: For Your Inspection

In the years before the attack on Pearl Harbor, battleships ruled the seas. Britain's HMS *Hood*, Germany's *Bismarck*, and America's USS *Missouri* were the titans of the seas. At Pearl Harbor, the Japanese proved that battleships could become nothing more than sitting ducks, and the golden age of aircraft carriers was born. Now, much of the U.S. Navy's force consists of ships that are designed to launch aerial attacks in the form of fighter jets and cruise missiles. The bulky battleships have been replaced with smaller, more maneuverable boats, including cruisers, destroyers, and amphibious vehicles.

To see how important aircraft have become to the Navy, look at the numbers. In 2003, the Navy had only 310 ships in operation, but more than 4,000 aircraft! Of the 310 ships in operation are more than 30 amphibious vehicles, 14 aircraft carriers, 27 cruisers, 65 destroyers, 58 attack submarines, and 18 ballistic missile launching submarines. The mission of the U.S. Navy is to give the United States a military presence in any part of the world.

The U.S. Coast Guard Close By

Although the Navy's primary mission is to give the United States a "forward presence," the U.S. Coast Guard prefers to stay closer to shore, protecting more than 95,000 miles of coastline and 361 ports. The U.S. Coast Guard has the following five objectives:

- **Maritime safety**   The Coast Guard ensures the safety of recreational watercraft, warns ships about icebergs and other hazards, and finds and rescues ships that are lost at sea.

- **Maritime mobility**   To improve navigation, the Coast Guard administers the operation of bridges, controls traffic, manages waterways, and performs polar icebreaking, when needed.

- **Maritime security**   As a law enforcement organization, the Coast Guard is responsible for drug interdiction, migrant interdiction, and treaty enforcement.

- **National defense**   Although the Navy has the big guns to protect the United States against attacks from foreign countries, the Coast Guard acts as a shield close to home. It is responsible for homeland security, general defense, as well as security of ports and waterways.

- **Protection of natural resources**   To protect our natural marine resources, the Coast Guard provides educational materials on pollution, acts to prevent pollution and enforce antipollution laws, inspects foreign vessels, and prevents the unlawful capture and transportation of protected marine life.

To perform its job, the Coast Guard is staffed by a highly trained, very motivated workforce and maintains a fleet of 48 buoy tenders, 4 icebreakers, 12 high-endurance cutters,

> **Underwater Eye**
>
> The U.S. Coast Guard is actually a branch of the military whose motto is *Semper Paratus*, "Always Ready." The Coast Guard operates under the Department of Transportation in times of peace, but upon declaration of war or upon orders from the U.S. president, the Coast Guard falls under the direction of the Secretary of the Navy.

32 medium-endurance cutters, 2 training cutters, 8 icebreaking tugs, 89 patrol boats, 12 construction tenders, 15 harbor tugs, 68 47-foot motor lifeboats, 44 44-foot motor surfboats, 173 41-foot utility boats, 71 fixed-wing aircraft, and 144 helicopters.

The British Navy—Still Royal After All These Years

At its height, the British Royal Navy was the most powerful navy in the world and played a large part in building and maintaining the British Empire. Although it's not quite as powerful as it was in its heyday, the British Royal Navy is still an influential force, providing support for international peacekeeping missions, UN sanctions enforcement, delivery of humanitarian aid, drug interdiction, policing of fishing areas, and search and rescue missions. Of course, its primary role is still the defense of the United Kingdom and its interests.

The British Royal Navy consists of 124 ships and submarines, 200 airplanes, and 42,000 dedicated men and women. The ships range in size from small patrol boats to huge aircraft carriers. The frigates and destroyers are the workhorses of the navy. Both are designed to be fast moving, maneuverable ships. The Royal Navy's Mine Countermeasure Vehicles, considered the best in the world, play an important role in ridding the oceans of new mines during wartime and old mines left over from previous wars. The Royal Navy also has several nuclear-powered submarines.

Russia, Canada, and the Netherlands

Several world powers have well-equipped navies of their own, including Russia, Canada, and the Netherlands. After the cold war, the Russian navy faced serious problems and an aging fleet, but fairly recently, it has shown signs of rebirth with cutting-edge nuclear submarines. Vladimir Putin seems determined to revitalize the Russian navy and has committed a good chunk of Russia's military budget to rebuilding the Russian navy.

Canada, too, has committed significant resources to developing its sea power and modernizing its fleet. Its destroyers, frigates, submarines, coastal defense vessels, attack helicopters, and airplanes are some of the most modern in the world and have made significant contributions not only to the defense of Canada, but also in international peacekeeping missions.

A Brief History of Maritime Law

Ever since nations began to trade with one another across the Mediterranean Sea, they have attempted to draw up rules to govern the seas. One of the earliest and most successful maritime trading nations was Phoenicia, a country that existed around 2500 B.C.E. in the area we now call Lebanon. The Phoenicians were master ship-builders and sailors, and their expertise placed them in high demand throughout the Mediterranean Sea and surrounding shores.

At the height of its power, Phoenicia developed a set of rules and regulations to govern maritime activity. These laws might have been loosely based on one of the earliest legal "documents" in history—Hammurabi's Code, composed by King Hammurabi of Babylon around 1700 B.C.E. These laws covered everything from commerce to marriage and from thievery to debts. Taking the eye-for-an-eye approach to punishment, penalties could be rather brutal—kiss another man's wife, and you lose a lip; build a house that collapses on its owner, and you die; take something that's not yours, and you lose a finger. Phoenicia adapted Hammurabi's Code to the seas to encourage free passage over the waterways, establish order on ships, and discourage piracy.

The Phoenician laws of the sea were so commonly accepted that the Greeks and Romans adopted them and continued to use them, with some amendments, long after Phoenicia became absorbed into the Greco-Macedonian Empire (around 330 B.C.E.). At about this time, the Greek city of Rhodes had become the central trading center for the countries bordering the Mediterranean Sea, so when the maritime laws finally became consolidated and made official, they were called the Rhodian Sea Law or Rhodian Code. Rhodian Code primarily dealt with lawsuits regarding marine loans, shipping contracts, construction of ships, cargo charges and damage, and arrangements for buying and selling ships.

With the fall of the Roman Empire, in the fifth century, overseas trading slowed considerably, and the shipping that remained was largely unregulated. In the Middle Ages, when shipping resumed, disputes again arose over shipping routes, free trade, and other issues. As disputes were resolved and solutions recorded, a systematic code of laws was constructed, which would later become known as the Laws of Oleron (in the twelfth century). Like the Phoenician laws of the sea, the Laws of Oleron pull no punches. If someone is convicted of murder, he is to be tied to the corpse and thrown into the sea; if he steals, he is to have his head tarred and feathered and to be cast ashore at the next landing; if he stabs a crewmate, he loses a hand. At the time of King Richard I, the Laws of Oleron were compiled into a handbook for England's navy called the *Black Book of Admiralty*. Many of these rules of conduct are still in practice today, though the punishments are a little less gruesome.

Freedom of the Seas

Although the Laws of Oleron and the *Black Book of Admiralty* guided the actions of crewmates, they placed few restrictions on how various nations could make use of the open oceans. Ships were allowed to cruise the oceans freely, fish in whatever waters they wanted, and explore the oceans for more convenient shipping routes. In the fifteenth and sixteenth centuries, when Spain and Portugal began exploring the world for new lands, they began to claim sovereignty over particular ocean areas. When the English and Dutch joined in, serious disputes arose.

To prevent and resolve disputes, a Dutch jurist by the name of Hugo Grotius published a treatise in the early seventeenth century called *Mare Liberum* (Free Sea), which set the basis for an international law, referred to as "Freedom of the Seas." Freedom of the Seas gave all nations the right to navigate, fish, and explore all ocean waters. (Later amendments accommodated fly overs, as well.) In the eighteenth century, another Dutch jurist by the name of Cornelius van Bynkershoek introduced an amendment to this law stating that a nation could claim a portion of water bordering it as territorial property. This was generally specified as a distance of 3 nautical miles or about 5.5 kilometers (approximately the distance that a nation's land defenses could reach out to sea). Some countries chose to claim a territorial boundary extending 6 or even 12 nautical miles from shore.

Although some lapses have occurred, most maritime nations adhere to the general notion that the seas should remain relatively free for all nations to cross. Of course, many nations choose to limit access to their surrounding waters in times of war, when other nations are exploiting their fish populations, or when other nations pollute their waters. During World War II, England, the United States, and Germany commonly tested their enemies' territorial waters to disrupt shipping routes and prevent their enemies from importing or exporting any products whatsoever, particularly munitions.

The Not-So-United Nations

As nations began to realize the economic importance of the ocean and as the world became more populated, nations became much more possessive of their territorial waters. The three-nautical-mile apron was no longer a sufficient buffer zone. In 1930, the League of Nations attempted to convince its members to agree to the three-nautical-mile limit, but the representatives of several nations walked out on the talks because of differences concerning overlapping borders.

In 1945, U.S. President Harry S. Truman declared unilaterally that the United States had the right to exploit any areas of its coastline up to and including the continental shelf—or about 200 nautical miles from shore. Other nations soon followed Truman's lead, declaring their own extended territories. In 1952, Chile, Ecuador, and Peru declared a 200-nautical-mile fishing zone to prevent foreign fishermen from exploiting their anchovies.

In an attempt to develop fair and equal rules for all nations, in 1958, the United Nations convened its first United Nations Conference on the Laws of the Sea (UNCLOS). This conference established articles defining just what the "continental shelf" constituted and how much of it each nation could claim. It also approved articles to ensure the safety of foreign vessels in territorial waters and attempted to set a limit on the extent of "territorial" waters. Many issues remained unresolved at the end of this conference and even after the second conference in 1960.

In 1973, the third conference convened and proceeded for nearly a decade. In addition to introducing several regulations to help preserve the oceans and their resources, the 148 participating states agreed to a 12-nautical-mile or less territorial limit around their coasts and a 200-nautical-mile "exclusive economic zone," which gave each nation the sole right to fish and mine minerals and oil in its economic zone. (Nations could then negotiate with other nations for fishing and mining rights in their exclusive economic zones.) This convention also adopted a host of maritime laws covering everything from conduct on the high seas to mining minerals in international waters.

Pirates, Privateers, and Other Opportunistic Villains

Wherever you find something of value, someone is ready and willing to take it, even on the high seas. When a captain and crew not associated with any legitimate government harass other boats and their crews and steal their cargo by force, they commit an act of piracy and are known as pirates.

Piracy is considered a crime against humanity and is prosecuted as a violation of international law. In cases in which a government sponsors the robbery, the offenders are known as privateers. Privateers were common in the days of Queen Elizabeth I, who encouraged privateers to raid the ships of competing nations and give her and her cronies a cut of the proceeds. Both pirates and privateers continue to raid ships even today.

> **Log Entry**
>
> **Piracy** is the crime of violence, robbery, or coercion for private benefit on the open ocean or in the airspace above the ocean committed by another ship or individual not sponsored by any legitimate government.

Yo Ho Ho on the High Seas

Since the days of the Phoenicians, pirates have shared the seas with navies and commercial vessels. Some of the first pirates were actually Phoenicians who moonlighted as pirates to earn a little supplemental income. Likewise, the Vikings of the early Middle Ages supplemented the booty they stole from coastal raids with a little piracy on the high seas. At the same time, in the Mediterranean Sea, the Muslims were hard at work terrorizing the shipping industry and filling their coffers with the cargo of legitimate vessels. By the early 1500s, the Algerians would hone their skills as pirates to terrorize the British, Americans, and other major commercial shipping nations. Operating from the Barbary Coast (the northern coast of Africa), these pirates menaced commercial vessels until the early 1800s, when American ships attacked Tripoli and Algiers.

During the 1600s, pirates from England, France, and the Netherlands sailed to the New World to harass the rich Spanish explorers who were busy conquering the lands of the natives and stealing their gold. These so-called buccaneers were led by the famous Captain Morgan. At their height, the buccaneers held near total control of the Caribbean Sea, and because they hassled only the Spanish, the superior English and Dutch navies left them alone. Later in their history, they were actually hired by the Dutch, French, and English to fight the Spanish in the New World.

When the British finally achieved supremacy on the high seas and the Americans had built a significant naval force (in the 1800s), they seriously curtailed the illegal activities of all pirates worldwide. Piracy was outlawed, and a couple of nations were finally capable of enforcing the law.

A Gallery of Rogues

Throughout the 1600s and into the early 1800s, piracy was rampant, especially in the waters off the coasts of the New World. Maritime traffic was at its peak, carrying gold and other valuables from the New World to Europe and carrying supplies and slaves from Europe and Africa to the Americas. To anyone with a well-armored ship and a lack of scruples, the sea was ripe for the picking. This was the golden age of piracy when the most infamous pirates sailed the seas.

One of the most famous pirates was Edward Drummond, alias Edward Teach or Blackbeard the Pirate, who lived from about 1680 to 1718. Known for his thick, black beard, Blackbeard was a maniacal marauder. To ready himself for a raid, Blackbeard would braid his beard into little pigtails tied up with ribbons. He would then tuck some lit hemp fuses under his hat so that smoke would encircle his head during the battle. Blackbeard was known to attack and defeat ships larger and better equipped than his own, giving him a reputation for being ruthless. He and his crews attacked ships up and down the eastern coast of North America and into the Caribbean, until he was killed in an attack that left him riddled with stab wounds and bullet holes.

Another bold pirate was the infamous Black Bart, Bartholomew Roberts, who pillaged more than 400 ships over the course of four years. Although Black Bart was a scrupulous thief, he was a fancy dresser who demanded honor among his crew. Black Bart himself did not drink alcoholic beverages, he expected his crew to be loyal to him and to one another, he enforced a strict code of contact, and he even led religious services on deck. In one of his most daring attacks, Black Bart's ship came upon a fleet of 42 Portuguese merchant vessels and two warships. He sailed his boat alongside the largest merchant vessel, fired a volley of shots, boarded and pillaged the vessel, and then headed out to sea before the other ships could respond.

Although men dominated the piracy scene, a couple of women crossed the gender barrier, most notably Anne Bonny and Mary Read. Both of these ladies spent some time disguised as boys in their early years and learned to survive as women in a male-dominated society. Eventually, Anne Bonny caught the wandering eye of a Captain Calico Jack Rackham and became his mistress. Later, they captured a ship bound for the West Indies, on which Mary Read was sailing, dressed as a man. Anne Bonny and Mary Read quickly became friends, which initially perturbed Captain Rackham, who thought that his mistress was in love with another man. Upon discovering that Mary Read was, in fact, a woman, Rackham was relieved and named her as the newest member of his crew.

Privateers, Pirates for Hire

Throughout the Middle Ages, small countries that did not have their own navies would hire privately owned vessels to carry out military operations on their behalf. The county would issue a letter of marque, giving a privateer the license to act on its behalf. In most cases, the privateer was a legitimate representative of the government, hired to carry out the same missions as an official naval vessel. However, some privateers were essentially legalized pirates, attacking not only military ships but also merchant vessels and stealing their cargo.

During the reign of Queen Elizabeth I (1558–1603), privateers were in their golden age. Queen Elizabeth commissioned privateers, including Sir Francis Drake, to raid Spanish ships and other merchant vessels in return for a portion of the profits. This made the good Queen and her fellow aristocrats very wealthy; however, it resulted in encouraging piracy and privateering to the point at which England's own merchant vessels were no longer safe. Many maritime nations, including the English and the Dutch, eventually needed to invest in navies to protect their merchant vessels from this rampant opportunism.

In 1856, privateering was condemned by the declaration of Paris. However, a few key nations refused to support the declaration, including Spain, the United States, and Mexico. Under the U.S. Constitution, Congress still has the right to issue letters of marque and enlist the aid of privateers.

Modern-Day Pirates, Modern-Day Equipment

The growth of the British and U.S. Navies during the latter part of the twentieth century nearly eradicated piracy. However, in isolated areas, especially where corrupt governments are at work, piracy once again has become a serious problem. In the waters of Southeast Asia, for example, where the British Royal Navy previously kept piracy in check, the pirates are back and are better equipped than ever before. Sporting their own satellite dishes, computers, high-tech communications gear, and automatic weapons, the modern-day pirate vessel is perfect for hit-and-run marauding operations.

Two factors contribute to making the waters of Southeast Asia a piracy hot spot— Southeast Asia is home of the busiest port in the world (the port of Singapore), and many of the governments in the area secretly condone and actually profit from these acts of piracy. Coastal patrols, navies, and marine officials from Indonesia, Thailand, Burma, Cambodia, the Philippines, Vietnam, and China receive their cut of the profits in exchange for looking the other way.

These New Age pirates are particularly ruthless and do not hesitate to wipe out an entire crew during a raid. Using speedboats, the pirates typically approach a slow-moving boat at night when most of the crew is asleep and ride quietly alongside it. They then hurl grappling hooks onto the deck, climb aboard, and subdue the captain and crew, often killing them outright and dumping their bodies overboard. After taking control of the boat, the pirates seize its cargo to sell on the black market. Sometimes, the pirates even steal the ship. Stolen ships often find their way to China and are then sold to individuals or companies in other countries around the world.

Environmental Pirates

Crime on the ocean isn't limited to robbery and murder. Illegal fishing, whaling, shipping, and dumping account for a great deal of criminal activity. Illegal fishing is especially common off the coasts of weaker nations that are unable to enforce their economic zones. In the decade following the collapse of Somalia's central government, for example, fishing boats from several nations freely fished Somalian waters without licenses or approval to do so. In addition, fishing boats commonly catch more than their quotas, placing fish populations in jeopardy. In some locations, satellite surveillance might someday help track fishing vessels and cut down on some of the illegal fishing, but detection and enforcement remain daunting.

Poaching and international trade in high-value invertebrate species on the black market is also a serious problem, affecting abalone, sea cucumbers, sea urchins, the

Chilean gastropod "loco," and other species whose fisheries have been restricted to protect depleted populations. In some countries such as South Africa, international criminal syndicates might even be involved in the systematic poaching of these animals.

Illegal (and sometimes legal) dumping is another serious problem affecting our oceans worldwide. Most of the pollution pouring into our oceans is actually in the form of legal dumping. Cities and states commonly pour their sewage right into the ocean or into rivers that flow to the ocean. In addition, chemical and manufacturing plants worldwide discharge toxic wastes directly into the oceans and seas, damaging not only their own marine environments but also the marine environments off the coasts of neighboring states and throughout the ocean basins. To add to the problem, some ships actually carry trash, metal drums full of toxic liquids, and other wastes out to sea for the sole purpose of dumping it, using the ocean as a huge landfill.

One of the more common ways to make money illegally on the seas is to deal in illegal shipments, including shipments of illegal immigrants or narcotics. Because of the vast amounts of cargo that are shipped daily, and the invention of containerized shipping, thorough inspections of every vessel crossing the seas is nearly impossible. To open and inspect every container that passes through the port of Los Angeles, for example, would take more personnel that could possibly be maintained. Every month, approximately a half million containers pass into or out of this one port! Ships can store huge amounts of weapons, artillery, illicit drugs, and other illegal cargo along with their legal loads without attracting even the slightest suspicion. Thousands of illegal immigrants have made their way to the United States in the hulls of ships.

> **Captain Clam's Comments**
>
> In 1988, Ronald Reagan signed the Ocean Dumping Ban Act, which prohibits municipalities and industries from dumping or disposing of any sewage sludge, toxic chemicals, nuclear wastes, and other types of wastes into the oceans.

The Least You Need to Know

♦ The navy with the biggest boats and best weapons typically makes and enforces the laws that govern the seas.

♦ The U.S. Coast Guard's primary responsibilities are to ensure the safety of the United States' territorial waters and to patrol its economic zone.

- "Freedom of the Seas" was the idea that all nations have the right to navigate, fish, explore, and fly over all ocean waters. All efforts to protect marine natural resources or domestic security must first confront this widely held doctrine.

- In general, every country bordering an ocean can claim as its territory the 12 nautical miles of ocean and continental shelf that extend from its shore.

- Most countries have a 200-nautical-mile apron extending from their shores, which they have the sole right to fish, mine, and explore—this is called an Exclusive Economic Zone (EEZ).

- Pirates are opportunistic criminals who steal and murder on the high seas for their own selfish gain—modern-day pirates are common in Southeast Asia.

- Privateers are bandits who have been given a mandate by a legitimate government to fight against another nation's navy or pillage their merchant ships.

20

Fishing and Restocking the World's Oceans

In This Chapter

◆ Who's eating all the fish

◆ Technology and overfishing

◆ Marine reserves: replenishing the fish supply

◆ Fish farming and genetically altered fish

The oceans collectively compose the world's largest fishing hole, serving up an enormous bounty of seafood, including tuna, anchovies, halibut, swordfish, lobsters, crabs, mussels, shrimp, and an array of other tasty and highly nutritious fish and shellfish. As our appetite for seafood grows and as commercial fishing industries become more adept at exploiting the ocean fisheries, fish populations are beginning to dwindle, and many species are currently on the road to depletion. To ease the burden on our oceans, people have begun to limit their harvests, farm fish (raise them in captivity), and limit the use of fishing gear that destroys habitat or affects other species. This chapter explores the current state of the world's fisheries and some of the ways humans can begin to help the oceans cope with our ever increasing demands.

The Not-So-Bottomless Oceans

From the early 1700s until the 1950s, the human population grew steadily from fewer than one billion people to nearly two billion. The oceans had no trouble keeping up with the seafood appetites of two billion people. From 1950 to the year 2000, the human population nearly tripled—to more than six billion—most of whom live on the coasts. Unable to feed themselves on what they produced on land, humans began to rely more and more on the oceans to supplement their diets. In addition, people began to realize that seafood was an excellent source of protein and essential fats. As a result, humans have begun to test the ocean's limits, and are now exploiting *fisheries* faster than they can replenish themselves. But who's doing all this fishing, and who's eating all this fish? The following sections supply the answers.

Log Entry

A **fishery** is an industry devoted to harvesting, processing, and selling fish, shellfish, or other aquatic animals. The term fishery can also be used to describe a place where fish are caught or a fishing business. Fisheries can be commercial, recreational, or local (for the subsistence of a community).

Who Catches the Most?

Long ago, seaside communities would catch only enough fish to feed themselves and would eat only the fish they caught. As populations grew, fish became an important commodity for trade. Early Phoenicians and Greeks relied on their fisheries as a source of income. Spain and Sicily relied on their fisheries in the Mediterranean Sea to trade with the Romans. For China, Japan, and other Eastern nations, fishing played an important role in their development.

Today, about 20 countries are responsible for catching most of the fish consumed throughout the world. China is the leading producer of fish, accounting for more than 30 to 40 million metric tons or 25 to 30 percent of the total fish harvested in the world; approximately 50 to 60 percent of their total harvest is from farm-raised fish. Although the catch for China might be overestimated, it still remains the largest producer by far. Peru is the second largest supplier of fish, harvesting more than 10 million metric tons of anchovies and other fish annually, followed by Japan, India, the United States, Indonesia, and Chile, each of which harvests between 4 and 6 million metric tons. (By the way, a metric ton is 1,000 kilograms, or about 2,205 pounds.)

Captain Clam's Comments

Fish production comes from three sources: marine fishing (about 72 percent), inland fishing (6 percent), and fish farms (22 percent). China dominates the world when it comes to fish farming, controlling nearly 70 percent of the total farmed fish market.

Who Eats the Most?

You can look at the question of who eats the most fish from two perspectives—by country or by individual (per capita). By country, China (which has about a quarter of the world's population) eats the most fish. However, if you examine fish consumption per capita, the Maldives (off the coast of India) lead the pack, where per-capita fish consumption is as high as 169 kilograms per year. That's more than a pound of fish per person per day! The inhabitants of several other isolated island nations eat a great deal of fish, as well. One of the larger countries that boasts a high per-capita fish consumption level is Iceland, with 90 kilograms annually. Japan, South Korea, and Malaysia follow up as the top fish eaters in the world, each of which has a per-capita consumption of between 50 and 60 kilograms annually. Compared with the average human, who consumes about 13 kilograms of fish per year, these numbers are extremely high.

The Most Popular Seafoods

Throughout the world, fisheries harvest more than 4,000 different types of fish and shellfish, some of which are ground into fish meal for use as livestock feed, whereas others find their way directly to the dinner table. These commercially valuable fish species can be broken down into the following five groups:

- **Ground fish**   Demersal (bottom-feeding) fish, such as cod, haddock, and pollock compose about 10 percent of the total global marine fish harvest. Flatfish, including sole, flounder, and halibut contribute another 1 percent to the total marine fish harvest. These species are some of the most heavily affected by overfishing. Atlantic cod has become the poster child for overfishing and has yet to recover to its historic levels. In 2003, groundfish fisheries were severely restricted in an attempt to rebuild depleted stocks along the Pacific coast of the United States.

- **Pelagic fish**   These open-ocean fish include sardines, herring, mackerel, anchovies, tuna, swordfish, and several other species. Large and small pelagic fish account for nearly 60 percent of the marine fish harvest. As you can see, the combined catch of ground and pelagic fish represent a huge portion of the total global fish harvest.

- **Crustaceans**   Shrimp, crabs, lobster, and other crispy critters make up this group, which adds a relatively small contribution to the total fish harvest—about 5 percent. However, in terms of money, the shrimp trade accounts for nearly 20 percent of the fish market. (The United States is the largest importer of shrimp, and shrimp has recently replaced tuna as American's fish of choice.)

◆ **Molluscs and cephalopods**   Molluscs include scallops, clams, and oysters, which are popular sea foods worldwide. Squid, cuttlefish, and octopus are harvested worldwide and are sold for human consumption in Japan, Mediterranean countries, and other countries throughout the world.

Captain Clam's Comments

Coastal pelagic fish (sardines and anchovies) have provided a rare success story in recovery from overfishing. After the sardine fishery made famous in John Steinbeck's book *Cannery Row* crashed in the 1950s, the fishery closed and a long-term research program was begun (known as CalCOFI). For the past 15 years, the sardine population has been on the upswing, growing by 30 percent each year.

◆ **Marine mammals**   In the past, whales contributed a significant chunk to the total harvest of marine animals, but overharvesting pretty much destroyed the whaling industry. By international agreement, there is a moratorium on commercial whaling. Japan and Norway continue their whaling industries despite this agreement, and some native peoples hunt whales, seals, and other marine mammals for traditional uses as food, oils, and furs. But, globally, this group contributes the least to the total "fish" harvest.

Commercial Fishing Techniques and Technologies

Fish is one of the few foods we humans still hunt for in the wild. And given the fact that we must find and catch about 120 million metric tons annually to satisfy our appetites for fish, there has been a great incentive to develop more efficient fishing techniques and technologies. The following sections reveal some of the key improvements in the fishing industry that have enabled it to keep up with the growing demand for fresh fish. Unfortunately, some of these techniques are so successful that they have led to the overexploitation of fish populations. You'll understand why as you read through these sections.

Fish Finders and Fathometers

Before you can catch fish, you must find fish. Some of the most significant improvements in the commercial fishing industry deal with fish finders and fathometers (depth finders). Using sonar equipment, fishing boats can scan surrounding waters for schools of fish and pinpoint their locations. They can also use depth finders to scan the ocean floor and find areas where fish are likely to gather in large numbers. Without having to spend a great deal of time searching for fish, commercial boats can go directly to where the fish hang out and drop their nets for a sure catch.

Many commercial fisheries also employ the use of helicopters, airplanes, and satellite technology in their search for fish. Helicopters and airplanes can spot schools of fish at or near the surface and call in their locations to the boats below. In addition, satellite services use computerized modeling software to determine the likely locations of schools of fish based on plankton maps, migration patterns, and water temperatures and currents gathered from satellites.

A Net for Every Occasion

Throughout history, people have caught fish using any of the following four methods: spear fishing, netting, angling (hook and line), or trapping. Of those four methods, netting is the most popular method and is used to catch the majority of fish. Several types of nets are currently used depending on the fish, the environment being fished, and on the rules and regulations regarding nets:

- **Purse seine nets**   A purse seine net is the most traditional type of net. A fishing boat lays the net down around a school of fish and then pulls a line that closes the net around the fish. The boat then hauls in its catch. These nets are commonly used to catch tuna, salmon, anchovies, and other types of fish that swim in large schools. Other species that swim among these schools can be caught incidentally—the most infamous example is the catch of dolphins with tuna. The number of dolphins killed by purse seine nets has been dramatically reduced in recent decades through international cooperation and changes in net designs and fishing techniques.

- **Straight drift or gill nets**   Outlawed by the United Nations in 1993 for use on the high seas, drift or gill nets are designed with holes large enough for a fish's head to poke through but too small for the fish's body to pass through. (The fish becomes caught by its gills.) Some kinds of gillnets can be used responsibly, but they can also cause large numbers of nontarget species (bycatch) to be caught. Drift nets are laid out in a line, sometimes as long as 60 meters and reaching depths of 8 to 12 meters, creating an underwater wall that fish cannot help but bump into. Drift nets were commonly used to catch salmon, tuna, squid, and many other types of fish. Some countries still allow drift nets to be used in their exclusive economic zones. Coastal gillnet fishing has been banned in California, Florida, and other locations.

- **Trawl nets**   Trawl nets are typically cone-shaped nets that are pulled behind a fishing boat either in the water column or along the bottom. These nets are commonly employed for catching shrimp, cod, and flounder. Bottom trawls can be extremely destructive when dragged through deep reefs and other important fish habitats.

◆ **Dredge nets**   To collect scallops, oysters, and other shellfish from benthic regions, fisheries commonly drag dredge nets along the ocean floor. The leading rim of the net is typically metal and digs down into the ocean floor, essentially scooping up any and all sand, dirt, rocks, corals, and shellfish on the bottom and sifting out the sediments. Like bottom trawling, this method of fishing disturbs both benthic habitats and nontarget species.

A purse-seine net encircles a school of fish.

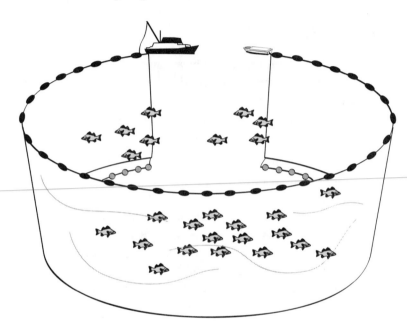

Ocean Alert

The United Nations banned drift nets for several reasons. First, the nets are highly effective, drifting with the currents and ensnaring any animal in their paths. Second, because the nets stay submerged for days, if they catch any air-breathing animals (such as turtles, dolphins, or albatross), they cause the animals to drown. Finally, these nylon nets commonly tear, but take a long time to break down. So lost sections of net (commonly called ghost nets) can float around the oceans for months, continuing to ensnare animals until their kill becomes too heavy to support, causing the nets to sink to the bottom.

Drop Me a Line

Except for fish caught by recreational anglers, few fish are pulled from the ocean on a hook. Fishing with hook, line, and sinker simply is not the quickest way to catch fish.

However, some fish are still harvested using hooks and lines, especially large deep-water fish, such as halibut, swordfish, and shark. The preferred tool for catching these fish is the *longline*—a rope weighted on both ends and at several points in between that has numerous baited lines along its length. Buoys attached to the rope float at the surface to help the fishermen locate the rope later. Trolling lines are also used to catch deepwater fish. These shorter lines, which are baited or have lures attached, are lowered into the water and dragged behind the boat. As fish are hooked, the lines are reeled in and fish are pulled into the boat using a gaff hook.

> ### Ocean Alert
>
> Some countries have outlawed longline fishing in some areas to protect sea turtles and birds, mainly the albatross. As the longlines are being set, albatrosses commonly take the bait, get hooked, and are dragged to the bottom with the line. Sea turtles are also attracted to the bait, and if they become hooked, they cannot reach the surface for air and eventually drown.

Trapping the Bottom Dwellers

Crabs and lobsters and other bottom-dwelling crustaceans are quite capable of removing the bait from a hook without getting caught, and they prefer to live in rocky areas, where nets are likely to become caught up and tangled. To harvest these creatures, fisheries employ the use of traps. A typical lobster trap consists of a wooden frame covered with strips of wood or a wire mesh. Each end of the trap has a cone-shaped entrance that narrows toward the inside of the trap. The lobster can crawl in to get the bait but cannot craw out through the narrow end of the entrance. Crab and shrimp traps, called pots, have a similar design, providing for easy entrance into the trap but no easy way to exit.

The pots used to capture octopuses are more pot-like than the wire-mesh pots used for trapping crabs and shrimp. Octopus harvesters commonly lower clay pots to the sea floor, which the octopuses use as temporary homes. After an octopus has settled into its new home, the harvester simply raises the pot, octopus included.

Fishing 'Round the Clock

In the past, fishing boats were severely limited in the amount of time they could spend at sea. Without onboard refrigeration units, boats had to unload their catch on shore soon after a harvest or risk having the fish spoil. In addition, if the boat had a particularly large catch, it would need to return to shore to unload.

Nowadays, large fishing boats can remain at sea for weeks. Many are equipped with their own refrigeration units and processing equipment, enabling them to can or freeze their catch on board. In addition, many fisheries keep larger boats at sea to fish for days on end and use smaller boats to shuttle the catch back to shore. All these developments have greatly amplified the range and capability of the fishing industry, and pushed the limits of formerly sustainable fisheries.

Fisheries Management and Conservation

The ever-increasing demand for fresh fish, improvements in fishing techniques and technologies, and poor fisheries management have led to the depletion of many fish stocks. According to the Food and Agriculture Organization (FAO) of the United Nations, more than half of the most popular 200 species of fish stocks are declining in population; that is, fisheries are harvesting these fish faster than the fish are able to reproduce.

As fish populations decline, the fishing industry has responded in two ways: by increasing the numbers of fishing boats and fishing for other types of fish. By increasing the number of boats, the fishing industry continues to place more stress on the fish populations, and by fishing for other types of fish, the industry has driven additional fish stocks to a state of decline. To stay on this path eventually would lead to the total collapse of the commercial fishing industry and leave us humans with few fish to eat.

Fisheries management remains extremely difficult because of the logistic challenges of predicting changes in fish populations and of enforcing laws on the open sea. Fortunately, many nations have begun to recognize these problems and have taken initial steps to reduce the amount of fishing and help fish stocks rebound to a level at which populations can be maintained and harvested for many years to come.

The following sections explain some of the more effective solutions that have been tried so far.

Reducing the Bycatch Blues

For every three fish that are caught and make their way to market, at least one fish is accidentally killed and wasted as *bycatch*. Bycatch is any fish or other creature that is unintentionally captured and usually killed in the attempt to catch a fish of a different species. When dolphins are captured in tuna nets and drown, for example, they are considered to be bycatch. Many other fish, mammals, sea turtles, and waterfowl become bycatch, as well.

To lower the bycatch rate, authorities have set limits not only on the target catch, but also on the bycatch. If a fishing vessel reaches its bycatch limit before reaching the target catch limit (the limit of fish it is trying to catch), it must stop fishing—thus reducing its harvest and income. One of the best ways to help fishing vessels avoid reaching their bycatch limits is to improve communications about bycatch hotspots. When a fishing boat experiences a high bycatch, it reports its bycatch to a centralized database that other fishing boats can access. These boats can then attempt to avoid areas where bycatch is particularly high. In many cases, management councils simply prohibit fishing in areas where large populations of nontarget species are known to live.

Several other techniques and technologies have helped reduce bycatch. By using nets with larger holes, fisheries can reduce the amount of smaller, juvenile fish they entrap by mistake. Some shrimp nets are equipped with special grids near the net's opening that allow shrimp to pass into the nets but block out larger fish and other animals. In addition, acoustic technology is used to repel marine mammals from lobster traps and submerged gill nets. To keep albatross away from longlines, fishermen frequently use scarelines equipped with waving ribbons that keep the birds away.

However, even with these innovations, bycatch remains a major problem. As with all marine fishery regulations, enforcement is a challenge, and it is not possible to have an observer on every ship. Some fishing vessels evade bycatch limits by discarding bycatch into the sea and not reporting it to the authorities.

Captain Clam's Comments

To ensure cooperation from fishermen, some management councils provide incentives for helping to reduce bycatch. If a particular fishery proves that it has reduced bycatch significantly, the council might reward the fishery with a higher target catch limit.

Downsizing the Fishing Fleets

As populations of commercially valuable fish have declined, the fishing industry has responded by adding more fishing boats to further exploit already dwindling resources. To help fish populations rebound and increase the harvests per boat, the industry needs to downsize—to reduce the number of boats by as much as 30 to 50 percent globally. However, with little or no financial incentive to downsize, individual fishers are not interested in leaving, and the fishing industry is reluctant to use fewer vessels—if one company cuts a vessel, others will add to fill the "gap."

Perhaps the best way to encourage the fishing industry to downsize is to stop subsidizing it, or at least substantially reduce subsidies. Traditionally, governments have subsidized the fishing industry in order to ensure a reliable fish supply, increase fish exports, and keep citizens employed. But fishing is an expensive business and does not always make a profit. Globally, the cost of fishing exceeds the revenue it earns by more than $50 billion (U.S.) annually. Cutting subsidies could force the industry to cut costs with fewer boats in order to achieve higher harvests per boat.

Improving and Enforcing International Agreements

Fish do not honor borders. They cross from one country's exclusive economic zone to another's at will and sometimes several times annually. If one country decides to prohibit the harvest of a particular fish in order to help the population rebound and other countries continue to harvest the fish, the population of the species will continue to decline. To stabilize the populations of migratory fish (so-called *straddling fish populations*), the United Nations drew up an agreement concerning the harvesting of these species. But so far only four of the top 20 fishing nations have signed it.

During the 1990s, the world has seen more conflicts over fishing rights than throughout the previous century. Disagreements in the Northwest Pacific over salmon, in the Northeast Atlantic over tuna, between Iceland and Norway over cod fishing, and between Canada and Spain over turbot have caused serious international tensions. Fortunately, the United Nations has led efforts to encourage agreements between nations to achieve *maximum sustainable yields*. The United Nations supports nations in establishing fishery management councils that can work with the United Nations to develop comprehensive and reasonable policies for managing their fisheries and to work together with other councils worldwide to resolve disagreements.

Log Entry

The goal of **maximum sustainable yields** (known as MSY) is to estimate a target harvest amount for all species ensuring that the populations remain at levels that produce fish now and for future generations. The MSY model has been widely used since the 1950s but is currently under fire because it is often difficult to implement due to a lack of information about the fishery (which hampers estimates of MSY) and a political tendency to continue fishing until MSY has been far exceeded.

Establishing No-Catch Zones

Fairly recently, scientists and marine biologists have been experimenting with no-catch zones or marine wildlife reserves. In a study organized by the National Centre for Ecological Analysis and Synthesis at the University of California in Santa Barbara, scientists studied more than 100 established no-catch zones for several years. Bigger, older, more fecund fish were found inside the marine reserves. Their findings also showed that not only did populations of depleted species nearly triple inside the reserve, but also populations nearly doubled in neighboring areas where fishing was allowed.

The results of this study and other related research suggests that by establishing a network of no-catch zones interspersed with fishing zones, fish populations can rebound and increase the harvests in open fishing zones. This kind of system has been set up on a small scale in New Zealand, and individual reserves currently operate around the world. However, ongoing political debates and outstanding questions concerning the optimum size and number of these no-catch zones and the best places to establish them have up to this point prevented this system from being implemented on a global scale.

Fish Farming and Frankenfish

One potentially helpful approach to reducing wild fish harvests is to farm fish (raise fish in captivity). This approach is commonly referred to as aquaculture. Slightly more than 20 percent of our fish supply currently is produced by fish farms, and this number is likely to grow. However, fish farms do have their drawbacks. To raise carnivorous species, such as shrimp, cod, and tuna, a fish farmer must feed the farmed fish between two and five pounds of wild fish for every pound of carnivorous fish harvested! (Fish food commonly consists of ground up herring, mackerel, sardines, or anchovies.) In addition, many species are farmed near the coasts, and waste products are dumped into the ocean, further polluting sensitive wildlife areas, including the all-important estuarine environments. For fish farming to be most productive, fish farms and consumers must focus more on raising vegetarian fish—such as tilapia, carp, catfish, or oysters—and reduce the pollution generated by fish farming.

Another controversial approach to preserving populations of wild fish is to genetically engineer "superior" fish—fish that reproduce more abundantly, grow faster, and have more meat on their bones. Genetically engineered salmon, for example, grow twice as fast as wild salmon,

> **Captain Clam's Comments**
>
> As a consumer, you can do your part to help restore wild fish populations by choosing to eat fish whose populations are not overfished. The Monterey Bay Aquarium's Seafood Watch (at www.mbayaq.org/cr/seafoodwatch. asp) and the Audubon Society's Seafood Lover's Guide (at www.audubon.org/campaign/lo/seafood/index.html) provide up-to-date descriptions and even wallet-sized cards to help you stay informed.

growing from 0 to 10 pounds in 14 months—half the time it takes a wild salmon to reach this weight. However, many scientists and ecologists fear that these "superior" fish (so-called *frankenfish*) could escape from captivity and drive the natural salmon populations to extinction. The frankenfish would outcompete their natural cousins for food, habitat, and mates. Even worse, zoologists fear that these fish, which are genetically *inferior* to their wild counterparts, could breed with the wild fish and dilute the gene pool.

Improving Shoreline Habitats

Although overfishing is the primary stressor driving down commercial fish populations, pollution and destruction of coastal habitats also affects fish populations off the coasts. Many commercial fish use estuaries, marshes, seagrass meadows, and even rivers to spawn and raise their young. As these coastal habitats are damaged—through pollution, overdevelopment, and fishing for bivalves and other coastal catches—spawning grounds and nurseries are quickly becoming limited. To ensure stable fish populations for future generations, coastal nations need to begin preserving these critical marine and semimarine environments.

As you learned in the previous chapter, several countries, including the United States, have banned the dumping of untreated municipal sewage and toxic industrial wastes into coastal areas or rivers that empty into oceans. However, the majority of developing countries still do not have wastewater treatment and continue to use the oceans as sewers. Much of the wastes concentrate in coastal environments, degrading the quality of the water and beaches.

The Least You Need to Know

- China is the biggest producer of fish in the world, and more than 50 percent of the fish it harvests are raised on fish farms.

- Worldwide, aquaculture makes up about 25 percent of all fish production.

- Island nations—such as the Maldives, Iceland, and Japan—typically have high per-capita fish consumption rates.

- One of the major problems faced by commercial fisheries is bycatch, the unintentional catching and killing of other fish, birds, invertebrates, and marine mammals.

- Scientists have discovered that by creating a network of no-catch zones, fish populations can be preserved while increasing the harvests in neighboring fisheries.

Chapter 21

Protecting Our Marine Ecosystems

In This Chapter

- ◆ Understanding the many problems that threaten marine ecosystems
- ◆ Compound problems require complex solutions
- ◆ Sorting out the good guys and the bad guys
- ◆ Identifying the tools, techniques, and discipline we need to solve the problems

With the ever-increasing population of humans, especially in coastal areas, and our increasing consumption of natural resources and production of wastes, we continue to threaten the habitat and survival of the plants and animals on which we depend. If we continue to use the oceans indiscriminately as we have in the past, we are certain to lose more than a few species that are important to the ecosystem. However, it's not too late to take some personal responsibility for the restoration and protection of critical ocean habitats.

Especially in the ocean, it might still be possible to help endangered species recover and halt their march toward extinction. From the continued low levels of Atlantic cod (a once abundant population of giant fish), to the overexploitation of abalone around the world, and ongoing efforts to boost sea turtle populations—there is plenty of work to be done. This chapter explores the ecological resources we are trying to save, the most prominent threats to ocean ecosystems, current efforts to counter those threats, and future challenges that we face. At the end of the day, raising awareness of these problems is an important first step to ensure that future generations can enjoy our ocean's bounty as we have.

The Need for a Holistic View

No single problem is causing the degradation of our oceans and sea life. Pollution, overfishing, overdevelopment, the introduction of non-native species, and other causes all contribute to the destruction of natural habitats, the decrease of populations of certain species, and the reduction of biodiversity. In addition, these causes are interconnected in such a way that they often compound the problems, making it difficult to identify specific causes and develop effective solutions.

Further compounding the problems is the fact that our oceans are not isolated bodies of water; they're connected to each other and to the land via air and rivers. Pollution in upstream New York State can eventually reach even the polar bears in Greenland. Sewage dumped in the Mississippi River or any of its tributaries flows right into the Gulf of Mexico. Oil spilled off the Eastern Coast of the United States can get sucked into the sargassum mats in the Sargasso Sea. Inland deforestation and urban development can often cause coastal erosion and excess silt near the coasts. One prime example of how pollution travels through the oceans environments is the accumulation of chlorinated hydrocarbons and other pollutants in the fatty tissue of top carnivores from dolphins to humans around the world.

Species are not isolated either; they form a food web and ecosystems in which various species rely on other species for food and shelter. Changes in populations of one or more species can perform a chain reaction through a particular community and ultimately through the ocean. For example, overfishing of one species (such as lobster) does more than merely decimate the lobster population. It can also result in increased populations of urchins, on which the lobster feeds, which can wipe out a kelp forest, which urchins eat.

This interconnectedness also exhibits itself in the relationships between various habitats and how some animals spend time in different habitats over the course of their lives. Many species spawn in estuaries, mangrove forests, and seagrass meadows, but live most of their lives in the open ocean. Some species, such as salmon, spawn in rivers and then migrate back to sea. This means that efforts to protect a particular species in just one of these critical habitats might not be successful, and collaboration between cities, states, and nations might become the limiting factor.

Identifying the Most Serious Problems

Although a host of interconnected problems threaten the health of our oceans, we cannot simply throw up our hands in despair. As with most complex situations, we must sort out the problems and identify them in order to develop and implement effective solutions. The following list identifies the most serious problems our oceans face and hints at some of the possible solutions:

◆ **Overfishing** Everyone, including the fishing industry, knows that commercial fish populations are being decimated by overfishing, yet nobody wants to make the sacrifices necessary to solve the problem. Several environmental organizations are pushing to have fisheries worldwide cut their fishing boat fleets in half by the year 2005 and encourage governments to stop importing fish from irresponsible (sometimes criminal) fleets. Reducing bycatch and fishing techniques such as trawling and dredging that destroy habitats are important components of establishing sustainable fisheries.

◆ **Overdevelopment** As the human population grows and coastal areas become more popular for their residential and recreational use, important coastal habitats are disappearing. Salt marshes, mudflats, salt flats, rocky coastal areas, and mangrove forests are commonly destroyed to make room for homes and hotels. In addition, development of coastal areas results in increased pollution, erosion, and siltation, further degrading ocean environments.

◆ **Destructive aquaculture** You might think that raising shrimp on a farm instead of catching them in the wild would be good for the environment. However, coastal shrimp aquaculture can result in the destruction of critical coastal environments, including mangrove forests and seagrass meadows. In addition, because shrimp eat fish meal (such as ground up anchovies), shrimp farming indirectly contributes to overfishing of certain fish species. Shrimp farms can be managed more sustainably, but this is not yet the norm, and most people do not realize how devastating the effects of irresponsible shrimp aquaculture can be.

◆ **Piracy** To avoid rules and regulations that apply to legal fisheries, some commercial ships sail with no markings or under flags of convenience (FOC means that they do not actually indicate which country the vessel is from) and exploit fish populations at will, completely ignoring no-catch zones, catch limits, and bycatch limits. Several nonprofit organizations are working to encourage governments to refuse these illegal fishing boats access to their ports, their markets, and other resources that subsidize piracy, and to improve enforcement of fishery regulations.

◆ **Marine pollution** Some companies and countries view the ocean as a dumping ground, thinking that the bottom of the ocean is a safe place to dump nuclear and toxic wastes. However, ocean currents carry these wastes throughout the ocean basin and cause considerable harm to individual species and ecosystems. International agreements against dumping and watchdog organizations to identify those who continue to dump toxins into the oceans are important ways of addressing this problem.

◆ **Invasive species** Over time, ecosystems establish a very sensitive balance between species. When a foreign species that evolved in different conditions is introduced, it can often tip the balance and take over an area, outcompeting other species for food and habitat. These invasive species commonly hitch rides in the ballast water of ships or by being intentionally released by pet owners. Only strict rules and vigilant adherence to these rules can prevent the introduction of invasive species.

◆ **Global warming** As the earth becomes warmer, the heat and the rising sea levels can cause additional problems for various ocean environments. One of the most obvious problems is the relatively recent increase in coral bleaching—the loss of photosynthetic zooxanthellae that live inside the coral polyps and provide them with much of their nutrition. Rising sea levels can often cause dramatic changes to various coastal habitats, and warmer waters can give rise to more violent storms, increasing coastal erosion. To help reduce the effects of global warming, we must reduce carbon emissions and develop and use more energy-efficient technologies and fuel.

The Role of Governments and Other Groups

Most of the problems that threaten the survival of our oceans must be attacked on two fronts: through lifestyle changes of individual human beings and through the action of governments, consumer groups, international organizations, environmental groups, and other groups of people working together to enact and enforce environmentally sound legislation. The following sections name and describe some of the more important governments and organizations involved in helping to restore ocean health and preserve their valuable resources.

International Organizations and Forums

Because oceans are connected and fish refuse to acknowledge the exclusive economic zone of any one country, international cooperation has become more and more important in preserving the oceans, conserving their resources, and encouraging an equitable distribution of the oceans' wealth. Two of the most influential groups are the United Nations and the World Trade Organization. The United Nations works to ensure sustainable fisheries by promoting agreements between nations and international laws. Specifically, its Food and Agriculture Organization (FAO) runs several programs to encourage responsible fisheries, collect accurate data concerning fisheries, and increase the contribution of aquaculture and fisheries to the world food supply.

The World Trade Organization works toward avoiding and resolving differences between nations concerning trade issues that may or may not be beneficial to the environment. In 1998, for example, the WTO ruled against a U.S. embargo on imported shrimp from countries that refused to use turtle-excluder devices on their shrimp nets. These devices are relatively inexpensive, 97 percent effective, and reduce shrimp harvests by only about 3 percent. Yet, the embargo was ruled to be unfair, because countries cannot impose their own standards on another country. A similar ruling was handed down on an attempt by the U.S. to enact an embargo on yellow-fin tuna caught in nondolphin-friendly nets. Other trade organizations, including the North American Free Trade Agreement (NAFTA) and the Asia Pacific Economic Cooperation (APEC) forum face similar conflicts between the desire for free trade and the need to protect species and preserve resources.

Nations and Unions

Although international cooperation is essential in protecting the oceans, individual nations and unions (groups of nations) often make unilateral decisions that affect the oceans and their fisheries in positive or negative ways. The European Union, for example, has developed a Common Fisheries Policy (CFP) that is working toward agreements on banning the use of drift nets, promoting the recovery of cod and northern hake, and studying aquaculture in the various nations that are part of the European Union. The European Union also works to establish agreements with other nations outside the Union.

The United States has also taken unilateral action to protect our oceans. The Pew Oceans Commission, for example, is "an independent group of American leaders conducting a national dialogue on the policies needed to restore and protect living marine resources in U.S. waters." The Commission has examined various aspects of ocean management, including aquaculture, fishing, coastal development, marine pollution, and threats from the introduction of non-native species. The Commission made its formal recommendations to Congress in the fall of 2002 with a series of reports.

During the summer of 2001, the U.S. Commission on Ocean Policy was formed to study ocean issues and "make recommendations to the President and Congress for a coordinated and comprehensive national ocean policy." The commission is responsible for providing recommendations on ocean resource management, pollution reduction, and regulation of commerce and transportation. The organization is also responsible for promoting and supporting various marine sciences and studies to collect accurate, useful data. The Commission is due to provide final recommendations to the President and Congress in June 2003.

State and Local Governments

State and local governments can have a significant impact on the oceans as well, by enacting and enforcing laws to prevent overdevelopment, pollution, and overfishing and to build infrastructure that promotes cleaner water and healthier environments. Local governments are often responsible for building and maintaining water-treatment plants, waste-management plants, and storm drains. If these systems fail, pollution typically finds its way to creeks and rivers that eventually flow to the ocean.

More directly, state and local governments of cities and states on the coasts or island states frequently take measures and enact legislation to ensure the sustainability of their own fisheries and the preservation of their marine environments. For example, the California Department of Fish and Game designated a network of marine protected areas in the Channel Islands in 2002 in the hopes of preserving these areas and increasing fish harvests in neighboring fisheries.

Nonprofit Organizations

Many nonprofit organizations work tirelessly at local, national, and international levels to improve the conditions of our oceans. These organizations include the Ocean Conservancy, Nature Conservancy, World Wildlife Fund, Conservation International, Environmental Defense, Surfrider, Baykeeper, Natural Resources Defense Council, and the Audubon Society. Each of these organizations plays an important role ranging from political advocacy to public education, fundraising, purchasing land to set aside for conservation, restoring habitats, working with endangered species, serving as watchdogs for government agencies and private companies, and pushing for legal protections for the environment. On high-profile issues such as fisheries, seemingly unrelated organizations may join the fray because of a broader legal and political agenda.

One of the most vocal and visible environmental activist groups is Greenpeace, whose members commonly refer to themselves as Warriors of the Rainbow. (*Rainbow Warrior* is the name of Greenpeace's flagship.) Greenpeace works in more than 40 countries and relies on public protests and direct action to force politicians and offending parties to acknowledge environmental concerns. Greenpeace and the Sierra Club also do important political work, including lobbying and waging legal battles to, to promote the enactment of environmentally friendly legislation.

Hundreds of ocean advocacy groups around the world are doing their part to ensure the survival of our oceans, including the Clean Ocean Foundation, the Australian Coral Reef Society, and the Australian Conservation Foundation in Australia; the Japan Marine Conservation Center, the Coral Reef Network, and Save Japan's Dolphins and Whales in Japan; International Dolphin Watch and Marine Conservation Society in the United Kingdom; and a host of other local and international organizations.

Ocean Industries

Many industry representatives participate in the U.S. Commission on Ocean Policy, as well, including representatives from shipping and fisheries industries. These representatives take part in deliberations over marine protected areas and other changes to state and federal policy that could affect their industries. As people who have a direct interest in using marine resources, some of those who profit from the ocean ultimately share an interest in continuing to use those resources for years to come.

In New Zealand, commercial fishers are directly involved in fisheries management as part of a quota system for fishing rights. They pay for and participate in all the research and are part of the decision-making process each year. While this isn't the way most fishery management works in the United States, the basic lesson that everyone who has a stake in the ocean resources has a potential role to play in using ocean resources wisely is an important concept.

Addressing the Issues with Legislation

Whenever issues affect more than one person or an area that is not isolated, laws are required to protect the rights and interests of all people involved, and I can't think of anything that affects more people and other beings than the health of our oceans. Local, state, national, and international laws are commonly passed to govern the oceans and the exploitation of their resources. The following sections explore some of the more important and visible laws.

Ocean Law

In many countries, national laws are in place to protect the habitat of endangered species, limit pollution, or prevent pirates from performing illegal operations on the sea. However, enforcing these laws can be expensive and difficult, rendering them ineffective. Because of this, some people working to protect ocean ecosystems focus on litigation (lawsuits) as a means to draw attention and cash to the problem of enforcement, making it possible for the government to take action. The creation of new national or state laws and funding to back them are an even more powerful tool, but can take much longer to advocate and campaign for their passage. Local Baykeeper chapters and the Natural Resources Defense Council are examples of non-profit groups that attempt to improve legal protections for the ocean by bringing lawsuits against both private and public parties.

International Law

To protect and preserve our oceans and their renewable resources worldwide, achieving cooperation between nations is essential. In order to develop a framework for future enforcement, and create leverage for ocean conservation in national-level politics, nations are sometimes able to reach agreement on particular issues—ever so slowly piecing together the international legal foundation necessary for conservation. Although international agreements are few and often lack the legal "teeth" to make them enforceable, they still represent progress toward equitable, sustainable, and pragmatic ocean governance. The following list describes some of the most notable examples of these treaties and conventions:

- ◆ **1973 Convention on International Trade in Endangered Species (CITES)** This voluntary agreement between 160 countries (referred to as "parties") prevents the trade of more than 30,000 protected species worldwide, both plants and animals both on land and in the water. CITES is one of the more successful examples of international environmental policies: Since it has been in effect, trade in endangered species has been significantly curtailed.

- ◆ **1973/1978 International Convention on the Prevention of Pollution from Ships (MARPOL)** A combination of two treaties agreed upon in 1973 and 1978, MARPOL is one of the most sweeping agreements ever written concerning the intentional and accidental dumping of wastes into the oceans from seagoing vessels. This agreement addresses the following six sources of pollution: oil from tankers as well as oil discharged during routine operations; dumping or discharge of noxious liquid substances; dumping of packaged harmful substances; dumping of sewage; dumping of garbage; and the discharge of air pollution from seagoing vessels.

◆ **1993 Convention on Biological Diversity**   This convention is one of the more important products that came out of the 1992 Earth Summit held in Rio de Janeiro. The Convention set three main goals: "The conservation of biological diversity, the sustainable use of its components, and the fair and equitable sharing of the benefits from the use of genetic resources." This treaty has not yet been signed by the United States and its capability to lead to real change has yet to be demonstrated.

◆ **1994 United Nations Convention on the Law of the Sea (UNCLOS)**   One of the most significant international agreements, the UNCLOS enabled nations to claim territorial waters extending up to 12 miles off their coasts and gave all nations the right to claim an exclusive economic zone extending 200 miles off their coasts. The idea was to encourage nations to conserve their natural resources and to reduce the number of conflicts over resources. Initially the exploitation of fisheries in many developing countries by foreign fleets was reduced by this law. However, in recent times overfishing by foreign fleets has been replaced by even heavier exploitation by each nation's own fishing industry—entrenching even more capital in the serial depletion of stocks worldwide.

◆ **1995 United Nations Conference on Straddling Stocks and Highly Migratory Fish Stocks**   Because fish do not acknowledge the exclusive economic zones of various countries, the United Nations drew up this agreement as an attempt to preserve populations of open ocean fish that are highly migratory, including tuna, swordfish, and cod. The agreement attempts to encourage nations to work together to maintain sustainable populations of migratory fish. This agreement initiated an international working group of scientists, managers, and policy-makers who have already had significant initial success in improving management of tuna stocks.

◆ **1995 UNEP Conference on Protection of the Marine Environment from Land-Based Activities**   This agreement stands as an implicit acknowledgment that land-based pollution has a detrimental effect on ocean habitats and wildlife. This Washington declaration calls on all parties, to develop national action programs, and cooperate on a regional basis to reduce or eliminate "emissions and discharges of sewage, persistent organic pollutants, radioactive substances, heavy metals, oils (hydrocarbons), nutrients, sediment, and litter," and to reduce physical alterations and destruction of habitats.

Global Problems, Local Solutions

Threats to ocean sustainability are increasingly multinational. For example, a super-trawler using nets the size of four football fields might be financed by a company in the United States, designed by a company in Norway, built in Spain, and licensed in Russia, to fish the already overfished waters of the Bering Sea. This diffused responsibility in complex chains of production makes it even less likely that the laws of any one country can be enforced on the open sea.

Because of this, some governments and conservation groups have decided to limit imports and encourage and educate consumers to stop purchasing threatened species. On a national scale, this was recently illustrated by the U.S. embargo on shrimp from countries that do not require turtle excluder devices on shrimp trawls. Ultimately this case was taken to the World Trade Organization (WTO) which is likely to be an increasingly important venue for creating international policy on marine resources.

Although government leverage can help on a national and international level, reducing pollution, slowing the spread of invasive species, and even encouraging sustainable fisheries can all begin at home. The seafood-choices-educational campaign and fisheries' efforts to provide "eco-labeling" and better information to consumers are prime examples of this focus on consumer power. From the convenience of your own kitchen, you can do your part to prevent overfishing—as mentioned in Chapter 20. The Monterey Bay's Seafood Watch program and the Audubon Society's Seafood Lover's Guide are good sources that can help you choose to eat more sustainable fish, whether dining out or cooking in.

Attacking Pollution on Two Fronts

Pollution is another problem that needs to be attacked on two fronts: both through governmental action and personal lifestyle changes. Environmentalists like to divide sources of pollution into two categories: *point source* and *nonpoint source* (NPS) pollution. Point-source pollution is easily identified, such as a manufacturing plant dumping used cleaning solution into a creek, or a pig farm flushing its wastes into the nearest river. NPS pollution is more difficult to trace and typically has several sources, such as the trash buildup along a river bank that results from illegal dumping and litter from multiple recreational boats.

Point-Source Pollution

Point source problems are relatively easy to solve. The environmental protection agency often can trace the problem to the responsible source and then fine the company or individual or even shut down whatever operation is producing the pollution. More frequently, government agencies develop ongoing relationships with potential polluters to gain compliance with the regulations—sometimes a better understanding of the problem and preventative measures are all that's necessary to improve business practices. In the case of severe violations, the EPA may require the company to clean up its mess and pay restitution to any individuals whose land, water, or air has been contaminated.

Captain Clam's Comments

For years, point source pollution was considered the primary source of pollution in the United States, but with more stringent regulations and better enforcement of the rules, point source pollution is on the decline. Unfortunately, nonpoint source pollution has become an even greater problem. Hopefully, by educating the public on the nature of the problem, we can all do our part to reduce non-point source pollution.

Nonpoint Source Pollution

NPS pollution can be extremely difficult to stop, because no one person or company can be held accountable. One of the major contributors of NPS pollution today comes from our storm drains. As rain falls, water washes over streets, lawns, and highways, and flows right down the drain, carrying with it oil, engine coolant, transmission fluid, fertilizer, animal wastes, soap from people who wash their cars in their driveways, cigarette butts, litter, and anything else that happens to fall on impervious surfaces, such as sidewalks and streets.

To help reduce nonpoint source pollution, dispose of trash and any toxic wastes properly; if your car is leaking oil or transmission fluid, repair the leaks; don't overflow your gas tank; don't dump animal wastes, including kitty litter, in the gutter; wash your car at a carwash instead of at home; avoid overusing lawn and garden fertilizers and pesticides; and don't wash paint brushes or other tools over or into storm drains. One person's irresponsible dumping might seem small, but when millions of people in a city act irresponsibly, these tiny drops of oil, transmission fluid, and other wastes add up to cause big problems.

Ocean Alert

Washing your car in the driveway can send pollutants from the oil, grit, and soap into the nearest river, lake, or ocean. Dirty water and soap run down the driveway and into the street or storm drain, eventually reaching the nearest waterway. This water is never treated and can cause problems for wildlife and for people enjoying the beach. Stick to washing your car at the car wash. If you prefer to wash it yourself, park the car on your lawn or another *permeable* surface that absorbs water—if the water forms large puddles or runs off quickly and does not soak in, it's not a good place to wash your car! Use a minimum of soap and discard dirty water in the toilet or the sink, never in the street or storm drain.

Establishing Marine Protected Areas

As introduced in Chapter 20, one of the most promising methods of preserving critical marine environments and helping wildlife populations rebound is to create a network of no-catch zones around the world. Studies have shown that within two years, fish populations in protected areas nearly tripled and populations nearly doubled in adjacent, unprotected areas. These so-called *marine protected areas* (MPAs) vary in size from a few acres to several thousand square miles, and their locations vary depending on where the most critical ocean environments are located.

Unfortunately, even though scientists are convinced that MPAs hold the key to preserving and restoring our oceans and establishing sustainable fish populations, the process of designating the zones and enforcing no-catch rules has proceeded extremely slowly, primarily because of local and regional politics. Only about one third of the recommended zones have been formally set aside and many of them are too small to produce the desired effect. Even those zones that have been designated as MPAs are often fished illegally, significantly slowing the recovery process. However, the world has been trying to implement this solution for only about two decades, so perhaps in the next two decades, broader public awareness of the need for ocean conservation will lead to the successful establishment and enforcement of these all-important conservation areas.

Ocean Restoration: Work in Progress

Most of the solutions discussed in this chapter up to this point deal with ocean conservation and maintenance. However, a great deal of damage already has been done. Pollution of various kinds (including DDT and oil spills) has damaged and continues to negatively affect many sensitive wildlife areas. Coral reefs have been chipped away by pollution, greedy coral collectors, and careless tourists. Wetlands have been sacrificed to create more beachfront property. And the human population continues to compete with ocean wildlife for living space and resources in coastal areas. Given the fact that more than 70 percent of the wildlife species spend at least part of their lives in coastal areas, we must prevent the loss and degradation of any more coastal habitats, but also restore degraded areas to the point where they can become healthy, functioning ecosystems.

Many restoration projects are currently being undertaken by private land owners, farmers, communities, volunteer organizations, and government organizations to restore wetlands, coral reefs, mangrove forests, and other critical environments, but these projects are not always easy. In many cases, wetlands have been filled in and/or drained. To restore them, any fill dirt must be removed, the areas must be refilled with water, and native species must be reintroduced. In many cases, volunteer groups work along with land owners and government organizations to clear non-native vegetation, replant the area, and restock it with fish and other native wildlife. In some coastal areas, residents gather on weekends to plant eel grass and other seagrass species to restore seagrass habitats, or remove invasive weeds that have taken over a native marsh.

Preservation of our remaining coastal environments together with the efforts to restore habitats that have been seriously damaged or destroyed are important steps to begin restoring the health of our oceans.

Encouraging Voluntary Conservation

Collaboration with fishing and other industry groups may seem counterintuitive, but in some situations this has turned out to be critical to success. In the face of so many challenges to the health of the ocean (only some of which are listed in this book), it just makes sense that the more people who are engaged, the more likely we are reach some of these goals.

For example, outreach programs that explain more sustainable ways of doing business are a key component to making shrimp aquaculture sustainable and fisheries less destructive, especially in developing countries. By providing information on reducing pollution and adding financial incentives to encourage reductions in pollution, governments, nonprofits, and even industry organizations can make ocean-friendly choices a way of doing business.

From the consumer's perspective, programs such as the seafood watch and the seafood lover's guide make it convenient to choose more sustainable fish. You can also do your part by using energy-efficient light bulbs and appliances in your home or saving gas when driving your car.

Educating the People

Just as nonprofits and businesses can do their part, everyone in the broader public has great potential as an ocean-friendly consumer, citizen, and voter. Raising awareness about the ocean is one of the most important tools for change, and by reading this book you have already expressed an interest in learning more. As governments, scientists, environmentalists, and private businesses attempt to develop solutions for the many problems the oceans face, they must also educate the public to the global nature of these problems. Until all citizens of the world work together to save our oceans, the oceans and the wildlife they support will remain at risk.

The Least You Need to Know

- Several interrelated problems threaten the health of our oceans, including pollution, overfishing, overdevelopment of coastal areas, destruction of wetlands, and the introduction of non-native species.

- Governments and local, national, and international organizations offer our best hope for restoring the health of our oceans and the sustainability of our fisheries.

- The primary role that governments play in preserving our ocean resources is to enact and enforce laws and international agreements that benefit the oceans and ensure sustainable fisheries.

- Hundreds of nonprofit environmental advocacy and activist groups play an important role in protecting and restoring the health of our oceans.

- Although pollution commonly is generated by easily identifiable sources, a significant source of pollution comes from storm drains—a source we all contribute to.

- One of the most promising methods to restore fish stocks is to create a network of Marine Protected Areas (MPAs) where fishing is prohibited.

- To ensure the future overall health of our oceans, we must restore critical habitats, including wetlands, seagrass meadows, kelp beds, and coral reefs, and make lifestyle changes that are environmentally friendly.

Stewardship Programs

If you are interested in getting more involved in monitoring, preserving, and restoring ocean environments and the various plants and organisms that call the oceans home, consider signing up for a stewardship training program or joining one of many nonprofit ocean advocacy groups. Following is a list of several ocean stewardship training programs and ocean advocacy groups in which you can obtain additional information on how you can get involved:

BlueVoice.org
1252 B Street
Petaluma, CA 94954
E-mail: contact@bluevoice.org
Web: www.bluevoice.org/

Boating Clean & Green
California Coastal Commission
45 Fremont Street, Suite 2000
San Francisco, CA 94105
E-mail: mgordon@coastal.ca.gov
Web: www.coastal.ca.gov/ccbn/
ccbndx.html

Caribbean Conservation Corporation
4424 N.W. 13th Street Suite #A1
Gainesville, FL 32609
Phone: 1-800-678-7853
E-mail: ccc@cccturtle.org
Web: www.cccturtle.org/

Coral Reef Alliance
417 Montgomery Street, Suite 205
San Francisco, CA 94104
Phone: 1-888-CORAL-REEF
Email: info@coral.org
Web: www.coral.org/

Environmental Defense Network
257 Park Avenue South
New York, NY 10010
Phone: 1-800-684-3322
E-mail: members@environmentaldefense.org
Web: www.environmentaldefense.org/

Friends of the Sea Otter
125 Ocean View Boulevard, Suite 204
Pacific Grove, CA 93950
Phone: 831-373-2747
E-mail: seaotters@seaotters.org
Web: www.seaotters.org/

Marine Conservation Biology Institute
15805 N.E. 47th Court
Redmond, WA 98052
Phone: 425-883-8914
Email: mcbiweb@mcbi.org
Web: www.mcbi.org/

Marine Environmental Research Institute
55 Main Street
P.O. Box 1652
Blue Hill, ME 04614
Phone: 207-374-2135
E-mail: meri@downeast.net

Marine Fish Conservation Network
600 Pennsylvania Avenue, SE, Suite 210
Washington, DC 20003
Phone: 866-823-8552
E-mail: network@conservefish.org
Web: www.conservefish.org/

National Marine Sanctuary Program
1305 East-West Highway, 11th Floor
Silver Spring, MD 20910
Phone: 301-713-3125
E-mail: nmscomments@noaa.gov
Web: www.sanctuaries.nos.noaa.gov/

Ocean Conservancy
1725 DeSales Street NW, Suite 600
Washington, DC 20036
Phone: 202-429-5609
Web: www.oceanconservancy.org/

Oceana
2501 M Street, NW
Suite 300
Washington, DC 20037-1311
Phone: 1-800-8-OCEAN-0 or 1-877-7-OCEANA
Fax: 202-833-2070
E-mail: info@oceana.org
Web: www.oceana.org

Reef Environmental Education Foundation
PO Box 246
Key Largo, FL 33037
Phone: 305-852-0030
E-mail: reefhq@reef.org
Web: www.reef.org

Reef Relief
PO Box 430
Key West, FL 33041
Phone: 305-294-3100
E-mail: reef@bellsouth.net
Web: www.reefrelief.org/

Santa Barbara Channel Keeper
120 W. Mission Street
Santa Barbara, CA 93101
Phone: 805-563-3377
E-mail: info@sbck.org
Web: www.sbck.org/

Sea Grant
841 National Press Building
529 14th Street NW
Washington, DC 20045-2277
Phone: 202-662-7095
E-mail: sherman@nasw.org
Web: www.seagrantnews.org

SeaWeb
1731 Connecticut Avenue, NW 4th Floor
Washington, DC 20009
Phone: 202-483-9570
E-mail: seaweb@seaweb.org
Web: www.seaweb.org/

SPARS
Sidney Pier Artificial Reef Science
c/o Gaye Sihin, SPARS coordinator
PO Box 6000 9860 West Saanich Road
Sidney, BC V8L 4B2
Phone: 250-363-6395
Fax: 250-363-6310
E-mail: sihing@pac.dfo-mpo.gc.ca
Web: www-sci.pac.dfo-mpo.gc.ca/
protocol/spars/default.htm

Tampa Baywatch
8401 9th Street, North
St. Petersburg, FL 33702
E-mail: info@tampabaywatch.org

The Most Popular Ocean Websites

This book provides an excellent introduction to the oceans from several different perspectives, but it cannot possibly teach you everything you need to know (or want to know) about our oceans. To continue your oceanic explorations, you can read additional books, watch videos about the oceans, take courses in oceanography or marine biology, volunteer to help an ocean activist group, and take up scuba diving. If you have a computer with an Internet connection, you can also access many resources on the web. The web features dozens of ocean sites packed with information about marine life, ocean weather, undersea geology, ocean ecology, and much more. Following is a list of excellent websites that focus on various aspects of our oceans:

- **Aquatic Network** (www.aquanet.com) functions as an information server for the aquatic world. This site includes information on aquaculture, conservation, fisheries, marine science and oceanography, maritime heritage, ocean engineering, and seafood. You can purchase everything from books to fish on this site!

- **Beneath the Sea** (www.beneaththesea.org) is a nonprofit organization that works toward increasing awareness of the earth's oceans and the sport of scuba diving. BTS helps promote the protection of marine wildlife via grants to other nonprofit groups. This site includes links to seminars, workshops, mailing lists, and other diving-related sites.

◆ **Enchanted Learning's Guide to the Oceans** (www.enchantedlearning.com/subjects/ocean/) is one of the best sites for children to begin their exploration of the oceans and the plant and animal life that live below sea level. Here, kids can learn about waves, tides, coral reefs, tidal zones, ocean explorers, and much more. They can also print diagrams to label and color and download instructions for fun and interesting projects.

◆ **How Sharks Work** (www.howstuffworks.com/shark.htm) provides an incredibly clear, illustrated description of shark anatomy and physiology. If you find sharks fascinating, check out this site to learn more about shark anatomy, eating habits, and sensory organs, as well as some of the threats to their survival.

◆ **National Oceanic and Atmospheric Administration** (www.noaa.gov) is packed with information not only about ocean weather patterns and currents, but also about fisheries, fishery management, preservation of coastal environments and coral reefs, and explanations of navigational tools and techniques. This site is very easy to navigate and features a hefty collection of colorful photos.

◆ **NOAA's Coral Reef Online** (www.coralreef.noaa.gov) is the home of the National Oceanic and Atmospheric Association's reef site, where you will find links to dozens of resources, including coral reef photos, areas where coral bleaching is a problem, locations of NOAA marine sanctuaries, information about biodiversity in coral reefs, and much more.

◆ **Ocean.com** (www.ocean.com) features the latest news, studies, and warnings about the condition of the earth's oceans. Here, you'll find information about ocean travel, a gallery of ocean photos, Poseidon's library of sea stories, and links to hundreds of sites featuring everything from ocean gear to conservation groups. Well-designed, easy to navigate, and packed with useful information and links to other resources, this site is my personal favorite.

◆ **The Ocean Alliance** (www.oceanalliance.org) is focused on protecting and conserving whales through research and international education initiatives. Here, you can follow the voyage of the *Odyssey* as it carries out its five-year mission to study the seas; you can learn more about the Ocean Alliance and its goals; you can contribute to the organization; and you can even shop online.

◆ **Ocean Planet** (seawifs.gsfc.nasa.gov/ocean_planet.html) is presented by the Smithsonian Institution as an archive of its traveling exhibition on the status of our oceans. This site might not provide the most up-to-date information, but its online exhibits of Oceans in Peril, Heroes (working to save the oceans), and Sea People are excellent.

◆ **Ocean Weather** (www.oceanweather.com) uses a unique hind-casting approach to forecast ocean weather including winds, waves, and surf. At this site, you can obtain current ocean data for various areas worldwide.

- **OceanLink** (oceanlink.island.net) is packed with information and resources for enthusiastic ocean explorers of all ages. Click **Ocean Info** to access more than a dozen links for a variety of fascinating ocean topics; click **AquaFacts** for the latest news and trivia about ocean life; or click **Records** to find out which marine creature is the largest or smallest, which can dive the deepest, which is the fastest, and which is the slowest. This site also features an excellent glossary.

- **Oceans Alive** (www.abc.net.au/oceans/alive.htm) focuses on marine life in the waters surrounding Australia and provides information on whale watching and marine biodiversity hot spots. It also provides general ocean information, including a list of ocean facts, information about seal training, links to schools that offer studies in marine biology, and links to other oceanic resources.

- **PADI: Professional Association of Diving Instructors** (www.padi.com) is a fantastic site with current information about diving. Updated daily, this site offers dive center listings, bulletin boards, product catalogs, news, and course listings, as well as a wide range of information beyond what you can find at most scuba-diving sites. PADI also offers a fish quiz to test your knowledge, a map of the ocean floor from NOAA, dive insurance, and more. If you plan on becoming a scuba diver, visit this site often.

- **Scuba Yellow Pages** (www.scubayellowpages.com) enables you to search a worldwide directory to find contacts and suppliers for all your scuba diving needs—from tour operators to airlines to clubs and certifications. The site also offers tons of information—a diver's directory, a search feature to help you quickly locate information, e-mail, and a lot of diver resources. If you are interested in diving for fun or profit, this is the place for locating equipment you need and other resources to make your dive much more successful, whether you dive for recreation or professionally.

- **Scripps Institution of Oceanography** (sio.ucsd.edu) is the Internet home of the world famous Scripps Institution of Oceanography, a part of the University of California, San Diego campus. Scripps has a 100-year history of helping various countries around the world research and solve problems relating to the oceans. Here, you can find information about the various programs and research projects that the Scripps Institution is involved in and explore its diverse collection of marine species and geophysical data. Its library is also searchable online.

- **Seafood Watch** (www.mbayaq.org/cr/seafoodwatch.asp) at the Monterey Bay Aquarium (www.mbayaq.org) has a wallet-sized card with recommended sustainable seafood choices, a list of different menu fish under green (for "go"), yellow, and red that is easy to use next time you eat out or at home. The Audubon Society has a similar site.

- **SeaWeb** (www.seaweb.org) provides headlines and links to the latest ocean news stories in addition to providing more in-depth information on their recent projects, including aquaculture, marine reserves, and swordfish. It also maintains an archive of recent scientific papers on particular ocean-related topics.

◆ **SeaWorld** (www.seaworld.org) is a great place for kids to learn about animals both in the oceans and on land. It's also a great place for teachers to obtain resources for their biology and science classes. Downloadable, printable teacher guides are available for all ages of students from kindergarten up to twelfth grade and cover a variety of topics ranging from arctic wildlife to sharks, wetlands, and species diversity. Parents can also obtain information about various adventure camps designed for kids.

◆ **Stephen Birch Aquarium Museum** (www.aquarium.ucsd.edu) is part of the Scripps Institution of Oceanography. This aquarium has information about volunteer opportunities, educational programs, and summer learning adventures. Here you can also find links to what's new at the aquarium, membership information, ocean quizzes, and articles and videos about various species of marine animals.

◆ **Surfrider Foundation USA** (www.surfrider.org) is the Internet home of the Surfrider Foundation, a nonprofit group dedicated to protecting, preserving, and restoring the world's oceans and beaches. Its site includes daily surf reports, weekly coastal factoids, policy updates, and an online membership form.

◆ **Titanic, the Official Archive** (www.titanic-online.com/titanic/index.html) explores the history of the *Titanic* from its conception and building to the time it sank and its discovery at the bottom of the ocean. This site also provides information about the passengers and crew, as well as descriptions and photos of many of the artifacts collected during the discovery. You can shop for *Titanic*-related merchandise online.

◆ **Whales Online** (www.whales-online.org) is an "information site dedicated to the conservation of whales, dolphins, and porpoises in the Southern Hemisphere." Here, you can find information about whales, dolphins, and porpoises by region; obtain information about responsible whale and dolphin watching; and learn about the numerous threats that our oceans and whales face.

◆ **Woods Hole Oceanographic Institution** (www.whoi.edu) is a private, nonprofit organization that studies the oceans and attempts to develop solutions for the most serious problems threatening the health of our oceans. At this site, you can learn about the Woods Hole programs and research projects, about their many interesting research vessels and vehicles (submersibles), and about its educational program offerings. This site also features fascinating articles about current expeditions and other ocean-related topics.

Appendix C

Glossary

abyss   The sea floor where the sun doesn't shine. This zone reaches from 2,250 meters down to the ocean floor. This area is characterized by cold, high-pressure, pitch-dark waters. *See also* zonation.

acoustic window   An opening typically located near the base of a cetacean's jaw that enables them to perceive sounds that they bounce off objects. *See also* cetacean and echolocation.

AGE   *See* arterial gas embolism.

aggressive mimicry   An evolutionary adaptation that makes a predator or parasite look like a beneficial creature, such as a cleaner fish, giving it easy access to its host or prey.

Agnatha   Jawless fish.

algae   Photosynthetic organisms that may take the form of single-cell microscopic plants or multicellular seaweeds, such as kelp. Algae are protists, not true plants. *See also* algae bloom and seaweed.

algae bloom (or algal bloom)   An explosive growth of algae that can sometimes kill other plant life or result in the depletion of the oxygen content of the water, leading to the deaths of fish and other sea creatures. *See also* algae and harmful algae bloom.

alginate   A thickening agent derived from algae.

algologist   A botanist or aquaculture scientist who specializes in growing algae.

amphibian A cold-blooded vertebrate with smooth, slimy skin that hatches from an egg, becomes a gill-breathing, free-swimming larva, and develops into an air-breathing adult. Because ocean water is so salty, no amphibians can tolerate it.

amphioxus This is the genus name for arrow worms, a taxonomic group in the same phylum as humans (Chordata). The term means "pointed at both ends" (like a toothpick) and describes their eel-like body shape.

ampullae of Lorenzini A sensory system that sharks and rays use to sense weak electrical signals in the water, typically emitted by prey. This is useful especially when a shark attacks because sharks typically roll their eyes back or close them tight for protection when they initiate an attack.

anadromous The ability to migrate from saltwater to freshwater in order to breed. *See also* catadromous.

anaerobic bacteria Single-celled organisms that live in oxygen-depleted environments, such as within the muck of an estuary. These bacteria use chemosynthesis to provide much of the food consumed by other bottom feeders in estuaries. *See also* anoxic.

angiosperm Another name for true plants or flowering plants—those plants that have a vascular system and reproduce sexually. Most familiar land plants are angiosperms.

animalcule Antoni van Leeuwenhoek's name for photosynthetic plant-like animals that could move. We now commonly refer to these organisms as protists. *See also* protist.

annelid Worm, including earthworms and tube worms.

anoxic The absence of oxygen; this term is commonly used to describe a layer of the ocean floor or water column where oxygen is unavailable and the bottom of the food chain consists of anaerobic bacteria, which do not require oxygen to survive.

archaeocetes Earliest whale-like mammals.

arribada A massive sea turtle nesting phenomenon in which marine turtles hit the shores to lay their eggs.

arterial gas embolism A condition that typically occurs when a diver ascends too quickly after a dive causing air bubbles to form in the bloodstream that are large enough to block the blood flow to the brain or another vital organ, resulting in serious injury or death. *See also* bends, oxygen toxicity, and nitrogen narcosis.

arthropod An invertebrate with an exoskeleton and jointed appendages, such as crabs, lobsters, and insects.

asthenosphere The layer of molten, liquid rock that lies beneath the earth's surface, below the lithosphere. As the asthenosphere heats up, molten rock pushes up between the spaces that separate the lithosphere's plates, causing the plates to move and the contents to drift. *See also* lithosphere.

atoll   A ring or partial ring of coral with a lagoon in the middle, which results in an island made of coral. Atolls likely form around volcanic islands, whose crater-like centers become the lagoon. *See also* fringing reef and barrier reef.

autotroph   An organism that can produce all the food it needs either by photosynthesis or chemosynthesis. *See also* photosynthesis and chemosynthesis.

axenic   An algae culture that is free from contaminants. *See also* oligoxenic.

backshore   The area of a beach that extends from the high tide level to the top of the beach—where you find most of the beachfront property. *See also* foreshore.

baleen plate   A whale's tooth that consists of a solid shield with a frayed edge composed of the same stuff that makes up fingernails. When a whale closes its mouth, the frayed edges of the teeth form a dense mesh through which the whale can strain the water out of its mouth and eat the plankton left behind.

bang stick   A rather nasty piece of diving equipment that a scuba diver might use to shoot and kill a shark or other adversary underwater.

barrier reef   A coral reef that is separated from the land by a shallow lagoon with a sandy bottom and patches of vegetation. *See also* fringing reef and atoll.

bathypelagic zone   An open-ocean zone that extends from the bottom of the mesopelagic zone to approximately 2,250 meters, but does not include the ocean floor. *See also* zonation.

bathyscaphe   An improved version of the bathysphere that could dive down and resurface under its own power. The first bathyscape (deep boat), called *Trieste*, enabled its inventor, Auguste Piccard, to descend to depths of 4,000 meters. *See also* bathysphere. The inventor's son later descended in the *Trieste* to 10,915 meters.

bathysphere   A hollow steel ball with windows that could be lowered down into the ocean from a ship. The bathysphere enabled Beebe and Barton to descend to a depth of 923 meters in 1934. *See also* bathyscaphe.

bay   A body of water partially enclosed by land, but with a wide mouth that opens to a larger body of water.

beach combing   The activity of walking along the beach and looking for animals, shells, wreckage, and other materials that have washed up on shore.

bends   A condition caused by absorbing too much nitrogen during a deep dive and ascending too quickly, causing nitrogen bubbles to form and expand in the diver's organs and joints and resulting in extreme pain. *See also* arterial gas embolism, oxygen toxicity, and nitrogen narcosis.

benthic   Attached or associated with the ocean floor. *See also* pelagic and zonation.

benthos   Plants and creatures that live in or on or rely on the ocean floor for their survival. *See also* plankton and nekton.

Bermuda Triangle   A mysterious area in the Atlantic Ocean defined by the points of Southeast Florida, Bermuda, and Puerto Rico, where planes and boats have been reported to mysteriously disappear or at least lose their bearings.

bilateral symmetry   The quality of having your left half look like a mirror image of your right half. People are bilaterally symmetric. *See also* radial symmetry.

bioluminescent   The condition of being lit up by a physiological/chemical reaction rather than by an energy source, such as electricity or gas. *See also* photophore.

bird   A warm-blooded vertebrate with wings that lays eggs. Birds do not necessarily fly, as the penguin proves.

bivalve   Clams, oysters, mussels, and other squishy molluscs that live in shells consisting of two hinged halves. *See also* mollusc.

blade   The leaf-like structure of a seaweed, whose purpose it is to catch the sunlight. Unlike the leaves of a true, vascular, plant, the blades have no veins running through them to carry water and nutrients. *See also* kelp, holdfast, and stipe.

brackish   A mixture of saltwater and freshwater that's less salty than water in the open ocean. Brackish waters are commonly found where rivers empty into oceans, bays, or gulfs.

buccaneers   Pirates from England, France, and the Netherlands who sailed to the New World in the 1600s to harass the rich Spanish explorers who were busy conquering the lands of the natives and stealing their gold.

buoyancy control device   An air-filled bladder, often worn as a vest, that enables a diver to control his or her buoyancy during a dive and avoid floating to the top or falling to the bottom.

bycatch   Fish or other marine creatures that are unintentionally caught while fishing for other species. Some estimates show that 25 percent or more of all fish caught are bycatch.

byssal threads   Strong, thin, sticky strands that anchor a mussel to a substrate, such as a rock.

carrageenan   A product derived from red seaweeds that is used primarily as a gel, food clarifier, and stabilizer.

catadromous   The ability to migrate from freshwater to saltwater in order to breed. *See also* anadromous.

caudal fin   Tail fin of sharks, rays, and fishes.

central ring canal In a sea star, the circular tube through which water is pumped to the lateral canals that radiate out from the central ring to the arms. *See also* lateral canal madreporite, and water vascular system.

cephalothorax A single anatomical unit consisting of a combination of the head and neck. A lobster has a cephalothorax.

cetaceans Pronounced *si-TAY-shins*; the group of marine mammals consisting of whales, dolphins, and porpoises.

chelicerae Jointed appendages near the mouth of a crab that sweep food into the mouth.

chemoautotroph A bacteria that can produce its own food through internal chemical reactions rather than through photosynthesis.

chemosynthesis The process by which certain bacteria and fungi convert carbon dioxide and water into carbohydrates using the oxidation of inorganic compounds to fuel the process. *See also* photosynthesis.

Chondrichthyes Fish that have a rubbery, cartilaginous skeleton, rather than a true bony skeleton.

chordate The major taxonomic group (phylum) that includes humans, including all vertebrates and some invertebrates that have a hollow nerve cord that runs through their bodies. *See also* vertebrate and invertebrate.

chronometer A reliable, portable timepiece, which helped navigators determine their longitudinal positions on the globe more accurately.

clasper The male reproductive organ of a shark. Male sharks have two claspers—either of which they can use when mating.

clavus Substitute for the tail fin in some species of fish, such as the ocean sunfish, consisting of extended and connected dorsal and anal fins.

cnidarian A group of sea creatures that have their own stingers, including jellyfish, anemones, and coral polyps. *See also* nematocysts.

cnidocytes A unique cell type found in all jellyfish, anemones, hydroids, and corals that have a bulb or nematocyst capsule that houses a cnidocil, the dart-like stinger.

coelom The central cavity in a worm, sea star, or other animal. In a sea star, the coelem carries water from outside into the central canal, which supplies pressurized water to operate the sea star's feet. *See also* water-vascular system.

commensalism A relationship between two organisms that benefits only one of the organisms without harming the other. The relationship between the man of war fish and the man-of-war jellyfish is an example of commensalism. The man of war fish swims around the man-of-war jellyfish's tentacles using them as its defense without harming the jellyfish. *See also* symbiosis.

conchology   A branch of zoology that studies the composition, design, and function of shells. *See also* malacology.

consecutive hermaphrodite   An organism that changes from male to female or female to male as it matures. A consecutive hermaphrodite that changes from male to female is called protandric, whereas one that changes from female to male is called protogynous. Rhythmical consecutive hermaphrodites can change sex several times during the course of their lives. *See also* hermaphrodite, protandric hermaphrodite, protogynous hermaphrodite, and serial hermaphrodite.

continental drift   The incremental movement of Earth's landmasses caused by the shifting of the plates that make up the earth's lithosphere. *See also* lithosphere.

continental shelf   The submerged edge of a continent, which includes some of the most biologically and geologically rich areas of the ocean. The width of the shelf varies from 1 kilometer to up to 750 kilometers.

continental slope   The furthermost edge of the continental shelf beyond the shelf break. In some cases, the slope dives straight down to the ocean depths. In other cases, it slopes somewhat gradually.

coral reef   A very diverse ecosystem built around a calcium carbonate base formed by the exoskeletons of coral polyps, calcium-producing red algae, and various molluscs. Coral reefs are found only in warmer areas and build up over thousands of years—the living layer growing on the skeletons of past generations.

corallite   The calcium-based skeletons created by coral polyps and used by them as their homes.

crest   The top of a wave. *See also* wave and trough.

crustose   Possessing a crusty surface. This term is used to describe some types of algae with crusty exteriors that make them look more like coral than algae.

crystalline style   A rotating rod inside the stomach of all bivalves and most gastropods that grinds up food against a hard plate called the gastric shield and mixes the food with enzymes to aid in digestion. *See also* gastric shield.

ctenophore   Pronounced *TEN-oh-four*, a creature with a watermelon-shaped, jelly-like body that has eight rows of cilia running the length of its body to help it swim and eat. Ctenophores also give off light.

current   The flow of water from one location to another. Surface currents describe the motion of water in the upper layer. Subsurface currents describe the motion of water beneath the surface. *See also* surface current, subsurface current, and rip current.

cuttlebone   The interior shell in cuttlefish that helps qualify them as molluscs and is sold in pet stores as a source of calcium for birds. (Most molluscs have an external shell.)

cyclostomes   Animals that have round mouths, typically jawless fish in the group Agnatha.

deep-scattering layer   A collection of plankton, fish, or other swarm of creatures that is dense enough to bounce sounds off of.

dermal denticles   Shark scales that are pointed like tiny teeth, with the points all facing the same direction—usually facing the tail of the fish.

detritus   Waste products or broken down, decomposing plants or animals that some bottom feeders, such as bivalves, like to eat.

diatom   Large single-celled algae that have glass-like exterior shells. *See also* diatomaceous earth and algae.

diatomaceous earth   A powdery natural material, similar to sand, that consists primarily of the discarded shells of diatoms (algae). Diatomaceous earth is commonly used in abrasives. *See also* diatom.

dinoflagellate   A single-celled organism typically equipped with two whip-like tails that it uses to move around in the water. Dinoflagellates make up a significant portion of plankton.

dioecious   Species in which each member of the species remains male or female its entire life rather than changing sexes over the course of its life. *See also* hermaphrodite, serial hermaphrodite, and protandric hermaphrodite.

disruptive coloration   A type of camouflage that breaks up the outline of an animal so that it blends in better with the background.

diurnal vertical migration   A daily movement of organisms from deeper regions (during the day) to the surface (at night). Reverse diurnal vertical migration means at the surface during the day and deeper at night.

dorsal nerve cord   The nerve chord that runs above the notochord in some vertebrates. The dorsal nerve cord is inside your spinal column. *See also* notochord.

downwelling   The flow of water from the surface down to the ocean floor. Downwelling usually occurs when water piles up on a coastline and then is pushed down by gravity causing a downward current.

dry suit   A variation of a scuba diving wetsuit that keeps the diver warm and dry when diving in extremely cold water. In very cold water, the diver might even wear insulated underwear under the suit. *See also* wetsuit.

echinoderm   Simple invertebrates that typically have an external skeleton, called a test, exhibit radial symmetry and have tubular feet. Sea stars, sea urchins, sea cucumbers, and sand dollars are all echinoderms.

echinoids   A subgroup of Echinoderms that have a velvety covering of short spines and pedicellariae, which help them burrow into and creep along the sandy bottom—for example, sea urchins, sand dollars (also known as sea biscuits), and heart urchins.

echolocation   A sophisticated navigational tool, used by dolphins and other toothed cetaceans, in which they bounce sounds off of objects to determine their locations. Scientists think that echolocation enables these animals to generate images in their brains similar to images generated by an ultrasound scan of a baby. *See also* cetacean and acoustic window.

ecosystem   An ecological community consisting of two or more organisms living in a shared environment. Ecosystems can be very complex and fragile, consisting of thousands of organisms living in very close proximity. The effects on one organism can cause a chain reaction throughout the ecosystem.

eddy   A current that moves in the opposite direction of the main current and typically in a circular path. *See also* current.

electro reception   A technique sharks and some other fish use to sense the changes in the electrical field that surrounds their bodies.

elver   An eel in its larval stage.

endangered species   Any plant or animal species that is facing the risk of extinction. More than 19,000 plants and animals, both in water and on land, are on the endangered species list.

environment   A plant's or an animal's surroundings.

epifauna   Animals that sit on top of the ocean floor. This term is commonly used to describe bivalves that sit atop the ocean floor rather than burying themselves in the mud or sand. *See also* infauna.

euphotic or **epipelagic zone**   The zone that sunlight penetrates well enough to support photosynthesis. This is typically 100 meters deep, but varies with water clarity and extends over the entire ocean surface. *See also* zonation.

epipelagic   The surface and near surface waters of the ocean where enough sunlight can penetrate for photosynthesis to occur. *See also* pelagic.

epiphytic   An organism that grows on top of a plant, relying on it for support but not for nutrients.

estuary   An area where freshwater sources, such as rivers and tributaries, mix with saltwater from the ocean body to create a unique habitat.

euphausiid   A group of crustaceans, also known as krill, that look like smaller versions of familiar crustaceans such as prawns or lobsters. *See also* krill.

euryhaline   Organisms that can tolerate very high as well as very low salinities. *See also* osmotic conformer and stenohaline.

eutrophication   The increase in nutrients, primarily nitrogen and phosphorous, in the ocean, typically near the coastline and typically caused by human-derived phosphates, fertilizers, and sewage washed down by rivers. Eutrophication creates conditions that favor blooms of algae—both harmful and not. *See also* harmful algae blooms.

fetch   The uninterrupted distance or area of water over which the wind blows to create waves. Fetch determines the size of the waves.

fibropapilloma   A common condition in sea turtles that causes them to grow large tumors around the sensitive areas of their bodies, including their necks.

fish   A cold-blooded aquatic vertebrate that has fins, gills, and (in most cases) a streamlined body.

fishery   An industry devoted to harvesting, processing, or selling fish, shellfish, or other aquatic animals. The term can also be used to describe a place where fish are caught, a fishing business, or a hatchery.

flippers   Analogous to fish fins, flippers are frontal appendages (such as arms) that have been modified by evolution to help animals maneuver in water. Penguins, dolphins, and seals all use flippers.

flotsam   The fragments of a ship and its cargo that remain floating after the ship has sunk. *See also* jetsam.

flukes   The pair of flattened appendages that make up the tail of a dolphin, porpoise, or whale.

foreshore   The area of a beach between the high tide and low tide levels. *See also* backshore.

frankenfish   A derogatory term used to describe fish that have been genetically engineered to make new food products.

fringing reef   A coral reef that commonly forms a skirt around an island or other landmass and appears as an extension of the landmass. *See also* barrier reef and atoll.

fusiform   Shaped like a torpedo, which is generally beneficial for creatures that need to move through water.

gamete   A reproductive cell that has half the number of chromosomes and can merge with a gamete from the opposite sex to form a fertilized egg. A sperm cell and an unfertilized egg are gametes.

gastric shield   A hard plate inside the stomachs of all bivalves and most gastropods that acts like a cutting board, allowing a rotating rod called the crystalline style to smash the food and mix it with digestive enzymes. *See also* crystalline style.

gill   An anatomical feature of most fish that enables the fish to extract oxygen from water.

glycoprotein   A solution that lowers the freezing point of the creature's blood so that it doesn't freeze solid when the water temperature dips below the freezing point.

gnathostome   Vertebrate fish with jaws. *See also* Agnatha.

gular pouch   Flabby skin at the base of the lower bill and/or neck on some birds, such as the pelican.

gulf   Any concavity in the shoreline into which a neighboring ocean or sea extends its reach.

gyre   Large-scale circular surface currents in the middle of each ocean created by the interaction of the wind, the spinning of the globe, and the effects caused when waters are deflected off the coastlines. Gyres typically follow a clockwise path in the Northern Hemisphere and a counterclockwise path in the Southern Hemisphere.

HAB   *See* harmful algae bloom.

habitat   An area where an organism lives.

HAM   *See* hypothetical ancestral mollusc.

hammock   A dense mat of mangrove trees. *See also* mangrove tree, propagule, prop roots, and pneumatophores.

hang ten   A surfing expression that means to stick all of your toes out on a surfboard and ride the curling wave into the adoring crowd viewing on the beach.

harem   A group of females protected and serviced by a single male of the same species. Dominant male walruses typically establish their own harems.

harmful algae bloom (HAB)   An explosive growth of algae that are nutritionally useless, produce toxins, or deplete an area of sunlight and oxygen. One of the most well-known harmful algae blooms is the red tide, which can kill fish and close beaches in the most serious cases.

hermatypic   Used to describe corals that are reef-building and require light. These corals have a symbiotic relationship with photosynthesizing zooxanthellae. Because the zooxanthellae are hermatypic, so are the coral that depend on them for their survival. *See also* zooxanthellae.

heterocercal   Asymmetric tail fin, characteristic of most sharks. *See also* caudal fin and homocercal.

high intertidal zone   The shoreline area that extends from mean high water to slightly below the mean sea level (where the higher of the two daily low tides reaches). This area remains exposed to the air for long periods of time twice a day and is flooded only during high tide. *See also* zonation.

holdfast   The root-like structure at the base of a seaweed plant, such as kelp, that anchors the seaweed to a rock or other substrate. Unlike the roots of a true plant, the holdfast does not suck minerals and water from the ground to feed the plant; it merely holds the seaweed in place. *See also* kelp, stipe, and blade.

homocercal   Symmetrical tail fin. This term is commonly used to describe the caudal (tail) fin of most fishes. *See also* caudal fin and heterocercal.

hydroid   A sessile cnidarian in which the tube-shaped base is anchored to a substrate and the finger-like tentacles stick out at the top. *See also* polyp, medusa, and cnidarian.

hydrologic cycle   The movement of water from surface to sky, via evaporation; from sky to land or sea, by the way of rain; and from land to sea, by the way of rivers and ground water.

hydrothermal vent   A hole or crack in the ocean floor through which a mixture of intensely hot water, sulfur, and other inorganic minerals spews.

hypothetical ancestral mollusc (HAM)   An imaginary creature that exhibits all the characteristics of a mollusc—a soft body, a shell, a single foot for locomotion, a rasp-like tongue, a mantle cavity, and gills.

ichthyosaurs   Early forms of reptiles that moved back to the seas. Also referred to as fish lizard.

infauna   Animals buried in the mud or sand. This term is commonly used to describe bivalves that bury themselves in the mud rather than sitting on top of the ocean floor. *See also* epifaunal.

interface   The border of two ecosystems—often used to describe the air-sea interface, the sediment-water interface, or the land-sea interface. *See also* zonation.

intertidal zone   The area between low and high tides. During high tide, this zone is covered with water. During low tide, it is exposed to the air. *See also* zonation.

invertebrate   Any animal that does not have a backbone, including anemones, sea stars, octopuses, squid, crabs, lobsters, molluscs, and any other animal that is not a vertebrate. *See also* vertebrate.

isopod   A small crustacean that feeds off decaying matter or other animals. You might be familiar with the pillbugs (a.k.a. roly-poly) in your garden—these are terrestrial isopods.

Jet Ski   A personal watercraft that carries only one rider who rides standing up. *See also* personal watercraft.

jetsam   Cargo or equipment that has been thrown overboard from a ship in distress and washed ashore (or sunk to the bottom). *See also* flotsam.

kelp   A multicellular form of algae that looks like a plant and acts like algae. Unlike a true, vascular plant, which has different types of cells to make up the roots, stem, and leaves, the cells that compose a kelp "plant" are all basically the same. Also, the kelp "plant" has no vascular system to carry water, gasses, and minerals from one part of the plant to another.

kitesurf   To ride along the surface of the water on a board while holding on to a kite that pulls you through the water.

krill   Small shrimp-like creatures that swim in thick swarms and are eaten by fish, birds, and (mostly) whales. Formally referred to as euphausid.

lateral canal   In a sea star, the tubes that run through the center of the legs and carry pressurized water to power the suction-cupped feet. *See also* central ring canal, madreporite, and water vascular system.

lateral line   A type of underwater radar used by fish to sense minute variations in water pressure. Along the sides of the fish are tiny organs called neuromasts, which sense water movement and variations in pressure. They can even pick up the movements of other fish. *See also* neuromast.

letter of marque   A letter bearing the official seal of a leader of a country and giving permission to the bearer to wage war on another country's ships or loot their merchant vessels. Privateers required a letter of marque to prove their legitimacy. *See also* privateer.

lithosphere   The outermost solid layer of the earth on which the continents and ocean ride. The lithosphere is made up of several plates that move in tiny increments as the surface of the world changes. *See also* plate tectonics.

littoral zone   The shoreline area between the low and high tide marks. *See also* zonation.

lobe-finned   The smaller of the two groups of bony fish, exhibiting rounded fins that are structured internally more like limbs than fins. Lobe-finned fish are formally referred to as composing the group Sarcopterygii. *See also* ray-finned.

longline   A rope weighted on both ends and at several points in between that has numerous baited lines along its length. Longline fishing is a method typically used to catch deepwater fish.

low intertidal zone   A shoreline area exposed to the air only during very low tides and remains flooded for long periods of time twice a day. *See also* zonation.

madreporite   A button typically located at the top of a sea star that enables it to draw in and release water to control its internal water pressure. *See also* lateral canal, central ring canal, and water vascular system.

magma   Melted, liquid rock below the earth's crust. When magma pushes up through cracks or holes in the earth's crust, sometimes forming volcanoes, it is called lava.

malacology   A branch of zoology that studies molluscs. *See also* conchology.

mammal   An animal that is warm blooded, breathes air, has hair (at least at some point in its life), gives birth to live young, and nurses its babies.

mangrove tree   Salt-tolerant trees commonly found partially submerged in coastal areas in tropical and subtropical regions. *See also* hammock, prop roots, pneumatophores, and propagule.

Mare Liberum   Translated as "Free Sees," and later giving rise to the notion of "Freedom of the Seas," it is the idea that all nations have the right to navigate, fish, and explore all ocean waters.

marine protected area (MPA)   A partially or completely protected preserve in the sea or coastline in which fishing is usually restricted. When protection is sufficient, marine protected areas can enable fish stocks to rebound.

marine reserve or no-take reserve   A marine protected area in which nobody is allowed to fish. Marine protected areas hold the most promise for enabling fish stocks to rebound.

maximum sustainable yield   A theoretical target amount of fish to harvest that yields the most fish possible without threatening the ability of the population to continue producing fish for future generations.

medusa   The free-swimming stage of cnidarian—for example, the adult stage of a jellyfish.

mesopelagic zone   Also known as the twilight or disphotic zone, an open ocean zone that extends from the bottom of the epipelagic zone down to about 1,000 meters. Some light, not much, reaches this zone. *See also* zonation.

metamerism   The segmentation of body into similar parts along the main trunk of a worm.

metazoan   Multicellular animals.

mitochondrial mass   The material in a cell that controls the genetic code and enzymes required for cell division and for maintaining a cell's metabolism. An enlarged mitochondrial mass in some fish enable the fish to produce heat, similar to warm-blooded animals. *See also* regional endothermy.

mollusc   Soft-bodied animals that typically have a hard external shell and a single foot used for locomotion, including clams, oysters, snails, limpets, and nudibranches. Squid, octopuses, and other soft-bodied creatures also fall into this group—even though evolution has stripped them of their outer shells and replaced the single foot with suction-cup–covered tentacles. *See also* bivalve.

MPA   *See* marine protected area.

mutualism   A relationship between two organisms that benefits both organisms. The relationship between the sea anemone and the anemone fish is a perfect example of mutualism; the anemone's stinging tentacles protect the fish while the territorial anemone fish protects the anemone from its enemies and might drop its extra food. *See also* symbiosis, parasitism, and commensalism.

myoglobin   Oxygen-storing protein found in muscle fibers. Some deep diving sea creatures have increased concentrations of myoglobin in their muscles, allowing them to shut down blood flow to their muscles during a dive and retain the ability to move.

neap tide   A phenomenon that occurs when the sun and the moon are at right angles to each other in relation to Earth, causing their forces to work against each other and resulting in less tidal variation around the globe. *See also* spring tide.

nekton   Animals that swim around in the ocean waters rather than floating at the surface (plankton) or crawling around on the bottom (benthos). *See also* plankton and benthos.

nematocysts   The stinging organs used by cnidarians to defend themselves and stun their prey. *See also* cnidarian.

neuromast   An organ on the sides of some fish that consists of hairs encased in a gelatinous cap and enables the fish to sense water movement and pressure variations in order to navigate. Neuromasts are typically arranged in grooves that run the length of the fish's body. As the fish swims, it creates pressure variations in the water and bounces waves off of surrounding objects. These pressure variations and waves move the caps of the neuromasts, which bend the hairs inside the neuromasts. *See also* lateral line system.

nitrogen narcosis   A condition that results from a high concentration of nitrogen in the bloodstream, which can make a diver feel (and act) drunk and can cause the diver eventually to pass out. *See also* bends, oxygen toxicity, and arterial gas embolism.

nonpoint source pollution   Pollution that cannot be traced to a single source, including pollution that runs down storm drains, which might contain oil, transmission fluid, cigarette butts, fertilizer, and kitty litter from several sources. *See also* point source pollution.

notochord   A rigid muscular rod that lies between a vertebrate's gut and the dorsal nerve cord, which runs down the back of the animal. *See also* dorsal nerve cord.

nudibranch   Fancy name for a sea slug.

ocean   The entire body of saltwater that covers nearly 71 percent of the earth's surface, or any of the five major divisions of the ocean: the Pacific, Atlantic, Indian, Arctic, and Southern.

oceanodromous   An ocean fish that spends its whole life in saltwater and actively migrates from one ocean to another.

Oceanus   Derived from Greek meaning "the river that flows around the earth," Oceanus is used to refer to Earth as the "water planet."

oligoxenic   A contaminated algae culture. *See also* axenic.

omnivore   A creature that eats just about anything.

operculum   1) A thin, hard disc that's attached to the foot of most snails and enables the snail to seal the opening of its shell when it retracts into the shell. 2) The thin layer of skin that seals the gills in fish.

osmoconformer   *See* osmotic conformer.

osmotic conformer   An organism that has the same internal salt concentrations as its surrounding environment. *See also* euryhaline and stenohaline.

ostracoderms   Ancient armor-plated fish thought to be the first animals with backbones.

overfishing   Catching so many fish that the populations begin to decline.

oxygen toxicity   A condition that occurs when the percentage of oxygen in the bloodstream becomes too high and begins to damage the lungs. This typically results when a diver remains submerged at depths greater than 30 meters for too long and/or uses an air mixture with an oxygen concentration that is too high. *See also* bends, oxygen toxicity, and nitrogen narcosis.

oyster drill   A snail that uses its radula to bore a hole through the shell of a bivalve and eat the soft flesh inside. *See also* radula.

parapodia   Long legs on a marine worm that make it appear feathery rather than worm-like.

parasail   A parachute that's attached to a boat by a strong cable and that lifts the rider off the deck of the boat high into the sky.

parasitism   A relationship between organisms in which one organism, the parasite, benefits at the expense of the other organism. Mosquitoes, ticks, fleas, tapeworms, leeches, and many bacteria and viruses are parasites. *See also* symbiosis, mutualism, and commensalism.

parts per thousand (ppt)   A unit of measure that describes the amount of a solute dissolved in a solvent, such as the amount of a particular nutrient dissolved in water. Formerly used as the unit of salinity.

pedicellariae   Cutting tools built into the anatomy of most echinoderms and used for eating and defense. Some pedicellariae have toxins that can paralyze small prey and keep the larger predators away.

pedipalp   The legs of a crab used for walking.

pelagic   An area that composes the entire ocean except for the ocean floor. *See also* benthic, epipelagic, and zonation.

pen   A long thin shell inside a squid that helps it qualify as a mollusc. (Most molluscs have an external shell.)

pentamerous radial symmetry   The characteristic of having a body arranged in five identical sections around a central point. A five-armed sea star is the perfect example.

period   The amount of time it takes a wave to pass a given point.

peristaltic   The wavelike contractions of a worm's tubular structure that enable it to move.

personal watercraft   A small vessel, usually less than 12 feet in length, that uses an inboard jet pump instead of a propeller for thrust. Instead of riding in the vehicle, as with a boat, the rider sits, kneels, or stands on the vehicle. *See also* WaveRunner and Jet Ski.

photic zone   The surface waters where light can penetrate.

photoperiod   An organism's daily exposure to light. Some organisms can sense the photoperiod and use it to determine the season for spawning or migrating.

photophore   Organs that create light through a physiological/chemical reaction. *See also* bioluminescent.

photoreceptors   Organs that can sense light.

photosynthesis   The process by which plants and plantlike organisms convert water and carbon dioxide into carbohydrates using sunlight. A main byproduct of photosynthesis is oxygen. *See also* chemosynthesis.

phylogeny   The evolutionary development and history of a species as described by their genealogy.

phylum   A major division of plant or animal life below a kingdom and above a class. All animals in the sea, for example, are in one kingdom. But those animals are broken down into phyla, including cnidarians, echinoderms, molluscs, and so on.

phytoplankton   Tiny photosynthetic organisms that float on and near the surface of the ocean and provide food for other organisms. *See also* plankton and zooplankton.

picoplankton   Plankton that's smaller than 10 microns. *See also* plankton.

pile   The mass of water that forms as wind blows over the surface of the water and creates waves.

pinniped   A group of carnivorous marine mammal that have flippers and tails they use for locomotion. Seals, walruses, and sea lions are pinnipeds.

piracy   The crime of violence, robbery, or coercion for private benefit on the open ocean or in the airspace above the ocean committed by another ship or individual not sponsored by any legitimate government. Piracy typically refers to the act of raiding another ship, but can also include the act of stealing sunken treasure or fishing in another country's waters without permission. *See also* privateer.

placoderm   Primitive, armor-plated shark with jaws and paired pectoral and pelvic fins (for improved balance and mobility).

placoid scales   *See also* dermal denticles.

plankton bloom   An explosion of plankton life that typically occurs near coastlines where upwellings carry nutrients from the ocean floor to the surface to feed the plankton. *See also* plankton.

plankton   From the Greek *planktos*, which means wandering. A diverse collection of tiny marine plants and animals that float in the upper layer of the ocean and make up a huge portion of the base of the ocean's food pyramid. *See also* plankton bloom, phytoplankton, and zooplankton.

plate tectonics   The theory of how the plates that make up the lithosphere move around the globe. *See also* lithosphere and tectonics.

pneumatophores   Mangrove tree roots that extend from trunk roots above the surface of the water, enabling the roots to obtain the gas the tree needs to survive. *See also* mangrove tree, hammock, prop roots, and propagule.

pod   A group of whales, dolphins, or porpoises.

point source pollution   Pollution that can be traced to a specific source, such as oil that spills from a pipeline. *See also* nonpoint source pollution.

polyp   The stage of cnidarians, particularly jellyfish, coral, and anemone, at which the animal is sessile (attached to a rock or other surface).

poriferans   Fancy name for sponges.

ppt   Abbreviation for parts per thousand. *See also* parts per thousand and salinity.

practical salinity units   *See* psu.

primary consumer   An organism that feeds on a primary producer. Primary consumers typically sit pretty low on the food chain. *See also* primary producer.

primary producer   An organism that converts inorganic minerals into organic materials that feed other organisms. No food pyramid could exist without a primary producer to form its base. *See also* primary consumer, photosynthesis, and chemosynthesis.

privateer   A captain of a ship hired by a country to fight its enemies or loot merchant vessels from other countries. A privateer is sort of like a legalized pirate. *See also* letter of marque and piracy.

prop roots   Mangrove tree roots that extend from the upper trunk of the tree down into the water and mud. *See also* mangrove tree, hammock, pneumatophores, and propagule.

propagule   The long, narrow seedling of the mangrove tree, this is actually a young plant that can drop straight down and take root in the mud or float many miles to more fertile ground. *See also* mangrove tree, hammock, prop roots, and pneumatophores.

protandric hermaphrodite   An organism that starts out as a male, but then develops into a female and stays that way for the rest of its life. *See also* dioecious, hermaphrodite, serial hermaphrodite, and consecutive hermaphrodite.

protist   A kingdom consisting primarily of single-celled, microscopic organisms. Some protists are actually multicellular beings; they do not exhibit specialized cells—each cell has the same basic structure and function.

protogynous hermaphrodite   An organism that changes from female to male over the course of its life. *See also* hermaphrodite, consecutive hermaphrodite, protandric hermaphrodite, and serial hermaphrodite.

psu (practical salinity units)   The unit of measure officially used to describe the salinity. *See also* salinity.

radial symmetry   The quality of having a body that can be divided into slices like a pizza with all the slices coming out looking identical. *See also* bilateral symmetry.

radiation   In evolution, the spreading of organisms into different locations and habitats resulting in increased diversity of species.

radula   A file-like tongue typically used by snails and other molluscs to scrape algae off the surface of rocks and other hard surfaces.

ram ventilation system   A system used by some fish to pass water over the gills that consists of swimming forward with its mouth open. Tuna use this system, so they must swim constantly.

raw bar   A seafood bar that serves up raw fish and shellfish.

ray-finned   The larger of the two groups of bony fish, exhibiting fins that consist of a thin membrane stretched over fanlike spines. The scientific name is *Actinopterygii*. *See also* lobe-finned.

regional endothermy   The ability to heat a specific area of one's anatomy. This ability is commonly exhibited in the swordfish, which can keep its eyes and brain warm when it dives deep, allowing it to remain alert. *See also* mitochondrial mass.

regulator   A device attached to the hoses of an air tank that automatically regulates the air pressure as a diver ascends and descends.

remote sensing   The study of oceans from satellite and aerial images.

reptile   A cold-blooded, scaly vertebrate that breathes using lungs and usually lays eggs.

rhumb line   The course a sailor plots from the point of departure to the destination. This is a common method of navigation for small vessels traveling short distances (1,000 nautical miles or less).

rip current   This is not really a true tide or current, but a subsurface flow of water created when the wind pushes water up on shore as a wave and the water flows back to the sea.

riptide   *See also* rip current.

rocky intertidal   The stony area on the shoreline between the low-tide and high-tide levels. *See also* zonation.

rookery   A breeding ground for large numbers of birds.

sailboard   A cross between a surfboard and a sailboat, which is powered by the wind. *See also* windsurfer.

salinity   The measure of the concentration of salt in water, typically expressed in terms of practical salinity units (psu), previously measured in ppt (parts per thousand).

salt marsh   A coastal grassy wetland that's typically filled by high tides flowing over sandbars.

Sargasso Sea   An elliptical body of water in the Atlantic Ocean, off the southeast coast of the United States, that slowly spins clockwise with the currents and is covered with thick mats of sargassum seaweed. *See also* sargassum.

sargassum   A type of seaweed that's independent, free floating, and commonly associated with the Sargassum Sea. *See also* Sargasso Sea and seaweed.

sea   A subdivision of an ocean, such as the Sargasso Sea, or a body of water that branches off from one of the oceans and might be partially enclosed by land, such as the Mediterranean Sea.

seagrass   Also referred to as submerged underwater vegetation, sea grass grows beneath the surface. Unlike kelp and other seaweeds, sea grass is a true, vascular, plant complete with roots and leaves (blades of grass). Sea grass grows close to shore and is an important food source for many animals, including manatees.

seaweed   Multicellular photosynthetic organisms that grow in saltwater but do not have the complex structure of true (vascular) plants. Instead of having roots, a stem, and leaves, seaweed, such as kelp, have a holdfast that anchors it in place, a stipe that supports it, and blades that catch the sunlight. *See also* vascular.

serial hermaphrodites   An organism, such as a scallop, that can produce both male and female gametes (the equivalent of sperm and eggs) throughout its life. *See also* dioecious, hermaphrodite, and consecutive hermaphrodite.

sessile   Planted in a fixed location. This term is commonly used to describe animals that choose to attach themselves to rocks, piers, and other surfaces rather than swim or crawl around.

shelf break   A drop-off near the outer edge of the continental shelf. Strong currents commonly cut deep canyons into the continental shelf and slope that run perpendicular to the shoreline.

shell gland   An anatomical feature that's common to all molluscs at some stage in their development and is used for creating a shell.

shoal   A raised portion of the ocean floor that creates an area that's shallower than surrounding areas.

siphon   A tube used (typically by bivalves) to suck in water and nutrients or dispose of wastes.

Sirenia   A group of marine mammals, including the dugong and manatees, that look like overweight walruses and commonly feed on sea grass.

sonar   The acronym for *so*und *na*vigation *r*anging, a technology that enables one to determine the positions of various objects in a body of water.

spicule   A spine-like skeleton created by sponges and some coral polyps, which differs from the standard cup-like skeletons most coral polyps form.

splash zone   *See* spray zone.

spray zone   An area above sea level that typically gets wet only at extreme high tides and during periods of jumbo wave action. *See also* zonation.

spring tide   A phenomenon that occurs when the sun, moon, and Earth are aligned in a straight line, resulting in higher high tides and lower low tides. *See also* neap tide.

stenohaline   Organisms that cannot handle extremely salty or fresh water but can tolerate a certain limited range of salinity fluctuation. *See also* euryhaline and osmotic conformer.

stipe   The stem-like structure of a seaweed that provides support for its blades. Unlike the stem of a true, vascular, plant, the stipe does not carry water and nutrients through the plant. *See also* kelp, holdfast, and blade.

stock   A population of fish or other marine life.

subduction   The bumping together of the plates that make up the earth's outer crust and result in the edge of one plate diving below another plate. *See also* lithosphere and plate tectonics.

submersible   A smaller version of a submarine typically used in exploring deep-sea areas and performing underwater rescues. Submersibles can be manned or unmanned.

substrate   A surface, typically solid, on which an organism grows.

subsurface current   The flow of water in the lower layers of the ocean typically caused by differences in water density, temperature, and salinity. *See also* current, surface current, and thermohaline.

subtidal zone   The area beyond the intertidal zone, but typically no deeper than 30 meters and within 1 kilometer of the shoreline. *See also* zonation.

supersaturated   A solution that is more full of a dissolvable solid than it can normally hold.

surface current   The flow of water in the upper layer of the ocean, typically powered by the wind. *See also* current and subsurface current.

surfboard   A wide, buoyant board that enables a surfer to ride atop a wave.

symbiosis   The interdependence of two species for the benefit of one or both species. Symbiosis takes on three forms: parasitism, which benefits one organism while harming the other; mutualism, which benefits both organisms; and commensalism, which benefits one or both organisms without harming either organism. *See* also parasitism, mutualism, and commensalism.

synchrony   A phenomenon that occurs when all male and female members of a given species living in close proximity release their eggs and sperm into the water at the same time.

syrinx   A bird's voice box.

taxa   Any scientific grouping of plants and animals, including kingdom, phylum, class, order, and species.

tectonic   Geological activity that results in changes to the earth's crust. *See also* lithosphere and plate tectonics.

test   The external skeleton of an echinoderm, such as a sea star, urchin, or sand dollar.

thermohaline   The combination of water temperature and salinity that determines the density of saltwater.

tidal wave   The false name given to a huge wave typically caused by an earthquake that occurs below sea level, near a coastline, or by volcanic activity at the bottom of the ocean.

Tidal waves are not caused by tides. The more appropriate name for a huge wave is tsunami.

tide   The rising or falling of water levels caused by the interactions of the earth's, sun's, and moon's gravitational fields.

torsion   An evolutionary modification in gastropods that causes the visceral mass (all the soft parts including the guts) to rotate 180 degrees. Rotating the midsection 180 degrees provides the gastropod with greater balance, making them less top heavy, and provides additional protection for creature's soft underbelly.

totipalmate   Having fully webbed feet, such as pelicans, gannets, boobies, cormorants, shags, frigate birds, and tropic birds.

trench   An area at the bottom of the sea where the seafloor dips to form a valley.

trophic level   The strata that make up a food chain. Typically, plants are placed on the lowest trophic level. Vegetarians eat the plants. Carnivores eat the vegetarians.

trough   The bottom of a wave. *See also* wave and crest.

tsunami   A huge wave typically caused by an earthquake that occurs below sea level, near a coastline, or by volcanic activity at the bottom of the ocean.

tunicate   A marine animal that resembles a tadpole in its larval stage, but anchors itself to a substrate and grows into a tubular animal as an adult. Tunicates adapt well to variations in the salinity of ocean water, making them common inhabitants of estuaries.

turbid   A term typically associated with muddy water.

upwelling   The flow of typically nutrient rich water from the bottom of the ocean to the surface waters typically caused when currents are deflected away from the coast by the Coriolis force, allowing deep water to rise to the surface. Upwellings typically cause plankton blooms. *See also* downwelling and plankton bloom.

vascular   Containing tubular vessels for carrying gasses, nutrients, and water from one part of an organism to another.

vertebrate   Any animal with a true backbone, including fish, reptiles, amphibians, birds, and mammals. *See also* invertebrate.

wakeboard   A wide ski-like board that a rider kneels or stands on while being pulled behind a boat.

water cycle   *See also* hydrologic cycle.

water-ski   To ride atop the water on one or two narrow skis while being pulled by a boat.

water-vascular system   An innovation that allows echinoderms to use hydraulic pressure to move their suction-cupped feet and grab onto objects. *See also* central ring canal, lateral canal, madreporite, water vascular system.

wave   The rise or fall of surface waters generated by an energy source, such as the wind blowing over the water's surface or Earth tremors from land or the ocean floor.

wavelength   The distance between the center points of two crests or two troughs. *See also* wave, crest, and trough.

WaveRunner   A personal watercraft that carries one to four riders in the sitting position. *See also* personal watercraft.

wetsuit   A neoprene covering that traps a thin layer of water between the covering and a scuba diver to keep the diver warm when diving in cold water. Neoprene is a layer of closed-cell synthetic rubber. *See also* dry suit.

windsurfer   A person who rides a sailboard—a recreational device that looks like a surfboard with a sail attached to it.

wrack line   A band of marine matter—consisting of sea grasses, litter, and other refuse—pushed up on shore by waves and tides. It is deposited at the daily high-tide line and can build up landward at higher tide intervals.

zonation   The division of the ocean into distinct areas in order to achieve a clearer understanding of the plants and animals that live in those areas and their interactions.

zooplankton   Tiny animals that float on and near the surface of the ocean or at depth, eat phytoplankton and other zooplankton, and serve as food for larger animals.

zooxanthellae   A photosynthetic, unicellular organism that commonly lives inside coral polyps and clams, absorbing carbon dioxide, producing sugars for its host, and receiving a place to live and perhaps some essential nutrients (such as phosphorous and nitrogen) in return.

Index